MW00784253

The Archaeology of Micronesia

This is the first book-length archaeological study of Micronesia, an island group in the western Pacific Ocean. Drawing on a wide range of archaeological, anthropological and historical sources, the author explores the various ways that the societies of these islands have been interpreted since European navigators first arrived there in the sixteenth century. Considering the process of initial colonization on the island groups of Marianas, Carolines, Marshalls and Kiribati, he examines the histories of these islands and explores how the neighbouring areas are drawn together through notions of fusion, fluidity and flux. The author places this region within the broader arena of Pacific island studies and addresses contemporary debates such as origins, processes of colonization, social organization, environmental change and the interpretation of material culture. This book will be essential reading for any scholar with an interest in the archaeology of the Pacific.

PAUL RAINBIRD is a Lecturer in Archaeology, Department of Archaeology and Anthropology, University of Wales, Lampeter. He has conducted archaeological fieldwork in the Pacific islands, Australia and Europe. He co-edited *Interrogating Pedagogies: Archaeology in Higher Education* (2001).

CAMBRIDGE WORLD ARCHAEOLOGY

Series editor
NORMAN YOFFEE, *University of Michigan*

Editorial board
SUSAN ALCOCK, *University of Michigan*
TOM DILLEHAY, *University of Kentucky*
STEPHEN SHENNAN, *University College, London*
CARLA SINOPOLI, *University of Michigan*

The Cambridge World Archaeology series is addressed to students and professional archaeologists, and to academics in related disciplines. Most volumes present a survey of the archaeology of a region of the world, providing an up-to-date account of research and integrating recent findings with new concerns of interpretation. While the focus is on a specific region, broader cultural trends are discussed and the implications of regional findings for cross-cultural interpretations considered. The authors also bring anthropological and historical expertise to bear on archaeological problems and show how both new data and changing intellectual trends in archaeology shape inferences about the past. More recently, the series has expanded to include thematic volumes.

Books in the series
A.F. HARDING, *European Societies in the Bronze Age*
RAYMOND ALLCHIN AND BRIDGET ALLCHIN, *The Rise of Civilization in India and Pakistan*
CLIVE GAMBLE, *The Palaeolithic Settlement of Europe*
CHARLES HIGHAM, *Archaeology of Mainland South East Asia*
SARAH MILLEDGE NELSON, *The Archaeology of Korea*
DAVID PHILLIPSON, *African Archaeology (second revised edition)*
OLIVER DICKINSON, *The Aegean Bronze Age*
KAREN OLSEN BRUHNS, *Ancient South America*
ALASDAIR WHITTLE, *Europe in the Neolithic*
CHARLES HIGHAM, *The Bronze Age of Southeast Asia*
CLIVE GAMBLE, *The Palaeolithic Societies of Europe*
DAN POTTS, *The Archaeology of Elam*
NICHOLAS DAVID AND CAROL KRAMER, *Ethnoarchaeology in Action*
CATHERINE PERLÈS, *The Early Neolithic in Greece*
JAMES WHITLEY, *The Archaeology of Ancient Greece*
PETER MITCHELL, *The Archaeology of Southern Africa*
HIMANSHU PRABHA RAY, *The Archaeology of Seafaring in Ancient South Asia*
TIMOTHY INSOLL, *The Archaeology of Islam in Sub-Saharan Africa*
M.M.G. AKKERMANS AND GLENN M. SCHWARTZ, *The Archaeology of Syria*
PAUL RAINBIRD, *The Archaeology of Micronesia*

CAMBRIDGE WORLD ARCHAEOLOGY

THE ARCHAEOLOGY OF MICRONESIA

PAUL RAINBIRD

Department of Archaeology and Anthropology
University of Wales, Lampeter

CAMBRIDGE
UNIVERSITY PRESS

PUBLISHED BY THE PRESS SYNDICATE OF THE UNIVERSITY OF CAMBRIDGE
The Pitt Building, Trumpington Street, Cambridge, United Kingdom

CAMBRIDGE UNIVERSITY PRESS
The Edinburgh Building, Cambridge, CB2 2RU, UK
40 West 20th Street, New York, NY 10011–4211, USA
477 Williamstown Road, Port Melbourne, VIC 3207, Australia
Ruiz de Alarcón 13, 28014 Madrid, Spain
Dock House, The Waterfront, Cape Town 8001, South Africa

http://www.cambridge.org

© Paul Rainbird 2004

This book is in copyright. Subject to statutory exception and to the
provisions of relevant collective licensing agreements, no reproduction of
any part may take place without the written permission of Cambridge
University Press.

First published 2004

Printed in the United Kingdom at the University Press, Cambridge

Typeface Trump Medieval 10/13 pt.   *System* LaTeX 2_ε [TB]

A catalogue record for this book is available from the British Library

ISBN 0 521 65188 3 hardback
ISBN 0 521 65630 3 paperback

Dedicated to the memory of my father,
Ronald Gregory Rainbird (1931–2003),
always a seafarer at heart

CONTENTS

FIGURES

PREFACE AND ACKNOWLEDGEMENTS

It feels as though this book has been a very long time in the making. My first trip to the region was in 1991 as part of a team working in contract archaeology and it was that experience, and discussion with John Craib, Peter White and Roland Fletcher at the University of Sydney, which led me to propose PhD research conducted between 1992 and 1995. Of course, I have continued to maintain my research interests in the region, and although I returned to Europe from Australia in 1997 I have found a new set of colleagues who have been energetic enough to organize colloquia and create a stimulating community through the European Colloquium on Micronesia and for that I thank Beatriz Moral and Anne Di Piazza.

My training in European archaeology, as an undergraduate at the University of Sheffield, has guided my research and interpretations, I think, in many ways not typical for the part of the world under discussion in this volume. As such, although I hope it provides a coherent and comprehensive account of the arch-aeology of the region, in its interpretative stance my intention is to provide a fresh understanding of the material evidence.

There are so many individuals and organizations that I have benefited from over the period of the preparation of this book that it is impossible to name them all here. Many I have acknowledged in previous publications, and I thank them again, but others have directly aided the production of the current volume. For reading and commenting on parts or all of the text I'd like to thank Atholl Anderson, Chris Ballard, John Craib, Sarah Daligan, Chris Gosden, Kate Howell, Anne Di Piazza, Miranda Richardson, Jim Specht, Matthew Spriggs, Peter White, Steve Wickler and Norman Yoffee. For answering questions and providing information I would like to thank Sophie Bickford, Paul D'Arcy, Roger Green, Scott Russell, Serge Tcherkézoff and the National Library of Australia.

I am very pleased to acknowledge a Research Leave Grant from the Arts and Humanities Research Board, which allowed me an extended period of time to complete this work as a Visiting Fellow in the Centre for Archaeological Research based in the Division of Archaeology and Natural History, Research School of Pacific and Asian Studies, The Australian National University. My Fellowship there provided an unparalleled environment for research and writing and I thank Professors Atholl Anderson and Geoff Hope for their hospitality.

My current and former colleagues in the Department of Archaeology, University of Wales, Lampeter have over many years provided a stimulating working environment where the range of expertise and geographical interests can only have served to keep critical thought alive, and I thank them.

A big debt of thanks is owed to Meredith 'Mem' Wilson, a stalwart friend, who is not afraid to ask difficult questions of me. Finally, I would like to thank Sarah and my family for their love, support and encouragement during the difficult times in which this book was completed.

CHAPTER I

MICRONESIAN/MACROFUSION

The story of Micronesia is one of fluidity and fusion. It is fluid in the basic sense of the sea as salt water, a body of fluid that allows for the passage of seacraft across what in the terms of Gilles Deleuze and Félix Guatarri (1988) we might understand as smooth space. The ocean is a space not striated by walls or fences as boundaries, but one where all the known world is the place of home; where nomads exist is large space from which they do not travel. We should be aware of the metaphorical use of some of these terms, the sea is not always smooth, but it is a space for movement, and the inhabitants of Micronesia are not regarded as nomads in the conventional sense, but their world has often been a large one allowing movement by judicious use of winds and currents that would often mean extended stays on islands that were not their homes: but, they were at home with the sea.

As salt and water fuse in the fluid of the ocean, so it is that I understand the story of Micronesia as one of fusion. As a concept in the study of human societies past and present, fusion allows us to think beyond boundaries, both of the body and of space. In regard to the body, if we accept fusion we can accept there is no expectation of finding pure types of people, no expectation that contacts between people from different places and with different histories produce hybrid forms, because each party in the process is already a fusion derived from meetings that occurred long before the several millennia that are the concern of this book. Fusion has the ability to allow us to think through intra- and inter-regional connections and is a concept that might stand as the motif for Micronesia and Micronesian studies. Whereas individual island worlds have often been invoked as microcosms of the Earth, perhaps best observed in the title of Paul Bahn and John Flenley's (1992) popular book *Easter Island, Earth Island* (see also Kirch 1997a; cf. Rainbird 2002a), in being sealed and localized eco-systems in which the humans are included, which is an extension of island biogeography and the now discredited concept of 'islands as laboratories' (cf. Rainbird 1999c). The connecting sea that ebbs and flows between the islands of Micronesia is also a connecting sea that pays little heed to supposed boundaries. Any boundaries that exist are social ones, and are of no less importance as a consequence, but have to be historically situated rather than assumed. Consequentially, with the seascapes of the Pacific Ocean in mind, it might be useful to look beyond the conventional boundary of the region under discussion here.

The following passage comes from the work of American ethnographer Fay-Cooper Cole in *The Wild Tribes of Davao District, Mindanao* and is derived from work conducted early last century:

Another possible source of outside blood is suggested by well verified stories of castaways on the east coast of Mindanao and adjacent islands. While working with the Mandaya in the region of Mayo Bay the writer was frequently told that three times, in the memory of the present inhabitants, strange boats filled with strange people had been driven to their coasts by storms. The informants insisted that these newcomers were not put to death but that such of them as survived were taken into the tribe. These stories are given strong substantiation by the fact that only a few months prior to my visit a boat load of people from the Carolines was driven to the shores of Mayo Bay and that their boat, as well as one survivor, was then at the village of Mati. I am indebted to Mr. Henry Hubbel for the following explicit account of these castaways: 'One native banca [single outrigger boat] of castaways arrived at Lucatan, N.E. corner of Mayo Bay, Mindinao, on January 2nd, 1909. The banca left the island of Ulithi for the island of Yap, two days' journey, on December 10th, 1908. They were blown out of their course and never sighted land until January 2nd, twenty-two days after setting sail. There were nine persons aboard, six men, two boys, and one woman, all natives of Yap except one man who was a Visayan from Capiz, Panay, P. I., who settled on the island of Yap in 1889. These people were nineteen days without food and water except what water could be caught during rainstorms. The Visayan, Victor Valenamo, died soon after his arrival, as a result of starvation. The natives recovered at once and all traces of their starvation disappeared within two weeks. The men were powerfully built, nearly six feet high. Their bodies were all covered with tattoo work. The woman was decorated even more than the men. (Cole 1913: 170–1).

Mindanao is one of the larger and most southerly of the Philippine Islands archipelago, a group of large Southeast Asian islands that has at no time been considered part of Micronesia. But to quote the report above is to highlight the fluidity of the boundaries and thus the difficulties inherent in such a project of labelling and identifying the region of Micronesia. Certainly in current geographical toponyms, the ocean expanse that forms the western seascape of the Mariana and Caroline Islands is the Philippine Sea. Part of this sea, with a greater area provided by a section of the Pacific Ocean, constitutes the 7 million square kilometres of area conventionally labelled Micronesia. Within this seascape there is 2700 square kilometres of land. Micronesia epitomizes what Epeli Hau'ofa (1993) has termed, in his highly influential essay, 'a sea of islands'. One sea connecting a multitude of islands both within and, as we have already seen, beyond conventional boundaries. The Philippines to the west of the study area (Fig. 1.1) have been the location for such stories of contact since the earliest reports by European visitors. As historian of Micronesia Fran Hezel (1983: 36–7) writes from the primary sources:

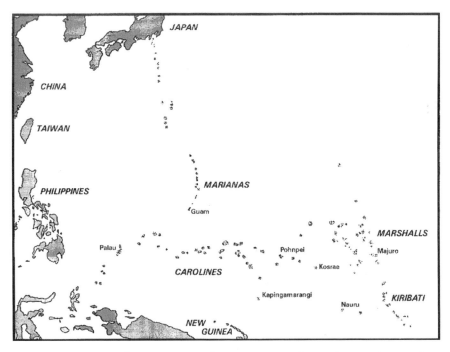

Fig. 1.1 Map of Micronesia. The current popular understanding is that Micronesia incorporates the island groups of the Marianas, Carolines and Marshalls, and the Gilberts in the Republic of Kiribati. A small number of other islands that fall outside of these main groups are also included.

One day in late December 1696, two strange-looking canoes appeared off the eastern coast of Samar, an island in the eastern Philippines . . . The villagers of Samar responded promptly and generously to the plight of the castaways. They brought coconuts, palm wine, and taro, all of which were greedily devoured by the strangers who . . . had been adrift for over two months. The villagers hurriedly summoned two women, who had themselves drifted to Samar some time before, in the hope that they would be able to communicate with the strangers. At the sight of one of these women, several of the castaways, who recognized her as a relative, burst into tears. By the time the parish priest arrived at the spot, communication between the Filipinos and the band of Carolinians was well under way, with the two women serving as interpreters.

Hezel continues that the 'castaways' were able, by placing pebbles on the beach, to tell of eighty-seven islands that they had visited, and provided the names and sailing times between them. They also had with them when they landed a piece of iron and were very keen to collect some more.

    This second account, more than 200 years prior to the first is, at least in its secondary reporting, apparently consistent in interpreting these 'strange' people on 'strange' boats arriving by accident through drifting from their prescribed course; the group arriving at Samar was supposed to have been sailing between Lamotrek and Fais in the Caroline Islands. But each of the groups had elements that were exotic to the Carolines (one had in their party a Filipino man, the other had a piece of iron), both crossing and re-crossing parameters of regional definition.

A third and final example from the Philippines is quite different from those reported above and is derived from the report of Fedor Jagor; whilst travelling through the Philippines in 1859, he states (Jagor 1875, quoted in Lessa 1962: 334):

In Guiuan [Guinan] I was visited by some Mikronesians [*sic*], who for the last fourteen days had been engaged at Sulangan on the small neck of land south-east from Guiuan, in diving for pearl mussels (mother-of-pearl), having undertaken the dangerous journey for the express purpose.

William Lessa (1962) in collecting this information has no problem with its reliability and accepts that the shell collectors were from Woleai in the Caroline Islands. And, indeed, why should we have a problem with accepting that Caroline Islanders were able to make many round trips of over 1000 kilometres each way in locally built outrigger vessels for the express purpose of collecting a resource not available nearby? Other resources to exploit might have included iron, but the Caroline Islanders, like the communities of the other Micronesian island groups, were users of shell over all other raw materials for portable tools until the general availability of iron, for most places not beginning until the twentieth century. Specific shell types would be intimately known, and the variety of colour, pattern and physical properties would be recognized by the majority of the community. Certainly, beyond apparently functional items, such as adzes and fishing lures, shell beads and whole half-bivalves were often valued as a type of money, strung together; and as I will discuss in detail in chapter 6, they often formed part of the cargo in inter-island exchange. But as we will see in chapter 7, in regard to the widespread distribution of particular adze types, fishing lures manufactured for trolling behind sailing craft can also have need of special raw materials that require contacts over large swathes of seascape. Robert Gillett (1987), in his study of tuna fishing on Satawal in the central Caroline Islands, found that pearl shell for fashioning lures was imported both from Chuuk Lagoon, which produced shell particularly prized for its rainbow-like colouring, and from much further asea in New Guinea, once again, like the Philippines, well beyond the supposed bounds of Micronesia.

The historical accounts, which I will review further in detail below, when read in relation to the later accounts of scientists and ethnographers, provide an understanding of the islands of Micronesia as situated within a seascape; although we should be wary of relative terms such as 'strangeness' or 'dangerous' that are used, as in some of the passages reviewed above, in outsider accounts of voyaging and encounter. Seascapes are knowable places, in the same way that landscapes have to be understood also as visionscapes, soundscapes, touchscapes, smellscapes (Tilley 1999) and even tastescapes. A person approaching the sea from the land in a strong onshore breeze can attest to the taste of bitter salt that is driven by the wind into the mouth and drying the throat. Seascapes are further nuanced and utterly knowable places for those that exist in them on a quotidian basis. Modern ethnography allied to historical reports provides an abundance of information that, through senses, lore, observation, technology, skill, mythology and myriad other ways, the ocean of the Micronesians was, and in some cases still is, an utterly knowable place in its form and texture and its link with the guiding heavens connecting the strange place that is always beyond the knowable world, the horizon, where spirits of below meet the spirits of above (Goodenough 1986). This is a seascape traversed by known seaways; a place of paths that linked communities.

Like landscapes, seascapes are not without their dangers and the large amount of recorded ritual relating to seafaring in the Micronesian sea of islands is as much to do with safe return as with successful, in an economic sense, trading or fishing expeditions. Journeys were taken when it was perceived safe to do so. They were not merely a necessity for the collection and exchange of mundane goods, but were instead part and parcel of communities who did not always perceive their boundaries as being at the edge of the reef, although at times, as we shall see in relation to the people of Pohnpei (chapter 7), they may have found it unnecessary to travel as people came to them. At other times, for example when the Spanish settled Guam in the late seventeenth century, islanders broke off the connections that had existed along well-traversed seaways.

Although occurring 250 years after the first European encounters with the people in the region now known as Micronesia, the voyages of Captain James Cook are often assumed to be the major turning point in Pacific history, the one that led to the colonial era which lasted up until the post-Second World War period (Rainbird 2001b). Scholarship concerning the Cook voyages has given apparent precedence to the map that was created from the information provided by the Raiatean navigator-priest Tupaia during the Second Voyage's visit to Tahiti as reported by Johann Forster (1996). Tupaia named eighty-four islands of which Tahiti was at the centre. The actual identity of these islands has been argued over ever since (see discussion in Lewis 1994), but for Forster it was simple to conclude that:

The foregoing account of the many islands mentioned by Tupaya [Tupaia] is sufficient to prove that the inhabitants of the islands in the South Seas have made very considerable navigations in their slight and weak canoes; navigations which many Europeans would think impossible to be performed, upon a careful view of the vessels themselves, their riggings, sails, &c. &c. also the provisions of the climate.

Unlike the potentially doubting Europeans, Forster had first-hand experience of the similarities of language and physical type of the people encountered on the second of Cook's first two voyages, which incorporated the two southerly angles of what later would become known as the Polynesian Triangle. The expeditions visited Aotearoa/New Zealand and Rapa Nui/Easter Island and the islands of the Equatorial zone of Tahiti and the Society Islands, the Marquesas in the east and the 'Friendly Islands' of Tonga in the west. The importance for Pacific scholarship that has been placed on this account and the chart that was prepared for Forster is quite different from the little-commented-upon chart constructed by Father Paul Klein of the eighty-seven islands identified by the Carolinian 'castaways' on Samar in 1696. Why are these received differently? The Spanish certainly appear to have become excited in regard to the prospect of many more souls to be saved on these previously unknown islands and an official inquiry found evidence of earlier 'castaway' groups that show, 'if the reports are to be believed, the traffic between the Palaos [as the Carolines were then known] and the Philippines was heavy. In the year 1664 alone, as many as thirty canoes reportedly drifted to the Philippines' (Hezel 1983: 40).

Klein's chart was reproduced many times, but as a measure of indigenous interaction prior to prolonged European contact with the region it has held little sway compared with the chart derived from the Cook voyage. Perhaps this reflects the fact that the area was generally a Spanish colonial concern until the nineteenth century. Even as late as the 1920s the anthropologist James Frazer (1924: 27) was able to say of Micronesia that 'on the whole this great archipelago has been more neglected [in scholarship] and is less known than any other in the Pacific'.

Another concern may have been the difficulty in grouping together these peoples who clearly were aware of each other's presence, and travelled beyond the putative region of Micronesia, but who also had distinctive differences in material expression and linguistics. Such problems are perhaps suggested in the musings of the French 'scientists' Grégoire Louis Domeny de Rienzi and Jules-Sébastien-César Dumont d'Urville. Although Dumont d'Urville is regarded as the founder of the boundaries of the division of the Pacific into three areas, or four if one includes the islands of South-East Asia and the appellation Malaysia, he had great arguments with his contemporary Domeny de Rienzi (see 1837). It was Domeny de Rienzi who coined the term Micronesia, a year ahead of Dumont d'Urville's tripartite division that used the term Melanesia for the first time, and was published in 1832.

Nicholas Thomas (1989; 1997) has highlighted the racist distinctions made in these divisions of the Pacific, at least in relation to Melanesia and Polynesia. Micronesia fits less comfortably into such arguments and this is probably due, at least in part, to what Serge Tcherkézoff (2001) has identified as a continuation of a fifteenth-century dualism separating dark skin/fair skin people. This has been identified as continuing today in Pacific scholarship (Terrell, Kelly and Rainbird 2001), but can be seen in other works such as Forster's significant work already mentioned above. In this, Forster links those people he had encountered in Polynesia as related to the Caroline Islanders and thus concludes that the Polynesians (although I use this term anachronistically in this case) were descendants of the Carolinians and quite distinct from the 'black' people that he had encountered in the New Hebrides (Vanuatu) and New Caledonia. Both the latter groups are today conventionally understood as part of Melanesia, that is, the 'Black islands'. Forster (1996 [1778]: 341) states in relation to the forming of the two distinct types of Pacific people that:

both would afterwards in the new climate preserve in some measure the hue and complexion they brought from the country which they left last: upon these premises we ventured to suppose that the two races of men in the South Sea arrived there by different routs [*sic*], and were descended from two different sets of men. [T]he five nations of [Tahiti/Society Islands, New Zealand/Aotearoa, Easter Island/Rapa Nui, Tonga, and the Marquesas] seem to come from Northward and by the Caroline-islands, Ladrones [Marianas], the Manilla [Philippines] and the island of Borneo, to have descended from the Malays: whereas on the contrary, the black race of men seems to have sprung from the people that originally inhabited the Moluccas, and on the approach of the Malay tribes withdrew into the interior parts of their isles and countries.

Forster was writing only a few decades prior to the advent of racial science that from the beginning of the nineteenth century attempted to systematize the attributes relating to the concept of divisions of people by race, and which eventually became linked to theories of social evolution through biology and social Darwinism (see, e.g., Stepan 1982). The intellectual milieu of Western discourse at this time was one in which the fusion of people from different places, evident in the population of Micronesia, provided a stumbling block in attempts to provide a definition of an actual Micronesian 'type' or 'race' as was desired. Consider these attempts for example:

We sometimes speak of the numerous colonies which have proceeded from Great Britain as being one people, inasmuch as they have issued from a single source; and in this sense we may apply the term to the tribes of Polynesia. We also speak of the inhabitants of the Roman Empire – at least after two or three centuries of conquest – as forming one people, inasmuch as the various nations and tribes to which they belonged had been cemented and fused together, by the general ascendancy and intermixture of one dominant race, – and in this sense alone the term is applicable to the natives of the Micronesian islands. Hence it will be seen that no general description can be given of the latter, which shall be every where equally correct, and which will not require many allowances and exceptions.

The Micronesians, as a people, do not differ greatly in complexion from their neighbours of Polynesia. Their colour varies from a light yellow, in some of the groups, particularly the western, to a reddish brown, which we find more common in the east and south-east. The features are usually high and bold, – the nose straight or aquiline, the cheek-bones projecting, the chin rounded and prominent. The nose is commonly widened at the lower part, as in the Polynesian race, but this is not a universal trait. The hair, which is black, is in some straight, in others curly. The beard is usually scanty, though among the darker tribes it is more abundant, and these have often whiskers and mustachios. In stature, the natives most often fall below than exceed the middle height, and they are naturally slender. (Hale 1968 [1846]: 71)

[For the Gilbertese] [p]roofs are abundant that the inhabitants of these islands belong to the same race as those of the Hawaiian, Marquesan, Tahitian and Samoan Islands. In appearance, they most strikingly resemble Hawaiians. There is evidently a mixture of people coming from different parts of Polynesia. Some strikingly resemble the Samoans, or Navigator Islanders. Not only does their appearance, cast of countenance, form of body, color of hair, eyes, teeth, and other characteristics indicate their origin to be the same, but also their language and many of their customs and practices. (Damon 1861: 6–7)

[The Carolines population is] an odd medley of the black, brown, and yellow races. It is a curious fact that, although Yap lies some 1500 miles nearer India and the Malay archipelago than Ponape [Pohnpei], the westernmost islands are much the darker and their language the more strange and barbarous. The great stream of Polynesian migration has passed further southward. Yet the dialect of Ulithi to the north of Yap, like that of the central Carolines, has a considerable Polynesian infiltration. These jagged or indented areas of speech are a peculiar puzzle to the philologist, showing a very irregular distribution of race-mixture. (Christian 1899a: 105)

It will be understood from their geographical position that mixture of races is inevitable in these islands. For instance, two different types may be distinguished in the natives of Truk [Chuuk]. On Yap and Palau, we notice that some of the natives have frizzy hair. We may possibly regard these facts as testifying to the mixture of races. (Matsumura 1918: 12–13)

All of these authors were writing on the basis of some direct experience of travelling and observing Micronesians first hand, but they all also relied on the writings of others for comparisons with places they had not visited, and the biases exhibited are not only their own but represent a long-established tradition of grouping and labelling people on the basis of similarity and difference. Of these authors only Horatio Hale and Akira Matsumura may be considered ethnographers proper of their quite different times, but the missionary Reverend Samuel Damon and the traveller F.W. Christian both adopt the common language for biological ascription prevalent at the time. In all cases, however, the complexity of the situations that they encountered did not allow for simple labelling.

The comment of Damon regarding the Gilbert Islanders (the I-Kiribati of the present Republic of Kiribati) having close affinities with Hawaiians is perhaps illustrative of a phenomenon exhibited by many travellers in their attempts to describe people and perhaps ought to be taken as a warning to the unwary. Damon was the pastor of the Bethel Church in Hawaii and had never previously visited Micronesia. The account of his trip on the missionary ship the *Morning Star* from which the quotation is taken makes it clear that the people of the Gilbert Islands were the first he made acquaintance with in Micronesia.

Thus, given his knowledge of Hawaii and Hawaiians, he is best able to make comparisons between these two groups. This is important, as the itinerary of voyaging requires consideration when assessing the various claims of people in describing the inhabitants of individual islands because it is likely that the comparison, although not always made explicit, will be with the people of the island previously visited. It has been argued in relation to this that the black/fair race divide of the South Sea made by Forster was particularly strong as the Melanesian New Hebrides (Vanuatu) was encountered by him for the first time directly after a stay in Tahiti (Jolly 1992; Douglas 1999).

Christian's reliance on linguistic variation as an indicator of complexity within the region is a continuation of a link between philology and race beginning in the eighteenth century with the discovery of the Indo-European family of languages (Ashcroft 2001). In our current understanding this would mean at least seven non-mutually intelligible language or dialect groupings in the region at the time of Magellan. Even within these there could be some difficulty in communication between different island communities, and within individual island communities there were also rank-accessed special ritual languages such as the *itang* of Chuuk. At another level however there are two main subgroupings (see Fig. 1.2) of the language family of Austronesian which covers the whole region. Thus, language could be used to separate or encompass at a variety of levels and with as much success in reality as physical characteristics. Of course, other languages such as Spanish, Tagalog, Japanese, German, English and American English all have had, or still do have, a presence in the islands, starting from at least the sixteenth century onwards according to historical reports. In the same way that today English has been incorporated as a second language, one of colonial government, while the local language has been maintained in many cases for the home and 'traditional' politics, neighbouring languages of the communities that were in regular contact with each other could also be learnt. 'Scientists' attempting to record the essential elements of a society rarely commented upon such occurrences, and this neglect in recording may also in part be a further consequence of treating individual islands as laboratories.

Fusion and fluidity do not in essence or as a consequence indicate sameness. In considering the contemporary consequences of globalization through multinational corporations and the forging of greater alliances between nation-states, many commentators have found that rather than the feared consequences realized in homogenization and the consequent single 'global village', such broader groupings have allowed different community identities to emerge as they imagine themselves differently when released from the confining dictates and boundaries of the nation-state (Bauman 1998; cf. Anderson 1991). It is possible, I believe, to envisage the history of Micronesia in a similar way, where social boundaries are maintained within a milieu of communication and contact across seaways and across putative language groupings.

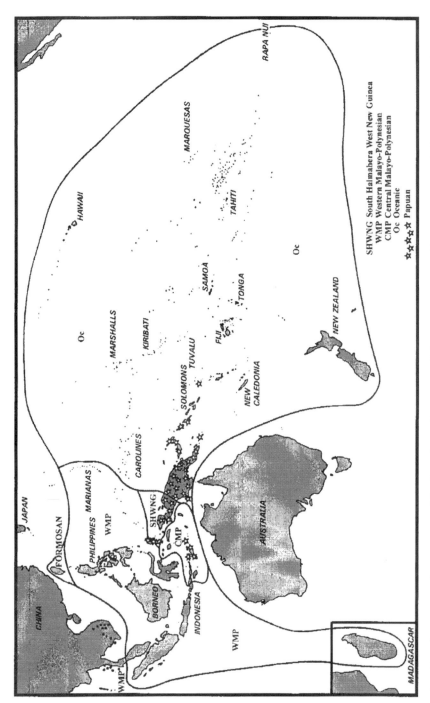

Fig. 1.2 The geographic range and high-order sub-groups of the Austronesian language group (after Tryon 1995). The solid lines indicating certain distributions should not be confused with the definite boundaries of nation-states or supposed 'culture groups'.

It is perhaps possible to identify such an issue from a local perspective by considering anthropologist Glenn Petersen's analysis in his monograph *Lost in the Weeds: Theme and Variation in Pohnpei Political Mythology*. Although Petersen's (1990a: 3) volume finds its title from a Pohnpeian saying that when trying to sort out the evidence of multiple versions derived from oral history 'the truth is *Nan tehlik* "Lost in the weeds" like a coconut that has fallen into the underbrush at the foot of a tree', he does find some consistency in some themes derived from local Pohnpeian history. One consistent aspect amongst the variety of stories related to the initial discovery, construction and settlement of Pohnpei is the continuing introduction of people and things from the outside. This theme of foreign introduction and incorporation is not without a certain ambivalence, but Petersen (1990a: 12) finds that '[t]he emphasis given by these early tales to Pohnpei's reliance on the outer world resonates in modern Pohnpei. The people see interaction with the rest of the world as fundamental to their own existence.'

Interaction with the outer world may indeed be fundamental to the people of Pohnpei in the past and present. In this Pohnpei is not alone, for all the other communities in Micronesia have similarly looked beyond their reefs. But the Pohnpeians, according to Petersen, jealously maintain the ability to control this interaction and may even go so far as to make the island 'invisible – hidden in a great mass of clouds – to anyone sailing past it on the open seas' (1990a: 12).

This theme of interaction allows the possibility of making sense of local understandings of a rock-art site on Pohnpei (Rainbird in press). In my work with Meredith Wilson (Rainbird and Wilson 1999) we found that along with ghosts and indigenous ancestors from mythical times, in the local understandings the engravings could also be attributed to Spaniards, Filipinos, 'Orientals' or 'Indians'. This provides, I suggest, further confirmation of the observations of Petersen.

Summary of the book

In examining the connectivity and resulting observations of similarities and differences in the material culture of the region and beyond, the motifs of fusion and fluidity, themselves linked, form two of the linking themes of this book. In chapter 2 I examine the intellectual and political milieu of Micronesian studies through a consideration of the historical and anthropological accounts of the region. Chapter 3 takes as its theme the fluid geographical, political and disciplinary boundaries of the area. This includes issues regarding seafaring and linguistics. Together the first three are introductory chapters.

Chapter 4 provides an assessment of the date of human arrivals in the region, and their possible direction of travel. The evidence from physical anthropology and archaeology is assessed in terms of its utility for providing evidence of origins for the people who first settled the islands of the region. This evidence inevitably leads to a consideration of broader themes of island colonization in the Pacific and critically discusses the issues of interpretation in relation to the evidence from the western Pacific more generally. Also considered are local understandings and the issue of what motivated people to settle the islands in the first place.

In order to provide as detailed an account as possible, in the next four chapters the region is split into island groups, with sections describing, where possible, smaller groups or individual islands. The latter is dependent on the amount of material available from each place, and is in itself a product of the history of archaeological research as discussed above. Chapters 5 to 8 therefore provide accounts of particular parts of the region. Chapter 5 focuses on the Mariana Islands archipelago from human settlement until the arrival of the Spanish. The history of the archipelago as a whole reveals differing connections through time within the region and beyond. Differences unique to the Marianas betray intra-archipelago community traits.

Chapter 6 takes the western end of the east–west chain of the Caroline Islands, along with the atolls of that group, and splits it into smaller areas of study. Each area is discussed in terms of its settlement history, archaeology and, where appropriate, rock-art. As is the case elsewhere in the book, ethnography and history are drawn upon where they appear appropriate as an aid to discussing the material remains. Chapter 7 focuses on the material remains of the high islands of the eastern Carolines.

The atoll island groups of the Marshalls and Gilberts and outlying islands in the region are brought together in chapter 8. Although relatively less is known about these islands, an overview and interpretation are provided, with the areas where evidence is lacking acknowledged.

Finally, chapter 9 draws together the three dominant themes, which are a thread throughout the text. These are fusion, fluidity and what will latterly be introduced as flux. Drawn together, such a synthesis provides a critical overview of the long-term history of the people in this part of Oceania and is further related to debates more commonly associated with other areas of Oceania. These other areas have, until now, often received greater attention from scholars.

CHAPTER 2

MICRONESIANS: THE PEOPLE IN HISTORY AND ANTHROPOLOGY

Archaeology is about people; it is about constructing an understanding concerning people in the past by using an array of resources. One way of attempting to understand the potential difference between the constructor, that is the archaeologist, and the lives of the past being constructed, is to look to the sources of the recent past, that is, the primary and secondary historical texts reporting encounters between outsiders and the people of the region. These direct texts begin with the arrival of Ferdinand Magellan in the sixteenth century. Another source, and one that has had as its aim the description of the differences of the lives of the people of these islands, is the ethnographic and synthetic texts of anthropologists.

It is less the case for the anthropological works, but still of some concern, that the majority of these texts are not vehicles for a direct hearing of islander voices. Some of the work, such as parts of the ethnohistorical work of David Hanlon, is drawn directly from oral history, and other works discussed in this book by Rufino Mauricio and Vicente Diaz are the work of islander academics. These are certainly the exceptions rather than the rule and we should constantly keep in mind the words of Epeli Hau'ofa, published nearly three decades ago, that '[w]hen [as anthropologists] we produce our articles and monographs and they [the people of the study] or their grandchildren read them, they often cannot see themselves or they see themselves being distorted or misrepresented' (1975: 284).

In this chapter I will review the anthropological and historical sources in relation to the region with two purposes in mind. The first is to provide further contextual information to allow for the building of a more detailed understanding of the region and the second is to develop further the themes of fusion and fluidity introduced in chapter 1.

Anthropology's history

As Marshall Sahlins (1995) has commented, supposed 'first contact' situations result in ambiguities amongst the reports. For example, translations of Pigafetta, the chronicler of Magellan's voyage, say of the Chamorro people of Guam that they indicated by gestures that they had no knowledge of people existing in the world beyond their own small group of islands (Lévesque 1992). But an account probably dictated by another in the company of Magellan and written in Portuguese states that the Chamorro approached their ship 'without any shyness as if they were good acquaintances' (Lévesque 1992: 249). In the Caroline Islands to the south of Guam, records of sixteenth- and seventeenth-century contacts between Europeans and islanders are sporadic, but none the less informative, with comparisons often made between the Carolinians and the Chamorro people of the Marianas.

There is documentary and cartographic evidence to suggest that Ulithi Atoll was sighted and contact made with the islanders during Diogo da Rocha's voyage in 1525 (Lévesque 1992; Lessa 1966). On a sixteenth-century Portuguese map the atoll is labelled 'momcgua' or 'momegug', which bears some similarity to the main islet name of Mogmog, indicating that a person with local knowledge had supplied this. Indeed, historical source work conducted by anthropologist William Lessa (1975a; also Lévesque 1992) found that a number of sixteenth-century works alluded to the European discovery of Ulithi, and Barros' *Terceira decada da Asia* published in 1563 provided additional detail. In this, Barros provides exact dates indicating not only that da Rocha's expedition had stayed on Ulithi for four months, but also that at least some of the Ulithians may have been familiar with the islands of the Philippines some 600 kilometres west. Familiarity with the Philippines appeared to be indicated by the Ulithian's knowledge of where to find gold when shown it by the Europeans, and the knowledge appears to be linked in Barros' account to the 'large *proas*', sailing vessels, possessed by the islanders. This Portuguese visit of 1525, only four years after Magellan led the Spanish expedition that landed at Guam, appears to be the earliest evidence of contact between Europeans and Caroline Islanders.

The Marshall Islanders had first contact with the Spanish when Alvaro de Saavedra stayed at an atoll (possibly Enewetak or Bikini) for eight days in 1529 (Hezel 1983). The eastern Carolines did not enter the European record for over another half-century, with the island of Pohnpei sighted in 1595 during the second Mendaña expedition. This brief encounter was reported by the expedition's Portuguese pilot, and later leader following Mendaña's death, Pedro Fernandez de Quiros, in the following statement:

When we reached a latitude of just over 6° N, we sighted an island, apparently about 25 leagues in circumference, thickly wooded and inhabited by many people who resemble those of the Ladrones [Marianas], and whom we saw coming towards us in canoes. (in Lévesque 1993: 26)

Moving back to the western Carolines, the islands of Yap are not first recorded until the seventeenth century. On 15 February 1625 the Dutch Nassau fleet reported the first sighting of Yap thus:

they saw another island, not laid down in the charts, in lat. 9°45′ N the natives of which came out to them in canoes with fruits and other refreshments, but as the ships were sailing at a great rate, they were not able to get on board. The people seemed much like those on Guam, and the island seemed very populous and highly cultivated. (Kerr's translation in Lévesque 1993: 574)

It appears from this quote that the Yapese had perhaps learned from elsewhere the appropriate response for extracting Western largesse: they came prepared with food to trade, even though they had apparently no direct experience of European contact up until this point. Could it be that already, a little over a century since Magellan and nearly two centuries before sustained European contact, the 'first contact' experience for the islanders had significantly changed in that the aliens had become knowable, or at least expected?

Earlier, in 1565, the small Spanish ship *San Lucas*, which had separated from the fleet led by Miguel de Legazpi, entered Chuuk Lagoon as the first recorded European craft. Here, as with the Dutch in Yap, the islanders came out to the ship with food and made gestures that they should follow them ashore. As the ship made for the anchorage as directed by a local pilot, 'the Spaniards noticed with alarm hundreds of canoes full of men armed with lances, clubs, and slings, rapidly bearing down on them' (Hezel 1983: 24). Making a hasty retreat across the lagoon, the crew of the *San Lucas* had two more violent confrontations before leaving the lagoon the next day and sailing westwards. However, on encountering two atolls, similar events occurred resulting in the death of two crew and countless islanders. The voyage through the Marshall and Caroline Islands is described by Hezel (1983: 27) as 'one harrowing escapade after another', but the ship survived to become the first to make the west to east journey back to New Spain (Mexico) from the Philippines, thus establishing the Manila Galleon route.

At the same time, we should try to be aware of the islanders' own frames of reference, which, in the Carolines, may be regarded as fine preparation for such encounters. As Glenn Petersen (2000: 26) explains:

When Europeans arrived on the scene, with their histories of imperial expansion, their technologies of domination, and their lusts for superordination, they did not encounter peoples who were unfamiliar with the possibilities of empire. Rather, they found populations who were not only committed traders but already possessed fairly sophisticated concepts concerning the possibilities of overlordship, well-developed commitments to making use of it, and skills and tactics for resisting it.

Many of the previously visited islands of the Carolines were not encountered again for a number of decades. The Spanish expedition led by Villalobos, which left Mexico in November 1542, visited a number of northern atolls of the Marshalls group before arriving in their westerly passage at the islands identified as Fais, never reportedly encountered previously by Europeans, and Ulithi, which had been. At both, the islanders confidently used Spanish or Portuguese greetings. A 1698 account of one of these encounters by Father Gaspar de San Augustin, although not to be regarded as a primary source, comments that (in Lévesque 1992: 580):

after a few days of navigation, they sighted a small, but very high, inhabited island, with many coconut palms [probably Fais]. They tried to come to an anchor at it, but they could not . . . When the natives of the island saw this, they went to the ships in a small boat, with six men aboard it, and as they came near they were making signs of friendship and offering fish, coconuts and other fruits. When paying attention to what they were repeatedly uttering, it was recognized that they were saying: '*Matelote buenos días*'. Then, making the sign of the cross with the fingers and kissing it; this caused no end of wonderment, because it was not known how they could have learned that, being as they were so isolated in such a remote region.

The allusions to Christianity may have been wishful thinking on the part of the author, but what is clear from the Villalobos expedition is that the community on Fais, which had had no previous recorded contact with Europeans, appear already to have been remotely affected within the eighteen years since the Portuguese had visited neighbouring Ulithi or the twenty-two years since Magellan had landed on Guam.

Encounters could indeed be fleeting, but on occasions the historical legacy can take on a much greater apparent importance. Such a case is that of Francis Drake and his 'island of thieves'. There is no primary report or journal surviving from the British buccaneer Drake's circumnavigation of the Globe in the *Golden Hind*. But secondary sources written decades after the event reported that several weeks after leaving the coast of New Albion (California) and heading west across the Pacific his first island landfall was an unhappy one. William Lessa (1975b) studied the specifics of this leg of Drake's voyage in detail and it is from this source that the following account is derived.

The geographical location of this landfall of islands on 30 September 1579 is variously reported as between 8 and 9 degrees north of the Equator. At this place, although the crew of the *Golden Hind* did not go ashore, they were becalmed and making little headway when approached by hundreds of 'canoes' each carrying between four and fifteen men. The watercraft were paddled rather than sailed, and were highly polished, with shiny white shells hanging from each prow. The islanders brought with them coconuts, fish, potatoes and fruit. They were apparently naked, with distended earlobes and black teeth, and they appear to have been chewing betel nut. At first there seems to have been brisk trade between the sailors and the islanders, but it is reported that over time this became particularly one-sided, with the islanders becoming more and more reluctant to part with goods for exchange. Eventually the islanders appear to have given up on exchange and resorted to taking anything that they could get their hands on, including a dagger and some knives from the belt of a sailor.

One report says that Drake had them fired upon and twenty of the islanders were killed. After three days the *Golden Hind* finally made headway beyond the islands that Drake decided to label 'The Island of Thieves' in order to warn future visitors.

As Lessa (1975b) reports, there have been many attempts, using the scanty historical documents, to identify the actual location of this island group. Yap, some western Carolinian atolls, and islands in the Philippines have all been suggested, along with Guam and the Marianas which Magellan had already labelled the Ladrones ('Islands of Thieves') in 1521. Lessa's own detailed assessment concludes that the Palau Archipelago is the one in question; this would be the first reported European contact with Palauans. He supports this proposal by assessing in detail the geographical and cultural elements of the historic reports, by assuming some confusion occurring in regard to later contacts on the same voyage in the islands of South-East Asia, and by assessing the behaviour of the islanders in relation to what Lessa regards as the already current role of exotic objects in the communities of these islands. In regard to the latter he states (Lessa 1975b: 254–5):

The natives already knew about iron because of their close proximity to Halmahera and other islands in the Indies, which obtained it from Chinese and European traders . . . More important, however, than their keen desire for iron could have been their interest in the beads the foreigners gave them. The Palauans already knew about beads, which from ancient times they used for money and valued with a deep and all-pervading passion. Coming entirely from Indonesia and the Philippines – and possibly ultimately from China, India, and the Mediterranean – vitreous and ceramic beads and other forms of ornaments, fashioned from both glass and clay, entered into the economic, social, political, and religious life of the people, and even acquired an extensive body of mythological tradition.

In chapter 6 I will consider these beads in more detail. For the time being it is important to note that the episodes that Western scholars have often perceived as dramatic examples of first and violent contact may often be a misperception of island peoples by alien voyagers new to the area. The islanders already had a strong tradition of encountering other people and in this had expectations and associated rules of behaviour in relation to such meetings. For the most part we can expect that these rules of behaviour were probably contravened by the uninitiated Europeans.

The second Dutch expedition to the Pacific was led by Olivier van Noort, a Rotterdam tavern-keeper. This expedition arrived at Guam in September 1600. In his own account van Noort reports of the Chamorros that 'some had their face eaten by the pox, so much so that they had only a small opening for the mouth' (in Lévesque 1993: 110). This is not direct evidence of smallpox, as 'pox' was used to describe a number of possible ailments; Lévesque believes it to be leprosy, even though he thinks that the Dutch thought syphilis was responsible.

Perhaps then we ought to be little surprised that in 1565 the voyagers on the *San Lucas* met hostility at every encounter with Carolinians, as this may have been at the height of knowledge that these aliens in European ships brought more than iron and beads. After all, up until this time Guam and the Marianas continued to feel the brunt of Spanish presence, and Glynn Barratt (1988a) makes a convincing case for continued Carolinian sailing expeditions to the Marianas with an especial interest in trading for iron. By 1700 the Carolinians had probably stopped communication with the Chamorro. By this time, the indigenous population of the Marianas may have been reduced by as much as 90 per cent through introduced diseases and war against the Spaniards. Barratt (1988a) believes that part of the massive population decline may be due to some Chamorros becoming refugees in the Caroline Islands, in the Woleai area or Ulithi and Fais.

The likelihood is that the reason for population decline due to illness was easily identified. In discussing the immediate post-contact consequences of venereal disease at the time of Cook, Margaret Jolly (1996: 203) states:

They [Cook's crew] were indeed the authors of the disease, a fact recognized by Hawaiians and Tahitians, and other Islanders ever since, not just in the immediate 'havock' of the first pains and pandemics but in the ensuing effects of infertility, dying and depopulation in subsequent generations. In many oral and written traditions authored by Hawaiians, venereal diseases are portrayed as the 'curse of Cook'.

Back in Micronesia in 1843, centuries after initial contact, the trader Andrew Cheyne recorded how the visit of his ship led to the death of several Yapese, and the illness of many others, from influenza (Morgan 1996).

It also ought to be acknowledged that the ripples in the Pacific seascape caused by Europeans were filtered through Mexico or South-East Asia, depending on the direction of travel. For example, the majority of Spanish expeditions after the 1540s were fitted out and crewed in the western ports of New Spain (Mexico), a Spanish colony torn from but encompassing the indigenous peoples since 1519, or Peru (Lima was founded in 1535), with a similar history. One of these ports, Acapulco, 'came to life in the 1570s and gradually acquired a small, permanent population of Negroes, Mulattoes, Filipinos, and a few Spaniards' (Gerhard 1972: 41). Thus, on the Pacific rim, colonial demands led rapidly to the development of what Ross Gibson (1994) has termed for early colonial Sydney 'ocean settlement', a mix of settler and diasporic communities, numbers of people born of the fusion of diverse ancestry, an entanglement of geographies and experiences realized through a European frame of governance.

Such a fusion is likely to have occurred much earlier in the islands of South-East Asia. With colonies established in the sixteenth century, the Portuguese expeditions emanating from there were joined to an earlier and long-established trade network linking south China through the islands to India, and almost certainly Arabia and Africa across the Indian Ocean in the west (Hall 1992). The wreck of a recently recorded Arabian or Indian vessel found in waters between Sumatra and Java serves to exemplify this in carrying Chinese pottery and dating to the ninth century (Flecker 2001). Manila, the Philippines colony formed by Spain in 1565, was apparently established to lure the Chinese market (Steinberg 1982). When the Dutch in the early seventeenth century established Batavia, their entrepôt in Java, they modelled it on Amsterdam, but in a short time the canals became breeding grounds for disease (Legge 1964), and by the time of Cook, according to John Beaglehole (1974: 257), 'with a mortality of something like 50,000 a year, the place was one of the deadliest on earth'.

So not only was a European traffic filtered through these places prior to entry into Micronesia, further complicating the fusion and redirecting the fluidity, but the filter in the west was one that already had strong maritime links over a vast area, and almost certainly on occasions these links connected with Micronesia. Each ship that entered the region from the sixteenth century onwards contained a diversity of people under one flag, a floating ocean settlement, which introduced islanders to a world much bigger than far-off Europe.

The eminent historian of Micronesia, Fran Hezel, has regarded the early phase of European exploration in the Caroline and Marshall Islands as a relatively short-lived episode that left little impact (Hezel 1983: 34–5):

The people on the islands that had been visited, for their part, had little to show for their encounter with the Spanish: a few iron nails, a word or two of Spanish, perhaps a scar from a musket ball, and invariably an interesting story to tell their grandchildren years later. Their lives were not changed by the occasional Spanish ship they had seen, and they could not have minded too much when they returned to the seclusion that they had known before Magellan's voyage.

However, an excellent assessment by Paul D'Arcy of the history of inter-island contacts between the years 1770 and 1870, with a focus on the western Caroline Islands, finds that there was no return to 'seclusion' as Hezel would have it, but '[w]hen a regional perspective is adopted, Carolinian indigenous history may be seen as more dynamic [with] inter-island exchanges [being] an integral part of that history' (D'Arcy 2001: 181). Thus, D'Arcy is calling for regional histories of Micronesia, ones that acknowledge the myriad contacts between islands and islanders, which do not privilege Europeans as the only possessors of technologies enabling change.

History's anthropology

Although it is clear that the era ushered in by the voyages of Cook has been overstated in relation to Micronesia, one change that did come about is the notoriety of Cook and the wish to emulate the 'floating academy' approach of expeditions as a matter of pride for seafaring countries and on occasions specific individuals. Ultimately deriving from Enlightenment ideals, the earliest 'scientific expeditions' that arrived in Micronesia were those emanating from Russia and France in the early nineteenth century. In the detail of their observations, they provide a striking contrast to the journals of previous aliens.

Otto von Kotzebue led Russian expeditions that visited Micronesia in 1815–16 in the *Riurik* and 1824 in the frigate *Predpriate*. He is credited with placing much of the Ratak Chain of the Marshall Islands on 'the map' and, along with the French botanist Adelbert de Chamisso who volunteered for the first voyage, he published detailed accounts of the Marshall Islands and visits to the Spanish colony in Guam (Kotzebue 1821; 1830; Chamisso 1836; Barratt 1984).

A French expedition of exploration led by Louis de Freycinet visited Guam and the Marianas in 1819. The voyage of the *Uranie* is reported not only by Louis (Barratt 1988a), but also by his wife Rose Marie, who, against regulations, had been smuggled aboard disguised as a man and through the voyage kept her own journal (Freycinet 1996).

Louis Isidore Duperrey captained the corvette *Coquille* for the French government, and in May and June 1824 he sailed through the Gilbert and Caroline Islands. On this voyage Duperrey was accompanied by Dumont d'Urville, who later became the renowned navigator and geographer responsible for the tripartite division of Oceania, as discussed in the previous chapter. Together, the writings of Duperrey, d'Urville and René Primevère Lesson, the ship's surgeon, provide the earliest reports of Kosrae and Kosraean society (Ritter and Ritter 1982). D'Urville returned to Micronesia in 1828 as commander of the *Coquille*, now renamed *Astrolabe*, visiting Guam and passing through the Carolines, and called again at Guam in 1839 on his last expedition (Dumont d'Urville 1987).

Fedor Petrovich Lütke led a Russian expedition to the Caroline Islands, spending almost a year there from November 1827. Pohnpei and the islands in its vicinity became known for some time as the Senyavin Islands after his sloop *Senyavin*. Lütke was probably the first European to record Eauripik Atoll (Dunmore 1992). He published detailed records of the work of his expedition (Lütke 1835–36), as did, although much after the event, Friedrich Heinrich von Kittlitz, a German member of the expedition with a particular interest in botany (Ritter and Ritter 1982; Barratt 1984).

Many other reports that have been drawn upon for insights into eighteenth- and nineteenth-century island life come from the journals of voyagers who were not on scientific expeditions, but rather going about business to which islanders were incidental curiosities or suppliers of water and food. These include whalers and naval ships of various nations that were playing out in the Pacific aspects of distant wars. An example is Captain George Anson of the British Royal Navy, who in 1742 spent nearly two months repairing his vessel, *HMS Centurion*, on the island of Tinian in the Mariana Islands (Barratt 1988b). Anson had been on a mission to disrupt Spanish activity in the Pacific.

Some merchant seafarers also stumbled into history: sailors such as the captains Gilbert and Marshall, who sailed through what became known as the Gilbert and Marshall Islands, providing a brief description of I-Kiribati (Gilbertese) they encountered on the way (Gilbert 1789). They had unloaded human convict cargo at the newly established British penal colony of Port Jackson in 1788 and were sailing the *Charlotte* and *Scarborough* north to pick up a cargo of tea from China. A more significant contribution was made when Captain Henry Wilson in another merchant vessel, the *Antelope*, was wrecked off Palau in 1783. Wilson and his crew stayed for three months, becoming embroiled in local warfare and documenting much detail of local life at that time, which provided the basis for a very popular account written by George Keate (1789).

Other early written accounts come from people shipwrecked, such as Edward Barnard, captain of an American whaling ship that was wrecked in Palau in 1832 (Martin 1980). James O'Connell (1836), an Irishman supposedly shipwrecked in Pohnpei, provided a detailed book-length account of his five years as a castaway. Karl Semper, a German stranded on Palau for ten months by a leaking boat in 1862, provided a detailed account of his sojourn (Semper 1982). Such accounts, however, ought to be treated with extreme caution as they were often written with a popular public audience in mind. As Dirk Spennemann and Jane Downing (2001: xliv) say of sailor and adventurer Handley Bathurst Sterndale in regard to his Pacific articles for the *Australian Town and Country Journal* published between January 1871 and February 1872, 'we can only speculate on what amongst his writing is accurate in a historical sense'.

Other independent observers and travellers who have provided historical information include those in the capacity of missionaries, colonial agents and independent travellers such as John (Johan) Stanislaw Kubary and F.W. Christian. Kubary, a naturalist and ethnologist of Polish birth, published detailed accounts of his wide travels in Micronesia. He spent a great deal of the twenty-five years up to his death in 1896 in Micronesia, initially arriving to collect specimens for the German company Godeffroy and Sons. He stayed in Palau for over two years, although relations with the locals deteriorated rapidly and he lived separately (Stocking 1991), and also had a house and plantation in Pohnpei. He is credited with the first detailed recordings of the monumental Nan Madol site in Pohnpei (Kubary 1874). Christian, a Briton, travelled through the Caroline Islands and also published descriptions of sites such as Nan Madol. His work is, rather more than that of Kubary, in the genre of travel writing, but his book (1899b) and paper presented to the Royal Geographic Society in December 1898 provide some useful information (1899a). However, I reiterate my previous warning in regard to using such sources; in his book Christian says of Tochobei (Tobi), one of the Southwest Islands in the Republic of Belau, that there are 'massive platforms topped by stone images of her *Yari*, or ancient heroes, gazing out upon the deep' (1899b: 170). There is no evidence of the existence of such structures surviving on Tochobei, and what is described here sounds more like the *moai* of Rapa Nui (Easter Island) than anything found on a Micronesian island. A small stone figurine is reported from Tochobei, but this squatting male is only 38 cm in height, and in style appears to relate to wooden carvings on the island called *sen*, which have occasionally been dubbed 'monkey men' (Black, Osborne and Patricio 1979).

Since the late nineteenth century many of the major anthropological works based on ethnographic research in Micronesia have been linked directly to histories of occupation. The *Südsee-Expedition* (1909–10), the Imperial University of Tokyo expedition (1915) and the Coordinated Investigation of Micronesian Anthropology (1947–48) are each linked to colonial control of the region by the country of origin of the expedition. As it is not possible to detach the history of anthropology from the political history of Micronesia, I will discuss them in tandem here.

Although nominally considered Spanish, the islands in the region, outside of the Marianas, were spared direct government control until the twilight days of Spanish control. The Spaniards appear not to have been greatly enthused by the prospect of further costly colonies and it was left to the Catholic missionaries to attempt to cajole the government into providing means to explore the little-known islands to the south of Guam. One such enthusiast was *padre* Juan Antonio Cantova, who in 1721 interrogated thirty Carolinians from Woleai Atoll who had arrived on Guam in two outrigger sailing craft (Barratt 1988a).

The islanders of Palau had a history of trade with Britain following the wreck of an English ship there in the late eighteenth century (Keate 1789). However, it was not until German colonial desires began to develop in the region during the late nineteenth century that the Spanish began to assert their supposed authority.

The Germans annexed the Marshall Islands in 1885, and in 1888, through a condominium agreement, allowed official control to be maintained by a group of German trading companies operating under the single banner of the Jaluit-Gesellschaft AG. Gerd Hardach (1997) reports that the Jaluit company saw the Marshall Islands as their own colony and took little notice of the weak government attempts to intervene in local affairs.

In response, the Spanish built a fort and colony on Pohnpei. The other islands in the region appear to have been little affected by the nominal Spanish control, although groups of traders, castaways and beachcombers were developing on many of them. Spain lost Guam to the United States of America in 1898 after the Spanish–American War and, apart from Japanese occupation during World War II, Guam has remained a US territory, with the Chamorros having few rights to self-determination (see Rainbird 2000a). In 1899 Spain sold the rest of its Pacific territories to Germany.

German administration

The German colonial period appears to have been half-hearted and short-lived. The Germans had little impact in the Marianas, which had already been transformed by centuries of direct Spanish rule. Perhaps German influence in the region was felt most in the Marshall Islands where, after the annexation of 1885, the Germans were able to force out all foreign traders who competed for copra and pearl shell (Firth 1973). With the exceptions of Palau and Nauru, where phosphate mining was established, the extraction and export of copra was the primary economic interest in the region. In the Carolines, where the Germans took over the Spanish colony on Pohnpei, renaming it Kolonia, the relationship established with the islanders was unstable to say the least. The Pohnpeians, who had resisted Spanish rule to a certain extent, continued in this vein, culminating in the Sokehs Rebellion which required the transport of German New Guinea troops to the island to restore order (see below).

In Chuuk Lagoon by the time of official German administration, Japanese, German, English and Chinese traders were established on the islands (King and Parker 1984). Although not exerting strict control, it appears that the Germans were the first to demonstrate their colonial might: this required what the historical anthropologist Greg Dening (1992) has aptly called a 'charade'. The performance apparently involved the presence in the lagoon of a warship, which bombarded and virtually destroyed a small islet (King and Parker 1984). As a consequence of this display, and probably other displays of military strength, the Chuukese surrendered to German authorities 436 guns that had been acquired by the islanders through traders (Fischer and Fischer 1957). The surrender of the weapons had been required since a ruling made by the German authorities in 1899; it had taken approximately five years for the Chuukese to comply, and perhaps illustrates not only the indirect nature of the German colonial rule, but resistance by the Chuukese to external control (Fig. 2.1).

In relation to Germany's colonial ambitions Stewart Firth (1973: 28) opines that:

It is a commonplace that Germany's colonial empire failed to realize the hopes held for it by the colonial enthusiasts of the 1880s, that German investors and emigrants largely avoided it, and that it was more of an economic burden to Germany than a source of strength . . . [T]heir usefulness to Germany was little more than to demonstrate [a] presence in the world . . . [H]owever some individuals benefited enormously from their investment in the Pacific islands . . . And that same economic process which enriched a select few in Germany was revolutionary in its consequences for tens of thousands of Pacific Islanders, for it meant access to European technology, loss of traditional lands, recruitment as labourers and subjection to foreign rule.

German rule allowed relatively easy access to the region for German collectors and 'scientists'. Richard Thurnwald, sponsored by the Berlin Ethnological

Fig. 2.1 A Chuukese chief from a painting made during the
Südsee-Expedition (after Krämer 1932). The Chuukese were
regarded as aggressive, supposedly feuding often between neighbours
within the Lagoon. Although the comb and shell ornaments
depicted here indicate high status, Chuukese social hierarchy
appears to have been very limited at the time of first European
records and as derived from oral testimony.

Museum, made brief visits to collect objects in the Carolines and Marshalls during 1907 (Branco 1988). This, however, paled into insignificance in comparison to the *Südsee-Expedition* of 1908–10. Jorge Branco (1988) has suggested that in scale and design the *Südsee-Expedition* drew inspiration from A.C. Haddon's 1898 Cambridge Expedition to the Torres Strait and Franz Boas' Jesup North Pacific Expedition. Both of these were of course formative in defining field research as a basic element of the discipline of anthropology.

The German expedition was led by Georg Thilenius, the Director of the Hamburg Ethnographic Museum. Mark Berg (1988) finds that Thilenius had no intention of investigating people in a 'pristine' state of existence, but sought rather to record the final stages of indigenous culture prior to its being lost forever under pressure from outside contact. But this is perhaps not the 'salvage ethnography' that had informed Haddon's expedition to the Torres Strait, as Glenn Penny (1998: 164) finds from Thilenius' documents:

the primary goals of this scientific expedition were to 'corner the market' in one area of material culture by gaining a collection that would retain its value and contribute to the prestige of Hamburg and its museum – a collection which was sure to never be reproduced by a culture guaranteed to perish.

Thus, according to Glenn Penny (1998: 158), the motor driving the desire to collect was 'a combination of scientific enthusiasm and civic self-promotion'. For Penny, then, the late nineteenth-century construction of great municipal museums in Germany, and elsewhere, was not for reasons of colonialism or nationalism, but for civic pride where a collection's reputation would bring fame to the individual city. Indeed, as it was often the burghers and councillors of the municipality who essentially funded these institutions, then the value had to be seen as something beyond its scientific worth. In picking the Sepik River of north mainland New Guinea, the Bismarck Archipelago, and the Caroline and Marshall Islands for the expedition, Thilenius was making an assumption that the people of these areas were to go through rapid and destructive cultural change before other collectors and thus museums would gain such an important collection. The *Südsee-Expedition* returned with 9400 objects from Melanesia and 8366 from Micronesia, though a large proportion of these were destroyed during the Second World War (Branco 1988).

Penny's (1998) interpretation of the motivation of German collectors runs counter to the popular thesis of colonialism as the motor for many museums and collections. Talking of collections made in German New Guinea, both Robert Welsch (2000) and Chris Gosden with Chantal Knowles (2001) emphasize the role of colonialism in making such collections. Obviously, access is one thing, and having a friendly government was important. Another was the ability to use the agents of colonialism, those people who become ordinarily situated in the colony, to the collector's advantage in acting as go-betweens with the local community. As Welsch (2000: 156–7) finds in regard to locating indigenous agency within objects in museum collections:

it is not simply that indigenous agency competes with the goals of a collector, but that both compete with other processes that occur outside the field context. In part these processes have to do with the structure of museum processes . . . But the colonial process itself – the competition among collectors of different nationalities working for competing institutions, and working with expatriate agents eager to profit economically from their dealings with museums – has also served to confuse and confound these processes and has shaped all early museum collections from Melanesia, no matter whether made by scholar, sea captain, or visiting sailor.

It is within this milieu that the *Südsee-Expedition* operated, one confused by local issues at either end of a chain of connections linking the ends of the earth. It explored Micronesia from July 1909 through to April 1910. Only two of the team had been in Melanesia: Wilhelm Müller, an ethnologist from the Berlin Museum, and F.E. Heilwig, a merchant, who stayed on for the Micronesian tour. Müller spent the entire Micronesian trip in Yap. They were joined by a new field leader, Augustin Krämer, an ethnographer, and his wife Elisabeth Krämer-Bannow who acted as expedition artist. They were also accompanied by two ethnologists, Paul Hambruch and Ernst Sarfert. Historian Mark Berg (1988) claims that Hambruch constantly got into trouble as he tried on every possible occasion to measure the islanders' bodily dimensions using calipers.

Aboard the expedition ship, the 710 ton motor vessel *Peiho*, the expedition stopped at forty-five islands. They started at Yap, headed south-west to Palau and the Southwest Islands and back north via Ngulu and along the low islands of the western Carolines to Chuuk Lagoon, back west to take in a few islands missed on the eastward passage and then returning to the east through the Mortlocks and down south to the outliers of Nukuoro and Kapingamarangi. They left the Carolines for the Marshalls through Pohnpei, Mokil, Pingelap and Kosrae. In the Marshalls they touched at the south of the Ralik Chain before passing through the Ratak Chain from south to north and then heading westwards to include four more Carolinian low islands previously missed. The voyage in Micronesia started in Yap on 31 July 1909 and finished in Palau on 15 April 1910 (Berg 1988).

The expedition scientists did not visit all of the islands and would stay for extended periods while the ship went elsewhere. Following the voyage part of the expedition, Hambruch, Sarfert and the Krämers stayed to conduct detailed research in particular island groups. Hambruch disembarked on Pohnpei as the *Peiho* steamed westwards back from the Marshalls and stayed for six months. He then continued outside of the original voyage itinerary and conducted fieldwork on Nauru, also a German possession at this time. Sarfert had already decided to conduct extended fieldwork on Kosrae and stayed from early February 1910 until May (although Berg (1988) notes a little doubt about this latter date). The Krämers spent three months on Palau.

The direct published output from the expedition was immense; twenty-three volumes with extremely high production values were published for the

Micronesian phase of the expedition over a period from 1914 to 1938. The volumes contain a variety of information from aspects of flora through material culture, language, folklore, religious beliefs, social structure, photographs, drawings, aquacolours and much more. Originally published in German, they were translated into English by the Human Relations Area Files at Yale during the Second World War. I discuss this further below, and these and more recent translations are available in a variety of libraries. As Berg (1988: 101) concludes in his brief paper spelling out the basics of the *Südsee-Expedition*:

For many islands, reliable historical records start with the volumes in the [*Ergebnisse der Südsee-Expedition, 1908–1910*, Thilenius 1913–38] series. As early as 1920, Thilenius foresaw these salutary benefits when he wrote: 'Even today it is certain that the expedition was able to gather a variety of sources that will not be available at all, or not to the same extent, in the near future . . . what had existed cannot be resurrected and culture change advances'.

Although there can be no doubt that the *Südsee-Expedition* legacy is a significant resource, there are cases where the results of this expedition have been used rather too uncritically in an effort by archaeologists to construct an understanding of 'traditional society' as the end point in a 'natural' social evolutionary process. Not that I would wish to deny their use where appropriate, but, like Berg (1988: 101), one also has to recognize their limitations:

in identifying certain Micronesians, in an overly rigid system of classification, in generalizing about Micronesians on the basis of too little information and in failing to consider inter-island relationships and influences.

These 'influences' included Europeans and other aliens from beyond the direct region. In the Marshall Islands during the generation before the *Südsee-Expedition*, Hardach (1997) finds that there was a population decline in Micronesia during the German administration. There was also a small but significant amount of in-migration with, by 1912, 425 'white' residents in German Micronesia, of whom 232 were Germans. Under German colonial law the definition of 'white' was fixed, as Hardach (1997: 237) explains:

'White' people were subject to laws, decrees and institutions that satisfied the standards of the civilized community of nations. Indigenous 'coloured' people were excluded from the sphere of civilized law, and were subject to a legal system of an inferior standard. [This under 'the presumption of "white" superiority and "coloured" inferiority' (1997: 236).] An imperial decree defined Japanese citizens who lived in German colonies as 'white' people. Chinese citizens, however, had the inferior legal status of 'coloured' people. In the twisted logic of colonialism, this strange discrimination was reasonable, and even necessary. Japanese traders and labourers in Micronesia had to be 'white' as they were citizens of an imperialist power. The Chinese were colonial subjects in Kiaochow, Germany's small colony on the Chinese coast, and thus had to be defined as 'coloured'.

This somewhat paradoxical 'colour-blind' racial distinction was not limited to the legal sphere. Hermann Hiery has found that, although it was not generally spoken of in Europe, in order to 'keep up appearances', it was common practice for European men in the German Pacific to take local 'wives' (1997: 301):

Even the Governor of New Guinea, Albert Hahl, is said to have lived with a Caroline Islander on Ponape [Pohnpei] before his marriage to a German baroness. His successor had hardly arrived when he already had a girl from the Marshall Islands as a 'housekeeper'. In fact she proved to be the real lady of government house.

The fusion and passing of fluids represented by such historical anecdote could not have been more intimate, at least in the sense of proximity, but of course within the relations of power in colonial contexts the 'colour-blindness' was more apparent than real. Even though James Gibbon, a black West Indian beachcomber resident of Palau, was made representative of the German administration for that island group and issued a proclamation declaring that polygamy was permitted (Hiery 1997), when colonial rule was threatened the might of colonial power was invoked. One instance of such a display comes from Pohnpei.

The German administration was aware of the Pohnpeians' resistance to Spanish colonialism, which required the Spanish to construct forts at strategic points around the island, and had maintained initially a moderate policy. But in 1910, later in the same year that Hambruch was on the island, and after two years of attempting to introduce land reforms, the German administration caused the harsh implementation of land and tax reform. These reforms took the land from the high-ranked owners and gave it to the occupiers, who, in limiting tribute to the ranked leaders in each district, now had to pay tax and unpaid labour to the German administration (Hardach 1997). These reforms were widely resented and led to the Sokehs Rebellion of 1910–11.

The Sokehs Rebellion started after the assassination of the German Governor, Gustav Boeder, on 18 October 1910. The people of Sokehs district besieged the German garrison in Kolonia, which was only supported by fifty policemen from German Melanesia and other Pohnpeians loyal to the administration (Hanlon 1981). The siege lasted for forty days, and even the Pohnpeians allied to the Germans took the opportunity to loot the colony. Reinforcements from New Guinea along with the warship *Siar* meant that in January the German forces were able to launch an offensive and defeat the rebels. In February 1911 fifteen of the leaders were publicly executed – a memorial marks the location in the present day. Four hundred men, women and children from Sokehs were exiled first to Yap and then to Palau and parcels of their land were given over to Carolinians from four low island communities (Hanlon 1981; Hezel 1995; Hardach 1997).

In the Mariana Islands, the people, long used to colonial government under the Spanish, appear to have been little affected by the presence of new colonial masters, apart from a migration scheme that resettled more than a thousand Carolinians from the low islands, on to vacant plots in the northern Marianas (Guam was already a US possession). But for those familiar with colonialism, the German period in the Marianas was a mere blip compared to the radical changes they were to encounter under the Japanese. Germany's domination of the region ended with the onset of the First World War in 1914.

Japan's South Sea colonies

At the commencement of the First World War, the Japanese military seized control of the German territories in the tropical north-west Pacific. The phosphate mines open and operational in the western Carolines were of particular economic interest to the Japanese, as was the potential for sugarcane and copra production on some of the other islands (Purcell 1976). The seizure was formalized in the post-First World War Treaty of Versailles, with the majority of German Micronesia being ceded to Japan (Hardach 1997). Initially, the economic interest in the region appeared to be the major attraction. Sugarcane production and its associated mills and railways transformed the environment of many of the northern Mariana Islands. Japanese and Asian workers were transported to the islands and settled in Japanese-style towns.

In 1920 the League of Nations granted all of the islands in the region (except Guam and the Gilberts including Banaba) to the Japanese as a 'Class C' mandate, and a civil administration took over from the military. Although the mandate required that the islands should be demilitarized and trade, other than with Japan, restricted, the ultimate consequence was tighter Japanese control of the region. Mark Peattie (1988: 57) observes that 'the islands were now to be administered as Japanese possessions, not as territories under quite temporary guardianship by the international community'.

The Japanese imposed on the inhabitants of the region their government, education and infrastructure. As Robert Kiste writes in an editorial note to Peattie's volume (1988: vii):

Japan's influence was pervasive and well orchestrated; the Japanese had clear objectives in mind. Micronesians were to be absorbed into the Japanese empire, and eventually Japanese and other Asians would come to outnumber islanders in their homeland by a ratio of two to one.

The Imperial University of Tokyo organized an expedition to Micronesia in the year following the annexation of the former German holdings in the region. Between March and May 1915 the three anthropologists on the expedition, Kotohito Hasabe, Akira Matsumura and Joukei (Tsunee) Shibata, sailed on the Imperial Navy steamship the *Kaga Maru* to Chuuk and Fiji, north to the Marshall Islands (only Jaluit), then west to the Caroline Islands of Pohnpei, Kosrae, Chuuk (where Hasabe left the expedition), Yap, Palau, Yap and Chuuk for a third time, and north to Saipan in the Mariana Islands where the Micronesian part of the trip concluded. The expedition incorporated the standard anthropological documentation of the time, including body measurements of living people, the collection and description of artefacts and some archaeological excavation in Pohnpei and Kosrae (Matsumura 1918; Intoh 1998).

The milieu from which the Tokyo researchers derived was one of a strong separation between the disciplines of anthropology and sociology. Anthropologists in the Imperial University of Tokyo taught anthropometry and biological evolution, while the sociologists were concerned with the social through the universalistic theories of Auguste Comte, Baldwin Spencer and Lewis Henry Morgan, to name a few (Beardsley and Takashi 1970). An assessment of Yosihiko Sinoto's (1988) collected abstracts of Japanese articles, if it can be regarded as representative, indicates that Japanese anthropological priorities continued to include anthropometry and biological evolution during the period of occupation. What may loosely be termed physical anthropology makes up approximately 22 per cent of the published papers, but standard concerns of social anthropology and material culture with specific and sometimes comparative descriptions make up the majority of the papers, with approximately 68 per cent devoted to such issues. The remaining papers, that is, five of the fifty assessed, were primarily concerned with archaeology. It appears that archaeology continued to play only a small part in the 'scientific' studies of the islands, with a contemporary understanding of the present population taking priority (but see Chapman 1968, who lists thirty-nine papers published in Japanese in regard to Micronesian archaeology; see also Chapman 1964). Indeed, as one begins to expect in a colonial situation, as late as 1940, the 'scientific work' including 'anthropology–ethnology' was being lauded as the 'basis for the development of the region' (Uchinomi 1952 in Sinoto 1988: vii).

Peter Chapman (1968: 73), in reviewing the Japanese contribution to archaeological interpretation in the region, concludes:

Funds and personnel for large-scale expeditions were not available. Surface collection and field survey were the usual archaeological methods of professionals in Japan and elsewhere. The circumstances of administration and transportation did not encourage long stays nor frequent visits to the islands. But while no extensive excavations were made, many of the known sites were visited often and protected. Pioneer work was done by Hijikata in the realm of myth and the stone images of Palau, and by Yawata throughout Micronesia, but particularly in the northern islands of the Marianas group.

During the Japanese period Guam had remained in the control of the US, apart from the Japanese occupation during the war, but the Gilbert Islands, including Banaba and Nauru, were following different trajectories as outposts of the British Empire, and apart from a brief period of Japanese occupation during the

Second World War the Gilbertese experience of colonial control has been restricted to relations with the British starting in 1892. There appears to have been little motivation for a British colony, but support came from the British colonial government in Australia who were becoming concerned about the growing possessions of other European countries in their region (Kiste 1994a). It was not necessarily a defensive concern, but one that wished to counter the trading activities of Europeans, especially of German companies (Hempenstall 1994). Banaba (Ocean Island) was part of these holdings, and from 1902 the British Pacific Phosphate Company began mining phosphate, with the eventual result that the islanders were displaced and in the 1930s and 1940s removed to Rabi Island in Fiji.

Nauru had escaped direct colonial rule until annexed by Germany in 1888, and in 1907 the first load of the extensive phosphate deposit of the island was shipped by the British Pacific Phosphate Company (Petit-Skinner 1981). At the outbreak of the First World War, Australia seized the island, and after the war it was mandated as a protectorate and remained controlled as such, apart from the Japanese occupation during the Second World War.

Post-Second World War

At the end of the Second World War the Japanese, Okinawans and Koreans, who in many instances were virtually starved, were repatriated to their home countries. This followed the massed bombing of Japan and the nuclear weapon attacks on Nagasaki and Hiroshima, which left from the huge airfield on the island of Tinian in the Marianas. All of the islands in the region now became administered by the USA as a Trust Territory under United Nations mandate. The USA found a strategic need for these outposts in the Pacific which required a trusteeship rather than full US incorporation as this would have set a 'bad example to the former USSR, and was out of step with the United States' anti-colonial self-image' (Smith 1991: 7). They returned to Guam and built an air-force base large enough to launch B-52 bombers on high-level raids to Vietnam during the US conflict in that country. In addition, between 1946 and 1958, the atolls of the Marshall Islands provided a location for detonating nuclear devices (sixty-six in total) for experimental purposes and another military base was later used for testing Inter-Continental Ballistic Missiles (Smith 1991). The displacement of indigenous people and loss of their land are subsequent results (Kiste 1974; Kluge 1991).

In the first twenty years as a trustee, the US did little else than use some of the islands as a military resource; the others it neglected, leading to some commentators inventing ironic labels such as the 'rust territory'. There was little opposition within or outside of the region, given the US casualties sustained in 'liberating' the islanders from the Japanese. As Robert Kiste (1994b: 229) notes, the '"blood on the sand" argument was popular', implying that the cost of American military personnel in battling to wrest the islands from the Japanese meant somehow that the region had become American by right. It was during this period that a huge amount of anthropological activity conducted by US-based scholars was undertaken.

The role of American anthropology in Micronesia has, at the end of the twentieth century, started to attract critical examination. Anthropologists Robert Kiste and Mac Marshall (1999; 2000) have brought together reviews of the anthropology of the region over the period from the Second World War until the late 1990s. However, the role that anthropologists played as agents of colonialism has yet to be fully explored. The lack of such an examination is surprising given both the reflexive mode of contemporary anthropology and the apparent direct nature of the colonial relationship with anthropology in the region as outlined briefly below.

The day after the Japanese attack on Pearl Harbor on 7 December 1941, the anthropologist George Murdock drew together the staff of the Cross-Cultural Survey, Institute of Human Relations at Yale University, and started the collection of all the material they could find about the peoples and islands of Micronesia. As Kiste and Marshall (2000: 265) highlight, in this 'act of incredible optimism . . . Murdock anticipated that the United States would need basic information on Micronesia. Unforeseen at the time, the Yale initiative was the beginning of the largest research effort in the history of American anthropology and a major program in applied anthropology.' From the information collected, and his request for translations of the German *Südsee-Expedition* volumes and available Japanese reports, Murdock produced handbooks for the military that proved useful for providing basic information on the people and places encountered during the push westwards across the Pacific towards Japan and through Japan's mandated territory, Micronesia. At the war's end, and while the region that in 1951 would become the Trust Territory was under US Navy rule,

There was optimism on all sides about the usefulness of anthropology, and Harvard anthropologist Douglas Oliver joined Murdock in planning Micronesia's future. Under Oliver's supervision, the navy sponsored a survey of economic conditions in Micronesia (U.S. Commercial Company, or USCC) in which several anthropologists were involved. More important, Murdock and Oliver planned the cardinal event that shaped the direction of American anthropology in Micronesia for years to come. (Kiste and Marshall 2000: 267)

This 'cardinal event' was the 1947–48 Coordinated Investigation of Micronesian Anthropology (CIMA), once again sponsored by the navy and involving a total of twenty-five sociocultural anthropologists and a smattering of geographers, linguists, botanists, physical anthropologists and psychiatrists, adding up to a team of over forty researchers (see Kiste and Marshall 1999: Appendix 1, for a full list of participants). That this shaped the direction of Micronesian anthropology 'for years to come' is not in doubt, but the Navy 'assumption that knowledge of Micronesians and their cultures would make for good administration' (Kiste and Marshall 2000: 267) is much harder to sustain. Certainly there must have been a perception that the colonial work of the anthropologists was worthwhile supporting through government funds, as CIMA was followed in 1949–51 by the Scientific Investigation of Micronesia (SIM) that included nine anthropologists as participants. Also beginning in 1949, and continuing until 1960, seventeen anthropologists served the US government as staff and district anthropologists in the region (Kiste and Marshall 1999: Appendix 1).

In the 1960s, as anti-colonial movements around the world gathered further momentum and doubts grew that US military bases in Okinawa and the Philippines could be maintained indefinitely, the US government began negotiations with island leaders in an effort to formalize its military use of the islands (Hanlon 1998). This decade also introduced a period of disjuncture within the US government in regard to the use of anthropology as an administrative tool in this colonial situation (it may also be a reflection of anthropologists' doubts as to the role of the discipline in colonial contexts). Up until this point, the input of anthropology in American Micronesia appears to have supported the policy of what has been reported as 'benign neglect'. The United Nations in 1961 severely criticized the US for this neglect, and a programme of infrastructure development leading to Americanization and a 'culture of dependence' was instigated (Hanlon 1998).

Kiste and Marshall (1999; 2000) report that, up until 1997, a total of ninety-eight doctoral theses had been awarded by US institutions for research in Micronesia conducted in the four fields of anthropology. These comprise seventy-eight in sociocultural anthropology, twelve in archaeology, six in biological anthropology and two in linguistics. Sociocultural anthropology, clearly the dominant field in American-led anthropology in Micronesia, has provided a wealth of anthropological information across the region in a range of environments and covering a wide variety of research topics. Although the effect of this research on the discipline more broadly is debatable, some of the most influential of twentieth-century US anthropologists worked in the region (through CIMA) and, to name a few, Murdock, Homer Barnett, David Schneider and Alexander Spoehr were each at the head of academic lineages that spawned a total of twenty-six anthropology doctorates on Micronesian topics (Kiste and Marshall 2000).

In comparison to anthropology, archaeology was a relatively late starter when it comes to doctoral research in Micronesia. Fred Reinman's (1965) doctorate incorporated Micronesian material, but was an Oceania-wide survey of fishing technology later published in revised form (Reinman 1967). According to Kiste and Marshall (1999), the first doctoral thesis completed in Micronesian archaeology was by Larry Goodwin (1983) from the University of Oregon, but this was actually a work of socioeconomic anthropology related to subsistence practices on Pohnpei. However, five archaeology theses have been produced in the same institution, all supervised by William Ayres (Haun 1984; Bryson 1989; Mauricio 1993; Kataoka 1996; Descantes 1998). George Gumerman of Southern Illinois University at Carbondale has supervised three doctorates all with topics focused on the Palau Archipelago (Masse 1989; Snyder 1989; Carucci 1992). Joyce Bath (1984b), Laurie Lucking (1984) and Takeshi Ueki (1984) completed Micronesian archaeology doctorates at the University of Hawaii, University of Minnesota and Brown University respectively.

Three doctorates have been completed outside the USA, the small number, in part, reflecting the colonial dominance of the USA in Micronesia over the second half of the twentieth century. John Craib (1986) working in the Marianas and Paul Rainbird (1995b) focusing on the eastern Caroline Islands completed doctorates at the University of Sydney in Australia. Michiko Intoh (1988), with a focus on the ceramic technology of Yap, produced the single doctorate on the archaeology of Micronesia to derive from the University of Otago in Aotearoa/New Zealand.

In total, fourteen doctoral theses have had their primary focus on Micronesian archaeology topics. All of these have been conducted within the area of the former Trust Territory, and significantly, all but one, Descantes (1998), have focused on the high islands. Even then, Descantes worked on both the high island of Yap and Ulithi Atoll. I will discuss further the issue of archaeological bias towards the high islands in relevant sections below, but note here that the focus of research has, at least in part, reflected the sphere of US colonial dominance, which has left out the low islands of the region to the south and east because of different political histories, particularly in the second half of the twentieth century.

Nauru became the independent Republic of Nauru on 31 January 1968. The remaining phosphate deposits and compensation paid by Australia and Britain resulted in Nauru being, *per capita*, one of the richest nations in the world. The Gilberts (including Banaba) split from the Ellice Islands (Polynesian Tuvalu) in 1974 and achieved independence in 1979, becoming the Republic of Kiribati.

Contemporary anthropology

Kiste and Marshall (2000) find that after half a century of intensive American anthropological research in Micronesia, making it one of the most studied of all world areas, a number of research topics remain neglected. They list the impact of 'Western-style formal education', medical anthropology (but see Martha Ward's engaging *Nest in the Winds* for a sideways view of medical anthropology in Pohnpei), legal anthropology (especially in relation to the introduction of Western-style jurisprudence), contemporary religious life, inter-ethnic relations, migration, gender issues, and visual and performing arts. I would suggest that the majority of these were neglected because they focused on issues of the effect of external influences. A study of such things as inter-ethnic relations and migration strained against the traditional anthropological purpose of studying island populations as bounded and pristine (this is much more obvious in archaeological approaches as I discuss in the next chapter; see also Rainbird 1999c). Medical anthropology would have to be included in this category in failing to assess the social issues related to the popular use of imported foodstuffs that are apparently responsible for high rates of obesity and diabetes in Micronesian communities, as reported elsewhere in Oceania. Gender issues have certainly come to the fore in Pacific studies more generally and I would tentatively suggest that anthropological and historical approaches are subsumed within these area studies. In Micronesia they have been particularly at the forefront of research since the 1980s.

After decades or even centuries of colonial attempts to introduce patriarchal regimes, the important political role of women at various points of historical and ethnographic contact in the majority of Micronesian societies can continue (see below) to be identified. Women have played a leading role in major political issues across the region (Teaiwa 1992). To name but a few, in Guam, women activists have been at the forefront of protecting Chamorro tradition through maintaining a strong family lead, and in the melding of Chamorro and Roman Catholic values that appropriates and rejects external influences through an identity forged from pre-colonial and colonial times (Souder 1987; Diaz 1993). In Chuuk Lagoon, the role of women in successfully campaigning to prohibit alcohol in the islands has been reported in detail (Marshall 1979; Marshall and Marshall 1990). In the Marshall Islands women have been at the forefront of the fight for the recognition of health problems and compensation associated with the nuclear bomb testing at Bikini Atoll; and also in part related to nuclear weapons issues is the stand made by Palauan women against the manipulation of the Palau constitution to enable the political deal which stalled the introduction of the Compact of Free Association with the USA (De Ishtar 1994; Wilson 1995).

The last of Kiste and Marshall's (2000) categories of neglected topics, that of the 'visual and performing arts', is certainly an important lacuna and one that impacts on archaeological studies in the region. There is a general view evident in the literature that Micronesian arts, especially of the visual material kind, are impoverished compared with those found elsewhere in Oceania. Most compilations of Oceanic art have only minor sections dedicated to Micronesia; as Karen Nero finds: 'Most books on Pacific art continue to slight Micronesian arts, partly because the books are based on museum collections, which are limited' (1999: 262). As Nero (1999) has detailed, in the first American anthropological study of Micronesian 'art', through his fieldwork on Ifaluk Atoll, Edwin Burrows (1963) basically had to redefine the study of arts in the face of the apparent lack of sculpture, painting and drawing as the material expressions of art in contemporary Western comprehension:

The stunted growth of art is apparently a matter of scant raw materials and a cramping of tradition. As to raw materials . . . stonework is hardly worthwhile in crumbly coral, nor wood carving in perversely cross-grained coconut or spongy breadfruit wood. There is only a little good hardwood, and not much pigment for painting. (Burrows 1963: 6)

Burrows soon found that there was much to be studied in the 'art' of Ifaluk when a broader understanding was adopted and detailed issues of body art, poetry, dance and song. Nero (1999: 263) identifies Burrows' work as pioneering in the history of anthropology (although apparently ignored by later practitioners) in its examination and explication of 'body and costuming arts combined . . . to create a multisensory perception that incorporated the audience in the performers' experience'.

Summary

The nuanced understandings exhibited in the work of anthropologists such as Burrows allow for the contextualizing of the understanding of the meaning and role of performance in constructing space and community in Micronesian societies. In considering such things, and in relation to the historical and anthropological texts discussed above, and my comments in regard to fusion and fluidity in the previous chapter, we might ask whether it makes any sense to talk of Micronesian societies as exhibiting specific intra-regional traits such as, for example, those related to the use of space. This issue, along with the geographical and other specifics from which the various notions of Micronesia are constructed is the subject of the first part of the next chapter. What I hope to have provided here is the historical milieu in which archaeology as a discipline is practised in the region and from which interpretations of the archaeology are constructed. These interpretative constructions are often based on specific readings of the types of material outlined and, without denying the value of this material if used with circumspection, in the second half of the next chapter I challenge some of these uses, especially as they relate to dominant intellectual paradigms in recent American anthropology and archaeology.

CHAPTER 3

FLUID BOUNDARIES: HORIZONS OF THE LOCAL, COLONIAL AND DISCIPLINARY

'Mike who?' is the response attributed to a US politician when asked about plans for Micronesia. Outside a closed circle of Pacific islanders, academics, military personnel, scuba divers and some politicians, the term Micronesia often elicits a similar response. But the appellation Micronesia is not without its own problems. In the first part of this chapter I explore what is meant by Micronesia, and the variety of possible answers to the 'Mike who?' question. This requires a consideration of geography, anthropology, history, voyaging and local self-definitions. Some of these issues have been raised in their historical contexts in the previous two chapters, but here they will be set as acutely contemporary issues, and, as such, I will consider the role that archaeology and heritage have to play within these debates. This archaeological role will be the subject of the second half of the chapter where it will be set within local and wider Pacific contexts. I will conclude by spelling out the main questions that archaeological understandings of Micronesia can be used to speak to at local regional and broader Pacific and global scales, and in particular the roles of fluidity and fusion in contesting and addressing these issues.

Geographical constructs

The basic contemporary understanding of Micronesia, at least the one first identified by anyone using an atlas, is of Micronesia as a geographical entity, one clearly marked as having boundaries in any atlas. These boundaries cross the swathes of blue on the double pages used to illustrate Oceania, that is, they cross the represented sea and the broken, dashed, natures of the lines allow the blue to flow in between. We can imagine the blue flowing under the black, as these lines are imposed from above and, dashed as they usually are, allow a hint of fluidity to be maintained. None of the Micronesian islands is linked by these cartographic devices, these conventions found throughout the atlas, but they allow the region and the islands to be described in general geographical terms.

Located predominantly north of the Equator in the north-western tropical Pacific Ocean (see Fig. 1.1), the region contains some 2373 islands ranging from a few high volcanic, mixed geology and raised limestone islands, to hundreds of sand and rubble coral islets in low coral atolls (Figs. 3.1 and 3.2). The islands

Fig. 3.1 Pohnpei from the sea. Pohnpei is a high island beyond the Andesite
Line. It is mountainous, with very high rainfall.

inhabited by humans vary in size between Guam, the largest, with a land area
of 544 square kilometres, to islets, such as the three that contribute to the total
land area of Lamotrek Atoll that have a combined surface area of 0.85 square
kilometres (Bryan 1971). It should be noted that sands can often be shifting
ones, and along with a rising sea level, which appears to be the current trend,
island morphology is ever changing and resistant to simple reliable description.
Although the land area of atolls may be relatively small, the lagoons, encircled
by the reef and islets, are often rich in marine life, and can be huge, the largest
in the world belonging to Kwajalein Atoll in the Marshall Islands. Together,
the islands of the region occupy an area of ocean greater than 7 million square
kilometres, larger in area than the USA, although the total combined land
area is only a fraction of this at approximately 2700 square kilometres (Karolle
1993).

   The long-term geological processes that have conveniently led to mountain
tops and coral growth surfacing above sea level have also produced distinct patterns that have allowed the identification of four island groups in Micronesia.
The Mariana Islands are the furthest north-west of these groups and, orientated in a north to south chain, are located directly on the edge of the infamous
Pacific 'rim of fire'. They are related geologically to the uplift of the earth's

Fig. 3.2 Ant Atoll from the sea. Ant (And) Atoll is in Pohnpei State and is typical of such island forms in rising only a few metres above sea level. Archaeological deposits have been found here of the same date as the oldest found on the neighbouring high island of Pohnpei.

continental crust at the point where the Pacific Plate pushes underneath the Philippine Plate, a location known to geographers as the subduction zone. The Marianas Trench located under the sea to the east of the islands is another direct manifestation of this zone and at its bed is the deepest point on the earth's surface. This is a geologically unstable area, with the most northerly islands volcanically active and all of the islands liable to earthquake. This further destabilizes a simple geographical definition, with the shifting tectonic plates moving the land in sometimes violent episodes of earthquakes. The 'nervous tension of plate tectonics' may act as a metaphor for the shifting ground of contemporary indigenous identity politics. Here there is a mixture of 'roots' in the land (and sea) and the 'routes' defined by travel and movement that create fusion. These routes often link to diasporic communities beyond the fluid boundaries of Micronesia (Clifford 1997; Diaz and Kauanui 2001; Jolly 2001).

To the south of the Mariana Islands is the east to west chain of the Caroline Islands. This chain has the high islands of the Palau Archipelago and Yap at its western end, which are once again formed by the activities of the subduction zone creating a mixed geology of volcanic, metamorphic and uplifted sedimentary limestones. In contrast, to the east of the Yap (and Marianas) Trench (another deep fissure in the Ocean bed), the island-forming geology is purely volcanic and the line of distinction between the islands formed on different tectonic plates is the Andesite Line. The Carolines, east of this line, consist of the high islands of Chuuk Lagoon, Pohnpei and Kosrae, which are interspersed by low atolls and a few raised limestone islands.

To the east of the Carolines is the Marshall Islands group formed by two archipelagos of low islands. The eastern chain is called Ratak, the islands of the sunrise, and the western Ralik, the islands of the sunset. To the south of the Marshalls, the group making up the Gilbert Islands, now part of the Republic of Kiribati, is also formed by low islands. The four islands of Banaba, Nauru, Nukuoro and Kapingamarani fall outside of these geographically distinct groups. The former two are upraised limestone islands, while the latter are coral atolls. They are all located south of the Caroline Islands and west of the Gilberts. Also to the south-west of the Palau Archipelago are the low islands of the south-west group.

Together the Marianas, Carolines, Marshalls, Gilberts, Southwest Islands and the four individual islands are commonly regarded as Micronesia. There are a few small islands off the coast of New Guinea, that have on occasion been claimed as part of Micronesia on the basis of cultural similarities and I will consider these in the relevant chapter. It is worth noting as an example of the contestation surrounding this geographical definition of Micronesia, that a little over 100 years ago F.W. Christian (1899a: 105) told the assembled members of the Royal Geographic Society in London that: 'the Marianne or Ladrone group [Mariana Islands], practically a prolongation of the Japanese chain, is not properly reckoned in the Micronesian area'. Such a geographic definition as this, based on a misreading of the map to suggest that the Mariana Islands are linked to Japan in the north through the Bonin and Ryuku islands, can in retrospect be seen as politically charged, given Japan's annexing of the islands within its Empire only fifteen years after Christian's publication.

A useful alternative to the tripartite division of Pacific islands has been set out by the archaeologist Roger Green (1991) and is based on biogeographic and geological criteria. In this case, the area formerly referred to as Micronesia finds itself in 'Remote Oceania' along with the islands of what is conventionally termed Polynesia. The other islands of the western Pacific are labelled 'Near Oceania'. However, conventional Micronesia straddles a geological division, the Andesite Line, with volcanically formed islands to the east and continental islands to the west. For Geoffrey Irwin (2000) this is a significant line that appears to mark a pause in the human colonization of Oceania for a number of centuries. Each of these approaches indicates the relativity of geographic description. In this book the term 'Micronesia' is used as shorthand for the region, without implying cultural homogeneity of the residents or diachronic maintenance of the boundaries; elsewhere I have proposed the appellation 'north-west tropical Pacific' as a less historically loaded label (Rainbird 1994a), and I return to this below.

The Pacific environment

The late Smithsonian Institute botanist/biogeographer F. Raymond Fosberg (1991) proposed a six-class division for Pacific islands, all of which are represented in Micronesia, with the majority being Class 4 Coral Atolls. Fosberg, the founding editor of the journal *Atoll Research Bulletin*, passed away in 1993 at the age of 85. The year before, I had met him in Kosrae where he was accompanying geographers on a fieldtrip. One obituary stated that he had probably visited more Pacific islands than any other man in the twentieth century.

The climate of the region is tropical maritime. Temperatures average in the mid-twenties Celcius all year, with few fluctuations. However, differences in rainfall patterns are pronounced. Islands in the west of the region (e.g., the Marianas, Yap, Palau and Chuuk) are affected by the Asian monsoon causing distinct rainy and dry seasons. The islands to the east (e.g., Pohnpei and Kosrae) are less seasonal and have very high rainfall all year round. The Marshalls have a slightly more complex rainfall pattern, with islands to the south of the group receiving more than their neighbours to the north, and in the Gilberts this operates in reverse, with the north receiving greater rainfall than the south.

The area of the central Caroline Islands is renowned as a spawning ground for typhoons, which often start in the vicinity of Chuuk before heading north-westward to wreak havoc in the Marianas or the atolls to the north and east of Yap. More rarely the typhoons develop further east and can affect the Marshalls and the islands of the east Carolines before continuing north-west.

The majority of the traditional staple crops in the region have in the past been typical Indo-Pacific varieties. Rosalind Hunter-Anderson (1991) has reviewed traditional high island horticultural practices in the Carolines. She finds that the typical staple crops are coconuts (*Cocos nucifera*), bananas (*Musa* spp.), taro (mainly *Colocasia esculenta* and *Cyrtosperma chamissonis* and some cultivation of *Alocasia macrorrhiza*), yams (*Dioscorea alata*, *D. nummularia*, *D. pentaphylla* or *cumingi*), and breadfruit (*Artocarpus altilis*), with the Polynesian chestnut (*Inocarpus edulis*) as an important supplementary tree crop. On the atolls and raised limestone islands (Fosberg's Classes 4 and 5) the fruit of the hardy pandanus tree has also provided a much relied upon staple crop. All of the staples have their origins in South-East Asia or Melanesia, and arguably pandanus, through its ethnographically attested use of the leaves for manufacturing sails, would have been one of the first to spread with people from those areas.

These crops are present throughout the Caroline Islands, but particular species are more favoured than others depending on the island. In general, Hunter-Anderson (1991) found that the islands of the west have a reliance on taro and yam, while in the islands to the east breadfruit is a main staple. Chuuk Lagoon in the middle appears to rely on the seasonal availability of both breadfruit and year-round taro. Protein sources derive mainly from marine species, although dogs, rats and possibly chickens were available to supplement the meat available from the indigenous delicacy of the fruit bat and the various species of land crab. Pigs do not appear to have been widespread prior to European contact (see Intoh 1986), although cases of prehistoric pig remains have been reported from Palau (Masse, Snyder and Gumerman 1984; Wickler 1998b) and Fais (Intoh 1991).

The environment of the Pacific islands has often been regarded as a critical factor determining social organization. Since the 1980s it has become clear that the environment, in respect to the flora, fauna and landscape of many, if not all, Pacific islands, has changed since human settlement (Kirch and Hunt 1997). Patrick Kirch (1993: 10) acknowledged that 'archaeologists have now abandoned an earlier perspective that viewed island ecosystems merely as static backdrops to cultural developments'; he (amongst others) has taken the view that island 'history is as much about environmental dynamics as of cultural changes in pottery types or adze forms'. The latter statement reinforces the nature/culture dichotomy, but this is a complex dialectic, and only an approach which contextualizes these aspects of island living can come close to gaining an understanding of island societies. I will return to the nature/culture issue below, but first it is necessary to continue the work of the previous two chapters and further place Micronesia within its historical context.

Historical constructs

In chapter 1 I discussed the nineteenth-century division of the Pacific that led to the establishment of the term Micronesia, 'the tiny islands', for the region. Unlike the putative racist root for the naming of Melanesia, the apparent physical geographical basis for Micronesia has, I would argue, allowed the term to slip outside of debates that have been more pronounced in relation to dichotomous divisions such as Melanesian/Polynesian or Melanesian/Malay. A number of commentators (e.g., Terrell 1986; Thomas 1989; 1997; Terrell, Kelly and Rainbird 2001) have recognized that the nineteenth-century division of Oceania was not purely on geographic criteria. Ward Goodenough (1957: 147), who conducted ethnographic fieldwork in Chuuk Lagoon as part of the Coordinated Investigation of Micronesian Anthropology (CIMA), was already questioning the reification of these boundaries in the 1950s:

It has been established practice to divide Oceania into three major areas: Melanesia, Micronesia, and Polynesia. Essentially geographical, these areas have often been treated as if they were comparable units culturally, linguistically, and racially. Nothing could be more misleading.

The French archaeologist José Garanger (1982: 3), famed for his pioneering work in Vanuatu, was equally critical thirty years ago:

Little by little the work of anthropologists, linguists and ethnologists, the abundance and complexity of the traditions that were collected and refinements of the comparative typology of stone tool assemblages, raised more problems than solutions. The previously defined boundaries between Melanesia, Micronesia and Polynesia appeared arbitrary to say the least.

As I stated above, the current concept of Micronesia is that it contains the island groups of the Carolines, Gilberts, Marianas and Marshalls, although the Gilbert Islands (the major component of the Republic of Kiribati) often fail to feature in reviews of the region. This is probably due to their different history, as outlined in the previous chapter, in that they were not administered as part of the US Trust Territory of the Pacific Islands (USTTPI). So, owing to the separate political administration to the north, the Gilberts (and Banaba and Nauru) have often been excluded from 'Micronesian' research. This is especially true in relation to American initiatives, such as CIMA, which virtually made the USTTPI area of Micronesia into an 'ethnographic zoo' (Kiste 1994b).

   From my adopted perspective of fusion and fluidity, the nineteenth-century divisions of Oceania have an inhibiting effect upon understanding the diverse culture histories of the region. Historical anthropologist David Hanlon (1989; 1999) has been one of the most consistently vocal academics in regard to highlighting how Micronesia has been a construct that does not bear much scrutiny. He remarks that, '[f]or the most part, Micronesia has existed only in the minds of people from the outside who have sought to create an administrative entity for purposes of control and rule' (Hanlon 1989: 1). If boundaries have existed in the pre-European past of the region they certainly are unlikely to have been static for the whole time, and archaeologists cannot afford to ignore the temporal significance, the fluidity, of boundaries, including the modern one under discussion here.

   Robert Kiste (1999), in summarizing and expanding on the collected works in Kiste and Marshall's edited volume *American Anthropology in Micronesia*, begins by asking whether Hanlon has a point when he argues that 'Micronesia is . . . a colonial construct located, bounded, defined, and described by a series of different colonial regimes whose efforts were self-serving and exploitative' (Hanlon 1999: 76). For Kiste (1999: 434), 'Hanlon, Rainbird and others would abandon the notion of Micronesia as a culture area.' Kiste would prefer to keep Micronesia and finds support for it as a distinct cultural concept in personal comments made by Ward Goodenough, ironic given the quote above, and in the contributions by William Alkire, Mac Marshall, Glenn Petersen and Karen Nero. Kiste (1999: 436) concludes that:

All of this does not invalidate Hanlon's basic point. The culture area notion is an abstraction derived from an attempt by anthropologists to make sense of and bring order to their ethnographic data. The data themselves, be they called cultural elements, traits, complexes, or something else, are the categories that anthropologists have found useful for purposes of ethnographic description and analysis.

It is these traits identified through ethnographic descriptions that I wish to move on to next. It is through a discussion of anthropological constructs that aspects of similarity and difference may be thrown into relief and highlight the diversity with elements of fusion, linked to fluid boundaries. This discussion will also provide further detail in regard to the people of the region within the scope of this book.

Anthropological constructs

A generation ago William Alkire (1977) provided a second edition of *An Introduction to the Peoples and Cultures of Micronesia*, his synthesis of Micronesian anthropology. It stands, as I write, as the only single-authored volume that incorporates the research from the American expeditions, and it also stands to symbolize a belief in the possibility of writing of Micronesia (including the Gilbert Islands) in a single volume. In this sense, that of a single regional volume, it shares similarities with this book. It is also similar in that Alkire dealt with the diversity of the region by discussing the evidence in geographical groupings. Being a work of its time, Alkire's book was not able to draw a great deal from archaeology, and the theoretical disposition of the author also differs from the present one in believing that 'the basic social institutions [of the region] have been molded by adaptation to the concept and reality of limited land' (1977: 88).

In a more recent treatment Kiste and Marshall (2000: 271) report that there is: 'support at least [for] a limited viability of the culture area concept for understanding the region known as Micronesia, even though there is clearly important variation, particularly when the three westernmost island groups are compared with the rest of the area'. This statement draws on evidence presented in the Kiste and Marshall (1999) volume, and in that book Kiste (1999: 434) indicates the 'problem' more clearly and it is useful to quote him at length:

At the 1993 conference . . . Ward H. Goodenough responded to Hanlon with the observation that several factors give the islands of Micronesia (in the broadest sense) a certain cohesiveness. He noted that a linguistic connectedness is found throughout most of the area, and it seems certain that this reference was to those languages that are classified as 'Nuclear Micronesian.' With the exception of the westernmost three, (Chamorro, Yapese, and Palauan), the two Polynesian outliers [Nukuoro and Kapingamarangi], and perhaps Nauruan, they are the languages of Micronesia. They are a dozen or so in number and they are historically related. Goodenough also argued that there were 'interactive spheres' that linked Micronesians prior to European times, by which he presumably meant connections through inter-island voyaging. There was two-way voyaging within the Caroline Islands and between the Carolinian atolls and the Marianas. Carolinians assisted the Yapese with their voyages to and from Palau. Marshallese navigators roamed throughout their own archipelago, the Eastern Carolines, Nauru, and Kiribati. Goodenough also suggested that the 'interactive spheres' did not regularly include parts of Polynesia and Melanesia.

There is a problem in the use of linguistics to suggest similarity while at the same time proposing putative 'spheres of interaction' that go well beyond those linguistic boundaries initially used to argue for a cultural cohesiveness. Certainly, some aspects of the spheres of interaction are well documented, and archaeology and cognate disciplines can further aid in identifying these and others (e.g., see Weisler and Swindler 2002). Interaction within the area of Micronesia is important to note, and must be carefully considered in relation to the linguistic evidence, but it is the presence of this interaction that makes the boundaries fluid. The final statement in the quote above, that interaction with Melanesia and Polynesia was not 'regular', presumably means outside of the normal and routine spheres of interaction, which is completely in keeping with understanding the region as connected, as open to fusion, but this should not be equated with homogeneity. The guarded terminology used by Kiste (1999), for example, in his 'certain cohesiveness' expresses, I suggest, a recognition of this distinction between interaction and sameness. Certainly, as I discuss further in the chapters to follow, we have clear examples of long-term interactions between people in the region classified to different language groups. Kiste (1999) argues that there are other elements discussed in *American Anthropology in Micronesia* that at least express a 'certain cohesiveness' over part of the region, and these include kinship and tenure, sociopolitical organization and art. I will examine each of these in turn. William Alkire (1999: 86, references removed) states in regard to kinship and tenure that anthropological studies in the region:

have highlighted both uniformities and contrasts in the ways Micronesians have adapted to their habitats: (1) Pie-slice subdivisions are typical of high islands in contrast to strip parcels on atoll islets; on both types of island, the larger subdivisions are analogous in form and function to the smaller land parcels (or estates); (2) Thus a universal conceptual unity inalienably ties people (kin groups) to land (their estates) in Micronesia; (3) The tenure system generally guarantees that all people have access to land of every important subsistence category (including reef and sea areas); (4) Each tenure system is inherently flexible (or processual) to accommodate shortages that might follow from demographic shifts or environmental disaster; And lastly, (5) it is often the case that landholdings on high islands are more localized (regionally restricted) than those of atoll residents, whose patterns of kinship, marriage and adoption frequently give them access to widely dispersed land parcels.

In its generality and within the concerns of ecological anthropology, Alkire's argument has a certain validity for certain places at certain times. The first of

Mac Marshall's (1999) chapters in the same volume explores the specifics of kinship and social organization (including tenure) in an attempt to identify the conventional elements that evoke a 'Micronesian-ness', that is, the repertoire of cultural traits that makes Micronesia distinct as a region. Micronesia for Marshall, appropriately for the volume in which this is published, is American Micronesia. It does not include Kiribati, and owing to the Spanish conquest the Chamorro culture has moved away from the Micronesian group, which leaves the Caroline Islands and Marshall Islands as the main groups exhibiting 'Micronesian-ness'. Marshall (1999: 108–9, references removed) finds that:

Throughout Micronesia, islands were divided into what usually are called districts in the literature, and these districts are major components of local social organization. Districts are named geographical entities occupied by members of named, ranked, nonlocalized, exogamous matriclans. The ranking of these clans is based on their putative order of settlement on the island and subsequent victories or defeats in interisland warfare, and their hereditary leaders hold positions in the traditional political order. These clans are divided into localized, property-holding matrilineages in most cases, with the following exceptions: the contemporary Chamorro, the contemporary Kosraeans [these two are regarded as having previously exhibited this trait]; on the two Polynesian outliers of Nukuoro and Kapingamarangi; on Yap; and on Pingelap and Mokil. The Chamorros, Kosraeans, Nukuoro, and Kapingamarangi have cognatic systems of descent; Mokil is patrilineal; and Yap and Pingelap are reported to have double descent, although this remains a matter of debate.

Matrilineality, the tracing of clan ancestry through the female line mother to daughter, and thus land ownership through the clan, is often flagged as a singular feature of Micronesian societies within Oceania. As Marshall notes, there are exceptions to this rule, even within the Caroline Islands. Yap also upsets Alkire's understanding of access to all resources for all groups, as here the lowest-ranking villages are traditionally situated inland and have no access to marine resources. A similar argument has been made for village groups in the larger of the Mariana Islands. I will discuss these issues further in the relevant chapters below. But, as I noted in the previous chapter, the power of women over land through the matrilineal system can perhaps be seen to have led to more obvious expressions in the contemporary political arena. Following Vicente Diaz, Margaret Jolly (2001) has made the point that in the Caroline atolls, with land passing through the mothers, women are linked to the land and men to the sea. And here I reiterate that the female roots to the land should not be expressed as indigeneity as opposed to routes as a synonym for diaspora. Rather, in the Caroline Islands, it might be best to conceive of roots and routes as both local and indigenous, in a place where this is a gender distinction rather than an economic or geographic one. If the power of land (not forgetting that tenure extends across reef and sea as well) exists with women, then the power of sea, in the male role as navigators and travellers, is another local means to power. As Jolly (2001: 431) states in relation to both past and present forms of travel, 'motivated mobility is good, especially for men. Past exchanges between islands in canoes, even shipboard journeys as indentured laborers and contemporary migrations to town . . . are seen as potentially empowering journeys, for men at least.'

Returning to the issue of anthropological constructions of Micronesia, from the above I think we can accept that there are some elements that exist within the bounds of what is commonly regarded as Micronesia, that may be distinct from elsewhere. However, it still has to be acknowledged that none of these cultural traits could actually be used to provide a boundary that would match the one established in the nineteenth century and still in general use today. Mapping each cultural trait, as assumed to represent 'Micronesian-ness', might be an interesting exercise to perform, but undoubtedly different configurations of Micronesia would be created.

Glenn Petersen asserts that he has identified a common underlying element of all Micronesians. Although in his study Petersen (1999) relies on ethnographic data from the Caroline Islands and 'occasionally the Marshall Islands' to represent Micronesia, in supporting the maintenance of a regional definition of Micronesia he paradoxically provides a strong argument that the sociopolitical organization in this region is a variation on a basic Oceanic theme. In his view all of Micronesian social organization is based on the conical clan, with the ideal of political power being inherited by the senior male closest to the ancestral lineage, usually a matrilineage, of the clan. Petersen clearly shows how this is only an ideal and is often manipulated for contemporary political purposes, but in arguing further against previous understandings of social variation in Micronesia, such as a medieval European 'feudal' type system on Pohnpei, he says all of the sociopolitical systems are based on the conical clan with variation in stratification usually expressed at district levels through reasons of demography and environment. I will consider this issue more closely in relation to particular island societies in the following chapters, but Petersen's analysis raises two issues that I need to comment on here.

The first is that Petersen traces the conical clan model of sociopolitical organization through historical linguistics to a Proto-Oceanic origin, which means that it is a basic element of all Austronesian-speaking populations in Oceania; that is, the basic underlying principle is thus the same in Polynesia as it is in Micronesia. At this level of analysis the boundaries of Micronesia must be considered to be broadened massively, but in relation to archaeology, if such a view is adopted, it would simplify our task in that any material indicators that might be interpreted as useful for constructing a notion of past political organization can begin with the basic knowledge of the existence of the conical clan as an organizing principle. From this knowledge an assessment of the population size and prevailing environment is all that is required to provide a likely scenario for the amount of stratification present at any particular time. A search for difference is thus limited to a few variations on a theme. As I discuss further below in the section on Pacific archaeological constructs, this brings us in a full circle back to the standard interpretative strategy adopted by archaeologists since applying neo-evolutionary models in the 1960s. It is no surprise then that Petersen pays homage to his former teacher and proponent of neo-evolutionary theoretical developments Morton Fried.

The second point I wish to make at this stage is that I do not wish to misrepresent Petersen, who provides a detailed and nuanced argument to support his analysis. He highlights excellently that within the grander theme many previous commentators have overlooked the messy detail of Micronesian socio-political organization (1999: 395): 'The ethnographic record establishes that any power or authority Micronesian leaders [chiefs] do exercise is profoundly complex, sophisticated, obscure, equivocal and contradictory, devilishly difficult, if not well nigh impossible, to describe, let alone define.' But this messy detail (my own, rather than Petersen's, phrasing) also creates for Petersen an inherent paradox that in its organization it both creates and resists centralizing forces, allowing a place for leaders, but also restricting their potential for absolute power. In assessing variability Petersen (1999: 391) does add to variables of population and environment the 'consequences of local historical processes'. It is these historical processes that require contextualization and the assessment of difference which is denied in neo-evolutionary modelling, but surely this obfuscation also further denies the existence of Micronesia as an ancestral construct, and it is this issue I return to here with a brief look at 'Micronesian art'.

For Robert Kiste, Karen Nero's assessment of the study of arts in American Micronesia provides further evidence of the cohesiveness of this thing called Micronesia. Nero (1999: 256–7) summarizes Micronesian arts thus:

The areas of artistic creativity practiced within Micronesia – performance arts, tattoos, costumes, architecture, stone monuments, sculpture, religious effigies, and rock art – nearly all fall outside [the] limited western view of visual arts . . . Micronesian aesthetics are even further removed from European sensibilities: the minimalist lines of its rare wooden sculpture; the force of its basalt architecture; the aesthetic attention paid to utilitarian objects such as bait boxes; or Micronesians' multisensory emphasis on the ephemeral arts of integrated chants, scents, and meditative movement – the composite impact of a line of dancers moving and chanting in unison, wearing hibiscus fiber skirts or geometrically woven *tur* cloths, their skins glistening with turmeric-spiced coconut oil, accented by garlands of rare shells and rustling coconut leaf decorations, crowned by richly scented floral wreathes.

The evocative description of dance and decoration as 'ephemeral art' apart, Nero's definition of Micronesian arts is one of absence, in its conventional sense, rather than illustrating clear connections. Certainly, as Nero and others have noted, a significant impact on perceptions of art in a conventional sense has been hindered by the vociferous appetite of ethnographic collectors in the early twentieth century. Unlike some examples from Melanesia (e.g., Thomas 1991; Torrence 1993), the presence of collectors does not appear to have stimulated further production of objects specifically with this market in mind. So the wooden statues of Nukuoro and the wooden masks from the Mortlocks, for example, were taken and there appears to have been no inspiration to create new ones. But even if we take some of Nero's examples from a broader definition of art – and I am not denying that such a definition should exist (indeed, I think it should) – are there specific pan-Micronesian styles?

In regard to tattooing, the traditions that existed across a large part of American Micronesia, but not the Mariana Islands (Russell 1998b), have recently been regarded as closely related to that of Polynesia. Indeed, Hage, Harary and Milicic (1996) were so struck by the similarities of tattooing between these regional constructs of Oceania that they prefer to merge the areas and name it 'Micro-Polynesia'. In the chapters to follow we will also find that in relation to architecture and stone monuments there is significant diversity across the region. The monumental basalt and coral constructed architecture of Pohnpei and Kosrae has no other parallels in the region. As much as Claude Lévi-Strauss (1987) is able to group these as 'house societies', the various types of traditional meeting houses, although known from each of the high islands, are completely different in form and bear very little resemblance, for example, to the large *maneaba* of the Gilbert Islands. The *latte* stones of the Mariana Islands are so different from anything found elsewhere that they have come to act as symbols of the modern political regimes in those islands. As a final example, and this will be returned to in detail in the relevant chapters below, the rock-art sites of the region, with the main groupings in Pohnpei, Palau and the Marianas, bear very little resemblance to each other, and in fact the Pohnpei motifs appear to be much more closely related to types found south of the Equator, while those of Palau exhibit similarities to types and sites found in western New Guinea and eastern Indonesia. In all then, the tattooing, architecture, stone monuments and rock-art do not provide evidence of a distinct 'Micronesian-ness'.

Indeed, the examples of kinship and tenure, sociopolitical organization and art that Kiste posits as illustrating a 'certain cohesiveness' in Micronesia can be seen to show a complex array of connections and differences possibly indicating a variety of geographical spheres, but none that comes close to the boundaries of contemporary Micronesia. One has to wonder, along with Hanlon (1999: 77), for whom: 'It seems . . . that American anthropology, in the particularism of its ethnographies, has always possessed the power to subvert the idea of Micronesia. Why it has not challenged the idea more aggressively and publicly is a topic for further reflection.' For Hanlon it is the taint of colonialism that has falsely bound these islands together as an object of study. As I have already discussed, the twentieth-century anthropological study of the people of these islands is one that has gone hand in hand with shifting colonial powers.

Generations of islanders in their 'strategically important' island homes have seen these powers come and go, have learnt and unlearnt various languages, and some have seen and survived the horror of war, and from this we can see a resilience that does make for distinct island ways, if not a 'Micronesian way'.

In regard to these distinct island ways that have emerged historically through fusion and fluidity the obvious thing to do is to turn to local understandings of the region. Vicente Diaz and J. Kehaulani Kauanui (2001: 319) have provided such a view:

[F]rom the region misnamed 'Micronesia', we find that Chamorros of the Mariana Islands refer to themselves as *Taotao Tano* (people of the land) amid the majority of nonindigenous residents of that archipelago, while atoll dwellers from the central Carolines prefer to distinguish themselves from their relatives on the high islands as *Re Metau* (people of the sea). Interestingly, 'high islanders', such as those who reside on the bigger islands in the Chuuk Lagoon, sometimes invert the originary category by referring to the *Re Metau* as 'Islanders'.

Here we have general, but separate, regional definitions, and Diaz and Kauanui continue, observing that:

In addition to these regional names, there are highly localized and politicized distinctions within each. For example, some Chamorros of Guam distinguish between the *Taotao Tatte* (people of the south) and those from elsewhere on the island, or between those who have remained, and the *po-asu*, who have grown up elsewhere. Among the *Re Metau* there is a distinction between those who have 'remained' (in the seafaring atolls!) and the *Refalawasch*, who have settled the islands of the Northern Marianas since the eighteenth and nineteenth centuries. In the Northern Marianas, the *Refalawasch* further distinguish themselves in fundamental terms of different voyaging histories and genealogical ties to the central Carolines.

The self-definition exhibited here is one that clearly illustrates different community identities within the region that, as Diaz and Kauanui say, is 'misnamed Micronesia'. Nero (1999) has noted that many Guamanians reject the appellation of Micronesian as a recent invention. Joakim Peter (2000: 263) further describes Carolinian distinctions:

The naming by outer islanders of the Chuuk lagoon in traditional chanting, or *ofanu*, as *Nomwirota* . . . can be literally translated as 'lagoon of reaching up', a sexual pun to illustrate the great availability of local resources. Lagoon people to this day still call outer islanders *re fenappi*, which means 'people of sandy isles', clearly to highlight the islands' limited resources.

Peter also makes the point (in part previously made by Ward Goodenough (1986)) that the horizon, locally termed *Ppaileng*, was the edge of the world, the space out there, one of ghosts and providing 'life-giving energy'. It was through the horizon, this dangerous space which required taming and making familiar, that the navigators travelled and in doing this they were in a local sense transcending fluid boundaries. Movement, travel, was in the lifeblood of *Re Metau/Re Fenappi*, where 'the dual concept of *waa* . . . as blood vessels that carry life through the body and as canoe' exists (Peter 2000: 266). I will return to navigation below, but first I will introduce the linguistic constructs of the region.

Linguistic constructs

The languages of the region fall within the Austronesian (AN) language group. Proto-Austronesian (PAN) language is likely to have developed either in South China, moving with people across the Taiwan Strait to the island of Taiwan 6000–5000 years ago (Tryon 1995), or in Taiwan itself after that date (Bellwood 1997b; cf. Chang and Goodenough 1996). The orthodox model is that, from Taiwan, the language was dispersed through the movement of people starting perhaps some 5000 to 4000 years ago (Bellwood 1997b; Spriggs 1999a). This dispersal led to the creation of the widest geographical distribution of any language group prior to the modern period, spreading as it does from Madagascar in the west through to Rapa Nui (Easter Island) in the east. However, linguists have identified many subgroups of Austronesian, and two of these are found in Micronesia (Fig. 1.2).

The indigenous languages of the Palau islands (Palauan) and the Marianas (Chamorro) are classified as being in the West Malayo-Polynesian (WMP) subgroup, while all the other languages of the region fall within the Oceanic (Oc) subgroup (Pawley and Ross 1995). This division has been interpreted by linguists and archaeologists as indicative of different patterns of migration into the region.

On the basis of historical linguistics and archaeology (discussed in detail in chapter 4), the first migration into the region was by WMP speakers. Speakers of this subgroup are distributed widely through most of the South-East Asian islands, peninsular Malaysia, Madagascar, and some pockets of mainland South-East Asia. Their only manifestation in the Pacific islands is in western Micronesia. Of the Micronesian languages that fall outside WMP into the Oc subgroup, these have all (with the exception of Yapese and Nauruan) been classified as Nuclear Micronesian (NMic), one of the nine high-order (and thus distinctive) subgroups of Oc (Pawley and Ross 1995).

Although in the past Nauruan, the language of the population of Nauru, was considered a linguistic isolate, Frederick Jackson (1986, cited in Rehg 1995) finds that it is close enough to NMic to be considered a sister language within a group he calls 'Greater Micronesian'. Yapese had also previously been considered an isolate. Its associations had been hindered by lack of research and also, perhaps, in that it falls west of the Andesite Line which, in the past, has made for a convenient boundary between WMP speakers in the west and the Oc speakers to the east.

Malcolm Ross (1996) has looked at the Yapese 'problem' and found that there are layers in Yapese that indicate significant contact with WMP speakers in Palau and Marianas (although not necessarily direct with the latter) and NMic speakers to the east. However, Ross finds that the underlying strand of Yapese is Oc, but not NMic; rather it is most probably connected to the Admiralties, a high-order subgroup of Oc located in present-day Papua New Guinea. The long history of contacts evident in the Yapese language is further confirmation of the thesis in this book that the seaways in the region have for millennia been busy with the movement of people, and further complicates the picture in regard to dating and direction of colonization. I will return to linguistics as part of the broader discussion of origins offered in the next chapter.

Constructed seascapes

From the Marshall Islands through to Vanuatu and beyond, the coastal people of Oceania exhibit a direct link with seacraft which provides a material metaphor for the direction and construction of social life. On the Marshallese atoll of Enewetak, Laurence Carucci (1995: 25) found that 'the canoe is the captain's island' and that, beyond metaphor, during the worst typhoons people would abandon the atoll and take their boats to sea. Once at sea, they would secure the rigging and fill the hull with water, creating a relatively stable platform, only bailing out once the storm had passed. Developing the maritime metaphor for Oceanic peoples, Diaz and Kauanui (2001: 317) draw on Carolinian ethnography to note that a perception of navigators is that the islands are moving in relation to them and the only stable point is one from which the position is gauged, that is, the seacraft itself. Such notional security in this fluid space provided by seacraft and the sea goes against common outsider notions of the ocean, but such reports have helped fuel a change in understanding the past in the Pacific. As Anne Di Piazza and Erik Pearthree (2001) have stridently asserted in regard to the quotidian nature of Carolinian sailing:

This banalization of voyaging allows one to think of the sea as an ally, to organize a world which extends beyond one's own island, and to satisfy the navigator's desires for the external world. This openness of the islanders to the world of the sea favors, perhaps more than elsewhere, communication in the direct as well as in the figurative sense. (Di Piazza 2001: 11)

In relation to such a perspective, as espoused by Di Piazza and Pearthree, Alfred Gell (1985: 272) asked:

Can one really assert that navigating a boat, without a chart or a magnetic compass, is really an 'everyday' task? Is it not rather a very special task, requiring long training, memorisation of a mass of detailed information, and considerable mental agility in applying this fund of information to the ever-changing circumstances of an actual sea voyage?

Gell attempts to answer these questions in relation to mental maps characterized as non-token-indexical statements, that is, representation of actual space
and the requirement of locating oneself as navigator through a token-indexical
spatial propositon, which is the literal perception of the stable position perceived by the navigator (as mentioned in a metaphorical sense above by Diaz
and Kauanui). Gell explores these issues in relation to Carolinian navigation
and in particular the system of *etak*, described by Gell (1985: 284):

The *etak* system is the means whereby Micronesian navigators contrive
to make star course maps generate token-indexical images. Lacking instruments such as chronometers and sextants, as well as charts, Micronesians
use dead-reckoning to estimate their whereabouts on the ocean, by continu-
ously monitoring their speed through the water and their heading. These dead-
reckoning 'fixes' are not directly identifiable from images of star course maps
because . . . star course maps do not generate locationally specific images.
Instead, token-indexical beliefs, arrived at by dead-reckoning, are cognitively
encoded as 'sightings' of an *etak* ('refuge') island lying perpendicularly to one
side of the desired inter-island course, so as to form the apex of an imaginary
triangle.

An example of how this might be illustrated in diagram form is provided in
Fig. 3.3.

Gell (1985: 286) finds in answer to his questions that: 'The *etak* system . . .
though of extraordinary refinement, is a system of images derived from a
[mental] map and is logically on par with the cognitive processes which under-
lie the most elementary kinds of way-finding in everyday contexts.' So,
although Gell acknowledges the great complexity and knowledge required to
operate the *etak* system, it is not beyond the 'everyday' in terms of experience.

In the atoll societies of the central Caroline Islands, Thomas Gladwin (1970),
David Lewis (1994) and others have recorded the skill, ability and something
of the cosmology of contemporary island maritime navigators. They have introduced us to an Oceanic seascape that had previously been ignored or poorly
appreciated. This oversight has led, in part, to the concept of Remote Oceanic
islands as isolated (e.g., see Terrell 1986; Broodbank 2000). Epeli Hau'ofa (1993)
has warned of the negative connotations implied by continent-centric scholars
who, unaware of the sailing skills of islanders, regard the islands as isolated
dots in the Pacific, rather than viewing their world as a mapped 'sea of islands'
(see Finney 1998). Thomas Eriksen (1993), in a discussion of the meaning of
the word island, has noted that deep continental valleys surrounded by mountains may indeed be more isolated from outside influence than an island in
an ocean. The sea can be both a barrier and a pathway, but either is socially
derived (for further discussion see Rainbird 1999c). If people had the ability to
sail and purposefully settle islands in Remote Oceania, then they could not
have perceived the sea as a barrier. Seascapes, like landscapes, are multivocal,
and as shown by Chris Gosden and Christina Pavlides (1994) for the Pacific

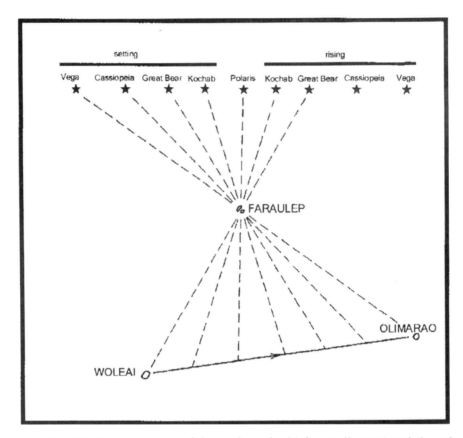

Fig. 3.3 Representation of the *etak* method (after Gell 1985): 'While sailing,
the navigator makes imaginary sightings of the *etak* island – which
is always invisible below the horizon – in order to formulate
token-indexical beliefs, arrived at by dead reckoning, as to his
current position. Thus at Woleai, Faraulep [the *etak* island] is under
"Great Bear rising". Some time later, if the canoe is still on course,
Faraulep is under "Kochab rising", and later still "Polaris" and
"Kochab setting" etc., until, on arrival at Olimarao, it is under
"Vega setting".'

islands, seascapes and landscapes should, at the very least, be considered in
their historical context as having a variety of possibilities of connection and
separation.

The simple term 'canoe' does little justice to describing the sophisticated and,
on occasion, large vessels that were constructed for long-distance voyages of
communication, exploration and colonization. The early Spanish visitors to the
Mariana Islands commented on the speed and manoeuvrability of the Chamorro
vessels that they named 'flying proas' (Fig. 3.4), and Pigafetta, who was with

Fig. 3.4 Painting of a 'flying proa' (from Freycinet 1996). The Marianas outrigger seacraft was dubbed the 'flying proa' when first encountered by the Magellan expeditioners in 1521, indicating their admiration for its speed and manoeuvrability. It was regarded as very similar to that in the Caroline Islands. Painting by Adrien Tauney (*c*. 1822), *Proh des Iles Carolines*, U8139/S, Rex Nan Kivell Collection. By permission of the National Library of Australia.

Magellan in 1521, added (quoted in Russell 1998: 199): 'The sail is made from palm leaves sewn together and shaped like a lateen sail. For rudders, they use a certain blade resembling a hearth shovel which has a piece of wood at the end. They can change stern and bow at will, and those boats resemble the dolphins which leap in water wave to wave.' The seacraft of the region, as historically and ethnographically recorded, are all equipped with a single outrigger. The outrigger was always kept to windward and tacking was achieved, as alluded to by Pigafetta in the quote above, by shifting the sail, usually made of woven pandanus leaves, and by this method changing ends so that the bow and stern were interchangeable; all the sailing vessels of the region can be called double-ended and, although there are variations between and within island groups, the basic design elements are shared across the region. The Chamorro vessels are recorded as being up to 15 metres in length, but they were narrow, little more than a metre at most, with the basic hull hollowed from a single log and the sides built up with planks. The planks were tied together with sennit twine and caulked. The hulls were painted with natural pigments available to the islands and often in red, black or white, with mangrove sap, coconut oil and lime, mentioned as possible binders for the pigment, which also aided in preserving the twine and wood (Robinson 1970; Russell 1998).

That the colouring of canoes is not likely to be simply a matter of preservative function and/or aesthetic taste may be illustrated by a story from Kosrae. The island of Kosrae has a mountainous interior and the shape in silhouette of the peaks and ridges, particularly when seen from the vantage point of Leluh Island on the eastern fringing reef, provides the outline of the torso and head of a lady, the 'Sleeping Lady', lying with her head to the north. Not so clear is that to the south the ridge line splits in two, becoming the lower limbs of the lady. That this observation is one with some local importance is suggested in that the four contemporary villages of Kosrae take part of their identity from their juxtaposition in regard to the Sleeping Lady. Alan Burns (1997: 7) reports that:

This identity was marked in residents' discussions of the 'Sleeping Lady' mountain and the qualities of women in each village. People from each village interpreted the location of village vis a vis 'Sleeping Lady' in terms of her attributes: Tafunsak women were said to have beautiful hair; Lelu[h] women were said to have beautiful faces and beautiful breasts; Malem women were said to have beautiful thighs; and Utwe women were said to have beautiful legs.

The female body metaphor for the island of Kosrae also extends into seafaring lore. At the point where the Sleeping Lady torso splits into the legs it is said that a fine red soil may be collected and it is this soil that was traditionally used to make the pigment for the red-coloured hulls of the sailing vessels. The location in relation to the Sleeping Lady's body and colour make for strong associations with blood from menstruation. In the Caroline Islands generally, menstruating women are reported to have been regarded as dangerous, particularly to men about to sail on fishing or inter-island travel expeditions. The direct application of such a pigment with dangerous associations may at first glance appear puzzling, but the inherent power within dangerous materials may perhaps be transformed and harnessed for successful sailing.

Double-hulled vessels were reported in 1832 as paddled 'war canoes' in Chuuk Lagoon and more recently remembered there as models that became 'sacred' objects (Haddon and Hornell 1936) and also in a sacred context in Tochobei. Double-hulled vessels, when equipped with sails, are more usually associated with Polynesia and are often regarded as having been introduced to the Pacific from the islands of South-East Asia over 3000 years ago (Spriggs 1999a). Atholl Anderson (2000) has detailed certain doubts about the antiquity of such vessels, and also the appropriateness of using experimental voyaging (both real and computer simulated) in support of ancient voyaging. In regard to experimental voyaging Anderson (2000: 22) says:

it is obvious that the problem inherent in simulated voyaging (by computer and by sailing) is the familiar epistemical difficulty of equifinality. In setting out to define the expected kinds of voyaging behaviour required to fit an observed chrono-geographical pattern of island discovery, the variables (vessel capability, navigational capability, frequency of voyaging etc.), can be adjusted to produce different voyaging behaviours that lead to the same result . . . The theoretical means of resolving this dilemma lies in evidence about which actual voyaging behaviour and frequency was employed at different times . . . but in practice no such evidence is available and . . . more than one proposition about the nature of prehistoric sailing vessels can be erected on the basis of proxy evidence.

Anderson continues that the technology chosen – and for the most part he is talking of the Polynesian types of double-hulled sailing vessels – is not of a type that was available throughout the process of colonizing Remote Oceania. Indeed he argues that, as reconstructed, the modern versions go beyond the technology available to the initial colonizers of even Hawaii and Aotearoa/New Zealand. The colonization of these archipelagos, he argues, was only possible through the introduction of new technology, from the west, and possibly even from Micronesia, 1200 to 1000 years ago.

Anderson makes some useful points that we need to be aware of, but there can be no denying that marine technology was developed to a sufficient extent to allow the majority of the Pacific islands to have been settled by 1200 years ago, and that, in the majority of cases, these colonization events were planned and purposeful. Colonizing oceanic islands successfully required introducing new plants, animals and a viable breeding population of humans (see chapter 4). There is also reason to suspect that the 'proxy evidence' provided by European explorers and more recent ethnographies has failed to elucidate the complete picture. For example, in relation to 'navigational capability', Robin Baker (1989; see Gell 1985), a biologist, has been controversial in showing that people can have a 'sixth sense', that of 'magnetoperception'. In this it is argued that human beings have the ability, like other species, to perceive the earth's magnetic field, and by so doing, orient themselves directionally in relation to geomagnetic forces. Ben Finney (1995) has specifically addressed the issue of magnetoperception in relation to Pacific voyaging, and contends that it may exist but has been mentally buried by years of neglect. Finney reports that it was during one of the voyages in *Hokulea*, a double-hulled reconstructed Polynesian vessel, that a circumstance possibly explained by magnetoperception arose. The experimental voyage was being navigated by Nainoa Thompson, a Hawaiian, who had been trained in non-instrument navigation by Mau Piailug from Satawal in the Caroline Islands. As the vessel sailed in the doldrums at about 6 to 7 degrees north of the Equator the thick cloud cover and switching wind during the night caused problems in navigation, as Nainoa Thompson recounts (in Finney 1995: 503):

It was just like I got so exhausted that I just got backed up against the rail, and it was almost as if, and I don't know if this was completely true, but there was something that allowed me to understand where the direction was without seeing it . . . I felt this warmth come over me and all of a sudden I knew where the moon was. But you couldn't see the moon it was so black, and then I directed the canoe with all this total confidence.

Finney reports that, following further experiences such as these, Nainoa Thompson told him that he has tried to cultivate the ability to find direction without using the visual cues that are commonly regarded as the basic elements of non-instrument navigation.

That the double-hulled vessel type does not appear to have been the most favoured for long-distance voyaging between the islands of the Micronesian region suggests that here the single outrigger type was honed to a particularly high level of technological sophistication from the time it was already capable of carrying people to these islands for initial settlement. We should take Anderson's critique of modern experimental voyaging and that of Margaret Jolly (2001), in relation to Epeli Hau'ofa's post-colonial classic 'sea of islands', in their warnings that we must be careful not to generalize too broadly across Oceania in regard to the islanders being people of the sea. As Jolly points out, some of the inhabitants of the large islands in Melanesia are not linked to the sea in the same way as people elsewhere in the Oceanic world, and similarly, the sailing and navigational expertise found in the Caroline Islands may be significantly different from that used in other parts of the Pacific. It appears that the ancient voyaging in Micronesia conforms very closely to that recorded in ethnographic studies of the Caroline Islands. At the same time, the power and role of experimental voyaging in developing a strong contemporary notion of identity and pride across many Pacific island communities should not be downplayed or belittled, as the spread of knowledge through fluid links is of supreme importance for the colonized, neocolonized and independent indigenous communities of Oceania.

Political constructs

In 1986, after many years of negotiation, the people of the Caroline Islands (except the Republic of Belau) became incorporated within the Federated States of Micronesia (FSM) under a Compact of Free Association with the USA. The Marshall islanders, not wishing to be subsumed by the relatively large population of the FSM, negotiated their own compact agreement that was ratified in the same year, and became the Republic of the Marshall Islands (RMI). The agreements provided money and other aid for a fifteen-year period, and in 2002 this was extended with negotiated changes for a further twenty years. In return the islanders allowed the US military use of their islands whenever required and they agreed not to enter into a similar agreement with a third party. The outcome allowed the USA to claim that they had met their obligations in relation to the United Nations Trust Territory in providing means towards local independence, but at the same time kept enough control for strategic purposes.

In the Republic of Belau, sections of the community put up great resistance to negotiating a deal that would allow the US military nuclear armaments rights to the archipelago; the death of two presidents, the division of Palauan society, and numerous referenda and court cases characterize this process (Parmentier 1991). Finally in 1994, as a result of US pressure and the lure of money, Palau's politicians finally succumbed and joined the USA in a separate compact agreement. Much of the recent archaeological work in Palau, discussed in the next chapter, is a direct result of this agreement in leading to an influx of money for capital improvements.

Two systems of government operate in the Mariana Islands. The people of Guam remain within a US Territory, and although there is a local movement for indigenous land rights and independence there is currently little prospect that colonial rule will change. The large military installations appear to remain of prime importance to the USA and the indigenous Chamorro are in a minority. However, their neighbours to the north, including large numbers of Carolinian-descended islanders who settled in Spanish times, opted for a US commonwealth at the end of the USTTPI, coming into effect in 1976. As the Commonwealth of the Northern Mariana Islands (CNMI), the residents have a similar status to Puerto Rico, although it appears that many would prefer full inclusion into the USA as a State.

The Carolines and Marshalls are in a relationship of dependence with the USA and the years of colonial control have not ended. The USA, in its forty years of administration (outside of Guam), has created a culture of dependence that has undermined indigenous subsistence strategies and replaced them with a cash culture. Now that the major source of money (through the Compact agreements) is drying up, the only door open is the one leading to a renegotiation with the USA. There is little possibility of full independence in sight, even though the FSM and RMI are slowly becoming recognized as independent states by other nations and were admitted to the United Nations in 1991.

The Marianas, particularly Guam and Saipan, have in recent years become popular tourist destinations. Accompanying this trend is an influx of Japanese investment that has led to major developments of tourist resorts, hotels and businesses (Fig. 3.5). Under US laws that aim to protect the environment and the cultural heritage, these commercial developments have led to an unprecedented

Fig. 3.5 View of Agana *c.* 1991. The capital of Guam has all the trappings of
modern urban America. This administrative district continues with
no perceptible boundary into the tourist area with the large hotels of
Tumon Bay.

upsurge in archaeological activity and the production of numerous unpublished
reports (Butler 1992b; Rainbird 1995a).

Not only is the majority of the region dominated politically by the USA,
but this has inevitably led to the archaeology being dominated by US archaeologists. For the most part, indigenous people are taking control of their own
historic preservation programmes, which manage archaeological and other historic work in their territory. But this is still partially funded by the US Department of Interior and the US National Park Service (USNPS) (John 1992). The
USNPS supplies policy and training to the indigenous participants, potentially
Americanizing their perceptions of the 'proper' way to deal with the past. This
situation may change in the FSM and RMI, following the renegotiation of the
Compact monies and requirements with the expectation that funding will be
reduced for cultural programmes in order to support basic health, education,
transport and commercial infrastructure. However, in relation to anthropology, and this might also be true for archaeology, Kiste (1999) argues that one
of the crucial issues as to why America has dominated research and applied
approaches in the last half-century is the intellectual parochialism of those

working from traditions of British social anthropology, and in these he includes scholars from Australia, Aotearoa/New Zealand and Canada. In this, American anthropologists are said to be interested in the work of anthropologists from other nations, while their own work is given cursory consideration by those coming from a British tradition.

Certainly there are issues of intra-disciplinary boundaries that are perhaps not as fluid as they ought to be, but Kiste also notes the role of the American governance in the region. During the early post-war administration, up until the early 1960s, access to American Micronesia was controlled by security restrictions, with foreign researchers discouraged from working there; the outside perception would have been one of an 'exclusively American enclave'. Another possible reason is that the mass of publication produced from CIMA and SIM, although through American publishers, may have presented the prospect of few opportunities left for new ethnography when compared to the 700 or so language groups and 'undiscovered' peoples of New Guinea. Finally, access and government funding was derived from the USA and it is from that direction that academics along established routes also flowed.

As for the case of archaeology alone, it might be worth considering the critical assessment of Geoffrey White and Ty Kāwika Tengan (2001: 392) in relation to the Hawaiian experience, when they conclude that a 'brief history of anthropological studies in Hawai'i suggests a logical progression: from salvage ethnography of disappearing natives, to acculturation studies of Hawaiians becoming Americans, to total absence from the cultural record'. The last stage is characterized by the post-war intensification of archaeology and physical anthropology and with it the 'implicit (and at times explicit) statement . . . that there were no Kanaka 'Oiwi left to study; the only place to find a Hawaiian was in the ground'.

Over a shorter period of time a similar pattern of development in the anthropology of American Micronesia might also be discerned. The initial programmes were very much concerned with a basic, perhaps 'salvage', ethnographic account; the 1970s saw a greater focus on aspects of development and acculturation in anthropological research; and with a few notable exceptions, archaeological research did not become common, certainly not for doctoral research, until the middle of the 1980s. The fact that archaeology in Hawai'i has often been the target of indigenous disdain and outright protest (see Spriggs 1990; 1991) supports such a view for that archipelago, but beyond similar comments by Chamorro people regarding archaeological desecration in Guam (see Rainbird 2000a), I am not aware of similar action elsewhere in Micronesia.

Archaeologists in their collaborative work with the various historic preservation staff have for many years been seen as participating in the development of potential benefits for the local communities in issues of preserving, enhancing and communicating heritage on various islands (e.g., see Gale and Fitzpatrick 2001). It is only in American archaeology's belated reflexive stage that much of this community archaeology has been deemed worthy of academic reporting. Scott Fitzpatrick has been working with the Palau Division of Cultural Affairs to enhance knowledge of the archaeology of cave sites on Palau, allowing for informed publicity and the proper steps to be taken in order that the sites chosen for touristic development are properly managed to preserve the cultural resource (Fitzpatrick and Kanai 2001). Such projects are likely to continue and a recent survey indicated that 'eco-tourism', with the focus on archaeological and natural landscapes, is going to be a particular aim of tourist development in the future (Spennemann, Look and Graham 2001). Indeed tourism is becoming a major facet of the local economy of some of the islands, as Terence Wesley-Smith (2000: 308) has noted in an introduction to a volume of papers on migrant labour and tourism in Palau:

[T]he number of tourists visiting the Northern Marianas annually rose fourfold in the decade after 1984 to more than a half-million. Visitor numbers in Palau [some 70,000 annually] rose by over 60 percent in the second half of the 1990s, and tourism's share of gross national product went from 15 percent in 1991 to 46 percent in 1996.

The Republic of Kiribati, at least as far as the Gilbert Islands are concerned, has not seen a significant influx of money, tourists or development since independence. In this case, archaeological work has been restricted to research projects instigated, for the most part, by foreign people.

Pacific archaeological constructs

Archaeology is a relatively young discipline and archaeology in the Pacific is younger than most, with a rapid increase in research since the 1970s (Kirch and Weisler 1994). Whereas anthropological information from the Pacific region has been used by social anthropologists and archaeologists around the world to inform interpretations of variation in human societies, there has been little reciprocal exchange. Most of the archaeological work in the region has received little input from more recent changes (gaining acceptance in the 1980s) in the nature of the disciplines of sociocultural anthropology, historical anthropology and archaeology: here I am concerned with archaeology.

   This is not the place to reproduce a history of Anglo-American archaeological thought but, in broad terms, it is possible to track general paradigms over the second half of the twentieth century. The immediate post-Second World War period was dominated by traditional archaeology, which can be considered as a culture-historical approach in which the archaeological data were reproduced in narrative form. In the 1960s archaeologists began to draw their inspiration for methodology and style of interpretation from the philosophy of science which stemmed from a positivist approach. This type of archaeology, coined 'New' or processual, drew upon the hypothetico-deductive method of analysis in an attempt to generate general cross-cultural models of human behaviour. Since the early 1980s there has been renewed interest in the historical approach to archaeological interpretation, with inspiration drawn from the social sciences. However, the processualist mode of enquiry still resonates strongly in Pacific archaeology.

A tenet of processualist (and neo-evolutionary) theories is that culture is an adaptive response to 'alterations in the natural environment or in adjacent and competing cultural systems' (Trigger 1989: 296). That is, all change in society must be a response to external pressure, otherwise the 'social system' would retain its equilibrium. This environmentally deterministic approach has been favoured in interpretations of island societies that were, and often still are, considered isolated and at the mercy of the island environment (Terrell, Hunt and Gosden 1997; for a general review see Rainbird 1999c). This approach spawned the concept of 'islands as laboratories' in which human adaptations to the island 'ecosystem' could be tested with little fear of influence from external sources (e.g., Goodenough 1957; Clark and Terrell 1978; Kirch 1986). Robert Bryson (1989: 7), in the introduction to his thesis on Pohnpei, exemplifies this attitude when he states that 'The islands of the Pacific have long been considered nearly ideal locations for the study of complex cultures evolving in relative isolation.' Michael Graves and Roger Green (1993b: 6) repeat this message, arguing that 'the "islands as natural laboratories" concept has considerable utility for archaeological research in this [Remote Pacific] region'.

As Chris Gosden (1994: 21) notes, in the highly influential early work of Marshall Sahlins (1958), generalizations about social forms could not begin without a consideration of adaptation to the environment. Energy from the environmental context was seen to determine the possibilities for the evolution of social stratification, so that 'impoverished' environments, such as atolls, would have low social differentiation, while large fertile islands would develop a complex social hierarchy. The social categories themselves were developed within neo-evolutionary frameworks during the 1960s (see e.g., Service 1962; Fried 1967).

Essentially having its roots in the Enlightenment, social evolutionary theory as we know it today was formed in the second half of the nineteenth century through the works of Morgan, Spencer, Tylor, Bachofen, Westermarck, Maine and Lubbock amongst others. In archaeology, it is possible to identify Gordon Childe as the first in the modern form of the discipline to introduce social evolutionary thought (Sanderson 1990). As a Marxist, Childe was aware of the social evolutionary stages proposed separately by Engels and Marx and, like them, he built upon the work of Lewis Morgan. Evolutionary theories came to

New Archaeology via social and cultural anthropology after renewed interest was shown in the latter discipline during the 1950s, by scholars such as Leslie White and Julian Steward, which became coined as 'neo-evolutionary'. A time lag meant that they were not adopted into archaeology until the late 1960s and early 1970s. Norman Yoffee (1993), in a review of the use of neo-evolutionary theory in archaeology, notes the ready adoption of ethnographic analogies to typologize societies into neat entities conforming to evolutionary stages. This occurred long after the social anthropologists had dropped the whole notion of unilineal social evolution, following the realization that each stage was represented by contemporary societies and therefore stages could not lead from one to another. It was also pointed out that finding acceptable cross-cultural criteria for defining each stage (except perhaps for states, which were of little concern for social anthropologists anyway) was impossible. However, archaeologists in the Pacific (and elsewhere, e.g., see contributions in Earle 1991) continued to apply these concepts to archaeology. Such works are exemplified in titles such as *The Evolution of the Polynesian Chiefdoms* (Kirch 1984a) and *The Evolution and Organisation of Prehistoric Society in Polynesia* (Graves and Green 1993a).

The more recent stage of archaeological study takes its lead in part from developments in the social sciences. The British sociologist Anthony Giddens, for example, has been particularly vocal in his dissatisfaction with social evolutionary models. He equates them with the worst of objectivist systems theories such as crude structuralism and functionalism, which deny the role played by human agency in society. These criticisms can be seen in the context of Giddens' prolonged attack on the American sociologist Talcott Parsons (Sica 1991). Parsons, a proponent of structural functionalism, is regarded even by some supporters of evolutionary theory as embracing 'the most extreme objectivist [form] of evolutionism' (Sanderson 1990: 213). However, many of Giddens' criticisms have broader validity.

First, Giddens (1984: 238) claims that the history of evolutionary thought is Occident-centric:

The voyage of the *Beagle* symbolized, as it were, the journeys that brought Europeans into contact with diverse and exotic cultures, subsumed and categorized within an embracing scheme in which the West naturally stood at the top. There is no sign that evolutionary schemes today are free from this sort of ethnocentrism. Where can one find such a scheme in Western social science which holds that traditional India is at the head of the scale? Or ancient China? Or, for that matter, modern India or China?

The consequence of this type of thought is the production of a normative association between contemporary Western societies and what is considered as progress or progressive. This Giddens (1984) identifies as the 'normative illusion'. He also identifies three other dangers in the social evolutionary scheme:

1. *unilineal compression*, the necessity of achieving one evolutionary stage prior to moving to the next;
2. *homological compression*, that identification of an evolutionary stage allows for the identification of the stage of individual personality development within that society;
3. *temporal distortion*, that history in evolutionary thought can only be a history of social change, that is, periods of relative stasis are likely to be ignored.

All of the above have the effect of masking difference between individual societies, difference that is created through the agency of individuals, who are otherwise considered subsumed under structuring principles. Agency has become a significant issue in archaeology (see, e.g., Dobres and Robb 2000). Evolutionary schema address only the structural level of society and thus ignore the effects of human actors who are involved in a dialectic relationship with that structure, in a recursive manner both shaping and being shaped. According to Giddens, 'there exists no necessary overall mechanism of social change, no universal "motor of history"' (Bryant and Jary 1991: 14). The corollary is that each social context must be considered historically upon its own merit, not by the application of a borrowed model. In regard to the sphere of Pacific archaeology Gosden writes (1994: 21–2, references removed):

Kirch provides an excellent statement of the evolutionary position, in which he charts the growth of social complexity from a putative Ancestral Polynesian Society. This ancestral form is seen already to exhibit some aspects of hierarchy when it first entered the Pacific in the shape of the Lapita cultural complex. Hierarchy bloomed or was curtailed depending upon the possibilities for subsistence intensification in different island groups. Hawai'i became the most clearly differentiated society because 'Hawai'i clearly offered the greatest range of environmental opportunity'.

Gosden's summary of Kirch's approach suggests that, in the final decades of the twentieth century, interpretation of Pacific archaeology and past island societies continued to use models first employed forty to fifty years earlier. This is particularly odd as it is actually not necessary for Kirch to invoke evolutionary models; in this theoretical construct all of Polynesia is represented by the 'chiefdom' evolutionary stage (see Yoffee 1993). According to Kirch this is the type of society which existed at the time of movement into the eastern Pacific. However, as we have seen, social evolutionary concepts are applied, the main criterion being adaptation to the environment. As chiefdoms already existed, Kirch's interest is in their 'evolutionary' prowess in maintaining the trajectory to greater hierarchy in varying island environments.

   All of the criticisms of progress, system and objectivism discussed above can be applied to Kirch's model, as they are all to be found there. In contrast, some other archaeologists in Oceania, presuming some sort of 'founder effect', suppose that society was necessarily reinvented each time an island was populated.

This concept produces developmental trajectories that see societies becoming progressively more complex as they adapt and grow (e.g., models proposed in Micronesia for Kosrae by Ueki 1984 and Cordy *et al.* 1985). These practitioners ignore history (homology, Gould 1986; *habitus*, Bourdieu 1977; or the possibility of structural tendency, Hodder 1990), and are equally as problematic in a critique of social evolution. It is these notions of history, and thus context, that have been introduced as part of a more critical archaeology, sometimes called 'post-processualism' or more recently and correctly interpretative archaeologies (Tilley 1993; Hodder *et al.* 1995; Thomas 2000), that has led some archaeologists in the Pacific away from evolutionary models. It is this type of approach that informs the interpretation in this book.

In my view, the application of typological stages to past societies only serves to blur the possibility of a clearer understanding of how individual societies operated. No *a priori* developmental sequence should be applied to the archaeologically derived histories. I prefer to avoid the term 'evolution' as it is imbued with too many preconceived meanings. It is clear that the style of evolutionism embraced by Spencer and Morgan to social circumstances is obsolete (Freeman 1974). As Yoffee (1993: 67) notes, even if some concept of social evolution is accepted, it is altogether possible 'that ethnographic chiefdoms lie in a different evolutionary line from states altogether'. Yoffee's statement follows the more complex forms of biological evolutionary thought which have become popular (e.g., Kirch and Green 1987; Terrell 1988; Graves and Ladefoged 1995). Recent approaches dissolve the culture/nature dichotomy by recognizing 'nature' as a cultural concept, the identification of natural changes from group to group. In highlighting the social and taking a lead from the social sciences this type of interpretative construction in archaeology, the type I am advocating in this book, may be termed 'archaeological anthropology'.

Micronesia, archaeological constructs

At the time Peter Buck (Te Rangi Hiroa), the Maori Director of the Bishop Museum in Honolulu, was writing his best-selling *Vikings of the Sunrise* (1938), the archaeology of the region was still poorly known. Outside of Japanese spheres, the majority of information was derived from Hans Hornbostel's notes and extensive collections of artefacts and human remains collected during the 1920s in the Mariana Islands. Hornbostel's collection was deposited in the Bishop Museum, but was poorly understood prior to the work of Laura Thompson published in 1932. Given the paucity of available research it is of little surprise that in strongly asserting his hypothesis that Polynesia had been colonized by humans using the 'northern Micronesian route', Buck relied wholly on racial characteristics, shared linguistic elements and mythology. However, in this scenario, the route bypasses the Mariana Islands, as it 'leads through Yap, Palau, and the Caroline Islands; then it branches, one line leading north-east through the Marshall Islands toward Hawaii, and one going south-east through the Gilbert and Phœnix Islands to enter Polynesia north of Samoa' (Buck 1938: 45). For Buck, the most positive argument for the identification of the Micronesian route to Polynesia was the lack of evidence for the 'southern Melanesian route'. The evidence available changed radically after the Second World War, making Buck's Micronesian hypothesis obsolete.

In her address to the Micronesian Archaeology Conference convened in Guam during September 1987, Janet Davidson (1988) was able to report what she considered to be 'remarkable progress' for a region that, when she conducted research in 1965, had been virtually unknown to archaeology. This was not entirely the case, as some significant primary work by American archaeologists had already been conducted: Alexander Spoehr (1957) and Hans Hornbostel (Thompson 1932; 1945) had worked in the Mariana Islands, while E.W. Gifford and D.S. Gifford (1959) had reported on their work on Yap. Also in 1965 Fred Reinman (1977) started archaeological work on Guam, and in Palau Douglas Osborne (1966; 1979) had already conducted extensive research, but their reports were not published until after Davidson's work on the atolls (1967b; 1971). Since Buck's hypothesis lost favour in regard to the broader models of Pacific (especially Polynesian) colonization, and the exciting developments following the discovery of the broad geographical distribution of Lapita pottery outside of Micronesia, the region had become regarded as rather a backwater for Pacific archaeology as a whole.

Rosalind Hunter-Anderson and Michael Graves (1990) in their introduction to the volume of papers from the Guam conference noted, with dramatic effect, that only thirty archaeological projects had been conducted in Micronesia by 1970. They also recognized that much of this work was 'exploratory' in nature. By 1990, however, they were able to estimate that another 300 projects had been either started or completed in the preceding two decades, but much of this work remains in 'discovery mode'. In reviewing the archaeology of the region, Hunter-Anderson and Graves (1990) found that archaeology from an American perspective, as noted above for elsewhere in Oceania, was mostly seen in attempts to identify processes leading to social complexity through archaeological correlates.

Hunter-Anderson and Graves (1990) identified two major paradigms that they believe had led archaeological thought in the region. The first was the culture history approach, which was dominated by issues of origins, that is, directions of migration and cultural changes indicated by diachronic variations in material culture. The second, an eminently Americanist approach, was a 'natural science-based adaptationist' one that places the environment in the forefront of cultural endeavours and evolutionary behavioural traits, and is thus located firmly within the processual paradigm.

In a mid-1990s publication that provided a synthesis of the archaeology of the region, I attempted to identify dominant themes in interpretative practice.

These were, for the most part, situated within the two paradigms identified above, and the list that I produced, and present again below, was intended to provide a direct critique of them as self-fulfilling and stagnant (partially modified from Rainbird 1994a: 300–2):

1. *Architecture*: Many of the island societies begin to use stone or coral rubble architecture at some point in their history. The archaeological recognition of this process has given rise to a number of related studies: dating the introduction (see 2); assessing the location of architectural types (see 6); and construction of settlement hierarchies (see 6 and 7).

2. *Chronology*: A basic understanding of culture history, the dating of artefacts and events, is still a major pursuit and is required for many of the islands within the region.

3. *Environment*: Often regarded as a determining factor in the making of island societies. The environment is often invoked in discussions of: adaptation (see 8); subsistence intensification (see 8); the poor understanding of culture-history (see 2 and 6), that is, the covering or disturbance of earlier sites through the process of adaptation or subsistence intensification; population, that is, the maximum carrying capacity of the environment (see 7); and the environmental necessity for some island societies to retain inter-island contacts (see 4). Little attention has been paid to the ability of island societies to manipulate and overcome what archaeologists perceive to be environmental constraints.

4. *Inter-island communication*: As the shackles of 'islands as laboratories' are shaken off, we are likely to see more consideration of prehistoric movement of people and materials between islands. Although most post-excavation analyses assess the provenance of materials from a site, little emphasis has been placed on attempting to explain the mechanisms by which exotic materials arrived. However, this is not the case when a network has been recorded ethnographically; in this instance, the material remains are simply considered in relation to the literature.

5. *Portable material culture*: A number of studies have considered a particular type of artefact, either for a particular island, or for a larger area for purposes of dating (see 2) or identification of ethnic groups. Few studies have considered the role of material culture within island societies, or the impetus for movement of material culture in other than purely functional terms (see 3 and 4).

6. *Settlement pattern*: A number of projects have been conducted on contemporary 'traditional' settlement patterns. On islands with well-preserved prehistoric settlement sites (see 1) efforts have been made to understand earlier settlement patterns. These attempts are limited by poor chronological control (see 2).

7. *Social organization*: Although many studies have relied on ethnohistory and oral histories for interpreting past social organization, a few have attempted to use material culture (see 1) and mortuary remains in an effort to understand earlier organization. Typically for Pacific prehistory, the imposition of neo-evolutionary and social

evolutionary models to the study of society has restricted a greater understanding of the potential variety of island societies (see 1, 3, and 8).

8. *Subsistence*: Although on occasion considered a topic worthy of research on its own merit, agricultural practice is often considered for the early periods in terms of adaptation (see 3), and for the later periods in terms of subsistence intensification which allows for the rise of social hierarchies (see 7).

Much work in the region continues to be informed by these themes and the two major paradigms identified by Hunter-Anderson and Graves. As archaeological work and reinterpretation has continued during the 1990s and beyond, the complexity of the evidence and the critique of such overriding paradigms from within the discipline as a whole, as noted above, has led to change. Many studies now take a more tempered approach, which contextualizes the evidence in relation to local historical contingencies.

The paper quoted above was published in the *Journal of World Prehistory* (Rainbird 1994a) and as such it did not incorporate issues regarding the archaeology of the periods of European contact and colonialism. In a similar vein these periods are not a focus of this book, but in keeping with the philosophy of this volume aspects of the later periods will be discussed in relation to particular topics as they arise. The identification of fluid boundaries also ought to include the boundary between what is often termed in archaeological parlance 'prehistory' and what in western academic and popular perception is called 'history', the period for which written records are available. Island histories through the oral, the narrative and the written flow across such boundaries and an absolute demarcation is impossible. Archaeologists have been active in researching the more recent archaeologies in the region, but I should state that coverage of such work is not as comprehensive in this volume as it intends to be for the earlier periods.

The next chapter introduces the detailed archaeological evidence that is interpreted to provide an understanding of the earliest human habitation of the islands in the region. In this, and the following chapters, by adopting an interpretative archaeological approach, one that attempts to construct an archaeological anthropology, it should become clear to the reader that alternative scenarios are being proposed to those that are normally derived from the dominant paradigms generally encountered in the region, and elsewhere in the archaeology of Oceania, to date. This does not mean that the 'baby is thrown out with the bathwater', as the methodologies of fieldwork practice are generally comparable amongst archaeologists and there is certainly very interesting work from all paradigms to be considered. But to begin with, the islands need to be peopled, and this is the role of the next chapter.

CHAPTER 4

SETTLING THE SEASCAPE: FUSING ISLANDS AND PEOPLE

The fluid boundaries discussed in the previous chapter did not come into existence, if indeed they can be said to exist beyond community imagination, by accident, and they are equally not the product of natural creation. These fluid boundaries became imagined in myriad different ways once people settled the islands in the region. All of the islands of this place called Micronesia, in the broadest sense of its imagined boundaries, were islands when people first set their eyes on them. That is, unlike some of the islands of the world in the present day, they were not connected to a continent by 'land bridges' at any time in the human past. In this the boundaries were always fluid ones; it was at all times in the past a requirement that the sea be crossed in order to travel to these islands, whether by boat or, beginning in the last century, by aircraft.

Debates surrounding the origins of the islanders of Oceania have been long and, on occasions, heated. The colonization of the islands of Oceania is generally accepted to be the most recent colonization of previously vacant (from a human perspective) land that provides the present distribution of the permanent settlement of our species on earth. (It might be argued that the camps in Antarctica have led to its permanent settlement since the last century.) Anthropologist Ben Finney (1992) suggests that the next great migration into uncolonized lands is likely to be into space, turning seafaring peoples into 'spacefaring' people and Polynesians into 'Cosmopolynesians'!

In this chapter I will first review local understandings of how the islands came into existence and consider a few examples of these understandings in relation to some specific colonization events. I will follow this with a consideration of academic discussion regarding the motivation behind the exploration and colonization of the islands in this part of Oceania. By necessity, and this is true for further discussions in this chapter, this will need to be addressed with due consideration to work conducted on island colonization elsewhere in Oceania. Following this I will present the archaeological evidence for the settlement of the region, in relation to the useful model proposed by Michiko Intoh (1997) as a structuring aid, and interpret this in relation to discussions regarding the perceived utility of palaeoenvironmental evidence versus direct archaeological data. Finally, I consider briefly the evidence for settlement strategies derived from biological and physical anthropology.

Local motifs

William Lessa (1961) in his broad consideration of Oceanic oral tradition finds that there are two common methods (or motifs) used to account for the origin of islands. The first is 'earth from object thrown on primeval water' and the second is 'island fished up by demigod (hero)'. The first method typically involves islands created by casting something on the sea; in Micronesia this is usually sand or stone. In western Micronesia Lessa finds that this island-strewing is often connected to an angry woman who wishes to make an island so that she can get away from those that have annoyed her. Lessa (1961: 282) provides an example from Ulithi Atoll:

Liomarr (Yap) and Ilabulue (Mogemog) were the sisters of Yonelap. Both of them lived in Numaui. One day, they caught a turtle and prepared it. All the people living in the house took their fill, except the women, who received part of the fins only. They hid their anger with great difficulty. The next day, they got another turtle. Again everyone had some, but one of the two women got very little. So she took a coconut and grated it, and got a turtle fin, a coconut husk, and a few [coconut] shavings. With these she went to a place between Gatsapar and Onean. She filled the husk with sand and walked out on the sea. She continued until she could no longer see Yap, and then she strewed the sand on the sea. Land appeared – a whole island group. Then she squeezed the shavings, and the milk ran over the land. In this way food came to the land. Next, she visited all the islands – Mogemog first of all. She took the turtle fin and went to Eor, where she laid it in the sand. Since that time this island has had many turtles. The woman thereupon returned to Mogemog.

This story was collected during the *Südsee-Expedition* (Damm 1938: 359) and, although not the only tradition related by Ulithians in regard to the origins of the atoll, it explains within it the motivation for island making and settlement, the necessity of introducing foodstuffs and a reason why turtles prefer one island over the others. Other stories in the Carolines, as might be expected given the strength of connection to spirits in the 'skyworld' (Goodenough 1986), have islands created from the sky often by the casting down of stones – similar creation stories reported by Lessa for the Marshall Islands also include stone, which is strange in an island group that could be defined by the lack of such material.

The second understanding derived from Oceanic cosmology as defined by Lessa (1961) is the 'island fished up by demigod'. Lessa identifies this strongly with the Maui tales of Polynesia, while the strewing of objects he finds is much more common in Melanesia. Lessa's Micronesian examples derive for the most part from the Caroline Islands, but examples from the Marshalls and Gilberts are also noted. He finds that there are often close similarities between the Maui-tikitiki (and dialect variations) fisher stories of Polynesia and the Motikitik (and dialect variations) of Micronesia. In both areas these stories often have the hero islander-fisher as a youngest brother, a descent into the

underworld, an 'Open Sesame' type formula that allows the gaining of knowledge, a transformation into a bird, and the fishing-up of food and islands with a
hook.

Lessa (1961: 296–7) provides an example of such a story from Palau, which is
once again derived from the *Südsee-Expedition* (Krämer 1929: 38–40):

Tmelogod, the earth fisher, was the grandson of a 'swan maiden' named
Dileteku. He acquired some brightly shining pearl shells that had been found
long ago by two *kalids*, or priests. The shells had been kept hidden from him by
his father and his father's palm-wine cutter; but one day he discovered them,
and his father reluctantly let him have them. He made a fishhook for Tmelogod from one of the shells. The young man used it every day to go fishing,
but once he lost the hook when it was bitten off by a large gold mackerel.
When his father, Ngirarois, discovered the loss of the hook he gave his son a
scolding and taunted him by saying that he had picked up his mother on the
beach. Tmelogod went to a priestess for advice. He did as she directed him and
went down beneath the sea to a beautiful place named Ngedip. There he saw
many women carrying water. He asked them where they were going, and why.
They told him Dileteku (his swan maiden grandmother) was seriously ill and
that they were going to wash her with hot water. He said, '*Audogul ma geuid.*'
When the women heard these words they returned to Dileteku and told her everything. She sent for Tmelogod, and when she saw him she at once noticed the
similarity between the boy and her daughter. When he asked her what was the
matter with her, she answered that she had eaten food from above and that it
was stuck in her throat. He said, 'That is my hook!' He removed the hook with
a stick that the priestess had advised him to take with him. Dileteku asked him
where he came from and he told her he was the son of Merupelau (Dileteku's
daughter). The old woman cried when she heard how her daughter had been
insulted. Then Dileteku told him to take the hook and go fishing, and to say,
when he was fishing up there, 'I want a bunch of bananas on the line.' After that
he was to pull up the line. The boy went back home and started fishing again
from his boat. When he hauled in the line a bunch of bananas was indeed on
it. Another time there were almonds with syrup. All this his grandmother sent
him. Later, he once threw out his hook at night and cried, 'I wish there were
land on it so that I would have a place.' His hook got caught in the depth. He
called his friends to help him, but warned them to keep silent. Together they
pulled on the line. Soon tree tops and the roofs of houses showed up, and then
the land itself. The men pulled up more and more, but before waiting until all
was there they jumped onto it and took possession of everything. Tmelogod got
only the houses in which his hook had caught. These still belong to his family.
He gave the hook to his father, who gave it to his palm-wine cutter. It is not
known where the hook is now.

Unlike the strewing of sand story from Ulithi recounted above, this Palauan
story has the island ready prepared for habitation, not only with plants, but with
houses as well. Another story recounted by Lessa, this time for the Marshall
Islands, should warn us that such stories of origins are not necessarily about
essentializing a distant past, but can identify the transformation of island environments and incorporate identifiable features of that process within the

landscape. This is a variation on the 'island fished up by demigod' motif (Lessa 1961: 314):

Edao came to the island of Mille (Mili) and told the chief about a reef that lay to the south-east. They organized a fleet to go out and investigate it but while everyone was searching, Edao returned to Mille and overturned and sank the island. He then rejoined the others, who had found the reef he had told them about; but he just kept on sailing when the fleet returned to look for Mille. They looked in vain for Mille until some ghost people from Eb (a mythical land from the west) came sailing by. The people from Eb were all sons of Iroijdrilik. They each made a different kind of augury to find where Mille was. Lanberan told them it was below and they must fish for it with a big shark hook. The people obeyed, and hauled up the island. But it was so full of water that they punched a hole in it with a canoe mast to let out the water . . . [I]t is said that the drain hole made with the mast is now a taro patch, and that because of being overturned Mille is a dangerous island with an unusual kind of lagoon, which is not enterable in rough weather.

In presenting these brief examples here, I wish to show how the world can be made sense of from different perspectives. In the final case presented above, identifiable features such as the taro patch are explained, and the specific attributes of the lagoon are conceived of and explained in historical discourses quite different from those normally produced by archaeologists. Obviously, the stories of islands raised from the sea or built by the tossing of sand can each be regarded from a geological perspective as emergence through volcanic or tectonic action or the building up of storm deposits on submerged reefs. Such a view, although important for understanding when the islands were available for settlement in the past, as I discuss below, is only one in a series of stories, each having value in particular contexts. The richness of life of the people in this sea of islands does not, at least for them, require a scientific explanation or an absolute date of origin. The stories that have been recounted from generation to generation have made sense of the world within which they live, and they are no less important when accounting for social life. Social life is, of course, in essence what archaeological anthropology is endeavouring to explore.

Motivations

As noted in the previous chapters, since the 1970s there has been a fundamental shift in mid-twentieth-century disquiet about the purposeful colonization of the islands in the Pacific Ocean. The earlier view, which supposed that people in unseaworthy and unnavigable boats could only have achieved occupation of the islands by accidental drift voyages, has taken a severe blow from ethnographic research and experimental voyaging. Although not without his critics (e.g., Anderson 2000), Geoff Irwin (1992) has shown in computer simulations, developed from ethnography, voyaging and current environmental conditions, that there is likely to have been a high success rate for those attempting to colonize the eastern Carolines from island Melanesia. He found that from the island of Buka, at the north-west end of the Solomon Island chain, of ten simulated voyages eight successfully reached landfalls in the Carolines. Similarly, of twenty simulated voyages from the Reef Santa Cruz islands, located at the opposite end of the Solomons chain to Buka, nine reached the Carolines, two landed in the Marshalls, eight returned safely without sighting land and the final one was lost at sea. Although it appears from these simulations that, based on recent prevailing weather conditions, settlement of the Caroline Islands from Near Oceania was probably highly plausible, and the people had to have come from somewhere and by sea, this knowledge does not provide information in regard to what motivated people to make the journeys of exploration and colonization in the first place.

It is unlikely that we will ever really be able to pinpoint what motivated people to take to the sea in order to find and colonize new islands. What we do know is that people had crossed the sea to settle Australia and New Guinea, at times of lower sea level always separated from South-East Asia and forming the continent we call Sahul or Greater Australia, tens of millennia prior to the discovery and settlement of the islands in the tropical north-west Pacific Ocean. By at least 35,000 years ago, people had moved across the sea gaps to settle the islands of the Bismarck Archipelago and at some point before 10,000 years ago appear to have purposely transported animals, perhaps for food, into these islands (Spriggs 1997b). At the end of the last Glacial period, between 10,000 and 8000 years ago, with the warming climate sea levels rose, separating New Guinea from Australia, and flooding large areas of land in South-East Asia.

The land flooded in South-East Asia is known as Sunda, and at the height of the last Glacial joined the Malay Peninsula with the present-day islands of Borneo, Java, Sumatra, Palawan and many of the smaller islands. These high points in the landscape were connected by large areas of lowland and river channels, the drowned area being some 2.2 million square kilometres in extent (Bellwood 1997a). It has been suggested that as this land became submerged at the end of the Pleistocene and beginning of the Holocene, so people in Sunda had to learn to adapt to a maritime environment, leading to innovative developments in marine technology and the packing of people into smaller areas of land. Such a scenario might lead people to develop a strategy for searching for and settling new land, but these consequences would have still to be being felt many millennia later if they are to be regarded as a motivating factor in the settlement of Micronesia.

Other scenarios may be considered in relation to what David Anthony (1990), borrowing from a range of modern migration studies, identifies as 'push–pull' effects in migration. Pushing people to migrate might be perceived overpopulation, war/feuding, expulsion, environmental catastrophe and/or adventure. Pull factors might be through the maintenance of contacts with sister communities that have already settled elsewhere, perhaps in diasporic ways as suggested by Ian Lilley (1999, following Spriggs 1995) as a scenario for Lapita pottery users. Other pull factors might be the need to develop new alliances through inter-marriage for political or population purposes and the developing knowledge of easy resource exploitation in pristine island environments.

Whatever the motivation, in accepting, as I do, that settlement of the Pacific was part of a conscious scheme of exploration and colonization by skilled sea-farers, the next question, and one that the archaeological evidence might be regarded as suited to have a bearing upon, ought to be where did the settlers come from?

Archaeological and proxy environmental evidence

It is possible to argue that the most direct example of origin is the languages spoken by the people of the region, which were discussed in the previous chapter. However, there is no consensus amongst Pacific archaeologists as to the valid-ity of historical linguistics in constructing models of islander origins. Matthew Spriggs (1999b: 113), an ardent supporter of using linguistic evidence, warns that:

historical linguistics can suggest likely places of 'origin' (in reality meaning the earliest deducible stage) of a language group, and the geography of its spread from such a point of origin . . . [But] on its own [it] cannot convincingly achieve a chronology for the spread of a language group or for the dating of a particular language stage or proto-language.

In regard to chronology, the problem is that language does not change at a constant rate and we do know that language replacement can occur rapidly; there are many relatively recent colonial instances of this, and other more distant ones (e.g., see Sather 1995). What is required is a material indicator of the language spoken to provide a correlation of language and date.

As might be imagined, such a correlation is very difficult to find, although much has been made of the South-East Asian Neolithic 'packages' and Lapita pottery found in the western Pacific in an effort to attach the Austronesian language group to eastward migration beginning perhaps 5000 years ago (Green 1999). These difficulties aside, it is important to assess the linguistic informa-tion for Micronesia in relation to the archaeological and biological/physical an-thropological evidence. The information gained from these disciplines enables the highlighting of the differences that exist between the current communities of the area, and warns of the complex associations between these communities in the present and the past. However, as noted above, it must be kept in mind that it is very difficult to associate historical linguistics directly with material evidence.

Here I consider the archaeology, the only direct indication of human presence on the islands in the past, and the palaeoenvironmental evidence, which may be used to provide a proxy (i.e., not direct) indication of human presence on the islands. The environmental evidence, like the historical linguistics, has problems related to its utility and interpretation and these issues are discussed below. In assessing the archaeological and palaeoenvironmental evidence, I utilize Intoh's (1997) transparent fourfold model of Micronesian settlement as a heuristic framework.

Intoh (1997) proposed four different colonizing episodes for the region (see Fig. 4.1). The first is to the Marianas, from a similar source as the contentious (see below) movement of people to the Lapita 'homeland'; this may mean from one or more of the South-East Asian islands. The second and third episodes are regarded as archaeologically simultaneous with people moving into Palau and Yap and then east to Fais, and possibly further east along the Caroline Islands, even as far as Pohnpei. At the same time people moved northwards from the south-east through the Gilbert, Marshall and Caroline Islands, bringing with them the languages that later became Nuclear Micronesian, and spread west along the atolls, including those closest to Yap. The fourth movement was by Polynesian speakers who settled on the Polynesian Outliers of Nukuoro and Kapingamarangi.

Intoh's model is not unusual and takes into account earliest archaeologically derived dates for settlement, material culture correlates and linguistics. Where Intoh does differ from the most recent accounts is in suggesting that the second phase may have involved a movement of people from Palau and Yap along the Caroline Islands to as far east as Pohnpei (the shared ceramic tradition argument she uses should mean that this can be extended further east to include Kosrae). In making this proposal, Intoh cites the shared trait of having pottery tempered by calcareous sand (CST) in the earliest phases of Yap, Chuuk Lagoon, Pohnpei and Kosrae, and draws on her findings from Fais. At the time of publication, Intoh was not able to consider her more recent work on Yap or the latest findings from Palau, which I discuss below.

On Fais, a raised coral island 180 kilometres east of Yap, Intoh (1991; 1996; 1997) found CST pottery, green schist stone from Yap, and bones from pig, dog, chicken and *Rattus tanezumi* (a close relative of *Rattus rattus* from Asia), all dating from earliest settlement at about 1900 years ago. These data are used to support an argument for the second-phase colonization of the region from west to east. But the archaeological evidence from the Caroline Islands to either the west or east of Fais provides little to support this. None of the animals has been reported from early deposits in Yap or Palau; indeed only dog is known at this date on the islands to the east: Chuuk Lagoon (Shutler, Sinoto and Takayama 1984), Pohnpei (Athens 1990b), Kosrae (Athens 1995) and the Marshall Islands (Weisler 1996). Intoh (1999) cites evidence of the unusual *Rattus tanezumi* from Pohnpei and Nukuoro, but these were recovered from deposits unlikely to be more than 1000 years old, and are therefore not directly associated with initial human (post-)colonization. The CST ceramic evidence is particularly difficult

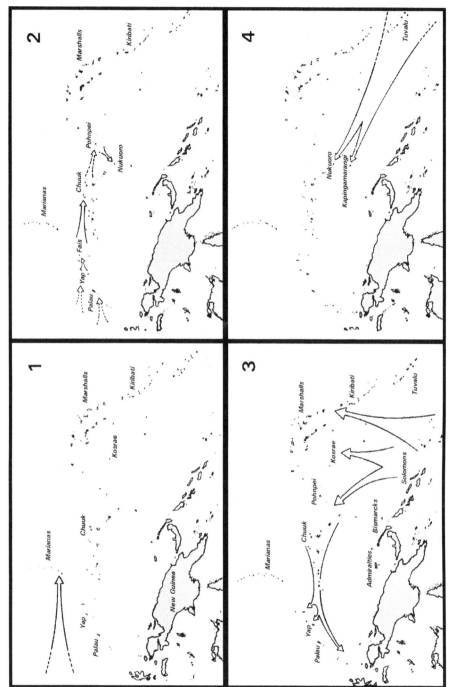

Fig. 4.1 Michiko Intoh's four-part model of the colonization of Micronesia (after Intoh 1997).

to interpret in regard to direction of colonization, owing to little in the way of distinctive decorative elements. In general terms, it may easily be included in the corpus of post-Lapita Plainware (Athens 1990a; Ayres 1990b), but a more direct or definitive association is very difficult to identify (see Rainbird 1999b). Intoh (1999) dismisses this possible southern association as she believes there is no indication of paddle and anvil technique in its manufacture; evidence for this technique is apparently common in the corpus of post-Lapita Plainware.

Intoh proposes no convincing alternative to a southern origin, and it is unlikely that the plain ceramics will ever allow this, but it should be noted that anvil marks are reported in the early assemblages from Pohnpei and Chuuk Lagoon (see below). William Dickinson and Richard Shutler (2000: 236) conclude that 'there is no temper trail [in the ceramics] that can be followed in either direction'. There is therefore little in the Fais material that can be taken beyond exhibiting contacts between Yap and Fais. Archaeological and palaeoenvironmental evidence obtained more recently by Intoh and others may also show that Fais was settled a great deal later than the neighbouring high islands to the west, and thus cannot be included in a colonization phase that encompasses them all. I will start by reviewing the evidence from western Micronesia and then turn to the east, which I will show is likely to have been settled later and from a different direction.

Western Micronesia

For Yap, Dodson and Intoh (1999) report findings from two pollen cores taken from inland taro swamps, one on the island in the group of four known as Yap Proper and the other from Gagil-Tomil. John Dodson interprets the deepest core as indicating a rise in charcoal particles and a reduction in tree species at around 3300 years ago, based on a radiocarbon date from peat. This, for Dodson and Intoh, is a proxy indication of the arrival of humans on Yap and, of course, disturbs Intoh's earlier colonization model, which includes a migration through to Fais at around 2000 years ago. However, the radiocarbon sample is derived from a depth of 235 to 245 centimetres, and the pollen diagram shows that charcoal particles are present below this depth, with a significant peak at 280 centimetres. Explanation for the presence of charcoal particles at the lower depth is not provided. It also appears clear from the pollen diagram that charcoal levels do not rise significantly, and become maintained at that density, until above the 160 centimetres level, when vegetation also appears to change dramatically. On the evidence presented, it seems difficult to argue for a palaeoenvironmental indication of human presence until somewhere within the 125–135 centimetre depth, which is bracketed between dates of 3300 and 250 years ago. This date range easily allows the maintenance of the settlement of Yap at approximately 2000 years ago. However, such a date becomes more problematic when considered in relation to the evidence from the neighbouring archipelago of Palau to the south.

Recent evidence from Palau requires us to make a radical rethinking of what may be termed the most recent orthodoxy regarding the settlement of western Micronesia (this orthodoxy may be found in Rainbird 1994a). Contract archaeological research conducted in advance of infrastructure development on the island of Babeldaob in the Palau group has yielded interesting results. David Welch (1998a; 1998b) reported on dates derived from integrated archaeological and palaeoenvironmental work, which indicate that we need to assume human colonization of the Palau group at 3500 years ago. Douglas Osborne's (1966) initial estimate appears to have been closer to the actual date of settlement, pushing the date back 1500 to 2000 years earlier than both the orthodox and Intoh's models.

The earliest Palau dates, like those from Yap, are derived from cores and, as elsewhere in the Pacific (e.g., see Anderson 1994; Kirch and Ellison 1994; Spriggs and Anderson 1993), are open to debate in regard to their interpretation. With this proviso in mind, however, Welch reports radiocarbon dates from cores where charcoal peaks or greater sedimentation occur, both perhaps indicating forest clearing by humans, which may have started 4000 years ago, and is strongly indicated by 3000 years ago. Preliminary results of work reported more recently are proposing to push dates for the settlement of Palau back further still. Steve Wickler (2000) cites evidence of taro (*Cyrtosperma chamissonis*) pollen dating to 4500 years ago, and cultural material remains from 3450 years ago. By 2000 years ago, deep ring ditches were being constructed around hilltops, and thin black ceramics with black paste appear to come into common usage (Welch 1998b; Wickler 1998a). In support of an anthropogenic explanation for tree decline between 4000 and 2000 years ago, Welch points out that in the fifteen cores taken from Babeldaob the decline does not coincide, indicating that broad environmental factors are not to blame. This does not, however, completely write off the possibility of individual local events.

Spriggs (1997c; 2000; 2001a) takes the view that for most islands in Oceania human life cannot be supported without the importation of subsistence plants and the development of an agricultural economy. Unlike Les Groube's (1971) earlier borrowing of the 'strandlooping model', which proposed that colonists initially relied on natural resources (discussed further below), Spriggs argues that the resources immediately available to people as they moved further into Oceania would be insufficient to sustain human life. Indeed, even for the larger islands of Melanesia, it has been identified that during early human settlement in the Pleistocene, animals and plants were introduced to enhance the rainforest subsistence systems (Spriggs 1997a; 1997b).

What has become clear (see papers in Kirch and Hunt 1997; *contra* Nunn 1993) is that people inhabiting Pacific islands will significantly change the local environment to, in most cases, enhance it for human existence (see also Rainbird 2002). What is not yet close to consensus is how to interpret such proxy data as palaeoenvironmental evidence when it comes to dating the human colonization of an island, and such issues are not easily resolved (see Kirch 1997b). In returning to Micronesia, it may be said that, owing to the amount of coring and the variety of data integrated with the archaeological programme, there is a stronger case to accept the earlier dates from Palau than there is for Yap, but I will discuss these important issues in more detail below.

Returning to Fais, it may be that what the evidence here shows is a later 'budding off' from Yap to the island in the east. This may have been a brief migration of people that did not go any further. What is important to note is that they appear to have had with them dog, pig and chicken that are not known to be present on Yap at this time. It may be that the distinct linguistic history of Yap may be linked with people arriving in the region from island Melanesia, where the full complement of introduced domestic animals did exist at this time. This can only be regarded as speculation, given the current evidence. However, if the initial settlement of Fais was a single-step colonization event, then it may, in part, be the result of the chronology of geological processes and we need to take these into account.

For western Micronesia, Fais is unusual in being a raised coral island, some 20 metres above sea level. Its atoll neighbours, to the east and west, are typical of the region in being raised only a few metres above sea level. Dating of archaeological deposits on Caroline Island atolls is far from satisfactory, but the few dates available may indicate that humans occupied Lamotrek less than 1000 years ago (Fujimara and Alkire 1984) and Ulithi, only 170 kilometres east of Yap, 1600 to 1200 years ago (Craib 1981; 1983). Ant Atoll, close to Pohnpei in the eastern Caroline Islands, has evidence of occupation at around 2000 years ago (Galipaud 2001). We need to consider the possibility that many of the Carolinian atolls, the majority of which were inhabited at European contact and still are, were not actually available for habitation when Fais was colonized. Irwin (1998) has reviewed some of the evidence and concludes that the settlement of western Micronesia did not proceed eastwards until a much later date. He suggests that the dozens of atolls that currently link the western high islands with the high islands of Chuuk Lagoon simply did not exist until after 2000 years ago.

From archaeological evidence we do know that at least some Marshall Island atolls and those of the Gilbert group in Kiribati were inhabited by 2000 years ago. I will return to this eastern area below, but first I need to complete the discussion of the settlement of western Micronesia by considering the evidence from the Mariana Islands.

Earlier models of colonization often considered the islands of Palau and Yap as 'stepping stones' to the Marianas. Until recently there was little chronological evidence to support this hypothesis, but, as discussed above, the early dates from Palau in particular could allow for a return to this model. However, the linguist Lawrence Reid (1998, but see 1997) considers the Chamorro language of the Marianas to be an early breakaway from the Austronesian spoken in the Philippines shortly after its spread from Taiwan between 5000 and 4000 years ago. Reid (1998; Spriggs 1999a) also found that the Palauan language is probably a later offshoot from the same general area of the Philippines, suggesting a later colonization event. Reid's linguistic analyses would thus place the settlement of the Mariana Islands ahead of that of the Palau archipelago and would mean that the earliest dates for the occupation of the Marianas have yet to be uncovered.

Following Reid's proposals, and based on the current preferred models for the movement of Austronesian speakers, this would provide a potential source of settlers to western Micronesia from Taiwan, or more likely the Philippines. If the contemporary linguistics can provide a clue to origins, and Irwin (1992) warns that it may only reflect the most recent pre-European contact history, then such a split should occur between 6000 and 3500 years ago. These dates are based on the supposed association of Austronesian speakers with the 'Neolithic' package in island South-East Asia (see Bellwood 1997a), and correlate well with the recent dates from Palau and, as I will show, also with those from the Marianas. The long curve of the Mariana archipelago would provide a wide target for early navigators sailing eastwards and it may still be a direct and separate sailing method of colonization of Palau and the Marianas that we should envisage, rather than that of a stepping stone, island-hopping movement.

The alternative, and less likely, model of colonization for western Micronesia is a movement of people through the Bird's Head of New Guinea and passing northward via the tiny south-west islands of Tochobei (Tobi), Pulo Anna and Sonsorol, as stepping stones to Palau and the Mariana Islands. The historical linguistics discussed above does not support a move from Palau to Yap, but the most recent dates for early settlement of Palau place it before that of the Marianas in the chronology of human settlement. In a recent assessment of accessibility and relative isolation – that is, amount of sea without islands around an archipelago – Irwin (2000: 397) finds:

If [the Marianas] had been settled directly from Island South-East Asia, then this would have been a very long and difficult offshore voyage. The accessibility of the Marianas directly from the Philippines . . . means that it approaches in difficulty voyages made into the margins of East Polynesia, at a much later time in prehistory. Therefore it may be deemed more likely that settlement of the Marianas followed an easier but indirect route *via* Palau, then to Yap, and on to Guam – which is the southernmost of the Marianas.

Archaeological sites in the Mariana Islands have yielded relatively secure dates of around 3500 years ago (Butler 1994; 1995; Amesbury, Moore and Hunter-Anderson 1996; Dilli *et al.* 1998; Haun, Jimenez and Kirkendall 1999). The dates are in association with two types of decorated pottery which appear to pre-date the generic red ware previously accepted as the earliest ceramic tradition (Craib 1993; Butler 1994). Their excavators have considered these newly identified ceramics as 'lapitoid' (e.g., Amesbury, Moore and Hunter-Anderson 1996). However, Brian Butler (1994; 1995) finds that the similarity with Lapita pottery is superficial and that no direct relationship can be proposed, although for him both ceramic traditions are derived from the late Neolithic peoples of Island South-East Asia. This proposition leads to a consideration of a debate in Pacific archaeology in which Butler clearly favours one side. The debate surrounds the question of the origins of Lapita pottery users in island Melanesia. First I will briefly introduce Lapita.

The highly decorated pottery known as Lapita is distributed widely in the tropical western Pacific from the Bismarck Archipelago to Fiji, Tonga and Samoa in the east, through to New Caledonia in the south (Anderson *et al.* 2001). The Lapita tradition, which includes undecorated as well as decorated ceramics, starts to appear at a date of approximately 3500 to 3300 years ago in island Melanesia (Kirch 1997c; Specht and Gosden 1997). The decorated ceramics are characterized by distinctive dentate stamping, with variations in motifs that have previously been thought to represent geographical regions (Far Western, Western and Eastern Lapita styles). More recently these variations have been reinterpreted as representing temporal distinctions (Early, Middle and Late) (Summerhayes 2000; 2001). In most areas of the Lapita distribution it appears that after approximately 2700 to 2500 years ago the majority of ceramics become either undecorated or minimally decorated, and although specific types have been identified these ceramics have been termed post-Lapita Plainware (Spriggs 1999a) and in island Melanesia, at least, exhibit broad similarities up to about 1500 years ago (Spriggs 2001b).

Archaeologists, along with linguists and geneticists, have been embroiled in a debate which questions the origin of Lapita pottery and related items, such as specific forms of shell artefacts, pigs, dogs and chickens (sometimes called the 'Lapita cultural complex'). The debate questions whether these items represent the arrival of people from the islands of South-East Asia, or the independent development and borrowing of techniques in place, by the autochthonous people of the Bismarck Archipelago (e.g., Smith 1995; Allen 1996; Spriggs 1997b; 1999b). Roger Green (see, e.g., 2000) has proposed a 'Triple I model' of intrusion, integration and innovation. The evidence from the Marianas (and Palau) plays a role in this debate.

In the Marianas, seven sites have been reported, that are distinguished by finely decorated ceramics and, in some cases, distinctive shell artefacts. Of the published sites, two are on the island of Saipan and the third is on Tinian and all date from between 3500 and 3000 years ago. Early dates from cultural deposits on the largest island, Guam (e.g., Bath 1986), have until recently been regarded as unreliable (e.g., Hunter-Anderson and Butler 1995: 29), and proxy data such as charcoal in a single core taken from a marsh on the Orote Peninsula were all that could be used, along with some typically early ceramics, to show evidence of people starting at 3550 years ago (Carucci 1993; Athens and Ward 1995). This anomalous situation has been overturned by excavations at Huchunao on the east coast, which revealed early-style ceramics in relation to four early radio-carbon dates conforming in period to those obtained elsewhere in the Mariana Islands (Dilli *et al.* 1998).

At Achugao on the western coastal plain of Saipan, excavations ahead of de-velopment located deposits of the rare decorated early ceramics. Brian Butler (1994; 1995), the excavator, was able to establish two separate pottery tradi-tions in the bottom layer. One of these decorative traditions, named Achugao by Butler, consists of parallel incised lines in rectilinear or curved patterns around the neck of the pot, with the spaces filled by stamped circles and/or del-icate punctuations that at first glance are reminiscent of the dentate stamping on Lapita pottery (Fig. 4.2). However, it must be stressed here that these do ap-pear to be individual punctuations rather than the groups of linear punctuations made by a comb-like implement on Lapita ceramics (e.g., turtle scute stamps, Ambrose 1997; cf. Moore and Hunter-Anderson 1999). The vessels exhibiting Achugao decoration may be slipped in red, black or buff-coloured material. Interestingly, although red slip is the most common colour treatment, being found on 60 per cent of all sherds (including undecorated ones), of the deco-rated sherds red and black slip accounted for approximately 40 per cent each, suggesting that as a percentage of type, black slip was preferred for decorative embellishment.

The second decorative type was named San Roque after a local village. This formed a much smaller percentage of the total decorated assemblage at 9.9 per cent (Butler 1995). The San Roque decoration consists of stamped cir-cles sometimes joined to a scroll formed by incised semi-circles (see Fig. 4.2). Butler (1995) finds that the two types are probably contemporaneous, and in comparison with other sites in the Marianas that they were extant over an ap-proximately 500-year period starting 3500 years ago. If there is a chronological distinction then it is likely that the San Roque style is the younger, as many of the decorative elements of this group continue in the ceramics of the Marianas Intermediate Period (see chapter 5). The decoration on both styles of pottery was filled with lime, although Butler finds that the Achugao pots had lime added after slipping while the San Roque pots were lime-filled prior to a slip being added. Both styles share the same vessel shape, being round-bottomed and small-shouldered (carinated), with everted rims.

On the south-west coast of Saipan, excavation in the vicinity has led to a reconsideration of Alexander Spoehr's (1957) attribution through radiocarbon of Chalan Piao as the oldest site in the Marianas. Doubt had been cast on Spoehr's attribution of a 3500-year-old date for the site when the shell that had been radiocarbon dated was redated to less than 2000 years old (Cloud, Schmidt and Burke 1956). Amesbury, Moore and Hunter-Anderson (1996) processed two

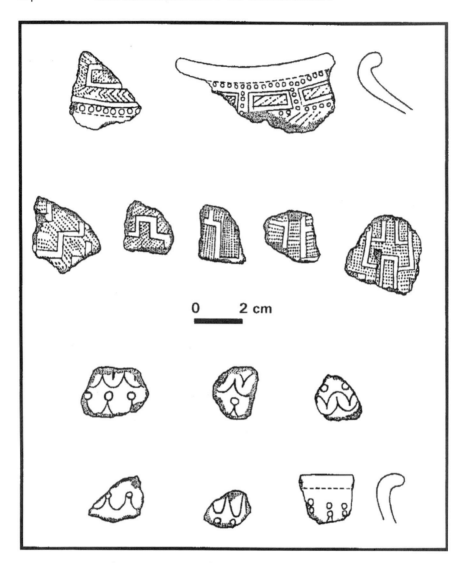

Fig. 4.2 Early ceramic types from the Mariana Islands (after Butler 1994). Examples of Achugao Incised sherds above the scale and San Roque Incised sherds below.

radiocarbon dates from dispersed charcoal collected in two layers, both containing examples of early decorated types described by Butler. The radiocarbon dates confirmed a date for the site beginning 3500 years ago.

Deposits excavated on the beach at Unai Chulu in north-west Tinian also recovered early decorated ceramics. John Craib (1993) found sherds of Achugao style, and the perhaps slightly longer-lasting stamped circles found at the other early sites in the Marianas. More recent excavations at Unai Chulu have presented a suite of dates related to the earliest deposits with decorated pottery, providing secure evidence of occupation starting some 3500 years ago (Haun, Jimenez and Kirkendall 1999).

Settlement at Chalan Piao, Achugao and Unai Chulu appears to be on sand spits at or very near sea level and this is typical for places believed to be the sites of earliest settlement in the region. A detailed discussion of the sites and relations in the Marianas will wait until chapter 5, as here we are identifying earliest settlement across the whole region.

What we find, based on present understanding, is that the Marianas are first settled at the same time as, or a few centuries prior to, the emergence of communities using Lapita pottery in the Bismarck Archipelago. Unlike the Lapita evidence, however, the Marianas material provides unequivocal evidence for the deliberate migration of pottery-using people into the Pacific. There is no evidence of people visiting these islands prior to this, so the first settlers must have taken with them the means to create a viable community. These people, who were presumably accomplished sailors in sophisticated seacraft, may have travelled a straight-line distance of at least 1800 kilometres. That they were motivated to do so a few centuries before Lapita pottery appears in island Melanesia shows that people were able to make colonizing expeditions from South-East Asia at this time. Though not proving conclusively that people using Lapita ceramics were derived from South-East Asia, it does show that people from that area did do such things. For Spriggs (1999a) this provides the 'smoking gun' evidence that favours the migration model for Lapita pottery-using communities.

If there is a single origin for the early settlers of the Marianas, then the linguistics and ceramic attributes point to a homeland in the Philippines region (Bellwood 1997a). Bellwood (1997b) finds that the red-slipped pottery in Yüan-shan assemblages of Taiwan, and dating from about 4000 years ago onwards, exhibits remarkable similarity to early examples from northern Luzon in the Philippines, the Marianas, and indeed Lapita itself.

The prevailing winds in this region are east and north-east (Karolle 1993: Fig. 30) and mean that the supposed direction of colonization from the Philippines fits into the model proposed by Irwin (1992). In Irwin's model the safest strategy for exploration and colonization is to sail against the direction of the prevailing wind; this reduces risk, as explorers are more able to return home downwind if no landfall is made. Direct colonization of the Marianas or Palau (depending on which happened first) in this manner would constitute the longest sea-crossing undertaken by that time in human history. However, we should not be unaware of the possibility that we are not dealing with single colonization events for each group of islands. Physical anthropologists using evidence from more recent late prehistoric and historical skeletal collections have in the past suggested links with the prehistoric population of Japan (e.g., Brace *et al.* 1990), and although more recent work has rejected this hypothesis (Ishida and Dodo 1997), further complexities should not be unexpected.

Eastern Micronesia

The islands of eastern Micronesia appear to possess a different history of human settlement compared to those of the west. It had been expected that the high islands would be settled prior to the atolls and raised limestone islands, which are often considered less attractive in terms of subsistence potential (Goodenough 1957). Excavations on separate atolls in the Marshall Islands have upset this model. Chuck Streck's results from excavations on Bikini Atoll have proved the most controversial.

Stratified archaeological deposits on Bikini, infamous as a site for nuclear bomb tests, have provided a series of very early radiocarbon dates, many older than the earliest dates for settlement of the central and eastern Carolines. Any contamination of the samples from bomb testing should make them younger rather than older. One determination from charcoal in an oven (*uhm*) at the base of the cultural deposits provided a date of approximately 3500 years ago (Streck 1990). This single date, which has no extra verification of authenticity such as further dates or diagnostic artefacts, is regarded as highly dubious and unacceptable (e.g., Kirch and Weisler 1994: 292); however, two charcoal samples from other cultural deposits provided dates with large standard deviations (> ± 200 years) centring around 2800 years ago. These too are much earlier than other dates in the Marshall Islands and may also be regarded as dubious, although in 1998 Streck (personal communication) still considered all of these early dates reliable.

Dates from Kwajalein Atoll appear to confirm at least a close to contemporary settlement with the high islands of the eastern Carolines. Shun and Athens (1990) recovered two dates on charcoal samples from a probable cultural layer indicating use of the atoll around 1800 years ago. More recent work on the atoll has identified what is interpreted as a taro swamp in association with earth ovens and portable artefacts dating to approximately 2000 years ago (Beardsley 1994). Marshall Weisler (1996; 1999b) has conducted a programme of excavations next to taro swamps at the centre of a number of atoll islands in the Marshalls and has also found earliest settlement dating to approximately 2000 years ago, confirming Riley's (1987) earlier findings for the southern atolls. On Maloelap Atoll, Weisler also found evidence for dog at this time.

To the south of the Marshalls, in the southern Gilbert Islands of the Republic of Kiribati, two dates suggesting human habitation at or a few centuries prior to 2000 years ago have been reported. Anne Di Piazza (1999) excavated two small test pits on the raised coral island of Nikunau. Each test pit revealed an earth oven at a depth of between 1 and 1.5 metres below the surface. The ovens contained the charred Pandanus keys (segments of the fruit) that were subsequently radiocarbon dated. Bones from a medium-sized mammal were also recovered, but closer identification was not possible because of the fragmentary nature of the remains. Excavations by Takayama, Takasugi and

Nakajima (1985) on the northern Gilbert Island of Makin recovered skeletal elements identified as dog in association with shell artefacts from a layer dating to approximately 1600 years ago. The radiocarbon dates were obtained from marine shell and should be treated with caution, but the stratified deposits, located just inland from the present beach, were excavated to a depth of 3.5 metres. The depth of the cultural material may indicate a long human presence somewhat consistent with the radiocarbon dates. The earliest deposits were located directly on the coral limestone bedrock and, interestingly, the shell artefacts are reported to have been water worn. I will return to this below.

As a matter of completeness, I should report here the findings from the other Kiribati groups, namely the Phoenix and Line Islands to the east of the Gilbert Islands. Both groups have evidence of human presence prior to European arrival in the Pacific, but they were deserted at the time Europeans encountered them, and thus have often been grouped with the 'mystery islands' of the Pacific (Bellwood 1978). Limited archaeological survey has revealed stone platform structures akin to those found in Polynesia. Carson (1998), who has reviewed the evidence from the Phoenix Islands, concludes that the architecture was constructed by east Polynesians during the period AD 950 to 1500. These islands are traditionally considered to be part not of Micronesia, but of Polynesia, and will not be considered further here.

To complete this review of the archaeology of human colonization of the region I will now track east to west along the high islands of the eastern and central Caroline Islands.

Earliest settlement of Kosrae is represented by Steve Athens' (1990a; 1995) excavations of submerged deposits at Leluh where pottery was recovered from a matrix of coralline sediments beneath the late prehistoric compound of Katem. Radiocarbon determinations provide dates ranging between 2000 and 1660 years ago (Athens 1995). The pottery from the submerged deposits is made up entirely of CST ware with no decoration. Analysis has shown that the pottery is derived from local clay sources (Dickinson 1995).

Other portable artefacts recovered from the pottery-bearing context include one or two *Tridacna* adzes, shell bracelet fragments, shell ring fragments and circular shell beads. Midden analysis showed a predominance of bivalve marine shell species, especially *Garfarium* sp., and a faunal assemblage dominated by bone from reef fish. There is also some evidence to suggest that dog was present at this time.

From the excavations at Katem and from another in the area of Finipea, also at Leluh, important evidence of early introduced subsistence species was recovered. Wood charcoal and pollen analyses allowed the identification of the taro aroids *Colocasia esculenta*, *Cyrtosperma chamissonis* and *Alocasia macrorrhiza*, showing that these species were introduced in this period along with breadfruit (Murakami 1995; Ward 1995). Evidence of coconut was identified but early dates were interpreted as indicating its introduction by natural means prior to human settlement.

Although Ayres (e.g., 1993) proposes earlier colonization, the earliest dated cultural deposits on Pohnpei derive from pre-islet surfaces at Nan Madol in the south-east of the island (Bryson 1989; Ayres 1990b). Athens (1990b: 21) provides dates ranging from 1970 to 1470 years ago from charcoal samples in association with CST ware. The excavation reports have yet to be made fully available, and the published reports focus on the ceramic component of the assemblage. Another possible site of this type has come to light at Ipwel on the north coast of Pohnpei, where pottery has been recovered from an old beach deposit 100 centimetres below the surface in mangrove swamp (Russell Brulotte, personal communication; Galipaud 2001).

The ceramics from Nan Madol are manufactured from local clay sources and reveal a variety of tempers. The majority of the earliest sherds are CST and these are replaced through time by other tempers broadly identified by Ayres (1990b) as 'plain' varieties. However, vessel form appears to change little, with open-mouthed globular pots and bowls predominating. Decoration is minimal, with parallel (interior and exterior) notching of the rim being most common and some punctuation along the inner rim surface. No definite slip has been identified, but anvil impressions provide a clue to technology (cf. Intoh 1999). Other than the ceramics, all that can be noted is the presence of dog remains in the earliest deposits. As has been described for elsewhere in the region, the palaeoenvironmental evidence from Pohnpei may indicate earlier occupation.

The Leh en Luhk pond is located at an elevation of 90 metres above sea level; four cores were taken, with a maximum depth of 2 metres reached from the surface of the lake bed. A further 1.4 metres of deposits were revealed by probing but not sampled. A peat layer at 1.3 to 1.4 metres in depth provided the earliest radiocarbon determination centring around 2500 years ago; below this layer was clay containing charcoal flecks and below that, down to 1.7 metres, a clay described as revealing 'some organic mottling' and leaves. Above the dated peat layer, a 10 centimetres thick band of clay was followed by another peat layer that was dated to approximately 2350 years ago. Although initially suggesting a natural origin for the dated peat deposits in this core (Ayres, Haun and Severance 1981; Ayres and Haun 1985), in a more recent publication the researchers attribute an anthropogenic origin to the organic material (following Spriggs 1982). Ayres and Haun (1990) propose that the peat deposits are likely to be caused by swamp cultivation or natural peat layers buried by rapid erosion resulting from forest clearance. If their reinterpretation is correct, then this would indicate anthropogenic disturbance of the vegetation by approximately 2250 years ago, if not substantially earlier. At two standard deviations there is no overlap between these dates and the earliest dated cultural assemblage from Pohnpei, at Nan Madol.

In Chuuk Lagoon, earliest dated deposits were excavated by Richard Shutler, Yosihiko Sinoto and Jun Takayama (1984) and may be split into two types as differences exist between the localities and the kinds of ceramic recovered. Nepi (TKFE-3) is the sole member of one type, and all of the other sites form the second.

The site at Nepi is located at the south end of Fefen Island within a long low dune separating the fringing reef and lagoon from a large taro swamp. The dune varies in width but is approximately 20 metres wide and reaches an approximate height of one metre above the beach and high tide level. Excavations uncovered pottery-bearing layers up to 2 metres below ground level in the first test pit and at rather shallower depths in the centre of the dune, suggesting an uneroded dune-like structure when the artefacts were initially deposited.

Artefacts collected from Nepi include 862 ceramic sherds, adzes (*Tridacna* and others), a *Conus* pendant (or possibly a lure shank), and *Tridacna* bracelets. Other finds from the archaeological deposits include bones of dog and fish and *Thespesia populnea* seeds. Most of the ceramic sherds are reported to be water worn, and anvil marks were detectable on the larger pieces. One decorated sherd had a pattern consisting of three incised parallel lines. The majority of the sherds were 'reddish' in colour and the excavator thought it likely that they had been finished in red slip. Robert Bryson (1989) has questioned the latter attribute. Most of the ceramics were of CST paste, and petrographic analysis showed that these sherds and the others collected from Fefen were manufactured using local clay sources (Dickinson 1984). Bryson (1989), in a reconsideration, suggests that the rim shapes indicate that both jars and bowls are represented.

Unfortunately, the single radiocarbon date from Nepi provides dubious dating for the ceramics, and the reported depth of the charcoal sample does not match the layer it is supposed to have come from. The date of this site thus remains open to debate. In this context it is perhaps interesting to note that two adzes manufactured of *Cypraecassis rufas* were collected from the pottery-bearing levels at Nepi while none was recovered from the neighbouring Sapota sites. The incorporation of these different artefact types may hint at the non-contemporary nature of the site at Nepi with those at Sapota.

The Sapota matrix was unlike Nepi in that the pottery-bearing layer was directly on top of relic reef and directly below the remnants of a mangrove swamp (Fig. 4.3). At the site of TKFE-1, in the village of Sapota, the archaeological deposits were reached at an estimated depth of 80–90 centimetres below ground surface. Between this and the coral limestone base rock appeared a layer containing prehistoric artefacts; the excavators noted that this layer could be divided on the criteria of fan coral fragments being predominant in the top half and finger coral in the bottom. Two usable radiocarbon dates were obtained from charcoal in the vicinity of this layer, providing a date for the context of between 2350 and 1650 years ago.

Fig. 4.3 The Sapota site, Fefen (Fefan) Island, Chuuk Lagoon. The ceramics and other artefacts derived from this, the earliest dated archaeological site in Chuuk Lagoon, were discovered on the fringing reef, having been exposed by the eroding of the formerly prograded coastline. This may have been the site of a settlement formed by buildings on stilts.

The ceramics collected were mostly of CST ware. Outcurved rim forms are the most common, with a small number of straight rims, and almost all lips have an outside bevel and are flat. Few sherds show any sign of decoration, but notched rims, and incised lines including one chevron design, were recorded. Markedly different from the Nepi ceramics is the colour of the Sapota sherds, which are predominantly black.

A varied collection of other material remains was recovered from the Sapota pottery-bearing layers, including tools manufactured from stone, shell and coral, and shell ornaments (Fig. 4.4). Of particular note are the typical *Tridacna* adzes, basalt stone saws (considering how few stone tools are recognized from Carolinian sites) and *Tridacna* bracelets or pendants, some with serrated edges with triangular cross-sections and others without serration but with triangular or rectangular cross-sections.

For the central and eastern Caroline high islands the major factors linking the site assemblages are the roughly contemporaneous nature of the dates, around 2000 years ago, similar site location and the presence of CST ceramics. The ceramics have so few diagnostic features that little more can be said other than that they have a broad similarity but maintain some differences. A few of the

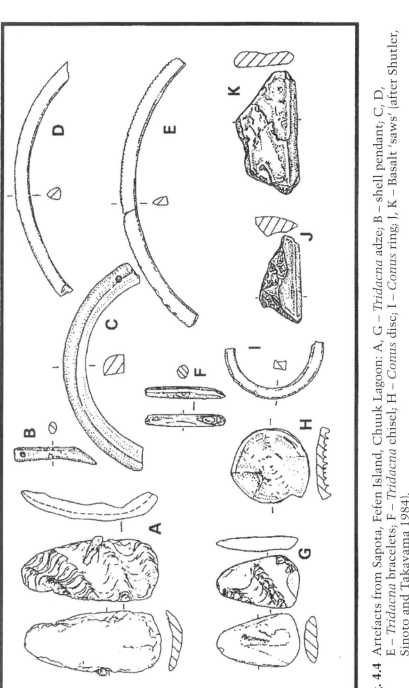

Fig. 4.4 Artefacts from Sapota, Fefen Island, Chuuk Lagoon: A, G – *Tridacna* adze; B – shell pendant; C, D, E – *Tridacna* bracelets; F – *Tridacna* chisel; H – *Conus* disc; I – *Conus* ring; J, K – Basalt 'saws' (after Shutler, Sinoto and Takayama 1984).

Sapota sherds exhibit carination, a feature I observed on three sherds from the Leluh assemblage held at the Bishop Museum, Honolulu; no carinated forms have been reported from Pohnpei. Water absorption tests conducted by Intoh (1989) on a number of prehistoric western Pacific sherds showed that within this corpus the Chuuk and Pohnpei sherds grouped close together (no sherds from Kosrae were tested).

Athens (1995) identifies some similarities between other types of material remains only found in the earliest deposits at Kosrae (Leluh) and Pohnpei (Nan Madol). These include a particular type of shell ring, possibly used as earrings, and quartz crystals that are not local to the islands.

On the basis of pottery characteristics, other material culture and linguistics, the colonizers of the eastern Carolines are thought to have emanated from the south. Ayres (1990b) suggests a homeland in south-east Melanesia and/or Fiji–West Polynesia. Athens (1990b) is more ambitious and suggests direct migration from areas in the south-east Solomons and Vanuatu areas. These hypotheses are based primarily on linguistic attributes. Little in material connections has been noted, except rather vague comparisons between the early Carolinian ceramics and post-Lapita Plainware. The latter makes impossible the identification, using ceramics, of a specific location from which the eastern Carolinians derived. Anywhere within the area settled by Lapita pottery users is a potential source. This is also the case for other types of portable material culture such as shell artefacts.

However, other aspects of the material remains, such as settlement type and location, may provide closer definition. Important to note is that all of the sites are coastal, semi-submerged and on the subsequently buried fringing reef. At Nan Madol and Leluh the locations continued to be a focus for human activities, while at Fefen, the Nepi site was abandoned and parts of the Sapota sites became mangrove swamp, as also occurred at Ipwel on Pohnpei.

A number of Lapita sites offer similarities with the earliest settlement evidence in the eastern Caroline Islands. There are two in the Bismarck Archipelago, one at Apalo (FOJ), Kumbun Island, Arawes group, off the south coast of West New Britain (Gosden et al. 1989; Gosden and Webb 1994) and the other at Talepakemalai (ECA), Eloaua Island, in the Mussau group (Kirch 1987; 1988b; 2001). There are also a number of possibly similar sites in the northern Solomon Islands (Wickler 1990a; 2001a). The Ferry Berth site at Mulifanua, Western Samoa, may be a candidate, but reinterpretation of the Lapita deposits, dredged from the seabed there in 1973, makes this unlikely (Leach and Green 1989; Dickinson and Green 1998).

All the sites listed above have Lapita pottery and date from the period when that style was current. The first two sites (Apalo and Talepakemalai) consist of waterlogged deposits and are interpreted by their excavators as the location of stilt-buildings constructed on the fringing reef of each island. At Apalo, the excavator revealed preserved posts and planks and a cultural layer estimated to have been deposited in sea water 1.5 to 2.0 metres deep at high tide (Gosden and Webb 1994). The stakes and post bases preserved at Talepakemalai represent the remains of a stilt-house village constructed some 30 to 40 metres from the contemporary shoreline (Kirch 1988b). In both cases it appears that these sites initiated coastal progradation by trapping sediments in the low-energy environments around their stilts; both sites were found below present-day beach deposits.

The similarity between the locations of these sites in island Melanesia and the earliest sites in the eastern Carolines is striking. The Carolinian sites are also located on the reef flat, and in two out of the three cases are adjacent to deep-water passages in the reef. Many of these sites have been identified as probable stilt-house settlements and there are a number of indications to suggest a similar interpretation for east Micronesian sites.

Although no preserved timbers have been recognized in the small areas of excavation carried out at the Carolinian sites, one aspect in particular, the sedimentological record, points to stilt-houses as a strong possibility. The Carolinian sites are characterized by the build-up of coastal sediments, whether they be the islets formed at Nan Madol, or the more typical progradation as observed at the Sapota site on Fefen. Stilt-buildings could have initiated this build-up, later purposefully added to in order to form coastal flatlands or artificial islets. Another similarity is that the pottery from Fefen and Leluh appeared to be a mixture of water-worn and that retaining integrity (the shell artefacts from the lowest levels on Makin Island, in the Gilberts, were also reported as water-worn); a similar condition was noted for the ceramic assemblage at Apalo (Chris Gosden, personal communication).

The existence of stilt-houses dating to the period of early settlement could be as a result of the dense primary vegetation of the islands when first encountered, having had no resident mammal to restrict growth. Settlement on the reef may have been the easiest location available for habitation until enough space had been cleared on the island proper to allow room for both subsistence crops and buildings – subsistence rather than habitation presumably being the primary concern. However, the development of settlement sites on the reef could not have been solely for this reason as earliest settlements in the islands east of the Solomon Islands do not take this form.

Spriggs (1999b), and others, have proposed that reef settlement at Lapita sites may have been necessitated by the presence of people already inhabiting the island, or in an effort to settle in areas with less malarial risk. Such a location for Lapita sites also supports the notion of the people who used such ceramics being maritime traders (e.g., Kirch 1988a). For the later architects of the Carolines, who viewed stilt-buildings as a cultural norm, it may be expected that earlier necessities of settlement location had dropped from community consciousness. Stilt-built settlements are still used in present-day Oceania.

The question of subsistence will need to be addressed next, but first, habitation should be explicated. That is, the early sites of eastern Micronesia are likely to have been settlements of stilt-houses located on reef flats. In turn, these types of site are known in the area of the Bismarck Archipelago and northern Solomon Islands during the period of Lapita pottery, suggesting further links between eastern Micronesia and the south.

Settlement and subsistence at initial colonization can further aid the search for origins. Here I venture into the realms of strandlooping versus transported landscapes and founder effect versus *habitus*. Strandlooping is a term borrowed from African contexts by Les Groube (1971) to describe the method of subsistence adopted by the first colonizers of Remote Oceanic islands. In this scenario, people were first restricted to a lagoonal/maritime economy until such time that a terrestrial subsistence base could be introduced or developed. Such a method would allow settlers of newly discovered islands to advance rapidly ahead of those attempting to establish more stable and permanent settlements. In Africa, this method allowed sealers and whalers to become established in areas ahead of full colonization by European agriculturalists.

At first glance, this hypothesis is an appealing explanation for settlements on the coral reefs, with the precocious inhabitants subsisting purely on the immediately local marine resources to await the impending arrival of agriculturalists (or setting about it themselves when the mood struck). However, this is an unrealistic proposition, as Spriggs (1997c; 2000; 2001a) has concluded; it is highly doubtful that survival would be possible without the introduction of subsistence crops and their immediate cultivation. Unlike islands of Remote Oceania, the African Continent was already replete with suitable flora and fauna to supplement subsistence requirements. An alternative scenario is that which involves what has been termed a 'transported landscape'.

The concept of a transported landscape was introduced to Pacific archaeology by Patrick Kirch (1984a). A transported landscape involves the conveyance of most, if not all, subsistence items found in the repertoire of the colonists' home island. In this case, although some animal species may die, and certain crops fail, at least elements of the package should flourish and allow a diverse subsistence base to be established. A corollary of this is that it may be possible to trace the origin of a settler community by the landscape they appear to have transported with them.

In general, the colonizers of the Pacific islands took with them all or some of the items from an available suite for subsistence of dog, pig, chicken, rat, taro, yam and breadfruit. Rats are included here in their role as a fast-breeding, self-feeding food source which has often been under-rated; they are commonly written off as stowaways which crept onto ocean-going seacraft under the cover of darkness. A review of the distribution of *Rattus praetor* in Oceania, and its apparent disjunctive similarity to domesticated animals, suggests that deliberate transport is most likely. As a corollary (White, Clark and Bedford 2000: 114):

Attribution of intentional translocation implies some function or purpose in the decision to translocate. What could this be in the case of *R. praetor*? When compared with other translocated animals, it is small, providing little food, and is not noted for its fine fur or other useful products . . . On the other hand, bones of the full range of available rodents are found in archaeological sites in contexts that suggest that all species could have been part of human meals . . . [E]ating rats is reported from a number of Pacific islands in the recent past.

Of the major animals transported, only dog has been reported from the early sites on Chuuk, Kosrae, the Marshalls and possibly the Gilberts. Dog and chicken have been reported in the earliest deposits on Pohnpei (Kataoka 1996). Dog, pig and chicken are present on Fais, but the generally limited ensemble of domesticates is typical of islands that are settled late in prehistory. The full complement of subsistence species is common in Near Oceania, but dwindles with distance from source (Kirch 1984a). Direct evidence for plant staples has only been reported from Kosrae. It cannot be assumed, but it is likely, that the first settlers of the neighbouring high islands introduced similar subsistence species.

By necessity then, the settlers, initially living on the reefs of islands, actively set about altering the landscape in order to create the conditions they perceived as suitable for settlement and subsistence. Their aim was to alter the very nature of the landscape, by manipulating the vegetation so as to cause erosion and thereby lay the foundations for the subsistence systems, in a landscape transported as much by mind as by seacraft. This approach to the landscape by the initial settlers would be responsible for creating conditions of high sediment transport and the progradation of the shoreline onto the reef flats underneath stilt-house settlements. This was the *habitus* of the settlers; it was an application of their habitual experience of island landscape alteration, an experience well attested at the Lapita pottery sites in Near Oceania.

A third possibility that I have introduced elsewhere (Rainbird 1995a) is that islands could be prepared, 'seeded', prior to permanent human colonization. The detailed evidence required to establish such a scenario is rarely forthcoming; however, analysis of palaeoenvironmental material from Kosrae may provide indications of seeding. This evidence may also provide proxy evidence for the human arrival in eastern Micronesia as a whole. Results from excavation within the Katem compound at Leluh report waterlogged deposits to a depth of 2.62 metres. At this depth archaeological deposits were identified including ceramics, other artefact types and large quantities of charcoal. Samples of the charcoal were taken for laboratory identification and found to include the major subsistence species of breadfruit (Athens 1995; Athens, Ward and Murakami

1996). The analysis indicated the presence of breadfruit trees at the earliest phase of the human settlement of Kosrae.

Coring elsewhere on Kosrae recovered pollen of *Cocos nucifera*, the coconut palm, indicating its presence prior to 2000 and perhaps as early as 2700 years ago. Jerome Ward (1995) regards this as evidence for the natural origin of this palm on Kosrae. Although previously Fosberg, Sachet and Oliver (1987) had considered coconut to be a species introduced by humans, there is evidence for the possibility of a natural diffusion of floating coconuts in the Pacific (Spriggs 1984; Parkes 1997). However, the use of palaeoenvironmental data in archaeology has to be considered in context if it is to be a useful tool for understanding the human past. The earliest dates for coconut on Kosrae are contemporaneous not only with the earliest (palaeoenvironmental) claimed evidence for human settlement on Pohnpei, but also with some of the earliest dates from cultural deposits on Bikini Atoll in the Marshall Islands, Kosrae's neighbour to the north-east. Can it be that coconuts arrived accidentally on Kosrae, owing to the presence of people who introduced them on the neighbouring islands that had already been settled? The currents and winds in the area of Kosrae in the present (Karolle 1993) suggest that if *Cocos nucifera* seeds had floated to the island they are most likely to have come from the east or north-east, that is, from the direction of the Marshall Islands. Could it be that the palaeoenvironmental data are corroborating the evidence for a human presence in the Marshall Islands some 2500 years ago? This date, as I have suggested above, may not be earlier than settlement in the Carolines, or at least Pohnpei, as previously believed.

This is, of course, assuming that the presence of coconut is not actually indicating the direct presence of humans on the island. However, few Pacific prehistorians are now under any illusion as to the efficacy of seacraft and navigators in the western Pacific by, at the very least, the beginning of the Lapita period. It was by this time that the Mariana and Palau archipelagos had been settled, requiring voyages over substantial distances and, to the south and east, people had reached New Caledonia and Samoa. Irwin (1992) argues for the possibility of sailing for exploration prior to an actual colonizing mission. A corollary to this is that it would have been possible for groups to sail to an island and prepare it *in advance* of a colony. In particular, coconut trees, banana plants and breadfruit trees require little maintenance once established. A reconnaissance group may locate an island, seed it and return home, while retaining or passing on the knowledge required to locate the island again for permanent or transitory settlement. In the terms of Irwin (2000), the palaeoenvironmental evidence might be regarded as an indication of *pre*-colonization events.

There are a few clues from Kosrae that perhaps indicate the possibility of a pre-colonization seeding process in the early history of human encounters with the island. The evidence for the introduction of coconut I have already noted above. In addition to this is the recovery of wood charcoal from the breadfruit tree in the earliest deposits, deposits regarded by Athens as possibly coming from the very earliest settlement of the island. Gail Murakami (1995) identified breadfruit wood charcoal in four out of the five samples from the early pottery-bearing deposits. Although not represented in the pollen record for Kosrae prior to 2000 years ago, and not substantially until after 1500 years ago, it is difficult to reconcile the burning of subsistence plants at an early stage in permanent settlement when there are many non-economic native plants waiting to be cleared. If it is not the case that they are burning their boats, then breadfruit may have been established at an early date, perhaps prior to what eventually became regarded as permanent settlement. The point here is not conclusive, but should lead to an awareness of the probably complex nature of island colonization, one that may have started in eastern Micronesia 2500 years ago, but may not have been complete for a further 1500 years.

The fourth colonization event identified by Intoh (1997) was that which brought Polynesian speakers to the atolls of Kapingamarangi and Nukuoro. These atoll communities have normally been termed Polynesian Outliers, as they are outside of the Polynesian Triangle defined by Aotearoa/New Zealand, Hawaii and Rapa Nui (Easter Island). Earliest dates for human settlement are *c*. 1250 years ago for Nukuoro (Davidson 1992) and 700 years ago for Kapinga-marangi (Leach and Ward 1981). More detailed discussion of the archaeology of these islands will wait until chapter 8. The final element of research that should be considered in this chapter is the biological evidence that, in recent years, has seen major developments.

Biological and physical anthropology

Although at a preliminary stage, it is important to note the use of genetic evidence in adding to debates regarding ancestral populations of Pacific islanders and the amount of mixing between the communities of Oceania. There are many potential pitfalls with the current biotechnology and it is clear that many of the questions asked by geneticists are led by archaeology and linguistics rather than presenting new information to challenge orthodox models (for a discussion see Terrell, Kelly and Rainbird 2001). At present, the best that can be said of the results is that the islands of Micronesia were settled by people having an ancestry, at some time in the past, in South-East Asia and to a much lesser extent in New Guinea. For Micronesia J. Koji Lum and Rebecca Cann (1998; 2000) have tried to push the genetic evidence further, using the mitochondrial DNA (mtDNA) evidence that is only transferred through the female line, mother to daughter. Their earlier work (Lum and Cann 1998) correlated with the linguistics, with the Oceanic (Oc) subgroup speaking populations of Austronesian being closely linked genetically, and indicating continued gene-sharing since colonization, while the populations of Palau and Yap are as different from each other, and the Oc-speaking populations, as they are linguistically, and the population of the Marianas largely isolated. However, Lum (1998), using the same dataset, found that for central and eastern Micronesia it is male biological transfer that is important, and is maintained constantly from initial colonization through to the present. Lum and Cann's (2000: 166) more recently published results have revealed a far more complicated picture of Micronesian populations, one that is consistent with fusion from widely dispersed geographical sources. They conclude that:

Our mtDNA lineage analyses have allowed us to identify some of these interactions. Central-Eastern Micronesians and Polynesians most likely shared a common origin in Island South-East Asia, and a common route into the Pacific along the north coast of New Guinea, but differences in specific group and cluster prevalence imply largely distinct prehistories. The three western Micronesian archipelagos appear to have had independent origins [in South-East Asia]. Since settlement, however, the Marianas, Yap Proper, and Palau have experienced an influx of mtDNA lineages from Central-Eastern Micronesia. As the ocean separating islands becomes viewed more as a means of communication than as a moat, the task becomes one of disentangling common origins from interactions to reconstruct the complex prehistory of the Pacific.

A major problem with such research programmes is that samples are taken from living humans whose genetic inheritance may have altered significantly, over the six or more generations, since the demographic effects caused by colonialism. Also, given the fluid boundaries that have been commonplace in the history of the region, and a relatively short time depth of occupation in human evolutionary terms, it is at present largely impossible for geneticists to tease out a chronology for genetic differences. To circumvent such problems requires the extraction of genetic information from ancient human remains, but this too is fraught with problems. Finding and extracting mtDNA from decayed bones is a difficult task, and where it is possible only incomplete strands are recovered. Comparisons then rely on reconstructing the full mtDNA strand sequence that, by necessity, is hypothetical and may or may not be a close approximation to the original. Researchers worldwide are struggling to develop improved techniques for the extraction of genetic information from human remains, and the real potential of such studies has yet to be realized. Earlier bold statements have in more recent years been toned down (e.g., Hagelberg *et al.* 1999). The ethical treatment of human remains is also an issue that is of concern to the people of the region (see Rainbird 2000a).

Summary

In considering the settling of the Micronesian seascape we have seen that perceptions of fusion are enacted in a number of ways. People sailing across fluid boundaries came from west, south and east to make island homes for themselves, their kin and community. In certain circumstances the first island discovered may have become the place to which they became tied, or they may have moved on or returned 'home' to tell others of the possibilities available beyond the horizon. From an archaeological perspective we cannot be sure that all the islands, scattered as if tossed like grains of sand across the sea, were actually there and suitable for habitation from the time that we have the earliest evidence of humans in the region. Some stories from the islands tell of the need to create islands, and, as has been broached in this chapter, the dynamics of island transformation introduces elements of flux that will be discussed elsewhere in the following chapters.

The human colonization of the islands in the tropical north-west Pacific was enacted in a number of events, some separated by many generations. All of the evidence points to an initial origin of these people, much later given the appellation Micronesian, somewhere in the myriad islands of South-East Asia. The first groups, of what must have been purposeful colonists, arrived skilfully from their former island homes to settle successfully the islands of Palau and the Marianas at around 4500 to 3500 years ago. The settlers of each of the island groups appear to have derived from different communities, and probably different islands altogether, and the motivations that led them to sail what today we consider vast distances may have also been quite different. Population pressure, owing to early Holocene sea level rise, may in part suggest a common reason for dispersal, but people and communities have methods of dealing with such issues, and social competition, or the desire to explore, amongst many other attempts to explain, should be considered as probably mixed into the complexities of human migration. When they left they took with them pottery technology and some staple plant foods, but what we currently know of these people derives mostly from the community that decided to colonize the Mariana Islands. Their distinctive ceramic styles indicate that a community spirit was maintained by contact across all of the inhabited islands of the group. These ties, ones that were linked to the homeland, maintained a community identity that aided co-operation and population growth that was probably necessary for survival, and lasted, at least as indicated by ceramic design, for up to twenty generations.

Given the evident seafaring skill of the first settlers, it is unlikely that Yap was not visited at some point during the 2000 to 1500 years prior to permanent settlement. The limited palaeoenvironmental evidence for forest disturbance at around 3300 BP may be indicative of this. But the permanent settlers, when they arrived on Yap, had traversed a different seascape, and although ultimately derived from South-East Asia, these people may have made their way from long-standing communities in Near Oceania. They brought with them pottery technology and they transported a landscape that included animal domesticates, pig, dog and chicken, that soon were also taken to Fais.

Archaeologically speaking, at about the same time, other people were moving out of Near Oceania and heading more directly north. The two or more migrations may actually be separated by up to half a millennium, but they rapidly moved through the Gilberts and possibly reached the northern end of the Marshalls by 2500 to 2000 years ago. There may have been a brief hesitation here, perhaps over a couple of generations, but not long enough to lose the knowledge of ceramics in these clay impoverished atolls, before the explorers located and seeded the eastern Carolines.

As the atolls of the central Carolines became habitable over 2000 to 1000 years ago, people moved from the high islands of the eastern Carolines in a westerly direction, until the disparate communities of west and east met and new alliances were forged. The seaways of the Pacific continued to function, and finally travellers from the east settled the remaining islands that disturb the currents between the Carolines and New Guinea.

Once islands were settled, new and different histories emerged, and it is the biographies of places, starting with the Marianas, that are attended to in the next four chapters.

CHAPTER 5

IDENTIFYING DIFFERENCE: THE MARIANA
ISLANDS

In geological terms the two arcs of islands that form the Mariana Islands archipelago (Fig. 5.1) are situated at the junction of two tectonic plates composing the
earth's crust. The islands are located on the edge of a subduction zone where
the Pacific Plate, moving westwards, dips below the Philippine Plate. Guam
is the largest island in the region, having a total land area of 544 square kilometres; the rest of the Marianas group has a combined land area of 478 square
kilometres. The islands generally diminish in size in a south to north direction,
and on a conventionally coloured map they appear to fade away to blue.

All of the islands north of Saipan, sometimes called the Gani group, are volcanic in origin, consisting of dark igneous rocks (Russell 1998a). The subduction
zone, although responsible for the creation of the islands in the first place, also
leads to an unstable archipelago, with many of the northern islands volcanically
active and all of the islands susceptible to earthquakes. The Marianas are also
known for the frequent occurrence of typhoons and droughts. Guam on average
experiences a typhoon every three and a half years, and a super-typhoon once a
decade. These storms can cause extensive and severe damage to both crops and
structures.

The majority of the archaeological evidence derives from the larger southern
islands, namely Guam, Rota, Tinian and Saipan. Guam is composed of a limestone plateau in the north and volcanic mountains in the south. Saipan, Tinian
and Aguiguan are geologically constituted of raised limestone, as is Rota except
for a small igneous component.

History of settlement

One of the local understandings of the creation and peopling of the Mariana
Islands was collected and presented by Mavis Warner van Peenen (1974: 3–4).
This story, although not featuring an angry woman, may be linked to the motif
identified by William Lessa, discussed in the previous chapter, of 'earth from
object thrown on primeval water'. Certainly there is included here a scattering
of elements that form earth and subsequently people:

Chaifi was the god who lived in Sasalaguan. He governed the winds, the waves
and the fire, but he did not govern the sun. He had a workshop in which he made
souls, and many slaves worked in it. One day hoping to speed up his work, he

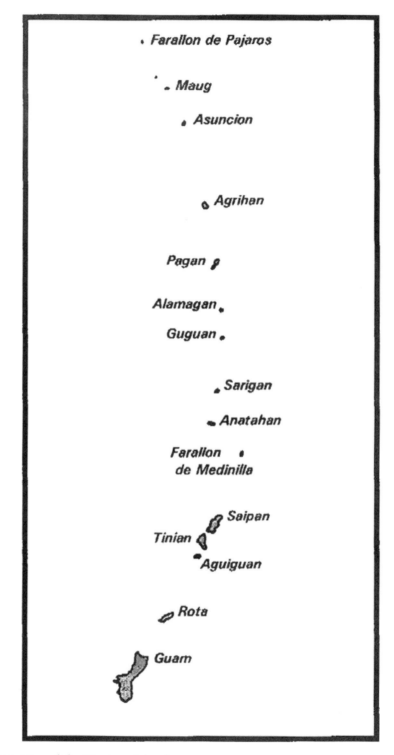

Fig. 5.1 Map of the Mariana Islands.

threw too much wood in the fire. An explosion ensued which was so great that it formed the earth. While all the excitement was taking place, a soul escaped and fell on Fua on the island of Guam, where it calcified. After a long time, the poor calcified soul became softened by the rain and sun and was converted into a man. Immediately, he set up his own shop in competition with Chaifi from whom he had learned the art of making souls. He took a little red earth and mixed it with water and moulded it into the form of a man, and he gave it a soul from the heat of the sun. Meanwhile Chaifi missed one of his souls, and he set out to search for it with the idea of killing it, however, when he did find it, he could not kill it because the soul of the man came from the sun which Chaifi did not control. He tried to kill the man by fire and by typhoons but without success. The first man remained alive so that he could produce other souls to replace him. So Chaifi gave up his persecution, but, from time to time, he remembers his escaped soul and starts out again to pursue him. It is then that the island of Guam is swept by typhoons which Chaifi wields.

The archaeologically derived settlement history of the Mariana Islands group is being clarified, but is less well understood until the appearance of *latte* stones and associated distinctive material culture, in what has been variously termed the Latte (Spoehr 1957; Moore 1983) or Protohistoric Period (Craib 1986; 1988; Craib and Ward 1988). The human history of the islands prior to the Latte Period, that is, the previous 3000 years or so, was initially simply termed Pre-Latte by Alexander Spoehr (1957), but has subsequently been treated to more sophisticated attempts to refine the chronology, as more evidence is brought to light. However, the initial chronological distinction was made between the earliest sites, containing ceramic types designated as Marianas Red Ware, and the later *latte* sites associated with a different ceramic type given the appellation Marianas Plainware (Spoehr 1957). Fred Reinman (1977) further attempted to identify and refine the ceramic sequence, and proposed a pattern that showed the earliest ceramics were tempered with calcareous sand (CST), while the later ceramics had volcanic sand temper (VST). Darlene Moore's (1983) detailed study of the ceramics from the excavations at Tarague Beach on Guam found that, although there is this trend in temper change, a strict distinction did not exist. Moore was able to develop a four-part ceramic chronology using a range of ceramic attributes.

With the increase in archaeological data production over the last two decades, Moore's model has been refined and has become the standard for the archipelago (Table 5.1). Temper types are not restricted to CST and VST but may sometimes be mixed, consist of grog or include calcareous sand and quartz grains (CSQT). None of these tempers is a chronologically distinct marker, but, along with other attributes, they have allowed for a four- or five-part sequence for the pre-contact history of the Marianas to be defined. In this chapter I follow the sequence defined by Moore and Hunter-Anderson (1999) but will give due consideration to the revisions proposed in Hunter-Anderson and Moore (2001). Apart from the very earliest phase, which is divided in two, these revisions have their biggest impact in proposing new names for each of the phases. It is

Table 5.1 *Comparison of five chronological sequences proposed for the Mariana Islands.*

	Spoehr (1957)	Craib (1990)	Moore (1983)	Moore and Hunter-Anderson (1999)	Hunter-Anderson and Moore (2001)
0 BP		Historic			
500 BP	1521 AD	1521 AD	1521 AD	1521 AD	1521 AD
1000 BP	Latte	Latte (Protohistoric)	Latte	Latte	Latte
		Mochong			
1500 BP			Transitional	Transitional	Huyong
2000 BP		Ypao		Intermediate Pre-Latte	Late Unai
2500 BP	Pre-Latte		Intermediate Pre-Latte		
3000 BP		Tarague	Early Pre-Latte	Early Pre-Latte	Middle Unai
3500 BP					Early Unai

important to provide these new phase names here, but time will tell whether they will be adopted more generally. I will now describe the archaeological evidence related to each of the phases.

Early Period

The sites of the Early Period in the Marianas were introduced in the previous chapter. Those on Saipan and Tinian appear to have been situated on sand spits close to breaks in the reef, but Tumon Bay has a wide fringing reef without breaks, and may not have been as attractive to early settlers. More likely areas for Early Period settlement on Guam may be at Pago Bay, or in the south-west in the area of Cocos Lagoon (Fig. 5.2). Early Period sites are usually recognized by their distinctive ceramics described in the previous chapter. However, decorated pottery on average only accounts for 2 per cent of sherds at each site (Hunter-Anderson and Moore 2001). Other material culture items related to

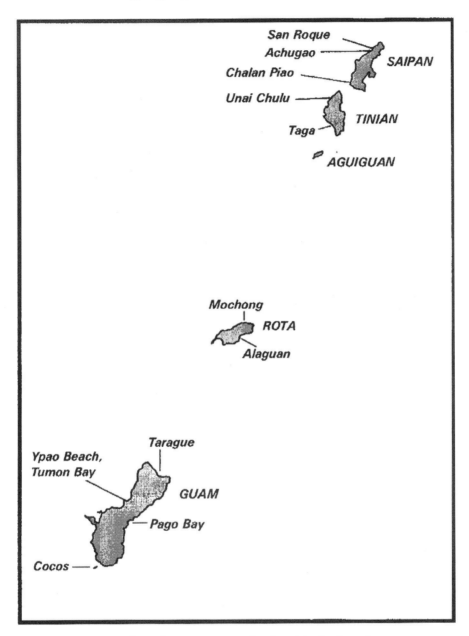

Fig. 5.2 Map of southern Mariana Islands with site locations

this period include *Conus* shell ornaments. Shell midden, probably related to subsistence practices, is typically dominated by *Anadara* and other bivalves, and indicates collection from a silty marine environment. The early sites, being located at the edge of lagoons and small estuaries, would provide such silt-laden environments in their vicinity. Judith Amesbury's (1998) diachronic analysis of shell species in Marianas archaeological sites finds the early dominance of bivalves is replaced by a later prevalence of gastropods, particularly *Strombus*, and concludes that environmental conditions favouring bivalve species, such as mangroves, may have been more widespread at the time of earliest settlement of the islands. However, although Amesbury (1998) finds the bivalve to gastropod change in Saipan and northern Guam, in southern Guam there is an increase in *Anadara* in sites of the Latte Period, perhaps suggesting an increase in mangrove there after its decline further north.

If mangroves did indeed exist at sites where evidence of earliest settlement has been recovered then our conception of site location needs to be modified accordingly. Rather than a small coastal settlement with open access to the lagoon and reef, these sites may have been tucked in behind mangrove strand. The reef passages adjacent to such sites may have to be envisaged as small openings through otherwise impenetrable mangrove, and may provide a further clue to the location of such sites.

The excavation at Unai Chulu (Haun, Jiminez and Kirkendall 1999) has confirmed the importance of marine resources at this time, with the local diet including shellfish, in-shore fish, and also the occasional turtle and shark. There is no evidence for the importation of animals, but birds and fruit bat appear to have been regularly exploited. Coconut (*Coco nuciferas*) was certainly present and the assumption is that some root and tree crops were introduced, but not rice.

Little else can be said of subsistence practices at this time. One sherd of CSQT red-slipped pottery, found in a cave on Aguiguan, has led Butler (1992a) to propose that this island was being used for temporary fishing camps. The sea around Aguiguan is regarded as a rich source of marine life in the present, and the quartz sand inclusions in the sherd temper point to a Saipan origin. Also indicative of seafaring at this time is the homogeneity of the early ceramics within the southern Marianas. The similarity in form and style of ceramics used in the Marianas up to the Latte Period is usually interpreted as revealing strong inter-community and inter-island ties.

Inter-island social ties are regarded as necessary in unstable environments, where a single typhoon can destroy a community's crops and disturb inshore fishing grounds. In extreme cases of environmental catastrophe, an impoverished community would be able to rely on their neighbours, with whom they have strong links, to support them until their own island could fully sustain them again. Such a scenario appears to be a practical and sensible explanation for similar pottery on each island. But the current evidence, with its poor chronological control, could equally support the notion of a shifting group or groups, seeding a variety of coastal areas, and moving at various times to exploit different ecological niches as they became known and understood. This may be a more typical scenario for these seafaring people until the end of the Transitional Period when, for the first time, evidence mounts for higher-density and sedentary settlement.

Indeed, Hunter-Anderson and Moore (2001) believe further definition of the Early Period is possible, with the final 500 years of the period yielding the simpler bold-line pottery decoration. They call this the Middle Unai Period, following on from the Early Unai Period. The appellation Unai is derived from the Chamorro term for beach, and links the locations of the currently known sites of this period.

Intermediate Period

Excavated archaeological deposits on Guam at Ypao Beach, Tumon Bay, are typical of the Intermediate Period, and consist of pottery with a small collection of lime-impressed decorated sherds, shell and a posthole (Olmo and Goodman 1994). Given that these deposits are located at the back of the beach, they support Joyce Bath's (1986; see also Amesbury 1998) hypothesis that the earliest settlement of Tumon Bay occurred here, prior to tectonic uplift and shoreline progradation. Bath had also found postholes relating to this period of occupation. Intermediate Period settlement evidence, although slightly more widespread, is found in similar locations to the Early Period sites, and suffers from similar problems of disturbance and disjunction. Aspects of continuity have led Hunter-Anderson and Moore (2001) to suggest renaming this the Late Unai Period.

Ceramics from this period become less complex, with bold impressed circles, bold lines and chevrons that are becoming common at the end of the Early Period (Fig. 5.3). Some of the decoration is lime-filled, but the overall impression is of a less delicate style than those of the Early Period, and through time they become even less decorated and this is restricted to the rim (Moore and Hunter-Anderson 1999). As decoration got simpler, so did the form, moving from the carinated bowl with round or flattened base to robust straight-sided 'pans' with flat bases. These pans appear late in the Intermediate Period, continuing into the Transitional Period, and are an evolving but new type of ceramic vessel, which eventually dominates the material record.

Butler (1995) sees this new style of pan pottery as indicating the gradual introduction of innovative forms of food preparation or consumption. Moore and Hunter-Anderson (1999) support Butler, and find that the new ceramics may indicate a move from hearth cooking to pit roasting, or greater utilization of preservation techniques, such as salting. They also note their suitability for larger community gatherings, where food was more readily shared from these broad bowls and pans. In all of these scenarios, they posit that population growth is responsible for these changes, and that this demographic growth was possible as a result of coastal progradation, allowing larger areas for terrestrial subsistence production.

Sherds recovered from a rock shelter in northern Guam provide an indication that people may have been intermittently using inland areas from about

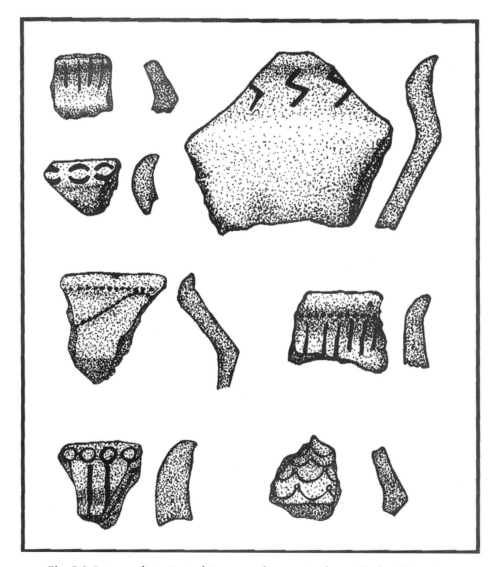

Fig. 5.3 Intermediate Period Decorated ceramics from Chalan Piao, Saipan, Commonwealth of the Northern Mariana Islands (after Hunter-Anderson and Butler 1995).

2500 years ago (Liston 1996; also see Moore and Hunter-Anderson 1999), and a similar picture is emerging from Tinian and Aguiguan (Bodner 1997).

Transitional Period

During excavations on the north coast of Rota, John Craib (1998a) recovered and identified a number of sherds of Transitional Period pottery, decorated with mat impressions and rim-notching. He recognized that these were identical to similarly dated sherds from Saipan, and proposes that they illustrate the existence of a 'communications network' during the early Transitional Period. One of the people who may have been involved in such a network was also found during the same excavation, in a rare example of a burial from this period. The inhumation, lacking cranial elements, was disarticulated and may have been interred as a bundle, along with the fragmentary remains of another person. (Bath (1986) also excavated a 'Pre-Latte' 'bundle burial' at Tumon Bay, Guam.) The main burial, according to Gary Heathcote (in Craib 1998a), was of a male around 170 centimetres (5 ft 7 in) in height, older than 35 years old, and suffering from osteoarthritis. There were also indications of the regular carrying of heavy loads with arms bent at the elbow, and changes to the hands that may be indicative of a net-weaver. Although midden analysis suggests that nets are more common for fishing in the Latte Period (Craib 1998a), they can be used for bird or bat collection as reported for the Marianas at the beginning of the twentieth century by Georg Fritz (2001: 67):

The most popular game is the fruitbat called *fanihi*. They occur in great numbers on all of the islands. During the day the bat is shot from the trees. In the evening, especially in the light of the moon, it is caught in flight with the *laguan fanihi* [fruitbat net]. This is a net made of rope or thorny twigs (*pakao*) attached to a pole four metres long.

Craib (1998a) notes that the burial is located outside of the area of Transitional Period cultural material, and proposes that human burial may have typically been at the edge of settlements at this time. However, the limited size of the sample, the missing cranium and the fragments of another individual may indicate that this was quite a different and unusual example of burial rite.

There is limited evidence to suggest that inter-island communication may have led to the first permanent settlement of Aguiguan at this time. Solely on the basis of ceramic attributes from surface collections, Butler (1992a) proposes that small-scale settlements were established on the interior plateau of Aguiguan after about 1200 years ago. The pottery style at this time was certainly showing attributes, such as the thickening of rims, that are common in the Latte Period, but this fledgling settlement would pre-date the actual construction of *latte* sets by some 200 to 400 years.

Across the settled islands of the archipelago, ceramics were generally changing from the open bowls and pans to plain vessels of round-based bowl or large jar varieties. These new ceramic types might suggest a return to hearth cooking, and possibly storage of grain or collection of water (Butler 1992a; Moore and Hunter-Anderson 1999). This ceramic alteration, including the thickened rim (Type B rim), is consistent with other items of material culture such as slingstones. It was previously thought to be typical of the Latte Period, but now appears to have been present towards the end of the Transitional Period (Butler 1995).

Butler does warn, however, that the coexistence of Transitional and Latte Period settlement on the same sites is likely to blur the chronological boundaries and also points out that *latte* sets, the main indicator of the Latte Period, may have been removed at later dates, making period identification more difficult.

There are proxy data that appear to indicate that change in Mariana island environments accelerated in the millennium prior to the Latte Period. The palaeoenvironmental data for Guam seem to show that landscape change was a major feature in the first millennium AD, and probably reflect similar environmental changes on the other islands of the southern Marianas (Cordy and Allen 1986; Athens *et al.* 1989; Hunter-Anderson 1989). Tom Dye and Paul Cleghorn (1990), using evidence from earlier excavations and survey (e.g., Osborne 1947) and more recent survey data (Dye, Price and Craib 1978; Dye 1979), postulate that the effects of settlement in the interior of southern Guam led to soil erosion and alluvial coastal sediment build-up. These changes occurred at various times from approximately 1500 years ago through to, and including, the Latte Period. Hunter-Anderson and Moore (2001) propose Huyong as an alternative name for this period, as it is the Chamorro term meaning to emerge or go out and reflects the move to exploit the inland along with the coast for subsistence purposes. The process of soil movement may have added to the problems of preservation of early coastal sites, which are susceptible to reworking by environmental action (Kurashina and Clayshulte 1983), but Craib, working with earth scientist Gary Mangold (1999), believes that these problems have been overstated.

Latte Period

In the second millennium AD, the people of the Marianas began to construct groups of paired quarried limestone, sandstone or basalt pillars, each supporting its own hemispherical capstone (Fig. 5.4). These pillars, ranging in number between three and seven pairs, are known as *latte* stones and are unique to the Marianas. Early foreign visitors commented on the *latte* stones structures and the Spanish named them *'casas de los antiguos'* (the 'houses of the ancients'); they were sketched and discussed in a number of published journals (see Russell 1998b).

Michael Graves (1986b), contradicting earlier supposition (e.g., Spoehr 1957), showed that there is no evidence of *latte* stones prior to 900–1000 years ago, with their use continuing up to and beyond encounters with the Spaniards in the sixteenth century. Owing to the perceived lack of historical reports concerning the use of these stones, a great deal of debate has surrounded their interpretation (see below). However, there are a number of historical texts.

A 1676 document by Juan Gayosa describes the Chamorro residences as sitting atop pyramid-shaped columns upon which are 'hemispheres' that hold the floor beams (quoted in Olmo 1995: 17). This historical report confirms the

Fig. 5.4 *Latte* stones at Latte Stone Park in Agana, Guam. These stones were removed from elsewhere in Guam and reconstructed here. Although they do not all belong to the same original group, they do provide a good example of the arrangement of *latte* sets.

general contemporary interpretation that the majority of *latte* sets supported a wooden and roofed superstructure, and constituted the dwelling place for all or some of society in the Latte Period. Many other historical sources report that houses and canoe houses were built on stone pillars, but do not mention the unique capstones (Thompson 1940).

The report of the 1565 Legaspi expedition provides quite a detailed account (in Plaza 1973: 6–7):

Their houses are high, well kept and well made. They stand at the height of a man off the ground, atop large stone pillars, upon which they lay the flooring. [There] they have the living room, [with] rooms and quarters on either side . . . Their sleeping platforms are high . . . These are the houses in which they sleep. They have other low houses, on the ground, where they cook and roast food. These have all the utensils and the platforms which the servants have for sleeping. Both types [of house] are thatched with palm fronds. They have other large houses which are used for boathouses. These are not dwellings, but communal [buildings] in which they store the large proas [i.e., sailing vessels] and shelter [their] canoes. In each 'barrio' [i.e., group of dwellings] there is one of these boathouses. There was one of these where we got our water. [It was] very handsome with four naves, constructed in the shape of a cross, easily capable of holding 200 men: fifty in each of the naves which were spacious, wide and high.

What have come to be regarded as *latte* villages are, for the most part, coastal, although many sites are located inland (e.g., see Henry, Boudreau and Haun 1994). The most favoured location appears to be low-lying sandy areas, such as the north coast of Rota and Tumon Bay on Guam. The west, leeward, coast of Saipan appears to have had almost continuous Latte Period settlement along the majority of its 16 kilometre length of narrow coastal lowland. This side of Saipan also boasts the island's major lagoon, with the barrier reef extending up to 3 kilometres from the shore at Tanapag Harbour. This area of Saipan remains the most popular residential zone in the present day, and consequently the archaeology is both well known through excavations in advance of development, but also highly disturbed by historical events.

The initial human settlement of Saipan, as evidenced at Achugao, appears to be on a sand spit but, as noted above, the majority of pre-Latte Period remains are found at the back of the beach, away from the modern coastline. It seems that significant progradation has occurred along this coast, beginning approximately 1000 years ago, and that late Transitional and Latte Period settlement followed the widening coastal strip towards the lagoon (Wickler 1990b; Butler 1992a; Henry, Ryan and Haun 1993). Similar processes have been reported for northern Guam (Dilli, Ryan and Workman 1993) and, as is the case for Saipan, the stabilizing of tectonic and isostatic processes has been invoked in explanation. The coastal strand of the north coast of Rota, although prograding, appears to have started developing around 3000 years ago, stabilizing about 2500 years ago, and making a push towards the present-day coastline at around 1800 years ago (Craib 1998). Owing to tectonic and exposure differences, there should be no expectation that coastal geomorphology in the Marianas has a shared history. Barbara White (cited in Olmo 1995) reports that the area around Achang Bay, on the southern tip of Guam, experiences a high frequency of storm surges. This high frequency is due to the local shallow waters of Cocos Lagoon and disturbs the processes of coastal sedimentation. In other areas, once relative geologic stability is reached, cultural processes will have a role to play in maintaining and developing the coastal zone.

Surveys in the southern interior of Guam from the late 1980s through to the middle of the 1990s have boosted knowledge of interior sites. The southern interior of Guam consists of uplands formed by volcanic rock that is dissected by deep river valleys. A review of archaeological surveys conducted in this region until 1994 found that 153 sites had been recorded in enough detail to allow comparison. The reviewers, Henry, Boudreau and Haun (1994), found that the inland sites typically date from the Latte Period and are located on ridge crests or plateaux overlooking drainages. The majority of sites (95 per cent) are found at altitudes of between 50 and 175 metres above sea level and between 0.75 and 5.5 kilometres from the coast. Only 20 per cent of these sites consisted of actual *latte* sets, and in 62 per cent of these cases the sites were small, with only one or two sets present. The other 80 per cent of southern interior sites were surface scatters of ceramics and flakes of siliceous stone.

Near Mount Sasalaguan, in the Inarajan Municipality of southern interior Guam, four artefact scatters were identified and sampled and, perhaps unusually here, half the artefacts recovered were slingstones (Highness *et al.* 1993). The conclusion of the 1994 reviewers was that the majority of the sites represented short-stay events for the procurement of stone and the exploitation of other natural resources. The slingstones may have been used in the hunting of avifauna. Felicia Beardsley (1993) reports the discovery of a chert and siltstone quarry, with associated reduction debris indicating hard-hammer percussion techniques, in the Manenggon Hills of Guam.

Of the inland sites containing *latte* structures, it was found that nearly all are situated in close proximity to soils rated as 'moderately to well-suited to agriculture' (Henry, Boudreau and Haun 1994). These appear to be, for the most part, small-scale permanent or semi-permanent settlements. Craib's (1994) extensive excavation of an inland site, consisting of two *latte* sets separated by a mound, found that one *latte* set was already abandoned prior to the second *latte* set and mound feature coming into existence. The whole site, located in the Manenggon Hills, exhibited a low intensity of occupation in the first instance, with more frequent occupation, or occupation for longer periods, in the second phase continuing into the Spanish Period. The second-phase 'mound' feature, although providing the focus for a few hearths/ovens, was not the expected midden (see below), but a natural topographic feature.

Although challenged by research in the southern interior of Guam, Tinian (Hunter-Anderson and Moore 1987) and Aguiguan (Butler 1992a), preliminary generalizations about *latte* set location were that they are often arranged linearly, and their orientation is aligned with natural features such as the coastline, cliff or river (Thompson 1940). A good example of this village arrangement is Site 5 on Aguiguan (Fig. 5.5). At Site 5, the surviving *latte* sets are orientated in relation to both landward and coastline topographic features. This pattern is only upset at the extreme ends of the settlement area, where the *latte* sets have a different orientation. Butler (1992a) sees this pattern, and the fact that the smallest three-pair sets occur here, as a purposeful indication of the parameters of the village area.

Craib (1986; 1998a) has proposed that Latte Period villages normally have three spatial components and that houses, represented by *latte* sets, cluster in groups around the largest houses (i.e., the largest *latte* sets). The three components consist of the *latte* sets themselves, mounds or cooking areas, and spaces in between that often reveal a low-density artefact scatter (see Fig. 5.6). Of these, the mounds or cooking areas are not well documented, and although Reinman (1977) reports them as common at Guam coastal sites, descriptions and interpretations vary (see Craib 1994). The spaces in between are defined by the *latte* set clusters and associated artefacts, of which much more can be said.

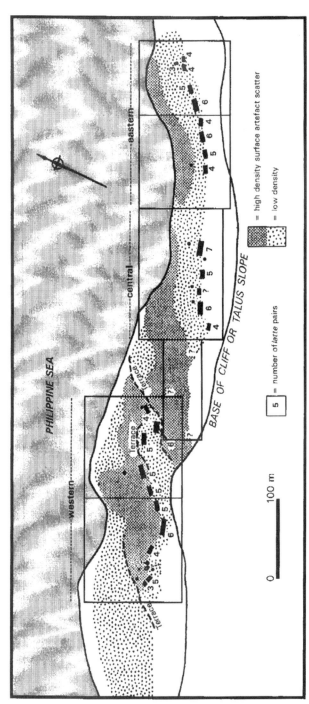

Fig. 5.5 Plan of Site 5, Aguiguan (after Butler 1992a). Here, the groupings identified at Site 5 on Aguiguan by Butler (1992a) can be seen. The three clusters identified as western, central and eastern are spatially separated. However, on the basis of the size of other *latte* sets, Butler posits further possible divisions. The eastern sector may have two groups each headed by a six-pair *latte* set, and the western group be divided in two and housing head persons in six-pair structures. There may also be a further grouping in the area of high-density surface artefact scatter between the western and central groups, where *latte* sets may have been removed by modern disturbance. Based on Craib's model, Butler's interpretation of Site 5 would thus lead to the conclusion that a large Latte Period village such as this consisted of between three and six semi-autonomous kin groups, each with a head person. One of the head persons would be higher ranked and residing with their kin group in the area of the seven-pair *latte* structure.

Fig. 5.6 Plan of the *latte* group at Tachogña, Tinian (after Russell 1998b). The ten *latte* sets are arranged parallel to the shoreline, and the set with most *lattes* and the two mounds appear to be spatially arranged central to settlement.

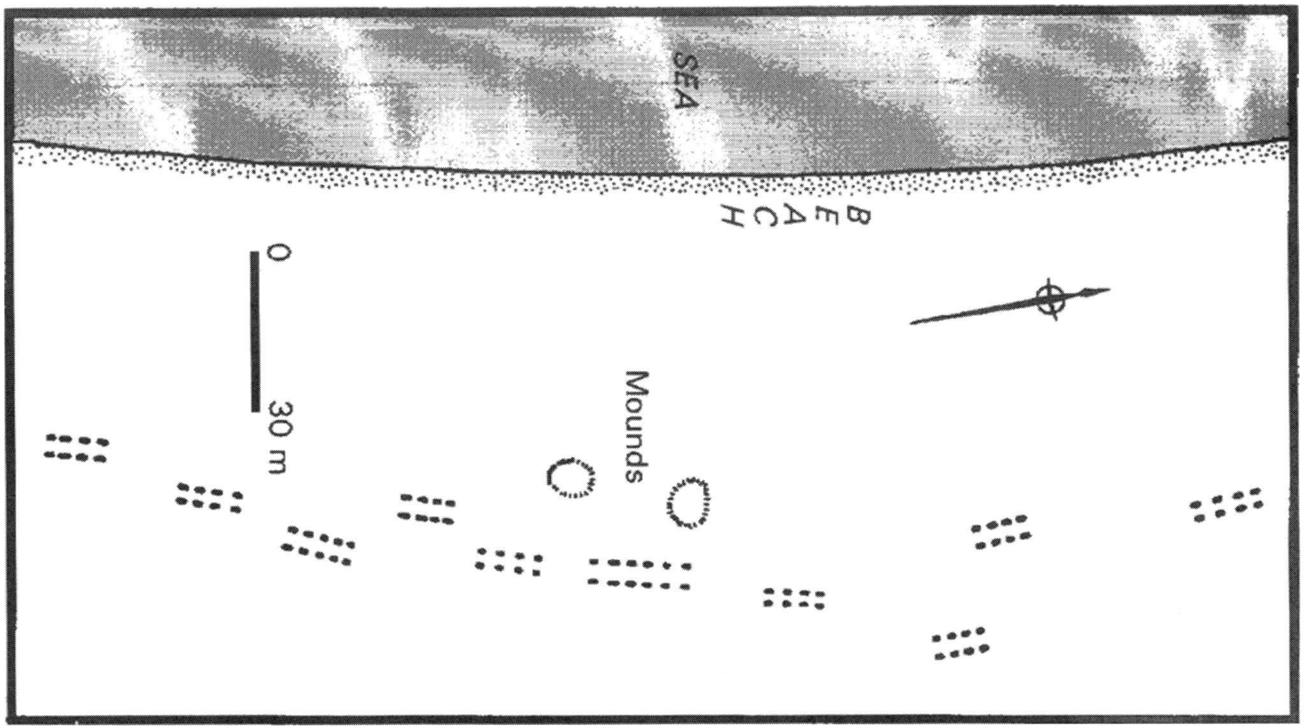

As Butler (1992a) has noted at Site 5, distinct groupings related to large *latte* sets may be discerned (see Fig. 5.5). Here, however, the *latte* are on the whole larger sets than those identified by Craib, and where he proposed five-pair sets as large, on Aguiguan, because of the higher distribution of sets larger than five, the six-pair sets and the centrally placed seven-pair set are seen to represent the important structures in the village hierarchy. Craib (1986) has proposed that clusters such as these represent descent group (kin-based) residential units, in which highest-ranked members of the group resided in the largest *latte*.

The *latte* sets with the most pillars (six or seven pairs) are often central to a settlement and are far less common than sets with four or five pairs of pillars. The corpus of material remains associated with the larger *latte* sets is the same as found with the smaller sets, and there is no material indication that they functioned as mens' or club houses as found elsewhere in Micronesia. That such buildings may have existed in the Marianas is hinted at when the head of the first mission to the Marianas, Father Diego Luis de Sanvitores, has bachelors' houses burned to the ground (Russell 1998).

Graves (1986b) in a study of 234 sets from Guam found that 84 per cent were four- or five-pair sets. The height of *latte* including capstones rarely exceeds 2.5 metres (Morgan 1988), although the perception of height for structures built on a slope would be accentuated when approached from below. Graves (1986b) found that, in general, there was little correlation between the height of the *latte* pillars and the number of pillars in the set. Although the presumed internal area of a *latte* structure did rise in relation to the number of pillars, increased area was achieved through the addition of more pillars, not by widening the distance between the rows.

The unique capstone, locally called *tasa*, may have been derived initially from the locally available coral heads, and may have been designed to exclude rats from the building superstructure (Thompson 1940). Certainly many of the journals of European visitors comment on the numbers of rats on the islands, and these rats will not have been native to the Marianas, but as in most cases in Oceania were introduced by people, possibly, as noted in the previous chapter, as a fast-breeding food source. In the case of the Marianas there is an interesting conjunction between the presence of *latte* stones and the introduction of rats.

David Steadman has for many years been working on the identification of bird bones from archaeological and other sites in Pacific islands. Across Oceania he has identified the remains of hundreds of extirpated and extinct species. Humans have often been held directly responsible for such losses, and this cannot be doubted in some cases, for example, the extinction through hunting of the moa in Aotearoa/New Zealand (Anderson 1989), but Steadman believes that other vertebrates, albeit commensal with humans, may be responsible. In the Marianas, where rats were the only mammals introduced prior to European imports, Steadman (1998) has found that many land birds, flightless rails, survived

Fig. 5.7 As Nieves *latte* stone quarry, Rota. If these part-quarried pillars and capstones had been erected they would have stood taller than those at the House of Taga on Tinian and may represent competitive emulation.

until approximately 1000 years ago when they drop out of the fossil record; coincidentally the evidence of rat, *Rattus exulans*, begins at this time. Also apparently contemporary with the loss of birds and introduction of rats is the beginning of *latte* architecture. Can it be that the rats and changes in material culture are indicating new contacts with people from outside the archipelago at this time? I will return to this issue below.

A unique example of *latte* architecture, which may represent a late elaborate manifestation of this phenomenon, is found on Tinian. The 'House of Taga', which during Anson's sojourn in 1742 had all twelve pairs of limestone pillars and capstones upright, has today only a single standing pillar and capstone together measuring nearly 5 metres in height. The pillars were well dressed, and narrow towards the top in trapezoidal shape. Nearby, Spoehr (1957), who excavated here, recorded the remains of the quarry and also noted that typically, given its size, the House of Taga had been the central *latte* structure in a village of eighteen *latte* sets. In central Rota, an even more massive structure had been planned, as is attested by the hewn vestiges of nine pillars and seven capstones still in place in the bedrock at the As Nieves Quarry (Fig. 5.7). Had it been completed, it probably would have been 50 centimetres taller than the House of Taga (Graves 1986b; Morgan 1988). It may be that these sites represent competitive emulation between island communities, but according to a legend collected by Spoehr in 1950 the two sites have linked origins, as it starts (1957: 89):

Taga was originally a chief on Guam. He was a very big man, at least ten feet tall. He came from Guam to Rota, fought the Rota chief, and defeated him. Then Taga became the Rota chief. He married a Rota woman and had a girl child by her. Taga commenced to build himself a house on Rota, and started to quarry the shafts and capstones at As Nieves. But he never finished the quarrying as he decided to go to Tinian instead [here he became chief and built himself a great house, the House of Taga].

What the House of Taga certainly does represent is a desire to be different. Whether it was the desire of an individual, a kin group or a community is not possible to define, but that the structure is at the centre of an apparent village, and that the material recorded by Spoehr in association with the *latte* set is no different from that found at other *latte* sites, may indicate that this elaboration represented a manifestation of community desire. In this case the House of Taga may provide an indication of inter-community or, with the As Nieves Quarry site in mind, inter-island social competition.

The monumental scale that *latte* sets could reach leads to speculation regarding the construction of these structures, which are inherently unstable (Godard 1995). Spoehr noted with apparent surprise that the House of Taga stones were set in sand, with no packing for support. He finds from Hornbostel's unpublished notes that at the As Nieves quarry the separate *latte* elements appear to have been lifted by levering and placing spoil underneath (Spoehr 1957). In Oceania the famous and much larger *moai* statues of Rapa Nui (Easter Island) bear some similarities to *latte*. There they also have an independent stone element, the *pukao* placed on the head of the statue in the form of a headdress, and speculation in regard to quarrying, transport and erection has been protracted and popularized (Bahn and Flenley 1992).

The ubiquity of *latte* structures has led to many further considerations as to how they may represent the constitution of Chamorro society in later prehistory. Earlier commentators (e.g., Thompson 1932) noted a relationship between the *latte* sets and human burial. They considered the *latte* as being monuments that demarcated a mortuary and ritual zone. More recently, excavations at *latte* settlements have shown that these sites served the whole range of typical domestic activity. This association of *latte* with quotidian domestic debris and artefacts prompted a reconsideration of these structures and their possible role in ancient society.

Ross Cordy (1983b) reviewed the earliest historical documentation of Chamorro society and discovered that, contrary to other opinions, there was little evidence before European contact of anything other than a bipartite society divided into chiefs and commoners. Although it is generally agreed that, at the time Magellan stumbled upon Guam, society was organized through matrilineal descent, the degree to which the society was stratified has been constantly a matter of debate. In a review of locally produced revisionist history, George Boughton (1992: 223) usefully provides the traditional and revisionist accounts:

The traditional interpretation contends that precontact society was organized into a three-tier class system. On the top of this system was the *matao*. This group had high status, controlled the use of land, and monopolized high status occupations (they were the warriors, navigators, canoe builders, deep water fishermen, etc.).

Below the *matao* was the *atcha'ot* . . . a middle group . . . It consisted of the family or close relatives of the *matao*, and it assisted [them] in high status occupations. The clan or lineage peers of a *matao* could demote him to *atcha'ot* status, either for life or for a specified period of time, as punishment for breaking customary law.

On the bottom of the social pyramid was the *manachang*. This group is set apart from the rest of the society by various restrictions, denied high status occupations, and relegated to the poorer lands. According to Spanish accounts they lived like slaves and were prohibited from cohabiting with members of the upper classes.

The revisionists argue that, since there was no social mobility between the *manachang* on the one hand and the *matao* and *atcha'ot* on the other, precontact society was characterised by a two-tiered caste system rather than a three-tiered class system. The high caste consisted of two groups, the *matao* and the *atcha'ot*, with at least some degree of social mobility possible between them. The *manachang*, however, were completely cut off from the high caste and were unable to change their status, at least during their lifetime.

It is difficult to reconcile either of these possible accounts with the material remains of the Latte Period, and historical reports, diluted through centuries of colonialism and ignorance of (or blindness to) the important role played by women, have probably downplayed social complexities. The complexities would have existed at local kin-based, clan and lineage levels, and have been replaced in the literature by assumed over-arching systems that may bear little resemblance to daily practice at the village level. Archaeologists have presented different interpretations based on the material remains.

Graves (1986b; 1991) regarded the *latte* as the house sites of the higher-status lineages in society, with the commoners living in wooden structures which have left little evidence in the archaeological record. Although not forming any recognizable foundation pattern, several postholes have been reported in association with possible Latte Period deposits in western Saipan and northern Rota (Butler 1988; Henry, Ryan and Haun 1993; Henry and Haun 1994). Twelve Latte Period postholes forming roughly parallel rows excavated at Tumon Bay, Guam, may represent rare evidence of a single structure (Workman and Haun

1993). Craib (1986) found little to support Graves' interpretation and concluded that all members of society were resident in the autonomous *latte* villages, with higher-status persons in the larger, centrally located *latte* sets, and lower-ranked kin in nearby smaller *latte* sets. In most cases it appears that postholes would most likely be related to structures built to cover cooking areas within *latte* villages and adjacent to *latte* sets (Craib 1998a).

Hunter-Anderson (1989; Hunter-Anderson and Butler 1995), while accepting the domestic function of *latte*, has resurrected the earlier idea of monumentality and ritual use of *latte*. She suggests that *latte* probably functioned in more ways than purely for habitation and status differentiation. The *latte* sets, which may not always have supported a wooden building, may have acted as territorial markers that symbolically laid claim to land and resources in a particular zone. Ancestors were buried within and in the vicinity of the set to further legitimate the claims to land rights. Butler (1992a) counters that the capstones could only have stayed in place on the shaft if the added weight of a wooden superstructure was present. In reply, Hunter-Anderson (personal communication) rejects the notion that the capstones need be upon the shafts in order for them to function symbolically, but agrees that without a heavy weight on the capstone these are unstable structures.

In relation to the ritual importance of house structures, and the impossibility of defining separate categories of domestic and ritual, it may be useful here to consider briefly the social aspects of the house in the Philippines. Connie Bodner (1997) has made comparisons between the various historical and archaeological understandings of Latte Period architecture and social organization with ethnographic evidence from the Bontoc region of northern Luzon. The 'Baley-style' traditional house Bodner describes has two floors (and occasionally an attic), with the first floor supported by large wooden posts with wooden disks attached to the top in order to prevent rats from eating the unpounded rice grain. Of further relevance here is that next to the entrance sits a mortar and pestle for pounding the rice grain. Anthropologist James Fox (1993), in a broader review of houses, found in traditional Austronesian-speaking societies, including the Philippines, some commonalities (many that also exist outside of Austronesian-speaking groups) that may at the very least allow us to develop more nuanced understandings of *latte* sets as buildings.

Fox (1993: 14) finds that: 'Posts and ladders, ridge-pole and hearth within an encompassing roof are the elements of the house most frequently marked as the foci of rituals for the house. They are the principal ritual attractors in the house.' The *latte* stones as house posts may well have been 'principal ritual attractors' and Fox further goes on to describe how house posts often take on a botanic metaphor related to rootedness and growth. This may be particularly important in relation to Hunter-Anderson's claims to linking *latte* stones and the ancestors. Laura Torres Souder (1992: 154) perhaps succinctly sums this up in stating: 'The spiritual world of the ancient Chamorros revolved around an ancestor cult. *Aniiti* (souls of ancestors) and *taotaomona* (people of before) were believed to be sacred and powerful and could cause great harm when crossed.' Christianity has not completely replaced such Chamorro views in regard to the ancestors, and many people are wary of approaching the sites of *latte* in the forest. However, as they are a symbol of Chamorro ancestry, the old proscriptions in relation to these remains can no longer be relied upon to protect *latte* sets from removal to provide garden ornaments. This is presumably not helped by local government using *latte* as a symbol and re-erecting them in the gardens of government offices (Godard 1995; Rainbird 2000a).

A further component of the Latte Period settlement system incorporates rock-lined paths. A detailed study of the Tarague Bay area of northern Guam found that a network of rock-lined trails served the whole area (Liston 1996). These trails appear to link the two local Latte Period villages with agricultural areas defined by clearance cairns and stone alignments.

There is an extremely strong association between coastal *latte* sets and human burials (Graves 1986b). Inland, for Guam at least, burials tend to occur at non-*latte* sites, and *latte* sites have no burials. At the coastal sites, a fairly consistent pattern has emerged, with inhumations being placed between the paired stones and on the seaward side of the *latte* set. There are many examples of exhumation of parts of the skeleton: usually the skull, including the mandible, and long bones. Two reasons for the exhumation of human bones have been proposed in relation to archaeology and ethnohistory.

Historic documentation notes the keeping of skulls of ancestors for purposes of communication with dead relatives. The ancestral skulls were symbolically displayed in Chamorro houses and this was a practice quickly expunged by Spanish missionaries (Russell 1998). Long bones, particularly of the lower limbs, were prized for fashioning into spearheads (see Hanson 1988). Typical spearheads were manufactured in the form of harpoons with barbs, and probably played a role in fishing, although use in interpersonal violence has been recorded.

A Latte Period burial of an adult male excavated at east Agana Bay, Guam, was found with ten spearpoints within the skeletal frame, and one had punctured the skull (Douglas, Pietrusewsky and Ikehara-Quebral 1997). Judith McNeill (1998) interprets this as the burial of a person who is more likely to have been ritually executed, rather than killed in warfare. Warfare is not well documented; however, the ubiquitous slingstones are often cited, along with the spearheads, as evidence of weaponry. In his survey of Aguiguan, Butler (1992a) proposed that the largest *latte* villages were sited in locations that allowed for the best defence of the island, but only two slingstones were found in a surface survey that collected 239 individual artefacts and noted many others.

Slingstones are manufactured from volcanic rock, limestone, coral or baked clay and are ovoid in shape with points at either end. Historical accounts report the great speed and accuracy achieved by the Chamorros, propelling the stones using slings made of either coconut or pandanus fibres (Russell 1998). Despite the deadly nature of slingstones reported in battles against the Spanish invaders (Russell 1998), prior to invasion they are just as likely to have been used for hunting birds.

Using data from collections made earlier in the century, Graves (1986b) found that although there was equal access to *latte* mortuary areas by sex, subadults were not included in the collections. This suggested to Graves that adult status was required for inclusion in these areas. However, Douglas Hanson (1988) warned that up until very recently mortuary data were only available from *latte* sets that were not completely excavated, and probably did not provide a full picture of cemetery population. Latte Period burials and related settlement were excavated in 1990 at Apurguan on Guam, and the analyses of the human remains provide an insight into pre-contact Chamorro demographics.

The 152 individuals recovered at Apurguan allowed the researchers plenty of scope for statistically meaningful analyses (Douglas, Pietrusewsky and Ikehara-Quebral 1997). The investigators found that subadults accounted for approximately 33 per cent of the cemetery population, providing a clear indication that burial in residential areas was open to all ages in society. Such open access appears available to both sexes, with a small under-representation of females. However, females were more likely than males to live beyond 50 years of age, with the average age at death for all adults being 43.5. In analyses of a larger collection of burials from the Tumon Bay–Hyatt Site, Melanie Ryan (1998: 237) found, that since

all demographic groups and both sexes are represented in *latte* set assemblages in relatively equal proportions, it seems likely that *latte* burial was kin based regardless of age or sex. No demographic group is conspicuously absent from any of the burial areas so it does not seem likely that differential access to spatially distinct burial areas was based on status.

Palaeopathological observations at Apurguan produced a list that shares common features with other Latte Period human remains, indicating the presence of treponemal infection, probably yaws – picked up by pre-pubescent children in contact with lesions in the lower legs – and also osteoarthritis and healed bone fractures. Typical of the Latte Period, dental pathology was good and this may be related to betel nut chewing, with staining from the nut often present on the teeth. Other cultural modification of teeth, that may include purposeful staining, includes the filing of the back of the teeth, and occasional engraving of the front incisors, that includes cross-hatching as the most sophisticated (Leigh 1929; Ikehara-Quebral and Douglas 1997).

The Latte Period ceramic corpus that in earlier times was glossed as Plainware has in more recent analysis provided an insight into the heterogeneity of Chamorro society and the contacts between the different communities which shared the tradition of *latte* architecture. Graves, Hunt and Moore (1990) have taken a geographical approach to the distribution of prehistoric ceramics in the southern Mariana islands. Their findings have necessitated some rethinking of the belief in a homogeneous Chamorro society prior to Spanish contact.

Graves, Hunt and Moore (1990) applied three analytical methods to eighteen Latte Period ceramic assemblages. The first, a study of the temper, revealed that a wide variety of types was used, but little in the way of geographical variation could be recognized. The second, a study of the exterior surface treatment of the pot, was more informative. The pottery from Guam, and probably Rota, had received much greater surface treatment than contemporary pottery on Saipan and Tinian, which tended to be only smoothed and scraped. The Guam assemblages, on the contrary, showed a wide variety of brushing, wiping and combing. The third method was compositional analysis of the pottery fabric and of two clay sources. Most of the pottery was found to cluster into four discrete groups, with only six of the thirty-six samples not included.

One group, from Tumon Bay on Guam, was made of clay probably collected at Mount San Rosa on the same island. In general, the analysis showed that local clay sources on individual islands were being exploited for pottery production. However, two sherds from Aguiguan cluster with a group from Guam, and two sherds from separate sites on Guam appear to have been derived from Saipan. These findings indicate, at the very least, limited movement of pottery or clay between communities on different islands in the southern Marianas. Butler (1992a) found that the Aguiguan pottery had similar surface treatment to that typical of Saipan and Tinian, but thickened rims that are a more diagnostic feature of Latte Period ceramics from Rota and Guam. He concludes by postulating that this fusion of form and style provides evidence of contact between Aguiguan and people in the archipelago to the north and south.

Craib (1998a) suspects that the ceramics only provide part of the picture regarding interaction between Mariana island communities, and points to the likely movement of basalt, *Isognonum* shell and exotic materials such as metal and glazed ceramics after Spanish contact, as potential indicators for more concerted inter-island contacts. Given that the southern Marianas are for the most part made up of limestone, the considerable amount of igneous rock found at Latte Period sites is likely to indicate transport from elsewhere. In his survey of the wholly limestone island of Aguiguan, Butler (1992a) found that nearly three-quarters (twenty-six of thirty-five) of the portable (i.e., non-earthfast) stone mortars were manufactured from imported volcanic rock. Craib (1998a) reports a pilot study of nine stone artefacts from Guam, Rota and Tinian that were subjected to x-ray fluorescence testing. This analysis found that at least seven, and possibly all, of the items are likely to have been manufactured from the same Umatac Formation of southern Guam. Furthermore, extensive testing may reveal other sources, and likely candidates are in the northern volcanic islands of the Marianas, where limited Latte Period settlement evidence has been found (e.g., Yawata 1963; Butler 1998a). The results from this limited study illustrate inter-island interaction involving the movement of materials, and reveal the potential through this method of greater definition of such communication.

Butler (1990; in part following Moore 1983) has highlighted the change in pottery morphology that occurs in the late Transition to Latte Period. Ceramic vessels change from open pan and bowl types into tall pots with constricted mouths. Butler proposed that this was a change in function, possibly related to an alteration in the subsistence base necessitated by an increase in population. He suggests that the boiling of starchy foods such as taro, yam or breadfruit may have become increasingly important. The expansion of population is inferred by the increase in settlement of inland sites, but changes in pot morphology may not necessarily indicate pan-Mariana subsistence changes. If the inland sites are examples of new settlement centres, rather than seasonal/occasional places related to coastal sites, then an agricultural subsistence base is the likely dominant mode, but other sites do not conform to such a pattern. Large Latte village sites, such as 3 and 5 on Aguiguan (Butler 1992a) and Alaguan (Craib 1988) on Rota, are situated in coastal zones at the base of steep cliffs without easy access to agricultural land. There is perhaps no other way of explaining such a dispersed settlement pattern other than assuming some form of symbiotic relationship between people in coastal and inland settlements. A seventeenth-century historical document by Fray Juan Pobre refers to the people of inland Rota exchanging rice with coastal dwelling people for fish (Driver 1989).

The question of the presence of rice in pre-Spanish contact times has been the subject of debate (e.g., Craib and Farrell 1981; Pollock 1983), which now seems to have been resolved. Takayama and Egami (1971) reported rice impressions on pottery from the Mochong *latte* village on Rota, although the temporal association of this sherd is unclear, and it may date to the historic period. There is mounting evidence, from more securely stratified contexts for rice impressed pottery, and from phytolith analysis, that rice was being grown in late prehistory (Hunter-Anderson, Thompson and Moore 1995). The current question is whether rice was a staple, as no agricultural features indicative of intensive rice production have been located. Through their study of the minimal documentary evidence, and the limited evidence derived from archaeological and palaeoenvironmental contexts, Hunter-Anderson, Thompson and Moore (1995) propose that during the Latte Period rice was introduced into the Marianas from South-East Asia, and served a limited role as a valued food for special occasions. The mortar stones common at *latte* sites may be linked to the introduction of rice, as they are typical of items used elsewhere for rice husking.

The mortars are often found placed between the end two pairs of a *latte* set, and may have more than one indentation pecked into them. The stone for the basalt mortars is often by necessity imported to a village either from a source on another island in the archipelago or, in the case of Guam, over a significant distance within the island. The procurement and movement of such weighty objects makes it likely that mortars were valued prestige items in the material culture corpus. At some village sites, the placing of the mortar at the end of *latte* sets may have been partly for display purposes to enhance the prestige of the residents. The link between the mortar stones and rice enhances the argument that it was a valued commodity. The Marianas are the only islands in the Pacific where there is evidence of rice production prior to the arrival of Europeans in the area.

The main subsistence crops appear to have consisted of breadfruit, taro, yams, bananas, sugar cane and coconuts. Other than humans (and I am not proposing the presence of cannibalism), the largest terrestrial mammal was the rat, and pig, chicken and dog, which are known elsewhere in the Pacific, were not present before European contact. Other available animals for subsistence purposes included land crabs, monitor lizards, fruit bats and several species of bird. Shellfish and marine fish were also taken, and remains of these form a major component of the assemblage at Latte Period sites. Stable isotope analysis of human bone samples from Latte Period burials finds that people in the Latte Period generally had a terrestrial plant-based diet, which was supplemented by small amounts of marine protein; on Saipan, compared with Rota and Guam, seaweed and/or sugarcane may have made a significant component to the diet (Ambrose *et al.* 1997). However, studies of samples from the north coast of Rota show that intake of marine elements of diet can vary between individuals from between 10 to 41 per cent, leading to the conclusion that some people had greater access to marine foods (assuming that is what was desired) than others (Pate, Craib and Heathcote 2001).

Although there has been no detailed study to date, the rock-art of the Marianas appears to be standardized in two ways: it normally occurs in caves, and it often consists of stick figures. Such figures have been reported from caves at Inarajan Bay, Talofofo, Ritidian, Mergagan Point and Hinapsu, all on Guam, Laulau on Saipan, and two caves at Aplog on Rota (Thompson 1932). Other motifs, including geometric and turtle images, have been reported. The figures can take the form of painted pictographs or engraved petroglyphs. At Fadian, in Mangilao Municipality of eastern Guam, thirteen pictographs and one petroglyph were recorded as a group creating a panel on a stalagmite within a cave (Highness, Brown and Haun 1992).

Typically, the stick figures are depicted without heads (Henrickson 1968). Scott Russell (1998) proposes that the figures were part of the ritual process of ancestor worship. As the worship of ancestors involved the curation of skulls of deceased relatives (noted in relation to archaeological evidence above), the headless human stick figures may be representations of the same ancestors. There are currently no dates for the rock-art, but many of the caves have evidence of long-term use starting before the Latte Period, and there are a number of examples of burials and modification of cave entrances. Walls at cave entrances may indicate their use for defence or habitation, or restricted access for ritual reasons. Once again, much of this is undated but it definitely includes the Latte Period.

The orthodox view is that there is little reason to believe that the existence of *latte* was anything other than a product of internal cultural development. The fact that some of the items of material culture associated with *latte* sites, such as slingstones and characteristic pottery, appear in the archaeological record during the late Transitional Period would appear to support this view. But other than the *latte* sets themselves, other material elements found for the first time at these sites are *Tridacna* shell adzes, which are ubiquitous at coastal *latte* settlements, shell fishhooks and gorges, pounding stones (pestles) and large basalt mortars. So only slingstones and some elements of the ceramic forms are present prior to the Latte Period. If we add to this the recently arrived rats discussed above and rice which also appears to arrive in the Latte Period and may be associated with the prestigious mortars, then a different picture may begin to emerge.

Commentators for the most part agree that the Latte Period ends with the arrival of Magellan in AD 1521. Although the permanent colonial settlement does not occur for nearly two centuries after this, the appearance of the Spanish expedition ushered in a period that saw visits from people hailing from many parts of the world not previously present in this region. According to an anonymous Genoese pilot, three sailors from the Spanish ships deserted in the Marianas during the visit of Magellan (Lévesque 1992). Hernanado de la Torre reports meeting one of these on Guam in 1526 during the Loaysa expedition; this former member of Magellan's expedition reported that by this time the two other deserters had been killed by islanders (Lévesque 1992). These deserters preceded many others, including beachcombers and missionaries, and prolonged stays for replenishment of Europeans in the Marianas, and their influence is likely to have been more than cultural.

Since the 'fatal impact' scenario constructed by Alan Moorehead (1966) anthropologists and historians have not failed to become aware of the important biological repercussions of colonial contact and there can be no doubt that such consequences were common (e.g., see Larsen and Milner 1994). The actual diseases are not easy to discern, but the point is often made that simple colds and influenza were deadly to islanders never exposed to such infections, along with the other diseases also deadly to Europeans.

We certainly know that the Europeans themselves were not in the best of health when they first encountered Pacific islanders. During the Spanish expedition led by Loaysa in 1526, following in Magellan's wake, the captain died of illness mid-Pacific on 30 July. Elcano, a hero survivor of Magellan's expedition, although already ill, took over command and was dead a few days later on 4 August. That is, the two highest-ranking and supposedly most cosseted members of the crew died of illness only weeks prior to the arrival of their ship in Guam on 4 September. We may wonder what new germs this visit introduced to the Chamorro. Although Urdaneta, a member of the crew, reported that forty men died during the Pacific crossing and this was 'either because of too much work, or of the bad food' (in Lévesque 1992: 456), he also reported that on leaving Guam they captured eleven islanders to stand in for sick crew and before they reached the Philippines another captain, de Salazar, had passed away. There can be no doubt that for the Chamorro the world had changed significantly.

Post-Latte flux

When the British man-of-war *HMS Centurion* commanded by George Anson finally made landfall at Tinian on 27 August 1742, having survived an ill-fated crossing of the Pacific that included the abandonment and scuttling of *HMS Gloucester*, the crew thought they had found paradise. Members of the expedition reported Tinian in terms that would attract the attention of the back-to-nature 'noble savage' philosopher Jean-Jacques Rousseau, who published his *Discourse on the Arts and Sciences* in 1750. Glynn Barratt (1988b: 18) finds:

the accounts of Tinian published by Anson's people were extremely favourable. They painted a beguiling picture of broad lawns and pleasant meadows, spring water, fruit in plenty, and abundant wild stock, and emphasised the speed and thoroughness of the recovery of men weakened by scurvy.

With the advantage of hindsight we should not forget the potential for exaggeration realized by sailors arriving at land. The heightened perceptions excited by the prospect of making landfall, with the anticipation of fresh provisions and other features of reduced privation afforded by a spell in a friendly port, can be identified in the following quote. Here von Kotzebue describes his arrival in the *Riurik* at Guam in 1817 (quoted in Barratt 1984: 19):

The northern reaches of Guam rise perpendicularly from the ocean to a moderate elevation, then run southward in a straight line as far as the eye can see. A splendid forest of various greens covers the upper part of the island, providing the mariner with a delightful sight . . . By 11 a.m. we had reached the northern extremity . . . Checked by the land, the winds died down almost to nothing. An occasional breeze, sufficient to move the ship along a little, carried out from the shore most delightful scents . . . The sailor who has long been at sea and deprived the sight of dry land well knows how to savour such sensations.

However, the chroniclers of Anson's voyage had indeed happened upon a garden island available for their satisfaction. They were greeted at Tinian by a single Spanish sergeant and a small group of Chamorros assigned to cull cattle for the supply of beef to the Spanish garrison on Guam. Apart from the cattle roaming freely they also commented on the wild hogs, citrus fruit, coconuts, breadfruit and wells full of water, all available to them. The island lacked permanent settlement, with the local Chamorros having, along with those on neighbouring islands, been removed to Guam as a result of the Spanish–Chamorro wars following the Spanish annexation of the Marianas in 1668. Accounts provided to Anson's crew by the Chamorros working on Tinian suggest that by the time of their eviction the inhabitants of Tinian were weak and few. An excerpt of an account written by either Reverend Richard Walters or Benjamin Robins (the authorship is disputed) provides an example (quoted in Barratt 1988b: 47):

I must observe, that it is not fifty years since the islands were depopulated. The Indians [i.e. Chamorros] we had in our custody assured us, that formerly the three islands of Tinian, Rota and Guam, were full of inhabitants; and that Tinian alone contained thirty thousand souls: But sickness raging amongst these islands, which destroyed multitudes of people, the Spaniards, to recruit their numbers at Guam, which was greatly diminished by this mortality, ordered all the inhabitants of Tinian thither; where, languishing for their former habitations, and their customary method of life, the greatest part of them in a few years died of grief. Indeed, independent of that attachment which all mankind have ever shown to the places of their birth and bringing up, it should seem, from what has already been said, that there were few countries more worthy to be regretted than this Tinian.

Writing of his experience seventy years after the above account of Tinian, von Kotzebue also appeared to feel the pain of Chamorros through their loss at the hands of the Spanish. Here he talks briefly of Guam's history and reflects, in essentialist, almost Rousseauian terms (quoted in Barratt 1984: 19):

Had I been there in the age when Magellan found these islands, our *Riurik* would already have been encircled by cheerful natives in canoes. The situation was very different for us: for no benign blessings have been spread here by the introduction of Christianity – on the contrary, the entire indigenous people of the Ladrones [Marianas] Islands have been extirpated. It was in vain that we looked around for any sign of canoes, or of men ashore. We might also have been coasting off an uninhabited island. I was much affected by the spectacle, well knowing that at one time these rich valleys had been the home of a nation, passing their days in tranquillity and contentment. Today, only palm groves remained to shelter the graves of those natives, and a deathlike silence reigned.

Although Chamorros did remain, von Kotzebue writes at a time when the late eighteenth-century literature of exploration, especially the passages related to the people of Tahiti, were extremely popular and created in the minds of Europeans the ideal elements of Pacific islands society. The island as wished for was not to be found in Guam, with the longest history of colonial contact in Oceania, and von Kotzebue was apparently bemoaning this.

    There was certainly abundant evidence of previous habitation in the depopulated areas of the Marianas. Anson's chroniclers dubbed Tinian variously an island of 'ruins' or 'ghosts'. In discussing the *latte* structures, which on Tinian include the monumental House of Taga, the Walters–Robins account also relates the view of the captive Chamorros (quoted in Barratt 1988b: 47):

If the account our prisoners gave us of these structures was true, the island must indeed have been extremely populous; for they assured us, that they were the foundations of particular buildings set apart for those Indians only, who had engaged in some religious vow; and monastic institutions are often to be met with in many Pagan nations. However, if these ruins were originally the basis of common dwelling houses of the natives, their numbers must have been considerable; for in many parts of the island they are extremely thick planted, and sufficiently evince the great plenty of former inhabitants.

These postulations in regard to the function of *latte* sets bear striking resemblance to some of the elements of interpretation of contemporary scholars of the structures outlined above. The modern writings are some 250 years younger than those related to the Anson visit, but the commentators from that expedition were themselves writing some 225 years since the arrival of Magellan. By this time Guam had already become a place linked into the economic world system.

On his first visit von Kotzebue had been informed that there were on occasion whole years when no foreign vessels arrived at Guam. Eight years later, in 1825, he found several English and North American ships at anchor in Apra Harbour. The ships turned out to be those of whalers who stopped for replenishment during their forays off the shores of Japan (Barratt 1984). The requirements of these whalers for food and water changed the frequency of foreign visits to many of the islands in the region during the 1820s and 1830s. This is not to say that Guam and the Marianas had been totally isolated in the late eighteenth and early nineteenth centuries. The galleons still arrived in most years, continuing to ply the trans-Pacific route from Mexico to the Philippines until 1811, but others came too.

Adelbert von Chamisso, a German in the company of von Kotzebue in 1817, made the acquaintance of Don Luis de Torres, a long-term resident of Guam who had developed a special interest in the people of the Caroline Islands to the south. While in the Marshall Islands von Chamisso had also developed a strong interest in these islands, having met a man named Kadu from the western Carolines. Von Chamisso (quoted in Barratt 1984: 32–3) reported this encounter on approaching Aur Atoll in the Radak Chain in these terms:

natives came out in their craft to welcome us, coming on board as soon as we dropped anchor. An individual stepped out from among them who was different in several ways . . . This was Kadu, a native of the Ulea [*sic*] group to the south of Guam. He was not a noble birth, but a confidant of his king, named Tua. The latter employed him to carry commissions to various islands, and in the course of these voyages Kadu had become well acquainted with the whole chain of islands with which Ulea traded, right from the Palau Islands in the west to Setoan [*sic*] in the east.

Sharing his knowledge of the Carolinians, de Torres told von Chamisso that a flotilla of people from the Caroline Islands had arrived in 1788 and contacts had been maintained ever since. Barratt (1988a: 23–4) paraphrases the primary sources thus:

a group of Lamotrekians deliberately planned a trading voyage to Guam, not to barter for turmeric, shell belts, and tortoise-plate as formerly, but to obtain iron and iron articles . . . A pilot named Luito led a mainly Lamotrekian [i.e. people from Lamotrek Atoll] flotilla north to Talafofo Bay, on Guam. He knew the route from ancient chant and from traditions he had heard in early manhood. Pleased by the native reappearance, the colonial authorities received Luito and his people kindly. Trade was speedily transacted and, on leaving, the well-rested islanders gave undertakings to return.

According to Barratt (1988a) this interaction had been typical of Carolinian–Chamorro relations that had existed for centuries prior to permanent settlement of the Marianas by the Spanish. Of course, Carolinians would eventually be allowed to settle on the depopulated island of Saipan, becoming the *Refalawasch*, but prior to that there are a couple of reports relating to unsanctioned settlement of an island in the Gani group of the northern Marianas, from quite a different direction.

   Both von Kotzebue and von Chamisso, in their reports of the 1817 visit to Guam, mention the presence of a number of Sandwich Islanders (Hawaiians) on the island (Barratt 1984). Although von Kotzebue's account that I present here differs a little from that of von Chamisso, the basic point I wish to make in regard to continuing fluid boundaries and the potential for further fusion is made in relation to the basic story of both. The account of von Kotzebue (quoted in Barratt 1984: 25) states:

Guam alone, in the whole Marianas chain, is inhabited [*contra* von Chamisso who says that Rota has a permanent village]. North Americans engaged in the fur trade between the North-west Coast of their own continent and Canton some years ago chose Agrigan and Saipan as resting points on their voyage. More than this, they brought several families of Sandwich Islanders with them and left them there, with a view to finding fresh provisions in the future: the Sandwich Islanders were made to till the earth and herd cattle. [On hearing of the enterprise Spanish] soldiers were dispatched who took the wretched natives prisoner and destroyed their plantations. I observed some of these Sandwich Islanders at the Governor's residence. They seem to have reconciled themselves to their fate . . . It recently came to the Governor's hearing that the Americans have attempted another settlement on Agrigan.

In his account, von Chamisso indicates that the Spanish had come to an agreement with the second group of American settlers, allowing them to maintain their settlement as long as they recognized Spanish sovereignty. A year after the visit of the *Riurik*, another Russian vessel, the *Kamchatka*, also called in at Guam. The captain, Vasilii Mikjailovich Golovnin, also provided a report of the two dozen Hawaiians he found there, noting that they were particularly melancholy owing to the lack of their favourite food, taro, which was not available to them in the Marianas (Barratt 1984)!

The southern islands of the Marianas have witnessed significant changes during the twentieth century. Japanese occupation of the islands, apart from Guam, led to industrial sugarcane production that swallowed up the majority of the arable land, and required the construction of supporting infrastructure such as mills, roads and railways. Over half (56 per cent) of the total land area of Tinian was taken into sugarcane production (Donham 1989), and even the available 300 hectares (*c.* 740 acres) of tiny neighbouring Aguiguan was cleared and planted (Butler 1992a). Phosphate deposits located in the hills of Rota added an extra dimension to the exploitation of that island (Peattie 1988). This large-scale exploitation undoubtedly destroyed many archaeological sites, and was compounded by the construction of fortifications and airfields, and the impacts of the American invasion in 1944. Tinian became a virtual, but static, aircraft carrier, with Americans expanding the former Japanese airfields to create, for a brief period, the largest active airfield in the world. Guam was further militarized following the Second World War and much land was grabbed for military use.

Summary

The history of human settlement of the Mariana Islands is one of fluidity and flux. The Early Period settlement is one that illustrates inter-community support and the reliance on sailing abilities to maintain these connections across fluid boundaries and to exploit deep-sea marine resources. It may well be that the communities regularly shifted their settlement sites, and in the process gradually altered pockets of the environment, making them more suitable for future settlement.

During the Intermediate Period it is clear from the ceramics that inter-community links were maintained. Evidence for the exploitation of inland areas of the islands at this time may hint at a broadening of the subsistence base. This use of the inland areas greatly increased during the Transitional Period and new areas, including the island of Aguiguan, may have been permanently settled at this time. The new open bowl and pan ceramics may indicate a greater emphasis on feasting or food preservation, both indicating growing population levels and a probable move to sedentary village patterns. The changes continue to be witnessed on a Marianas-wide basis, indicating continual seafaring. This seafaring ability may have allowed people to collect rice from South-East Asia at the beginning of the Latte Period, or alternatively mariners from outside of the archipelago may have introduced it.

Contacts with rice producing areas, probably the Philippines, must have existed at the beginning of the Latte Period. Do the significant changes in the Latte Period indicate a significant migration of new people, or can the rice, rats, fishhooks, gorges and megaliths be regarded as changes through diffusion and internal innovation? Sarah Nelson (1999), writing of the introduction of rice into Korea some 3000 years prior to the beginning of the Latte Period, considers the link between rice and the rise of megaliths that appear to be roughly contemporary in that peninsula. She finds that the rice probably came from north-east China, along with two new tool types that may be associated with grain harvesting and paddy clearing. On chronological grounds Nelson argues that the megaliths, mostly dolmen types for individual burials, developed only once rice had been established across the majority of the peninsula. At this time the productivity of rice, in the classic argument for agricultural intensification and surplus production, allows for the development of a social elite who were marked out in death by burial under megalithic structures. Thus Nelson rejects an interpretation of the arrival of a new staple, new items of portable material culture and new megalithic architecture as emblematic of the arrival of new people into the region. What is impossible to deny is that such evidence at the very least requires contact with other peoples, the selective borrowing of elements across fluid boundaries allowing the fusion of certain elements into the pre-existing corpus. These elements introduce a state of flux and lead to rapid material change as best identified in megalithic structures, in the Marianas represented by the *latte* sets.

It appears that rice did not replace the subsistence staples in the Mariana Islands and cannot then be considered in the same way that Nelson outlines for Korea. However, rice does appear to become a component of prestige items including mortar stones and differentially sized *latte* sets. The ability of smaller elements of the community to provide for special feasting food may have led to minor ranking developing, with the *latte*, initially constructed for dealing with the rat problem, becoming entwined as a further prestige component within the system.

By the time the Spanish arrived, the people of the Marianas were using all areas of their archipelago and exploiting a variety of resources, including the complex processing of the toxic nuts of the *Cycad* plant. They appear also to have developed an intense reverence for the ancestors, indicated by burial practices and rock-art, and lacked any form of large-scale conflict or warring. Although living in large villages, they maintained their close link with the sea that had existed for over three millennia and were able to amaze the early Spanish visitors, who dubbed the Chamorro seacraft the 'flying proa'.

The Spanish, and subsequent occupations by the Japanese and the Americans, decimated the local population and introduced others, leading to the current situation where the Chamorros are in the minority. However, the Chamorro language continues to be spoken and traditional features of Chamorro life are maintained in an increasingly Americanized environment. Following a break in voyaging between the Marianas and Carolines as a result of the political upheavals of colonial rule, navigational knowledge was maintained and used to cross the fluid boundaries once again in 1969 when Hippour, a navigator from Puluwat Atoll, guided David Lewis' yacht to Saipan, without the aid of modern instruments (Lewis 1994).

In the following chapters it will become clear that the archaeological anthropology of the Mariana Islands is quite distinct, especially in the last 1000 years, from that of the other archipelagos in Micronesia. Because of this difference it may be regarded as reasonable to consider the Marianas an outlier of Micronesia. I will return to this issue in the final chapter.

CHAPTER 6

A SEA OF ISLANDS: PALAU, YAP AND THE CAROLINIAN ATOLLS

The Carolines form a string of islands paralleling and approximately 7 to 9 degrees to the north of the Equator (Fig. 6.1). Covering two time zones, they straddle the Andesite Line, stretching from 132 to 164 degrees longitude. The 3000 kilometres between the Palau Archipelago in the west and the high igneous peaks of Kosrae in the east are broken for the most part by small islets on atoll reefs, and the occasional 'high' island. In fact, most of the Palau group and the island of Kosrae at either end are high islands and, with Pohnpei and those within Chuuk Lagoon, constitute all of the high islands of the group. In this chapter, I will review the archaeology of the western Caroline Islands of the Palau Archipelago, the Southwest Islands (also part of the Republic of Belau), Yap and the atolls of the Caroline chain as a whole.

Palau (Belau)

As noted in chapter 3, linguistically Palau (or Belau) appears to have a distinct history of settlement when compared to elsewhere in Micronesia. In earlier models this history was assumed to be one of the oldest, as a necessary staging point in the 'stepping stone' colonization of the region. As I have mentioned in chapters 4 and 5, this model envisaged the settlement of western Micronesia as a series of moves from the Celebes or Bird's Head of New Guinea areas north through Palau, Yap and finally the Marianas. The zoologist and ethnologist Karl Semper, while *en route* to Palau in 1862, staying there ten months, considered the early ponderings in regard to this model of colonization (1982 [1873]: 17–18):

If Quatrefages' proposed theories about the various migrations of the Polynesian peoples are true, the equatorial countercurrent has played just as important a part in the eastern hemisphere, of course in a different respect, as the Gulf Stream has played in the western hemisphere.

It is known that Carolinians were frequently cast away on the Philippines; each time they reached Samar Island or south Luzon, as a proof that the north equatorial current breaks right at the barrier of the Philippines. On the contrary, no Filipinos appear to have reached the Palau Islands, while people from the Celebes Islands and islands in the Celebes Strait have. According to Johnson's testimony, it was in 1859 or 1860 that a sailless boat with six passengers was

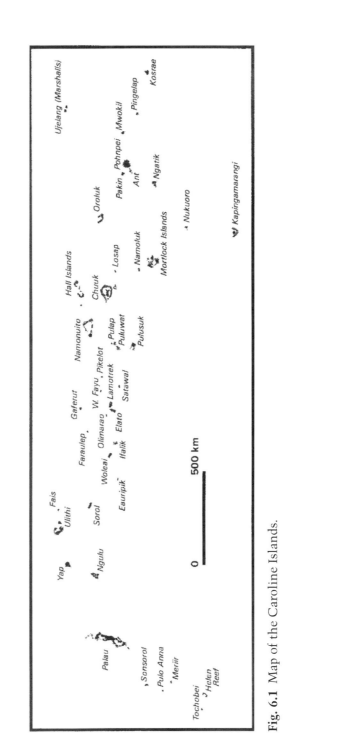

Fig. 6.1 Map of the Caroline Islands.

driven to the north-west side of Palau . . . The six maintained they had left
Salibago Island three days before . . . Also at the time of the well-known Captain
Wilson – whose account of the shipwreck of the *Antilope* [*Antelope*] and of the
amiable people of Palau awakened a universal sympathetic interest – came in
touch with these people, he found a Malayan from an island near the Celebes,
who had been driven to Palau by the westerly current.

Indeed George Keate's (1789) account of the 1783 wreck of Wilson's East India
Company packet, the *Antelope*, shows that without the assistance of the
'Malay', cross-cultural communication would have been far more difficult, as
this man was able to act as intermediary. In regard to evidence of previous
contact, the fact that the 'king' of Koror, Ibedul (Keate's Abbé Thulle), arrived
with an iron hatchet, clearly a prestige item, draped over his shoulder, is also
telling. Palau had seen passing contact with Europeans since the early days of
Spanish presence, but the crash landing of Wilson and his men in their alien
craft ushered in major changes in the sociopolitical dynamics of the archipelago,
of which Ibedul and his people initially appeared to be the major beneficiaries.

   Nicholas Thomas (2000; see also Martin 1980) suggests that the popularity
of Keate's *Account of the Pelew Islands*, alluded to in Semper's 'well-known
Captain Wilson' phrase above, was in providing a reassurance in Europe that
friendly cross-cultural relations with islanders in the Pacific could still be possible less than a decade after the shocking news of the death of Captain Cook
in Hawaii. Thomas also finds that Ibedul cleverly manipulated Wilson into
providing military support for his military campaigns using European men and
weapons that placed Ibedul's *beluu* in the ascendancy.

   The primary *beluu* of contact period Palau were the main polities that later
became known as 'districts' and 'states' (Reed Smith 1997). Each of the fifteen
or so had a chief, although there were two main confederacies, one headed by
the Ibedul's *beluu* Koror in the south and the other rallying around Melekeok
in the north. The chance event that led Wilson to be under the influence of
Koror provided the opportunity to monopolize trade, including the protection
of English warships if required, for at least eighty years. Semper (1982 [1873]:
184), who spent most of his time in a *beluu* of the northern confederacy, could
not disguise his surprise at the material difference he witnessed on his first
visit to Koror:

We soon reached Aidil, Ebadul's [Ibedul's] house. The path ascended the hill
steeply with a few curves. It was well maintained. Everywhere there were traces
of Corore's [Koror's] extensive trade. Whenever I looked into houses along the
path, I noticed a number of chests and large cooking pots, all kinds of European
vessels, knives and forks in profusion, and even porcelain plates . . . numerous
turkeys and geese ran about in the village.

Once in the house of the Ibedul, Semper was shown another element of Western
influence, a carefully curated seventy-year-old copy of Keate's *Account of
the Pelew Islands*, sent shortly after its publication. Semper notes with great

sensitivity the importance placed on this volume, particularly on the illustrations of the people now passed away. Here, of course, is a very early example of a publication being sent to the subject community and it playing an important social role, something that ethnographers have so often been accused of not doing. I will return to issues related to the history and ethnography of Palau at the end of this section, but first I will introduce local understandings of the origin of the islands and people and then describe the archaeology.

DeVerne Reed Smith (1997) makes the important point that the social and political organization of Palau in the historical past can be seen in the mythology of an earlier time. The geography, the hierarchies of *beluu* and villages among other things can be traced to the origin myths. In general the stories of origin have three phases, beginning with the creation of the archipelago as found today, followed by a flood which removes the first people who had become bad, and the repopulation through the single survivor, Milad. Richard Parmentier (1987) in his historical ethnography *The Sacred Remains* provides the detail of these origin stories from elders in Ngeremlengui district on the west coast of Babeldaob, the largest island in the archipelago, but Reed Smith (1983: 10) provides a useful brief synopsis of the first phase of island building:

Uab was a child, born in Angaur, who was greedy and ate too much food. He grew into a giant who demanded that people feed him. Like all greedy and selfish people, Uab had a mean temper. Fearing Uab might destroy their gardens and trees, or harm their children, the people set him afire. Uab kicked mightily, so hard that he kicked himself into many pieces, large and small. The pieces scattered far and near, and they settled into the ocean as islands. Many people went to live on these islands, saying 'We fed Uab – now let him feed us.' Uab's head is one part of Ngarchelong (Babeldaob Island), and the people who live there talk too much. Peleliu is part of his legs, and for that reason it is rocky and rugged. Other people say that Aimeliik is formed of Uab's legs, pulled up and kicking in anger. The large island of Babeldaob is the trunk of Uab's body. The people of Ngiwal live in the middle of his stomach, and they eat seven times a day. Melekeok is Uab's navel. The group that holds the chiefly title of Reklai has its home in Melekeok, and its name is said to mean 'umbilical cord'.

Until recently the early history as derived from archaeology has proved elusive. Japanese anthropologists, prior to the Second World War (e.g., Hijikata 1956), started small-scale archaeological investigations in the archipelago, but it was Douglas Osborne, commencing in the 1950s, who described the variety of archaeological remains (1966; 1979). In the 1970s and 1980s, excavation and survey campaigns were mounted under the direction of Jun Takayama (1979; Takayama and Takasugi 1978; Takayama, Intoh and Takasugi 1980) and Laurie Lucking (1984). During the 1980s, archaeologists (most under the supervision of George Gumerman from the University of Southern Illinois) clarified aspects of the last two millennia, but did not find evidence of the expected greater antiquity of human settlement (e.g., Gumerman, Snyder and Masse 1981; Masse and Snyder 1982; Carucci 1984; 1992; Masse, Snyder and Gumerman 1984; Snyder 1985; 1989; Masse 1989; Snyder and Butler 1997).

The archaeological evidence from the main island group of Palau comes from two geologically distinct areas (Fig. 6.2). In the south are the raised limestone islands of Angaur and Peleliu and between them and the mixed geology islands beyond are the stunning and rugged coralline islands known locally as the 'Rock Islands'. While Angaur and Peleliu have resident populations in the present day, the Rock Islands are largely uninhabited and are difficult of access, with steep cliffs that are often undercut close to sea level, providing the islands with a mushroom shaped profile with a bulbous top standing on a narrower waist. To the north of the limestone islands are islands, including Koror, that are of mixed geologic origin. The northern group includes the large island of Babeldaob which, with an area of 363 square kilometres, constitutes 75 per cent of the archipelago. The interior of Babeldaob rises to an elevation of 120 metres, with rolling hills descending to mangrove swamps on the coast. North of Babeldaob is the atoll of Kayangel.

On the northern islands there are substantial terraced hillsides constructed on a monumental scale (Fig. 6.3). These terraces were subject to excavation by Osborne (1966; 1979), and later by Lucking (1984) for her doctoral research. The conclusion of these investigators was that they served a dual function for both agriculture and defence between 1500 and 700 years ago. In many cases, steep terraces completely cover hillsides and often end in a high-sided 'crown' at the peak. Lucking later played down the defence attribute, by noting that many of the presumed ditches and 'footcatchers' can be bypassed, and in some instances actually aid ascent to the summit (Lucking and Parmentier 1990).

It has become increasingly clear (e.g. Ito 1998) that terracing and summit modification have transformed large areas of the northern islands into sculpted landscapes, and indicate considerable effort employed in modifying the island environment. Gumerman (1986) proposed that the terraces indicate a dense population that was reaching the limits of its carrying capacity. The monumental scale of construction certainly indicated that a substantial labour force was available in this period. But the archaeology at the time was not able to show a direct relationship between settlement sites and the terraces. Pottery recovered from the construction fill of the terraces did not appear to relate to actual settlement on the terraces. Investigation of the Rock Islands appeared to provide partial clarification of the settlement pattern at the time the terraces were in use.

The Rock Islands consist of more than 200 raised limestone islands ranging in elevation from only a few metres to over 200 metres above sea level. Aerial photographs of these islands provide some of the classic glossy magazine images of tropical islands. The interiors are densely vegetated, they have no historically recorded permanent human settlement, their rock surfaces are uneven and rugged, and water is restricted to the brackish lakes that are hidden

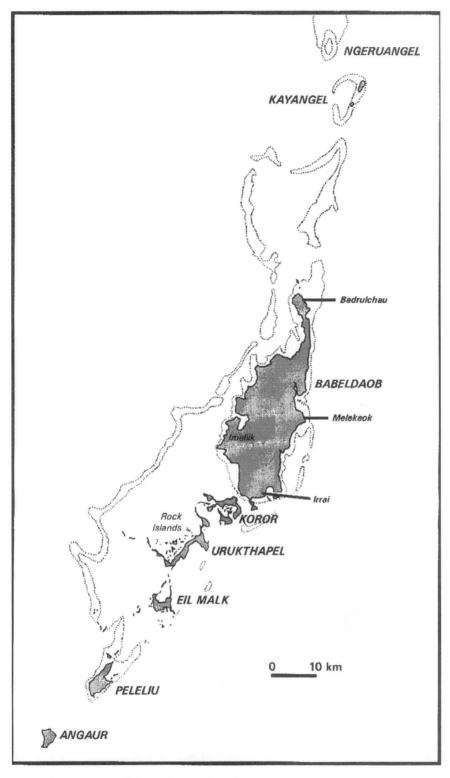

Fig. 6.2 Map of the Palau Archipelago.

Fig. 6.3 The monumental terraces of Imelik on Babeldaob Island, Republic of Belau. The landscape of Babeldaob and neighbouring islands was sculpted in spectacular fashion over a period of 1000 years, finishing approximately 800 years ago.

within the interior of the islands. Many of these lakes have been isolated long enough to allow the evolution of unique creatures such as the non-stinging sun-following jellyfish of Eil Malk.

Although the Rock Islands may appear in the present as an unlikely environment for human habitation, there is evidence of long-term settlement that corresponds with information from the Pacific as a whole, that these seafaring people have visited virtually every piece of dry land to be found. The use of these islands, as derived from the excavation of middens, is dated by Bruce Masse (1990) to between 1350 and 350 years ago. The midden contents indicate that the inhabitants of the Rock Islands relied on marine resources (Masse, Snyder and Gumerman 1984) and provide evidence for the over-harvesting of specific molluscan species (Carucci 1992).

Further evidence of human occupation, although of more limited duration, is provided by at least eleven village sites dated to between 800 and 550 years ago (Masse, Snyder and Gumerman 1984; Masse 1990). That these villages are in many cases generally contemporaneous with each other is indicated by linking stone paths (Gumerman 1986). The location of these settlements in the Rock Islands, on limestone ridges, and with walls at points of access to a number of the villages, makes clear that limiting access to them was a significant consideration in their location. There is much still to be learned about these sites, but their apparent overlapping contemporaneity with the terraces of Babeldaob has been seriously brought into question by more recent investigations.

Following the signing of the Compact Agreement in 1994, major US investment in developing the infrastructure of Babeldaob has required extensive archaeological mitigation projects (e.g., Wickler 1994; Beardsley 1996; Wickler *et al.* 1997; 1998; Liston, Kaschko and Welch 1998; Liston, Tuggle *et al.* 1998; Liston *et al.* 1998; Liston 1999). Over seventy new radiocarbon dates have been processed and many areas surveyed in detail for the first time. Excavations and coring for palaeoenvironmental samples have also been a major feature of these projects. These have led not only to a reassessment of the earliest colonization date of Palau, as discussed in chapter 4, but to a new and evolving chronology for the major features in the archaeology of the northern islands of Palau.

Archaeologists working for the International Archaeological Research Institute, Inc. have provided an outline of the chronology based on their most recent research and dates. Following the initial human settlement of Palau dating somewhere between 4500 and 3500 years ago, the next earliest artefactual evidence has been derived from a cave on Koror. Here, on a limestone ridge that leads south from the volcanic core of Koror Island, are located a number of caves, one of which has been investigated and found to contain inhumations and apparently related ceramics. The ceramics are Painted Ware and have a single associated radiocarbon date of approximately 2700 years ago (Beardsley and Basilius 1998). A few Painted Ware bowls had been reported from elsewhere in Palau (Osborne 1979), but are now lost, and Peter Bellwood (personal communication) has observed that they bear a striking resemblance to ceramics of a similar date in Taiwan. However, painted ceramics have been recovered from burial pits in Babeldaob and are dated to between approximately 2000 and 1500 years old. These ceramics may be tantalizing but inconclusive evidence of distant contacts.

At about 2500 to 1500 years ago, thin black ceramics with black paste seem to come into common usage, and are also associated with deep-ditched hilltop enclosures (Welch 1998b; Wickler 1998a; in press). The painted ware and black ceramics have added new dimensions to the Palauan ceramic sequence that had previously frustrated attempts at seriation (Snyder 1989) and chemical analysis (Pavlish *et al.* 1986).

Hilltop enclosures, of which two are now known in Melekeok State of Babeldaob Island, have not previously been identified outside the 'crown and brim' summits of the terrace systems. One of the sites was found to be 100 metres in diameter, enclosing an area of approximately 1 hectare. The ditch was excavated and found to be substantial, with a depth of 7 metres (Welch 1998b). These enclosures were clearly designed to produce a definite barrier that made a distinction between the area inside and that outside, and linear ditches, apparently related, have been found crossing the ridges approaching the bounded summits, further defining the upland space. By naming these enclosures 'ring forts' Welch has interpreted these as defensive sites. Such a view is supported by the many 'forts' that have been identified elsewhere in Oceania. In Micronesia, though, hilltops have been identified as sacred space, and it should be kept in mind that the enclosures may relate more to this than to warfare (Rainbird 1996).

The earth-altering activities of the islanders indicated by the hilltop enclosures appear to presage the terracing which apparently begins during the period in which hilltop ring-ditch enclosures were still being used. Steve Wickler (in press) proposes that construction of terraces, with multiple uses in agriculture, burial, boundary marking, defence, ceremony, social display and as house platforms, begins around 2000 years ago. From about 1800 to 800 years ago Wickler argues as the principal period of terrace construction. This is *contra* Jolie Liston (1999) who agrees with the end point but prefers an earlier start, some 2200 years ago for the main period of terrace construction.

These tentative sequences can be seen as deceptively simple in view of the enormous undertaking and multiple uses that these terraces and transformation of the landscape actually represent. The earlier simple functional models of agriculture and/or defence have been replaced by the realization of the complex use and symbolic potential of such undertakings: these earthworks must surely reflect deeper early Palauan perspectives about landscape and experience. I have discussed this issue in relation to Pierre Bourdieu's concept of *habitus*, and how this unique manifestation of monumental terraces in Micronesia must reflect distinctly different histories and experiences of the terrace-building Palauans, compared with the other high island communities of the Caroline Islands (Rainbird 1995b; 1999b) where relation to landscape was apparently quite different. Felicia Beardsley (1998) has given preliminary consideration to the terraces in relation to the architecture of symbolic space. Contemporary local understandings relate the terraces to the Story of Milad, where the land was flooded by the gods, with only Milad surviving, who gave birth to one girl and three sons who became the cornerstones of a new Palauan population (Lucking and Parmentier 1990).

Wickler (in press) has proposed that the construction of the terraces had a great deal to do with competitive emulation in developing power relations between neighbouring polities. Of course, although perhaps an extreme example, but one worked out through local understandings, the changes in sociopolitical organization and archipelago-wide hierarchies caused by the arrival of the *Antelope* represent only one episode of flux in what undoubtedly was a changing and transforming system. DeVerne Reed Smith (1983: 35) in reviewing Palauan social organization is keen to make the point that it 'was never static'.

In his tentative sequence, Wickler (1998a; 1998b) proposes that terrace construction and traditional use stops, to be replaced by formal nucleated villages at around 800 years ago. It is only at this time that the villages of the Rock

Islands are being constructed, and thus the new dates upset the notion of contemporaneous use of these villages and the terraces. However, on Babeldaob,
direct evidence for village structures has not been dated to before 550 years
ago, although apparent nucleation at these sites does appear to begin 800 years
ago. Lucking confirmed that the construction and use of the abandoned village of Uluang dated to after the abandonment of what was supposed to be an
agricultural use for terraces, on which the buildings were located (Lucking and
Parmentier 1990). Nevertheless, the date of 550 years ago for the construction
of formal village structures is a century or so earlier than previous estimates.

   The village sites were the focus of settlement in Palau until early in the
twentieth century. They typically contained several *bai* (men's or community
houses) adjacent to or behind large platforms, which are connected to the rest of
the village by stone-paved pathways (Fig. 6.4). These villages, including houses
on smaller stone platforms, are usually situated a little above the shoreline,
with easy access to a canoe dock at the shore. Directly contradicting a number
of previous commentators, Wickler (1998b) has found that the villages are commonly found to be built on terraces. It should not be thought that terraces are
abandoned completely after 800 years ago; it is only that their construction is
severely reduced, and Wickler (in press) argues that the sociopolitical role that
the terraces had in inter-district power struggles was replaced by the prestige
of village construction. The terraces were built upon, the crowns and ditches
continued to be used for defended look-out posts, and potentially ceremonial
and other social activities were continued in these social landscapes, but the
memory of them as humanly constructed soon began to wane. In villages and
across the landscape, structures in stone were emerging and the power of stone
should not be underestimated, as Reed Smith (1997: 10–11) confirms:

A traditional *beluu* constructed impressive stone complexes, with stone paths
and stone backrests for *rubak* [high-ranking people] along the paths. A *bai*
would have a stone platform and a stone outdoor meeting place . . . Many
beluu had stone platforms at *beluu* entries or near *bai* on which to display
trophy heads; most *beluu* have a set of stones that are significant gods or spirits
that can act upon human behaviour. Stones marked the entries and exits to a
beluu, and the stairs along a path ascending to the traditional residences on
the hillside (for defensive purposes) were not only named but often stones of
special historic significance.

Since the 1980s, oral history projects instigated, and in many cases conducted,
by local people have sought to record Palauan traditions. Many of the stories
relate to the traditional villages, many now abandoned, four of which formed
the 'corner stones' (children of Milad – Palauan notions of matrilineality are
of course linked to this, see Force and Force 1972; Rainbird 2001a) of Palauan
politics and society. As expressed in these oral histories, the idealized notion of
Palauan society and politics is one of symmetry, a symmetry that is purported
to exist in the material remains of the abandoned traditional villages. Rita

Fig. 6.4 The *bai* in the village of Irrai, Babeldaob Island, Republic of Belau. Several *bai* meeting houses often formed the focus of 'traditional' village settlement in the Palau Archipelago until the early twentieth century. As in this case, they were often painted with images from Palauan stories. The traditional village appears to have become the standard settlement pattern for Palauans around 550 years ago.

Olsudong (1995; and later Wickler 1998c) has assessed the local claims that the villages were organized with a *bai* central and the ranked chiefs' houses (of which there were usually ten in each village) positioned with alternately ranked chiefs living on either side, that is, five chief's residences on each side of the *bai*. The studies have shown that this is an idealized model that appears not to have been rigidly enforced. Further testing of the friction between the oral history and the material remains has highlighted other discrepancies. Olsudong (1998) found from interviews that there were certain conventions that needed to be met in the construction of stone platforms to support buildings. One such prescription stated that to avoid bad omens 'the sun must not cross the width of a *bai*'. To avoid this situation it would be expected that the long axis of *bai* platforms would be east–west, but Olsudong found that an equal number of platforms from archaeological sites were orientated north–south.

Although work with oral historians is useful to develop questions for archaeological analysis, such discrepancies serve to highlight a problem with the archaeology. Improved immeasurably in recent years, the current status of archaeological knowledge of village sites still means that there is poor chronological control, and an assumption that all villages, sites and stone plat-forms are generally contemporary (Wickler 1998c). What the archaeology does indicate is that these villages were occupied for at least 400 to 500 years, and there should be no expectation that they remained the same over that period. Perhaps an indication of this is the local perception that the villages, although now for the most part abandoned, remain very important to Palauan people, who trace their ancestry back to particular villages and stone house platforms, that have often formed repositories for dead kin. As Reed Smith (1997: 1) notes: 'ancestors buried in house platforms still influence the living'.

The direct evidence for subsistence practices indicates a typical Micronesian reliance on marine fauna and terrestrial flora, with one unusual excep-tion. Mounting archaeological evidence indicates that pig was present in the archipelago before European contact, and possibly for a number of centuries be-tween approximately 1250 to 500 years ago (Osborne 1979; Masse and Snyder 1982; Masse, Snyder and Gumerman 1984; Masse 1990; Wickler 1998b). There is no record of the presence of pig in Palau at the time of European contact (Intoh 1986), and apart from the examples excavated on Fais (see chapter 4 and below), these are the only prehistoric specimens known in Micronesia. Patrick Kirch (2000) has discussed the issue of local extirpation of pig elsewhere in Oceania and finds that they become unsustainable in relation to four variables: small island size and relative isolation, high human population density, inten-sive resource competition, and internal social strife and warfare. These factors, according to Kirch, lead humans and pigs into direct competition for resources and inevitably the pigs are removed. However, only the last variable of social strife and warfare can be attested for Palau and thus Kirch's model of 'trophic competition' does not appear able to explain the demise of pigs there. The ques-tion is left begging as to why pigs survived for 750 years and were then allowed to die out.

Although stone adzes have been collected from Palauan archaeological sites, Craib (1977) has noted the predominance of shell adzes manufactured from the *Terebra* shell, rather than from the ubiquitous giant *Tridacna* clam that is more typical of the rest of the region. In fact, *Terebra* shell adzes are consid-ered to have appeared relatively late (second millennium AD) in most of the Carolines and Marshalls (e.g., Ayres 1993). The same is also true of the distinc-tive beaked adzes that are relatively common on Palau, but rare elsewhere in the region (Craib 1977). These artefacts have some bearing on issues of con-tact and communication in the region as a whole and I discuss these further in chapter 9.

Present-day men's houses, and those recorded directly after European contact, are well known for their painted decoration. The *bai* paintings are figurative and often illustrate stories from Palauan history and myth. The carved Palauan storyboards, that are popular souvenirs of the islands for tourists, maintain elements of this distinctive art style (Jernigan 1973; Nero 1999). Other Palauan images have been recorded in the form of parietal art at six locations in the archipelago. This rock-art is painted and at five sites is produced from red ferrous oxide while the other is white ochre (McKnight 1964; cf. Schmidt 1974 who states that all the pictographs are red). The images at these sites, located on the walls of rock shelters and often difficult of access, bear no resemblance to the paintings found at the men's houses and consist mostly of geometric shapes, hand prints and highly stylized figures.

The general conclusion is that the rock-art is of ancient origin, and the closest similarities have been found with images recorded in eastern Indonesia (West Papua) (Gregory and Osborne 1979). These sites, in the Bird's Head and MacCluer Gulf areas for the most part, are similarly located to the Palauan ones, being in coastal rock shelters that are relatively difficult of access (Schmidt 1974). A common element in Palau rock-art is the four-pointed star (Simmons 1970), and although not obviously related, comparison has been made with the enveloped cross image typical of Melanesia; this form is also found in Micronesia in Pohnpei (see chapter 7). The four-pointed star is not found in the east Indonesian corpus.

Some features unique to Micronesia are found in Palau. Monolithic stone carvings of human faces, some over 2.5 metres in height (Hijikata 1956; Osborne 1979; Morgan 1988), are more reminiscent of Oceania with the carvings of the Marquesas or Rapa Nui (Easter Island), than of anything found in Micronesia. These carved stones are often associated with the later villages, and Jo Anne Van Tilburg (1991) identifies similarities with the *bai* paintings discussed above, but carved stone heads are also found at the enigmatic site of Badrulchau. In his visit of 1876, the Russian naturalist and ethnographer Nikolai Miklouho-Maclay, described by Tolstoy as 'the first to prove indubitably by experience that man was the same everywhere' (see Stocking 1991), found that the carved heads are related to *chelid*, which is hard to define, but can loosely be translated as a spiritual thing. Miklouho-Maclay describes the local understanding of these carvings (Parmentier and Kopnina-Geyer 1996: 87):

There are a few stone-chelid in the archipelago. In Melekeok I have heard of three of them. One is called *Mengachui*: it has a human face and eats the hair of passing women if their hair is not properly combed. *Olekeok*, which is located near the rubak's meeting house inside the village, has a habit of rising out of the ground when the *cheldebechel* [men's club] of Melekeok takes an enemy head, before people in the village find out about it. *Odalemelech*, the third stone-chelid, also called chelid klou-klou (big-big chelid), is not described as anything particularly remarkable. Here we have an example of how the stages of religious development are intertwined with each other. Together with shamanism there are ancestral cults, close to idol worship. The stone-chelid . . . lacks only a temple and fulltime worshippers around it to be called an idol in the full sense of the word.

Badrulchau, a site that has so far defied convincing interpretation, is located at the northern end of Babeldaob. The site consists of rows of andesite monoliths with grooves pecked in their tops, as if to hold a wooden beam. Osborne (1966; 1979) conducted excavations, but was unable to provide a date for the set. A number of scholars believe that the stones were the supports for a large community structure, perhaps the precursor to the *bai* (Osborne 1979; Masse, Gumerman and Snyder 1984; Morgan 1988). Bellwood (1978) has commented on a slight similarity with the *latte* stone structures of the Mariana Islands. Osborne (1980) noted another set of stone uprights at the southern end of Babeldaob, although these were apparently not identified in a more recent survey of the area (Snyder and Butler 1997).

Another interesting item of the Palauan material culture repertoire, although partly shared with Yap, is the presence of non-indigenous glass beads and bracelet fragments (Kubary 1895; Ritzenthaler 1954; Osborne 1966; Masse 1990). These beads are regarded as having high value, and their use in exchange events has led some scholars to regard them as a form of currency or money. Inez de Beauclair (1963) finds that they are also present on Yap and proposes that they may have arrived in Palau from there although they are not indigenous to Yap, and, along with Palau, the presence of the glass valuables forms the north-eastern edge of the larger 'Indonesian bead area'. Similar beads have been found in the Philippines in graves dating between 800 and 400 years ago (Force 1959), but they appear in the islands of South-East Asia at around 2000 years ago (Swadling 1996). As with rice in the Marianas, the beads of Palau and Yap may indicate contact with South-East Asia a long time after initial settlement of western Micronesia.

During the Japanese colonial period Palau, particularly Koror, which became dubbed 'Little Tokyo', was heavily developed with Japanese military and civilian infrastructure. Vestiges of this are still to be seen today, but the consequent defensive structures and violent invasion by the Americans as they island-hopped towards Japan in the final stages of World War II, has led to the disturbance of earlier archaeological deposits. On Peleliu, the site of a bloody US invasion, Beardsley (1997) found shell midden deposits dating to between approximately 950 and 500 years ago, but evidence of the war in the form of bomb craters and post-war clean-up features constituted ubiquitous elements of the archaeological record. In assessing cave sites for fossil and archaeological deposits Gregory Pregill and David Steadman (2000) found that activities associated with the use of caves in World War II had destroyed the potential of caves that otherwise might have been regarded as promising for preserved deposits.

The Southwest Islands

In Robert Johannes' (1981) excellent ethnography of fishing in Palau, *Words of the Lagoon*, a chapter co-authored with Peter Black (Johannes and Black 1981) provides an introduction to the islands south of Palau, known as the Southwest Islands (Fig. 6.1). The local language is Chuukic, and extends the distribution of that central Carolinian dialect almost to Indonesia, bypassing Palau. The five islands extend from north to south over a distance of nearly 200 kilometres, but collectively they maintain a culture known as Sonsorolese after the north-ernmost island, Sonsorol. The other islands are Pulo Anna, Meriir, Fana and Tochobei (Tobi). Another member of this group is Helen Reef (or Atoll) but this is composed only of a recently formed sand bar, although traditionally Tochobeians sailed there to collect the large *Tridacna* clams for raw ma-terials and food (Hunter-Anderson 2000). This group has long held a fas-cination for Pacific archaeologists as possible components in the chain of 'stepping stones' allowing island colonization. Because of this notion of step-ping stones, both for initial colonization and for later long-distance contacts, it has been hoped that the archaeological remains would include evidence of such events.

Osborne (1966) conducted limited archaeological survey in the group in 1954, reporting some mounds, platforms and pathways. Most recently, in a brief sur-vey including limited excavation on the islands, Hunter-Anderson (2000) found archaeological remains on all of the Southwest Islands except Helen Reef, which she did not visit. She recorded residential mounds on Tochobei, Meriir and Pulo Anna. Some mounds were found in association with shell artefacts and fish and turtle bones. A number of single dates from a variety of materials and various archaeological deposits are generally unreliable, but indicate that some of these features have an antiquity of at least 300 years. Ceramics of Palauan style were observed on Tochobei and Fana and indicate links with that archipelago.

The low coralline limestone nature of the Southwest Islands with fringing reefs rather than lagoons meant that fishing was of the deep ocean. Taro was undoubtedly a major staple, but phosphate mining on Tochobei and Sonsorol during the German and Japanese colonial period removed large portions of the central areas of the islands where taro pits might be expected to have been placed. People inhabiting these islands are by necessity extremely adept sea-farers. An indication of the Sonsorolese familiarity with the sea is provided by Johannes (1981) in relation to one of the methods used to catch sharks. A shark was attracted by rattling a line of shells under the water next to the boat, and when alongside a noose was placed over its head and it was cap-tured once this caught behind the gills. Further archaeological study may find evidence of contacts in directions other than that of Palau; however, items collected from elsewhere may not have stayed long in the possession of the Sonsorolese as they may have passed along the chain in exchange for foreign fruits. Hunter-Anderson (2000: 37–8) in considering further contacts states: 'A prehistory of contacts between the islands of Indonesia and Tobi [Tochobei], and possibly other islands in the south-west group, is indicated by linguistics, oral history and marriage patterns, as well as physical characteristics of the people.' Although Hunter-Anderson (2000) found none of the mounds typical of Tochobei on Sonsorol, believing that Japanese industrial activities may have been responsible for their removal, she was able to record a stone setting, previously recorded as Osborne's Site 1, locally regarded as the site where a chiefly meeting house had once stood. The low perimeter wall appears ovoid in plan and some 25 metres across its longest axis. A small test pit within the enclosure found that it had a coral rubble floor some 40 centimetres in depth, and directly below this, on top of sand, a layer of turtle and fish bones, charcoal and dark sand mixed with burnt pieces of coral. A radiocarbon date from this layer gave a modern date. Along the perimeter wall was a head carved from phosphate stone, and, taken with the 'monkey-man' figure from Tochobei mentioned in chapter 2, this is further evidence of the carving tradition in the Southwest Islands.

Tochobei became a place exoticized as one of fear amongst seafarers and Americans in the nineteenth century (Buschmann 1996). The *Mentor*, a New Bedford whaler under the command of Edward C. Barnard, passed through the Atlantic and Indian oceans and in the chase for whale oil entered the Pacific. Following a storm the ship foundered on the reefs north of Babeldaob in the Palau islands during May 1832. In the following December, seven of the surviving crew and three Palauans set out in the ship's boat and a vessel in local style constructed in Babeldaob, in an attempt to reach the ports of the Philippines or Celebes. They became hopelessly lost in storms and eventually washed up on Tochobei. There are two eyewitness accounts in regard to the treatment of these castaways, one by the ship's captain, Barnard (Martin 1980), and the other by Horace Holden, a crew member (Holden 1975 [1836]).

The accounts concur that from the moment of contact the castaways were roughly treated, became enslaved by individual islanders and were forced to exist on meager rations. Two of the party, Barnard and Rollins, managed to escape within two months, but over a two-year period the rest perished through starvation or execution, leaving only Holden and Nute to find passage in November 1834, and the last surviving Palauan was not repatriated until December 1835. The deprivations the survivors described became further embellished in the popular press, and Tochobeians became known as cannibals (Huntress 1975). The situation that led to the apparent poor treatment of the shipwrecked crew is difficult to tease out from the available texts, but it can certainly be assumed that the castaways were in a particularly poor state of mind, having presumably thought that on their departure from Palau they were finally on their way home and relieved to be leaving a potentially dangerous political situation on that island. What is interesting to note is that over seventy years later the German *Südsee-Expedition* was met with antagonism and resistance from some of the non-secular members of the society, 'shamans' in particular (Buschmann 1996).

Such a problem of representation was not an issue for all of the Southwest Islands. Alfred Tetens (1958), in stopping at Sonsorol in late 1865 or early 1866, although wary at first, found an unprecedented welcome in which he was carried to the shore on paddles, was treated to dances in the village and left replenished with fruits and fish.

Beyond the Southwest Islands, to the south-east of Tochobei and outside of the bounds of what is normally regarded as Micronesia, is the atoll of Mapia, located off the north coast of the island of New Guinea and within Indonesia. Mapia, along with a number of other small islands off the north New Guinea coast, is reported to have had a Micronesian population when first recorded by Europeans (de Beauclair 1963). The anthropologist William Lessa (1978) has studied the historical journals to assess the affinities of the Mapia islanders in relation to physical appearance and material culture, dating prior to the 1859 introduction of plantation workers from Yap and elsewhere. Lessa finds that although there are some discrepancies, and contacts must have been maintained with other areas, the closest similarities with the original inhabitants of Mapia appear to be with the Sonsorolese. These islands would have been in good locations to link between island South-East Asian and Melanesian trade and exchange systems.

The other islands often claimed to have a certain Micronesian-ness about their inhabitants are the Western Islands of the Manus District of Papua New Guinea. The main Western Islands are Hermit, Wuvulu (Maty), Aua and the Ninigo Group. In assessing the affiliations of Wuvulu islanders through material culture collections and in the work of others, Edge-Partington (1896) was able to report that these people were not Melanesians, but 'not descendants but brothers of the Micronesians'. By 1925, and based on fieldwork and the notes from Parkinson's 1899 visit, George Lane Fox Pitt-Rivers (1925: 428) was able to state:

The natives of Aua and Wuwuloo [Wuvulu] are usually referred to as Micronesians. Parkinson, in using that term, describes them as a branch of the Malayo-Polynesian race. In their folk-lore they have apparently no tradition of any migration nor of any former racial home which might suggest that they migrated south from Micronesia.

Pitt-Rivers (1925: 426) was not alone in imagining that here, in Aua Island, he 'had an opportunity of studying a highly developed Stone-Age culture, as yet but slightly contaminated by direct contact with Europeans'. But there are indications that he, along with the others espousing such views, was wrong. The German entrepreneur Tetens (1958: 67) records how in the 1860s he visited the Western Islands 'after taking on one hundred [Yapese] with their twenty-five canoes'. They went in order to collect *bêche de mer* and large pearl shells, setting up a settlement on land and getting into violent confrontation with the locals. Tetens provides little in the way of details, but his account provides a warning in regard to the movement of island people in crossing fluid boundaries that may have been becoming quite different as world system economics continued to shrink the globe, a world that ethnographers such as Pitt-Rivers was attempting to attend to by finding the pristine; here as elsewhere where ethnographers have tried to claim such things, they are too late, if indeed what they were searching for ever existed at all. However, the history of these communities, like those of Mapia, remains poorly known outside of the islands at present.

Ngulu

Ngulu is an atoll situated between the islands of Palau and Yap and slightly east of a direct line between them (Fig. 6.1). It is endowed with an extensive and productive lagoon, but a habitable land area of only approximately 0.43 square kilometres. The highest point is 2.64 metres above sea level. Given the location of Ngulu between the two major high islands of the western Carolines, Jun Takayama and Michiko Intoh thought that its archaeology might yield information as to possible contacts between the people of the larger islands. During 1980 they conducted excavations and survey on the atoll islands (Intoh 1981; Takayama 1982). Intoh (1981) reports that the survey of the only currently inhabited island in the group revealed thirteen coral house platforms built in the hexagonal-plan style typical of Yap. The platforms raised the wooden superstructures approximately 60 centimetres off the ground. Other platforms of slightly different construction, in that the coral blocks only lined the platform while retaining the same hexagonal shape, were found abandoned, suggesting a diachronic change in the style of platform architecture.

Petrological analysis of pottery sherds recovered confirmed the presence of both Yapese and Palauan wares on Ngulu (Dickinson 1982). Pottery from Palau was rare in comparison to that from Yap. More recently Intoh (1992b) has suggested, on the basis of the limited ethnographic accounts, that pottery was functionally important for the successful processing of toxic *Alocasia* (dry taro), the major subsistence crop on the atoll, through the ability to simmer coconut sap. Intoh (1992b: 166) concludes:

If Ngulu had been rich in plant resources, earth-oven cooking could have been the main cooking method, and pottery would not have been necessary for survival. However, the severe natural environment of this atoll forced the Ngulu people to rely on a highly toxic variety of *Alocasia* that could be grown locally. The addition of coconut syrup during sustained cooking made it possible for Ngulu residents to eat this carbohydrate-rich plant without adverse effects. In addition, surplus coconut syrup was produced in order to trade with nearby high islands to obtain other food resources and natural materials important for life on the atoll. Among the imported items, of greatest importance was the continued supply of earthenware vessels for producing coconut syrup in the first place.

Radiocarbon dates from the archaeological excavations are inconclusive, but on the basis of the pottery sequence, Intoh (1981) postulates settlement beginning prior to 1200 years ago. The excavations revealed archaeological deposits of over 3 metres in depth and comprising quantities of turtle, fish and rat bones, along with shell midden and shell artefacts. A complete skeleton of a small dog was recovered, and tentatively dated to 700 years ago, from its stratigraphic relationship with a dated *Tridacna* shell.

The ceramics are indicators of contacts over at least a millennium with the neighbouring high islands, but linguistically the inhabitants of Ngulu are, like the Sonsorolese, Chuukic speakers and their stories of origin link with the Carolinian atolls, especially Ulithi. The material culture and linguistic evidence point to contacts with and beyond the high islands of Palau or Yap. This is further exemplified by Lessa (1961: 45–6) in his report of Ulithi oral history on 'how Ngulu was settled'. His informant, Melchethal, told Lessa that essentially the same story was told on Yap and Ngulu and reads in part:

A man called Halengloi lived on the island of Mogmog in Ulithi Atoll. One day, there was a typhoon, so when it was over he went to Gagil District in Yap and stayed with the clan known as Pebinau at the village of Gatchepar [he had *sawei* relations with this clan; for a discussion of the *sawei* see the Yap section below]. He lived there for a while, and one day the chief of Guror village in the district of Galiman came to Gatchepar and asked the man who was host to Halengloi if Halengloi wished to go to live with him in Guror. The Ulithian was willing and went back with him. He fished, collected palm sap, and did other work for the village chief. After some time had passed the chief felt that the Ulithian had helped him considerably, so in gratitude he found a woman for Halengloi to marry. She was from Hachlau in the same district.

[Halengloi expressed a wish to sail and catch a fish called *likh*, so the chiefs gave him a canoe.] Halengloi was now a *pelü*, or navigator. He had never before been to the island of Ngulu but he knew about it. The people of Yap, however, did not. Halengloi wanted to go there, so he sailed far to the south, but he did not tell the others of his intention. Suddenly, all the people on the canoe shouted, saying there was something in the distance. Halengloi told them it was the island of Ngulu, and it was then that the people from Yap realized that he had set sail, not in order to catch fish, but to reach the small atoll.

[They gathered shells, fish and bird wings at Ngulu and returned with them to Yap.] When they got there, the Yap people talked to their village chief at Guror, telling him they had been to an island to the south . . . They took the *sar* [shells], *likh* [fish], and *hataf* [frigate birds] and gave them to the chief. After a day had passed the chief of Guror went to Gatchepar to see the man who had been host to Halengloi. He told him the Ulithian had been to an island to the south. He said he wanted the host (who was the owner of the island because he had the status of 'father' to the man from Ulithi, who was his 'child') to give him, the chief, the island. The man from Gatchepar consented, saying the chief could have the island. The chief returned to Guror. Halengloi and his wife told him they would like to go to live on Ngulu. Thus, the two went to the atoll to stay for good. They had children, and then grandchildren, until the island became populated with a number of people.

This is why Ngulu belongs to the chief of Guror in the district of Galiman on Yap. And this is why the people of Ngulu have the customs of both Ulithi and Yap and also speak both these languages. For their ancestors come from there.

Lessa (1961) classifies this story as a 'historical legend', suggesting that there are elements of historical fact embedded within it. This may be the case, or it may also be a *post hoc* construction in order to legitimate more recent regimes. Whatever the case, there are certainly parts of the story worth highlighting, particularly in relation to the current chapter.

That the Ulithians already knew of the existence of Ngulu, and the Yapese did not, concurs with much ethnography that records the Carolinians as the sailors and the Yapese as more or less landlubbers. But we do know that Yapese people were sailing in return voyages between Yap and Palau to quarry and remove the stone money valuables and in so doing would have to pass in the vicinity of Ngulu. However, as I will discuss in more detail below, the Yapese involved with the atolls to the east and those involved in the quarrying of stone valuables in Palau may have been members of quite distinct confederacies and geographical knowledge would undoubtedly be restricted. In such a scenario it would be less surprising for the people of Gagil to be unaware of Ngulu, while other Yapese were.

A point less directly related to the story, but of extreme resonance in regard to the apparent amount of contact between people generally regarded as having non-mutually intelligible languages in the western Micronesia region, is the comment in the final paragraph that the people of Ngulu speak both Chuukic and Yapese. In my opinion, as non-linguists archaeologists are often confused by distribution maps that present distinct boundaries between neighbouring language groups. Undoubtedly, the primary or first language of an individual is an indicator of community and ethnic identity, although even these may be divided by specialized language restricted to initiated individuals, such as the *itang* of Chuuk Lagoon, but we should not believe that this is the sole language possessed by all members of the community at all times. It is clear from situations such as are found in northern New Guinea or central Australia that people will also speak a number of neighbouring languages, the primary languages of the people they are most often in contact with. In regard to this, and this is especially relevant to aspects of the following section regarding Yap, we should not give too high an importance to the significant differences in primary languages spoken in western Micronesia.

Yap

Yap is a group consisting of four major islands and several smaller ones located in the western Carolines, south-west of Guam and north-east of Palau, and is comprised of sedimentary, metamorphic and volcanic rocks. The major islands of Rumung, Gagil-Tomil, Map and Yap are tightly clustered and share a fringing reef (Fig. 6.5). In the present day, only Rumung requires crossing water from an adjacent island, modern bridges having been constructed between the remaining islands. Together they have an approximate land area of 80 square

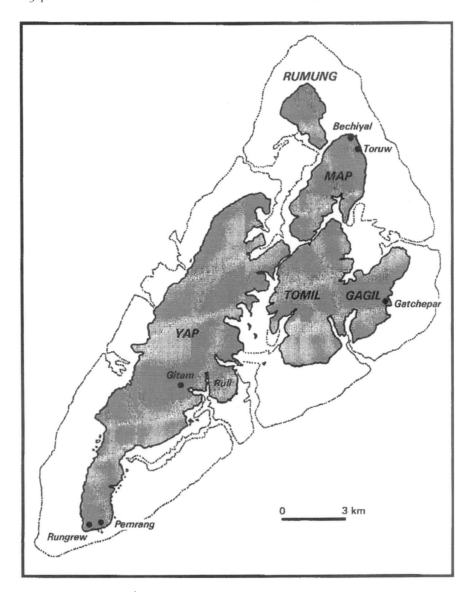

Fig. 6.5 Map of Yap.

kilometres, and reach an elevation of a little over 170 metres in the rolling hills of the interior.

In chapter 4 the possibility that Yap was originally settled around 3000 years ago was considered, but the earliest evidence for human presence is poorly understood at present. Following Edward and Mary Gifford (1959), work conducted by Takayama and Intoh (Intoh 1981; Takayama 1982) and more recently by Intoh (Intoh and Leach 1985; Intoh 1988) has provided a chronological sequence of ceramic production for Yap. Excavations in the south of Yap, at Rungrew and Pemrang, have both revealed sequences of ceramics spanning the presently known history of human settlement on the island. A rough tripartite ceramic typology has been developed, often aided by the discovery of pottery on islands beyond Yap (see below).

The three pottery types identified reveal that the earliest is Calcareous Sand Tempered (CST), which overlaps with Plain Ware, and the most recent is Laminated Ware (Takayama 1982). On present evidence the CST ceramics span the period from possible earliest settlement (between *c.* 3300 to 2000 years ago) to around 650 years ago. Plain Ware is most common between about 850 and 650 years ago, followed by the laminated ceramics (Intoh 1992a). This work has dispelled the suggestion of Gifford and Gifford (1959), on the advice of Spoehr, that a close relationship could be observed between the Plain Ware pottery of Yap and that of the Marianas (Intoh and Leach 1985). Ethnoarchaeological studies of the production of Laminated Ware (Gifford and Gifford 1959; Intoh and Leach 1985; Intoh 1990) have demonstrated the peculiar practices in the open firing of these ceramics that appear to go against normal understandings of pottery production. For example, every effort is made to remove non-plastic materials from the highly plastic clay, and a further three 'peculiar practices' are noted by Intoh (1990: 47): 'wetting the pot just before firing, building a big fire before the pot is put on, and putting the pot on a very hot fire'. The methods of construction and firing are responsible for the laminated structure of the ceramics and make the sherds easily recognizable in the region. The ethnoarchaeological studies also found that pottery production is only practised by females and that they are from the lower caste of society. Of the other portable material culture, stone tools are considered rare, and many of the other artefacts of shell and bone resemble those typical of the Carolines.

Little is known of settlement patterns prior to the 'traditional' village system, which have been recorded in a number of ethnoarchaeological studies (e.g., Craib and Price 1978; Hunter-Anderson 1983, 1985; Cordy 1986a; Pickering 1990). According to these studies most villages appear to fit roughly into concentric environmental zones. The *faluw* (men's house) is located facing, or adjacent to, the lagoon, with a taro swamp located inland (Fig. 6.6). On the other side of the taro swamp, on the lower slopes of the hills, is the main village area consisting of house platforms, at least one *pebaey* (community building), stone paths, tombs (depending on the rank of the village), dancing areas (*malal*, where the *rai* 'stone money' are normally displayed) and a number of *wunabey* (stone-paved platforms with stone-slab backrests). Higher up the slope, above the village, are found the mounds which form the yam and swidden gardens and this is also the location of the menstrual houses. The village area also extends out in the other direction, beyond the *faluw*, onto the fringing reef, and in this zone are located a variety of stone-built fish traps (Hunter-Anderson 1981).

Fig. 6.6 A Yapese *faluw* or men's house, Balabat, Yap Proper. Built on a stone
platform, and often the focus for stone money (*fai/rei*), they do not
appear to have an antiquity greater than 600 years and quite possibly
250 years, given the vagaries of dating.

William Adams, through the archaeological survey of Gachlaw Village in
Gilman Municipality at the south end of Yap, has challenged this, as he believes,
simplistic model of village organization, and states (1997: 24):

One of the problems in trying to develop a model with application throughout
Yap is that Yap is a high volcanic island with diverse soils, plants, and topography. Secondly, the natural topography has been greatly modified by humans.
What was once reef area or mangrove has been systematically filled in by building a retaining wall and hauling basket-loads of sand to fill behind it. Hundreds
of acres of land have been created by this process.

What has become known as the Yapese 'caste system' is exhibited through
village ranking, amongst other things. There are four ranks of village, with
the first three translated in descending hierarchical order as 'Chief', 'Noble'
and 'Commoner'. The first two may control the land of a lower-ranked village,
but the 'Commoner' village stands alone as a single unit. A fourth and lower,
presumably 'Outcaste' group is constituted by small upland 'serf' settlements.
Intermarriage between castes is traditionally not permitted and individual rank
is ascribed by village of birth. Within villages ranking also exists and is normally
restricted to 'Chief' and 'Commoner' (Lingenfelter 1975; Cordy 1986a). The

lower-ranked members of society were required to pay tribute and labour to the higher-ranked. This is, of course, extremely simplified and there were many crosscutting alliances, but the basic structure appears to have been robust and all pervading.

The basic relationship of Yapese people to land and place is through *tabinaw*. The *tabinaw* is land owned by a single patrilineage and is maintained through patrilocal residence; both circumstances are unusual in Micronesia (see chapter 3). Each *tabinaw* has a *dayif*, which is a house platform of hexagonal plan. These house platforms, in their perceived permanence as opposed to the corporeality of humans, play extremely strong roles in maintaining the social identity of the *tabinaw* (Lingenfelter 1975; Descantes 1998).

The chronology for the associated architecture and village sites and the social structures they represent is not well understood. Hunter-Anderson (1983) conducted a small excavation in a probable cookhouse mound, in the putatively oldest part of Toruw Village, at the north end of Map Island. Three radiocarbon dates were processed and were found not to be stratigraphically consistent, probably because of crab burrowing. The oldest determination was on charcoal and dated to approximately 350 years ago.

Michiko Intoh and Foss Leach (1985) attempted to date some of the traditional village features at Gatchepar Village, on the east coast of Gagil-Tomil Island. The partial excavation of a house mound revealed that it had probably been constructed utilizing a double stone wall, whose cavity was 65 centimetres wide and filled with earth and acted to retain the fill of the mound. No dates were retrieved from the mound itself, but the construction deposits were dominated by pottery of Laminated Ware type, suggesting a date of no earlier than 550 years ago, but possibly as late as 150 years ago (Intoh and Leach 1985; Intoh 1992a). They were able to achieve more secure dating for a platform and house mound they excavated in Gitam Village, on the east of Yap Proper. Of two radiocarbon dates on charcoal, one provided a determination of 550–360 years ago, and dates deposits below the stone construction on the site. Another five dates from the site all fall within the last 250 years. The dates tentatively indicate that the traditional village type settlement on Yap is a relatively recent phenomenon, unlikely to have originated more than 600 years ago, and possibly within the last 250 years.

The supra-political organization of Yap appears to have been one of shifting confederacies in the years leading up to and including European contact. Although not altogether clear, owing to the conflicting histories available, it appears that north-eastern districts of the group, Gagil, Map and Rumung, were usually at odds with the southern districts, especially Rull on Yap Proper. Tomil, the western half of Gagil-Tomil island, appears to have been at times incorporated within the north-eastern group or separate from them both.

Gagil district, and in particular the village of Gatchepar (and sometimes Wonyan), has been described by the anthropologist William Lessa (1950),

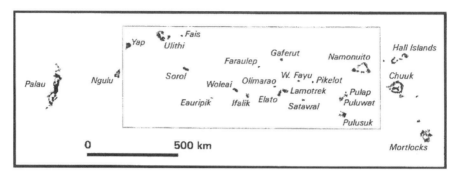

Fig. 6.7 Map of participants in the *sawei* system. The *sawei* linked communities on the atolls of the western Caroline Islands with 'parent' communities on the high island of Yap.

perhaps rather over-evocatively, as at the head of a 'Yapese Empire' (but for support of the use of this appellation see Petersen 2000). Lessa was here describing a system of tribute paid to the ranking members of Gagil district by people from the atolls and raised limestone islands stretching over 1000 kilometres east of Yap, almost as far as Chuuk Lagoon. This system, known as the *sawei*, linked these central Carolinian communities in order of ascending rank from Namonuito Atoll westwards (Fig. 6.7).

In this system, the people of the 'Outer Islands', as these low islands are generally known, were subordinate to the Gagil people, within the fictive idiom of a 'parent–child' relationship. Whenever requested by the Yapese 'parents', the outer islanders were required to sail westwards, collecting others on the way, until the final fleet sailed from Mogmog in Ulithi Atoll closest to Yap (Ushijima 1982). Because of restrictions placed on the movement of Carolinians in the German and Japanese colonial periods (1898 to 1945), the system, known from oral history, was not ethnographically recorded and details are at times contradictory. It appears however that the tribute was paid on a cycle of approximately every three years (cf. Alkire 1977; 1978, who says annually). The ranked relations between the outer islanders and the Gagil community do remain in some form to the present day (Alkire 1993).

The Outer Islanders gave gifts, either directly to the chief of Gatchepar village, or to particular Gagil people who were notionally regarded as 'owners' of particular low islands or parts of them. The gifts included fibre skirts and loincloths, shell valuables, sennit twine, coconut- and turtle-shell belts, pandanus mats and coconut oil. In return, the Yapese gave their 'children' ceramic pots, wood for canoe building, red-earth pigment, turmeric, *Tridacna* clamshells and a variety of foodstuffs.

William Alkire's (1965; 1977; 1978) initial assessment of the *sawei* was one of functional utility, in that the people of the low islands needed to maintain formal contacts in case of crop devastation by a typhoon or drought. In such a case, Alkire believed it would be possible to call on *sawei* partners to aid the community through lean times. Later, Alkire (e.g., 1980) saw the *sawei* as an indication that the Yapese were following a trajectory towards political centralization.

Sherwood Lingenfelter (1975) tied the *sawei* to political rivalry, which allowed the people of Gagil to claim and control the Outer Island products as special and prestige goods. These 'products' also included the navigational knowledge possessed by the Outer Islanders. In particular, Lingenfelter thought that the *lavalava* (loincloths) and certain shells were scarce on Yap. In both the Alkire and Lingenfelter scenarios, the full system would not work without the threat of retribution if tribute was not paid. The expected retribution was the sending of typhoons, as the Outer Islanders believed that their Yapese possessed 'magic' that could control the weather.

Hunter-Anderson and Yigal Zan (1996) have reviewed these interpretations and proposed an alternative scenario. They criticize Alkire for his attempt to force a social evolutionary model on an inappropriate case. They find that there is no evidence for a trajectory towards political centralization and, indeed, propose that the Yapese system of shifting confederacies was a long-term and relatively stable scheme. They also argue that the low islands are not as environmentally impoverished as Alkire would like to propound, and are resilient to environmental damage with the ability to regenerate quickly.

In regard to the model proposed by Lingenfelter, they find that a high value placed on *lavalava* is unlikely, in that the raw material and ability to produce them was also held on Yap. Hunter-Anderson and Zan also downplay the role that would have been played by the threat of divine retribution, arguing instead that being overlorded by the Yapese was a small price to pay for the goods they received in return for their comparatively meagre tribute. The Outer Islanders would return home with items, such as pottery and turmeric, not available in their coral and limestone worlds. In this scenario, what Gagil received was local prestige in Yap for being able to maintain and support a dependency over a large portion of the Caroline Islands. However, Hunter-Anderson and Zan fail to discount, or even discuss, the passing of shell 'valuables' as important and prestigious tribute as proposed by Lingenfelter.

Mark Berg (1992), in discussing the *sawei*, has placed a much greater emphasis on the shell tribute, while contextualizing the Gagil-centred system in relation to the 'stone money' system that linked the other major Yapese confederacy, centred on Rull, with Ngulu Atoll and the Palau Archipelago, 400 kilometres to the south. In the scenario identified here, Berg proposes that two main types of 'money' existed on Yap. The first, and most valuable, consisted of small *Spondylus* shell beads known as *gau* that came from Eauripik Atoll, Udot Island in Chuuk Lagoon, and Etal Atoll in the Mortlocks group, south-east of Chuuk. The second was stone discs quarried and transported from caves in Palau by the Yapese. These stone discs are known as *rai* in the north of Yap and *fei* in the south; they are made of calcite and range from a few centimetres to metres in diameter. In a story recorded by Lessa (1980: 27) on Ulithi, the bringing of *rai/fei* to Yap was first achieved by a Yapese navigator and passengers stopping at Palau on a return voyage from Pohnpei in the eastern Caroline Islands. The part of the story concerning the stone discs states:

When they reached the island of Palau they lived there. They started to make some *palang* [close to the Palauan term for *rai/fei*], or stone 'money', in the shape of monitor lizards, fish, and other animal forms. But all of them broke as they made them, so they stopped. One night they saw the full moon rising in the east and said, 'Let us make an image of the moon.' The next day they started on this work and made images of the moon. Everyone liked the images when they were through, and none broke. They had made holes in the middle of the stones because they could put a stick through the holes and carry them on their shoulders. After they had carried them to their canoe they set sail for Yap. When they reached there and the people heard about the stones, they came to look at them. After that people went to Palau to make these stones.

Palau is outside of the *sawei* network as usually compiled. Within are the *gau* producers of Eauripik, but although those of Udot and Etal are not, they were undoubtedly involved in inter-community relations that in one direction led to Gagil on Yap. Gagil controlled the *gau* resource, while Rull had access to the quarries of Palau, and thus the stone discs that have made Yap famous as the 'island of stone money'. This balanced access to valuables promoted stability between the main confederacies, although the introduction of European shipping resulted in 'inflation' as larger *rai/fei* were transported from Palau. Although Berg attempts to draw in results from archaeology, the chronology presented is weak, but it is possible that this dual system operated prior to European contact, and the main challenge is to Hunter-Anderson and Zan's claim to an imbalance in gift-giving. It may well be, given this scenario, that the Gagil community was exchanging like with like, rare valuables for a rare valuable, in each party's perception.

Possible archaeological indicators of the *sawei*, in the form of Yapese pottery, have been identified from excavations at Ulithi (Craib 1980, 1981; Descantes 1998), Fais (Intoh 1996) and Lamotrek (Fujimura and Alkire 1984). However, an understanding of the origins of the *sawei* is very difficult to gain, and as we have seen, the fledgling archaeology in the islands can place (Descantes *et al.* 2001) and date some exotics, but the social processes by which they arrived are far more difficult to unearth. Both Berg (1992) and Descantes (1998) date the intensification of contact between Yap and the Outer Islands to the fourteenth and fifteenth centuries, and this may represent the inception of the *sawei*, with less intensive contact occurring for many centuries prior to this.

Hunter-Anderson and Zan (1996) have proposed that the ranking of the outer islands indicates a spread from Yap east over time. Their logic is that, as other island communities realized the benefits of the *sawei*, they too would want to join, but so as not to undermine the prestige of the already participating communities, they had to join as subordinates. This is a possibility, but it is not totally clear that the geographic limits and temporal flexibility of the system have been properly established.

Per Hage and Frank Harary (1991) find that the regular exchange network in the Carolines goes beyond Chuuk Lagoon to the east of the expected *sawei*, and at times included communities in the Marshall Islands, the Gilbert Islands (Kiribati) and on into Polynesian Tuvalu. Indeed, there is other Carolinian evidence to indicate exchange contact beyond the traditional boundaries of the *sawei*.

The islanders from Woleai Atoll, in the east of the *sawei* distribution, are also recorded as making regular trips to Chuuk Lagoon, where they exchanged for goods similar to those extracted from Yap (Sudo 1996). Indeed, in terms of language and cultural similarities, it made more sense for the outer islanders to visit Chuuk. In 1961, Alkire (1965) recorded a trading expedition from Lamotrek Atoll to Chuuk Lagoon, a distance of over 600 kilometres. They took with them items to trade such as cordage and tobacco and hoped to return with, amongst items like steel wire for fishhooks, turmeric. Turmeric, given its use in many Carolinian rites of passage (see Rainbird 2001a), was clearly an important commodity, and was apparently available from either Yap or Chuuk Lagoon.

The southern system, that linked the 400 kilometres between Yap and Palau, is also difficult to date, even on the evidence of recent, but as yet not fully published, work at the *rai/fei* quarry sites in Palau (Fitzpatrick 2000; 2001). Cora Gillilland's (1975) detailed study of the *rai/fei* phenomenon shows that it is little commented upon in visitors' reports prior to the second half of the nineteenth century. It may be that the shiny stone discs were much smaller and less common prior to European intervention, and this rarity may only have served to enhance their value in comparison to *gau* shell valuables. Between 1872 and 1901 Captain David Sean O'Keefe used steamships to import ever larger and supposedly more valuable *rai/fei*, in exchange for copra and labour in copra production. The largest *rai/fei* undoubtedly date to this time. Earlier Yapese trips collected smaller discs of the highly valued stone, and de Beauclair (1963, see also 1961 and 1962) proposes that many of the glass bead valuables found on Palau were brought by the Yapese in payment for the right to quarry in the caves.

Yap was undoubtedly at the centre of a number of networks, many of which are now lost to history. The material remains of the hundreds of *rai/fei* and evidence of quarry sites in Palau, the exotic materials excavated in the outer islands, along with the ethnography indicating the vast distances travelled in the *sawei*, and elsewhere, using traditional seacraft and navigational techniques, must be regarded as echoes of regular inter-island voyaging, at least over the last 1000 years or so.

Yap of the present day is popularly regarded as the most traditional of the high islands in the region. Betel nut is a national passion, and the red painted floor at the modern terminal building at the airfield is purportedly a concession to this. People certainly still value their ancestral land as Adams and his co-workers found when surveying the largely abandoned Gachlaw village. Many former residents returned to renew ties and make sure proper ownership was recorded, they state (Adams, Campbell and Ross 1997: 30):

It was a roving town meeting in which everyone used their machetes to expand our jungle clearings more to their aesthetic liking or to clear out areas we had overlooked. In the process only two more house sites were discovered. The end result was that each site has been identified by traditional name and landownership and a site history collected for many. The villagers have already benefited by our project stimulating them to come back to the village and reach a consensus about who owns what.

Of course, Yap has also felt the impact of colonialism, and beginning in the early 1800s the reefs were being exploited for *bêche de mer* by foreign traders. By 1880 Yap was producing 1500 tons of copra and was a centre for commercial activities (Hezel 1983). Direct colonial rule did not arrive in Yap until the German period, beginning in 1899, but the biggest enforced changes occurred during the Japanese period, which also witnessed a continuing decline in population that had started much earlier. Gorenflo and Levin (1991: 101, references removed) find that:

The immediate reasons for this decline appeared to be a high death rate, linked to tuberculosis and infant diarrhea, and a low birth rate due to gonorrhea. In addition to carrying out economic, cultural, and social changes in establishing its authority and improving commerce in the area, Japan introduced better health care and related training in 1915 to help stem depopulation. But these efforts were unsuccessful; by 1937 the [Indigenous] population of [Yap] had declined to roughly 3,400 [from 6,200 in 1911].

Although not of the highest military priority, preparations for armed conflict leading up to World War II did take place on Yap. Adams (1997) notes at Gachlaw Village how trenches were constructed in house platforms and even the valuable *rai/fei* were broken up and used as road material. Lin Poyer (1995: 234) in interviews found that the greatest wartime havoc was by the defending Japanese rather than through military attacks:

Quartering soldiers, building fortifications, and clearing land for gardens for military use all caused widespread damage. Soldiers destroyed taro patches, cut betel nut trees for buildings and lampposts, cut coconut trees to eat the palm hearts, and used stone money to anchor floating strings of copra. Soldiers lived in churches, and sacred areas were destroyed by searches for firewood and other materials. Outside the main target areas, it was occupation troops, not bombing, that caused the most destruction.

In their archaeological survey of a Second World War Japanese lighthouse in the Gagil area of Yap, Hunter-Anderson and Moore (1995) were also able to record the oral history related to the site. They found that the Japanese had chosen the site of a Yapese cemetery, and the forced labourers, mostly Outer Islanders, collected the bones and gave them to the Yapese community for reburial. The lighthouse was never completed, and apparently in an attempt to remove it as a target for US bombing, the Japanese dynamited it. In the present it is extant as a tumbled ruin, and Hunter-Anderson and Moore note the irony in the fact that the Yapese landowners wish to present the site as a tourist attraction for Japanese visitors.

Carolinian atolls

Images of atolls often capture the imagination by providing the picture postcard version of an archetypal desert island of sand and palms. From the air, the ring of islets and reef provides a yellow and green frame to the myriad iridescent blues created by the sandy shallows of the lagoon. These tropical blues contrast with the deep and dark blues that lap, or crash, at the outside of a solid ring, providing an extra band of foaming white. Ecologically, atolls have often been regarded as marginal environments for human populations (e.g., Alkire 1978). The small land area, poor coralline soils and vulnerability to environmental catastrophe have in the past led archaeologists to believe that atolls are also impoverished archaeologically.

As noted above, Hunter-Anderson and Zan (1996) have collated evidence from a number of researchers that challenges the notion of atolls as impoverished environments in terms of food production. Typically, atoll islands (or islets) have a central taro patch that has been mulched and developed over centuries, and breadfruit and coconut trees circle this. It is also the case that, distinct from the *sawei* connections, the Carolinian atolls were involved in smaller-scale exchange systems, at inter-island or intra-atoll scale that, amongst other things, mutually benefited the participants at times of localized food shortage (Hage and Harary 1991). It also should be noted that inter-community interaction was not always friendly and for the sharing of aid, as the historical reports of fighting between atoll communities attest.

Janet Davidson's 1965 excavations on Nukuoro found that, like former notions of environmentally impoverished atolls, the opposite was also true of the archaeology, and suggested the possibility of finding stratified archaeological deposits on other atolls. Following her success on Nukuoro (see chapter 8), Davidson (1967b) conducted brief surveys on the Carolinian atolls of Ngatik, Pakin, Mwokil and Pingelap (see Fig. 6.1). This work allowed her to conclude that there was great potential for archaeological investigation, but a decade passed before further archaeological investigations of Carolinian atolls commenced.

Fujimura and Alkire (1984) were mostly concerned with issues of social anthropological significance during their 1975–76 fieldwork in the atolls of Woleai, Faralaup and Lamotrek. However, excavations allied to their research represented the first test of Davidson's optimistic reports. The poor results from their small excavations on the atolls of Woleai and Faralaup did not support Davidson's assertions, but the final excavations conducted on Lamotrek were more fruitful.

Lamotrek Atoll, consisting of three islands with a total land area of 0.85 square kilometres, is situated approximately 950 kilometres east of Yap. The two trenches excavated produced evidence of archaeological deposits to a depth of almost 2 metres, although no absolute dates were obtained. Through petrographic analyses of the pottery and stone, they were able to suggest that Lamotrek received ceramics produced on Yap and Palau, and volcanic rock derived from Chuuk Lagoon (Fujimura and Alkire 1984). The attribution of Palauan ceramics has since been dismissed, but the links with Yap remain (Dickinson and Shutler 2000). Other imports may have included the extremely large *Tridacna gigas* shells, either unmodified or in the form of the adzes recovered, as this species is not known historically in the waters of the atoll.

Stratigraphic relationships showed that large *Tridacna* shell adzes only appear early in the sequence, while *Cassis* shell scrapers are a more recent phenomenon. Although it is clear that certain items were being imported, stone artefacts are rare on the atolls, with food pounders created from local coral being most common. Peter Steager (1979) reported that on Puluwat Atoll the manufacture of coral pounders was recognized as a specialized and time-consuming craft.

The overriding, and ethnographically observed, use of shell for durable material culture was highlighted when an extended inhumation of a young female was discovered, buried beneath 1.8 metres of deposits. Her head was resting on a large *Tridacna* adze blade, and on her wrists were bracelets manufactured from either *Conus* or *Trochus* shell. Perforated shell discs, possibly of *Lambis*, scattered around the neck and head suggest she was buried wearing a necklace. A single, and thus unreliable, radiocarbon date from a toe bone suggests that she may have died approximately 780 years ago. It appears that twenty-five *Cassis* shells may have marked the grave site. These shells had their centre wall removed to create simple containers, two of which held small fish and mammal bones, perhaps the last remaining vestiges of a funeral feast.

Ulithi is the largest of the Carolinian atolls, and consists of a lagoon with an area of approximately 460 square kilometres, and forty-one fringing islets that have a combined land area of 4.7 square kilometres (Bryan 1971). Craib (1980; 1981; Craib and Mangold 1999) conducted three seasons of archaeological fieldwork, which included minimal excavation, but midden deposits dating back some 1400 years were detected, and surface features and artefact scatters identified. The surface features included abandoned village sites, identified by the presence of low coral stone platforms and coral slab graves. Of particular interest were surface scatters of large quantities of Yapese Laminated Ware, which attest to a certain amount of contact with the high island (located 120 kilometres west) in later prehistory: perhaps in the form of the *sawei* tribute system, as discussed above. In the small excavations conducted by Christophe Descantes (1998) on Mogmog islet, he found the earliest cultural deposits, associated with Yapese Plainware, to be some 1400 years old.

Ant (And) Atoll is currently uninhabited, and only visited occasionally by fishermen and day-trippers from the large high island of Pohnpei, which is located 15 kilometres to the north-east. During 1978, William Ayres, Alan Haun and Craig Severance (1981) conducted a brief survey of Ant and, as expected, links with the high island were shown. Abandoned basalt prism platforms and basalt *sakau* (*Piper methysticum*) pounding stones and flaked stone tools indicated that a considerable amount of basalt had been transported by seacraft to the atoll. Surface artefacts recovered consisted mainly of adze blades manufactured from *Terebra* and *Tridacna* shells.

On Imwinyap Islet, directly south of the only pass into Ant Atoll's lagoon, an abandoned settlement consisting of five platforms and a coral rubble enclosure was surveyed and excavated. A small test pit yielded what was interpreted as food refuse, including remains of dog, rat, bird, shellfish and fish, in four layers down to 85 centimetres below ground level. A single radiocarbon date on charcoal, derived from the bottom layer, dated to approximately 1100 years ago. As discussed in chapter 4, Jean-Christophe Galipaud (2001) has more recently found a ceramic deposit dated to 2000 years ago.

The interiors of the larger islets of Ant were modified for the pit cultivation of giant swamp taro (*Cyrtosperma chamissonis*). Further modification of the islet for subsistence purposes was also indicated by the presence of stone-lined wells; such wells have also been reported in the Carolines from Namoluk Atoll in the Mortlocks group (Hunter-Anderson 1987). The researchers concluded that site densities on Ant reflect intensive settlement over at least a millennium.

The Lower Mortlocks group is located to the south-west of Ant and south-east of Chuuk Lagoon (Fig. 6.1). Takayama and Intoh conducted archaeological survey on the atolls of Satawan, Lukunor and Etal in 1979. Although surface collection produced numerous portable artefacts, the majority being shell adze blades of *Tridacna*, *Terebra* and *Cassis*, small excavations on Moch and Satawan Islets recovered little in the way of artefacts or features (Takayama and Intoh 1980). They found evidence of external contacts in the style of coral breadfruit pounders, that were similar to those found on Chuuk Lagoon, 300 kilometres to the north-west, and in the form of *Cassis* peelers, that they believed were indicative of contacts with atolls in the central Carolines.

Intoh (1991; 1996) has conducted archaeological investigations at Fais, a raised coral island about 80 kilometres east of Ulithi, in the western Caroline Islands (Fig. 6.1). It is included in this section because its small land area

(2.8 square kilometres) and porous rock make it more similar to the atolls than the high islands. However, there are two major differences between Fais and atolls: the plateau, at 20 metres, has a much higher altitude than any atoll, and Fais has a fringing reef, and thus lacks the typical atoll lagoon rich in marine life. The porous rock allows for good natural subterranean storage of fresh water, but the lack of a lagoon contributes to a limited subsistence base. Phosphate mining during the first half of the twentieth century has caused a somewhat depleted picture of the terrestrial environment, which was once described as having 'the richest soil, and the most luxuriant flora' (Chamisso 1821: 183, quoted in Steadman and Intoh 1994: 116). Nevertheless, prior to 1850, when sweet potato was introduced from Yap, subsistence was based mainly on dry-land taro (*Colocasia esculenta* and *Alocasia macrorrhiza*) and banana (Intoh 1991).

Fais has probably been settled for at least 1900 years, and pottery, pigs and possibly dogs were present throughout most of this occupation (Intoh 1991). As there is no local clay source, pottery must have been imported, and much of it appears to have come from Yap. The Yapese imports include the whole range of pottery types known from that island (see above) and other sherds originate from Palau. Green schist stone was introduced from Yap at the time of earliest known settlement. Intoh (1996; 1999) has been keen to highlight the multiple and long-distance contacts exhibited by the material found in her excavations on Fais. She notes possible contact with the Philippines to the west, and the Solomon Islands to the south-east. The latter is suggested by the similarity of trolling lure types, and the contact is proposed by Intoh to have taken place sometime between 1500 and 600 years ago.

In the stories provided in oral histories there appears to be no apparent problem in imagining a time when inter-island communication across the Caroline Islands was not a normal practice. In his collection of oral testimonies relating to the spread of knot divination in the Caroline Islands, a complicated practice by which knots in palm leaves are used as a form of oracle, Lessa (1959) found that the stories linked many islands. One myth from Namoluk Atoll links a spirit journey in a sailing vessel with Ulithi in the west through to Pohnpei in the east, with most of the islands in between, including the Mortlocks, named as places visited.

Summary

The archaeological work of recent years now makes the Palau archipelago stand out as having a very distinctive and different history among the islands of western Micronesia. The dramatic terraces that were sculpted by people in the northern islands of the group are now seen to be a continuation of earlier hill-top enclosures surrounded by deep ditches. The previously intractable ceramic typology has been completely altered by the discovery of other ceramic types.

But this is a history not isolated from other islands within the region and there is plenty of material evidence for contacts with the Southwest Islands, Yap and the low islands to the east.

Yap, linguistically distinct, has probably yet to reveal its earliest history, but contacts with Palau are exhibited through the quarrying and collection of stone discs, and historically documented intense relations with the low atolls and islands to the east and further indicated by the distribution of Yapese pottery. This is an emerging picture of complex relations requiring further clarification, but the present level of knowledge indicates multiple possibilities in regard to exchange networks crossing the fluid boundaries that are likely to go beyond that indicated by the *sawei*.

The Carolinian atolls have so far only partially lived up to Davidson's optimism of 1967, but new understandings of atoll subsistence practices, and greater awareness of the extent and achievements of inter-island communication developed since the 1960s, provide for new interpretations beyond the earlier notions of isolated and impoverished communities. We now see these atolls as part of a sea of islands, connected by seascapes that incorporate not only reefs and other islands, but mythical creatures and 'ghost' islands; both of the latter aid navigation, but the ghost islands sink from view as people approach (see e.g., Gunn 1980).

The arrival of Europeans and others in the region had different effects on the communities over this vast spread of islands. These ranged from that of benign neglect through to the forced removal of people for their required labour in phosphate mines. However, the most shocking event during the earliest period of contact for many of the Caroline Islands occurred in 1837 with the complete massacre of the adult male population of Ngatik Atoll. This at the hands of the crew of the *Lambton*, in order to seize a cache of tortoise shell (Poyer 1993).

The next chapter completes the review of the Caroline Islands with a consideration of the islands in Chuuk Lagoon and the other high islands of Pohnpei and Kosrae.

CHAPTER 7

'HOW THE PAST SPEAKS HERE!' – THE EASTERN CAROLINE ISLANDS

In this chapter, I consider the archaeology of the three high islands of the eastern Caroline Islands, starting with Chuuk Lagoon, which is located just east of the centre of the Carolines chain, and then moving eastwards through Pohnpei and then on to Kosrae, the easternmost of the Carolines. These islands do not stand alone, and a number of the atolls, mentioned in the previous chapter, are located in the eastern Caroline Islands (Fig. 6.1).

Chuuk Lagoon

Chuuk Lagoon is the 'almost-atoll' of the Carolines, with the islands of volcanic origin clustered in the southern half of an immense lagoon, with an area of 2125 square kilometres, formed by a barrier reef (Fig. 7.1). Surveys of the reef islands have provided some evidence to indicate long-term human occupation of, at least, Piis Moen at the very north, and Ruo to the north-east (CSHPO 1981; Rainbird 1994b). However, as is the case today, the main centres of settlement were probably within the lagoon on the often steep-sided volcanic islands, with the reef islands occasionally visited for fishing camps and other activities. For example, the coral rubble and sand reef islet of Ruo has a dense and aged capping of pandanus trees, and may have been exploited as an occasional resource for fruit and leaf procurement.

American interest in the post-Second World War period led to the first tentative reports regarding the archaeology of the islands (Gosda 1958; Smith 1958). Francis Clune (1974; 1977) conducted extensive research but, like the work conducted before this, it is not reported in detail and only minimally published. Jun Takayama and his colleagues picked out a few hilltop sites for intensive archaeological investigation (Takayama and Seki 1973; Takayama and Intoh 1978). At the same time, an injection of US money for infrastructure improvements led to archaeological projects on Moen (Craib 1978a; Parker 1981; Parker and King 1981; King and Parker 1984) and Tol (Edwards 1978).

Tom King and Patricia Parker's interest in Chuuk instigated a series of surveys on Moen by local members of the Chuuk State Historic Preservation Office team, which resulted in several short reports (e.g., Bukea 1979a; 1979b; Cordy 1980; CSHPO 1980a; 1980b; 1980b; King and Parker 1984; Parker and King

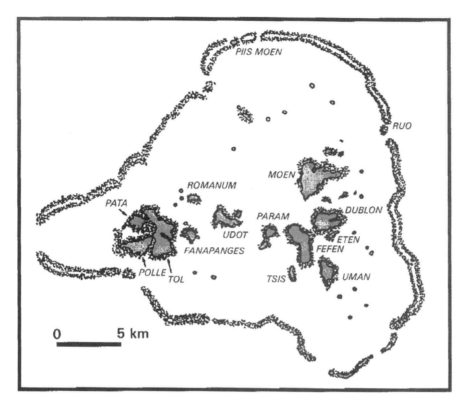

Fig. 7.1 Map of Chuuk Lagoon.

1987). The 1970s and early 1980s remain the busiest times for archaeological research on Chuuk, with only a few projects pursued since then. The Micronesian Endowment for Historic Preservation funded an archaeological survey of Pwene Village, on the island of Dublon (Tonowas) (Craib 1997), and a transect survey was conducted across Fefen Island as part of doctoral research (Rainbird 1994b).

In Chuuk stories regarding the origin of humans state that the people came from the high island of Kosrae at the eastern end of the Caroline Islands. Goodenough (1986) preferred to interpret the legends less specifically, as discussed by Mark Berg (1993: 200):

Three Chuukese legends dealing with early settlement of the lagoon mention migration from Kosrae to Chuuk; Kosrae was often referred to as 'Adjau'; the same word is also a common noun meaning 'basalt'. According to Ward Goodenough 'Kachaw' or Adjau refers to a sky-world rather than to the island of Kosrae. On Yap, Wilhelm Müller noted in 1909–10 that the word *atsau* was a rare word used to mean 'rainbow' which supports Goodenough's contention. But the sets of sailing directions obtained from Satawalese and Puluwatese captains at the same time listed courses for 'Adjau', that is, Kosrae . . . Perhaps it is best to think of Kosrae as just a stop along migration routes followed by people who eventually settled in Chuuk and on the coral islands, so that mention of Kosrae in the legends is just a shorthand method of saying 'from the direction of Kosrae', that is, out of the east or the south-east.

As discussed in chapter 4, the earliest known sites for human settlement on the high islands of Chuuk Lagoon are located on the island of Fefen: according to the radiocarbon dates and stratigraphy they ceased to be occupied after about 500 years (Shutler, Sinoto and Takayama 1984). At this time, approximately 1500 years ago, the use of pottery, a distinctive material marker of human settlement, apparently ceases. The discontinuance of pottery use is not unusual in the Pacific islands, but following its loss in Chuuk, Parker and King (1981) identify a 1000-year break in the archaeological evidence, that they designate the 'long gap'. During this period, up to approximately 500 years ago, they find no evidence of human settlement on the islands within the lagoon. An intensive review of the available dates from Chuuk Lagoon, conducted in the early 1990s, revealed that the long gap, although not as unique to Chuuk as commentators previously supposed, certainly did exist and requires some explanation (Rainbird 1995b).

As reconstructed from the accrued palaeoenvironmental research (Bloom 1970a; 1970b; Curray, Sheperd and Veeh 1970; Brooks 1981; King and Parker 1984; Shutler, Sinoto and Takayama 1984; Matsumoto *et al.* 1986 cited in Athens *et al.* 1989) it appears that, by approximately 3000 years ago, progradation of the coastal flatlands had commenced in Chuuk Lagoon. It is possible that this was due to the slowing rate of submergence, and a consequent equalling out of fringing-reef growth, creating a trap for sea-borne and alluvial sediments. After 1000 years, some locations on the fringing reefs may have offered environments attractive to human settlers. Also at this time, development of the Iras coastal lowlands started, though the evidence from Fefen suggests that it is likely that much of the fringing reefs still remained free from progradation. During the next 1000 years, from the middle of the first millennium AD to the middle of the second, enough sediment was trapped on the reef to allow for the spread of mangrove tree communities. This build-up of sediments also appears to have allowed the formation of freshwater swamps (as at Sapotiu) suitable for the cultivation of taro. The mangroves remain in many places, although Margie Falanruw *et al.* (1987) regard them as not well developed, owing to small land area and therefore to the amount of runoff and silt deposits about the islands. In other places the trapped sediments have been used as a substrate for further filling and use as habitable land. The deep deposits around Tonaachaw suggest this apparent long-term filling and use.

In a soil survey, William Laird (1983b) found that in general terms, 27 per cent of the land area of the islands in Chuuk Lagoon consists of level or nearly level bottom lands and mangrove swamps formed by organic deposits and coral sand

Fig. 7.2 Coastal transgression on Polle, Chuuk Lagoon: palm trees falling in to the mangrove forest and an undermined stone platform are indicators of coastal transgression on this Chuukese island.

(0–3 metres above sea level). The remainder of the land consists of soils of upland varieties, ranging from shallow to very deep and formed by colluvium and residuum from the bedrock.

Currently, on unmaintained coasts, the reverse of progradation is occurring, with coastal transgression clearly a recent phenomenon. This latter phase may be indicative of a rise in the normal minor fluctuations in long-term sea level change, or perhaps an indicator of the proposed recent advent of global warming with consequent sea level rise. But could it be that traditional practices of coastal maintenance have ceased, allowing for consequent erosive effects? I return to this question below.

Environmental change, including coastal progradation, on the islands within Chuuk Lagoon (Moen at least) started before there is any evidence of humans arriving to settle the island; equally, it is clear at both Fefen and Moen, that coastal progradation occurred following the appearance of humans on the islands. Indeed at Iras on Moen, the presence of logs upon the beach suggests either that to ensure their preservation they were quickly covered after arriving on the beach, or that they were actually part of the mixed fill, and may be direct evidence of forest clearance.

On Polle, in the west side of the lagoon, transgression is clearly occurring in the present day (Fig. 7.2). I have suggested some possible reasons for this phenomenon above, but prefer an interpretation that regards this transgression as due to the rupture in traditional practices created by, amongst other things, a reliance on introduced non-local subsistence strategies. Habitual practices, which would traditionally maintain the coastal flats, have been significantly affected by appropriation of a western (mainly American) cash economy. Because of these changes, the coastal lowlands are not being maintained and consequently the sea is reclaiming the space it had enjoyed prior to human intervention. The 'long gap', and similar chronological gaps identified on other islands in the region, may be related to these practices. That is, the manipulation of the environment in order to favour coastal lowland development will in itself destroy or bury much of the archaeological evidence. I will return to this issue, in a comparative discussion with the other islands, in the final chapter.

At the end of the chronological gap, beginning about 500 years ago and lasting until and beyond the arrival of Europeans in the islands, there appears to be a move to settle inland areas, as well as the already established coastal zones. Evidence for hilltop occupation, in the form of middens and enclosed settlements, appears on most of the islands within the lagoon. Many scholars have viewed these sites as material indicators of the commencement of the endemic inter-group and inter-island violent conflict reported in post-European contact texts. Of warfare in the Chuuk islands, Thomas Gladwin and Seymore Sarason (1953: 40) reported that:

Intermittent wars between and within the peoples of various islands characterized the Trukese society as far back as we know it, and along with these organized battles of conquest and revenge there were sporadic fights between individuals and lineages over more personal matters.

Goodenough (1951) found that much of the warring was related to arguments over access to women, and did not appear to relate to the gaining of land or excessive political power. Indeed, the society of Chuuk Lagoon, as recorded post-European contact, was apparently the least hierarchical of all the Carolinian high island societies. It appears that, in general, the senior male of the founding lineage in each district (of approximately 100 persons) was ranked above others, but received little recognition and only the occasional pleasure of receiving periodic food gifts (Alkire 1977). James Peoples (1990; 1993) has argued that the lack of political centralization in Chuuk results from the small size of the islands and their close proximity to each other, which allows people to change allegiances very quickly.

There are few references to battles or warfare relating to the hilltop sites and it may be that the origins of the hilltop sites relate to broader cosmological changes within Chuukese societies. The earliest hilltop sites are little more than piles of discarded shells (midden), which may represent the remnants of meals. Mount Tonaachaw on Moen, which according to oral history appears to play a significant symbolic role in Chuukese history (e.g., Goodenough 1986), had a small shell midden deposit surviving on its summit (King and Parker 1984) (Fig. 7.3). A firepit at the base of the midden yielded a radiocarbon date from charcoal of between 660 and 500 years ago. Elsewhere, excavation by Takayama and Intoh (1978) on Chukienu, a hilltop site on Tol, revealed stone paving directly beneath a shell midden. Radiocarbon dates are inconclusive but indicate that these features may be anything up to 500 years old. A different area of shell midden at Chukienu, which was not related to the stone paving, provided a radiocarbon date from charcoal of between 640 and 310 years ago. These dates may indicate that, prior to the stone paving, this summit was a focus of activity similar to that on Tonaachaw.

Elsewhere, I have proposed that these hilltop sites at Tonaachaw and Chukienu, and others presumably now lost under the more recent hilltop sites discussed below, represent a fundamental change in the Chuukese perception of their island home (Rainbird 1996). No longer were they actively promoting the extension of their lowlands, which suited a cosmology that linked their lives to a coastal and outward direction, but instead they now started to claim the core of their islands, using white shell and fire in the dark and green interiors. The shell symbolically linked the seascape with the landscape and, indeed, it may be at this stage that more rigid territories were being defined.

At a later stage the tops of at least twenty-six, and probably more, of the hills and mountain ridges within Chuuk Lagoon were furnished with stone walls and in a number of cases stone platforms (Fig. 7.4). These hilltop sites take a variety of forms, and walls rarely form a complete circuit, but either cut off ridges or utilize natural topographic features, such as high cliff faces, to complete the definition of the internal area. The platforms may have been constructed as bases for large wooden buildings, possibly community buildings, known in Chuuk as *wuut*, although as recorded by ethnographic observers these are normally built directly on the ground. Frank LeBar (1964: 110) in his CIMA funded research also found that orientation was a significant element of such structures; this does not appear to be the case with the variety of alignments of hilltop stone platforms, as he described it:

Correct orientation was considered an essential part of building operations, and all meeting houses and lineage houses were oriented east–west. This same pattern is observed today in the case of meeting houses; residential units built along aboriginal lines also have the old orientation.

A number of these sites have been investigated (Gosda 1958; Takayama and Seki 1973; Clune 1974; 1977; King 1984; Rainbird 1994b), the most thorough study taking place at Fauba on Tol (Takayama and Seki 1973; Seki 1977; Edwards 1978; Edwards and Edwards 1978). These sites are poorly dated, but where dates are available, they appear to be placed in the period a few centuries before and including the years of early European contact. Researchers commenting on

Fig. 7.3 Mount Tonaachaw, Moen Island, Chuuk Lagoon: excavation on this peak has revealed evidence for ancient occupation in a place regarded in local cosmology as linked to the Thunder God, Soukachaw.

Fig. 7.4 Platform at the Fauba hilltop enclosure with Mount Ulibot in the background, Tol Island, Chuuk Lagoon: the Fauba enclosure is one of the best known on the islands of the lagoon. Another possible example has been recognised on Mount Ulibot, the highest peak in Chuuk Lagoon.

these sites have usually privileged a notion of defence, linked to the historical reports of feuding and warfare. This may be a facet of their role, and they certainly appear to be in close proximity to village boundaries, at least as indicated by mid-twentieth-century mapping. But boundaries are also special places in many cosmological schemes, and much oral history relates to these places as the abodes of spirits and ghosts, and a spiritual role within defined summit space should not be ruled out (see Rainbird 1996).

Augustin Krämer (1932, quoted in Berg 1993: 196) during the *Südsee-Expedition* reported in relation to a hilltop site on Tol island that:

According to legend, the people who lived at the top were long besieged by the coastal dwellers because of their haughtiness. They fled from Chuuk at long last and settled nearby islands, such as Puluwat, Satawal, Lamotrek, Ifaluk, Elato and so on, whose residents they slew so they could take their places. Only a few returned. Some returned from Puluwat, which is why the Puluwatese always call at Tol first when visiting Chuuk.

During this late period, domestic structures were built utilizing an ever-increasing amount of stone for walls and house platforms. King and Parker (1984) have suggested that this late pre-European phase can be explained by a change in subsistence, related to the adoption of breadfruit as the staple crop. The ability to store breadfruit in pits meant a year-round source of food. This allowed for the creation of thoroughly sedentary communities. An investment was made in a plot of land not only by the construction of buildings, but also by the digging of pits for the storage of breadfruit.

In the study of the archaeology of Chuuk Lagoon based on previous work and their own extensive study of the Tonaachaw area of Moen Island, King and Parker (1984) draw at length on the oral accounts of modern informants, and ethnographic and ethnohistorical literature to interpret the material evidence. They provide a culture-historical schema for the lagoon, identifying four phases (King and Parker 1984: 419):

1. *Winas Pattern*   *c.* 500 BC–AD 500
   Sites on the shore with pottery a distinctive feature, also shell ornaments particularly *Conus* rings.
2. *Long Gap*   AD 500–1300
   Little, if any, evidence of settlement within the lagoon.
3. *Tonaachaw Pattern*   post 1300–*c.* 1900
   Characterized by the full range of artefacts associated with ethnographic Chuuk. Includes the full range of archaeological sites recorded for Chuuk with no pottery present.
4. *Historic Period*   *c.* 1900–present
   Colonial rule onwards.

King and Parker concern themselves little with the first two phases and concentrate their research on the final two. They are happy to account for the Tonaachaw Pattern, the last 700 years, by using the accounts of modern informants and ethnography. They were able to suggest that this period was little different from the early historic period and the present. The conclusions of King and Parker are perplexing in that they appear to ignore the evidence of construction, use and abandonment of hilltop enclosures during the period labelled the Tonaachaw Pattern. The archaeological evidence along with the oral history and earlier ethnography can contribute to an understanding of the use of these sites (see Rainbird 1996) and provide a richer appreciation of the recent phases of their culture-historical schema.

From the earliest recorded European encounters with the Chuukese, violence appears to be a common theme. In 1565, the Spaniard Alonso de Arellano entered the lagoon aboard his ship the *San Lucas* and was alarmed by some of the Chuukese, who tried, unsuccessfully, to detach the ship's launch and in apparent frustration hurled spears, while the Spaniards replied with musket shot (Hezel 1973). Arellano anchored and overnighted in a remote part of the lagoon, and made his escape at first light; it was over 250 years before the next recorded visit of a European ship. Although earlier Duperrey had mapped the barrier reef from outside of the lagoon, it was his French compatriot Dumont d'Urville who next visited Chuuk, and entered the lagoon in December 1838. Although items of warfare had been noted amongst the possessions of the Chuukese, such as spears tipped with stingray tails and wooden clubs, Dumont d'Urville's initial impression was one in which 'the natives live together in harmony and are gentle and peaceful by temperament' (Dumont d'Urville 1843 quoted in Hezel 1983: 100). This peaceful impression was shattered when a party from his ship was attacked by a group of Chuukese emanating from another island in the lagoon.

Francis Hezel (1979; 1983) points out that it is likely that Dumont d'Urville found himself embroiled in the endemic local warfare assumed to be typical of the time. The visitors did not wait to confirm that this was the case, but left the day after the attack. Throughout the nineteenth century, as the neighbouring islands became commercial and colonial enclaves, the islands of Chuuk Lagoon were avoided for fear of violence. By the end of the nineteenth century, traders had established stations on Chuuk, but the reputation for violence continued until the late twentieth century (e.g., see Marshall 1979), and may even have deterred western interest in the history and archaeology of the islands.

Apart from a little interest shown in an assessment of possible marine-life exploitation (Purcell 1976), the islands of Chuuk Lagoon do not appear to have been favoured in terms of economic potential by the Japanese. Instead the lagoon became the headquarters for Japanese military operations in the region. By 1935 there were almost 2000 Japanese living there (King and Parker 1984). Most lived on the island of Dublon (Tonowas), where the fishing industry flourished (Young, Rosenberger and Harding 1997). The militarization of Chuuk began with the establishment of a major naval base for the Japanese Fourth Fleet headquarters (Peattie 1988). In addition three airfields were constructed, with the tiny island of Etten physically converted to resemble an aircraft carrier (Fig. 7.5). During 1944 the American advance and bombardment of

Fig. 7.5 Etten Island, Chuuk Lagoon: part of the fringing reef of Etten was
covered by Japanese engineers in order to create an aircraft runway
and this gives the island a form resembling a floating aircraft carrier.

Chuuk isolated it from outside contact and annihilated its offensive capabilities; these were times of incredible hardship for the Chuukese, the Japanese and especially the forced labourers imported from elsewhere (Rainbird 2000b). Jemima Garrett (1996) provides an extremely moving account of this period of Chuukese history, based on interviews with Nauruans transferred to Chuuk by the Japanese. The Japanese forces surrendered in September 1945 and the US Navy took over administration of the islands, beginning a new stage of colonial government.

In archaeology, I have considered the material remains relating to the period of Japanese colonial occupation of Fefen Island, in Chuuk Lagoon, in connection to meaning and transformation in regard to both the Chuukese and the Japanese (Rainbird 2000b). The material landscape of one upland plateau of Fefen has a mnemonic effect. Memory is activated in two different ways. The first is by the Japanese who, after repatriation to Japan following World War II, returned to construct a monument to their dead colleagues. The second is by the Chuukese, who avoid the area and through loss of the place enhance the memory of the hardships of the period. Such studies are not commonplace, but many surveys have reported on the abundant material remains on the islands dating to Second World War military activities (see Denfield 1981b).

Pohnpei

Pohnpei, with an area of 330 square kilometres, is the third largest of the islands in the region, and by far the largest of the eastern Carolines (Fig. 7.6). Pohnpei is mountainous and consequently annual rainfall is extremely high, allowing for large rivers and dense vegetation; the mountains reach an elevation of 790 metres and support cloud forest. The majority of the island is surrounded by a barrier reef, creating a large lagoon with several smaller islands.

Recounting local histories of origin with a specific emphasis on the role played by women, Kimberlee Kihleng (1992: 169–70; see also Hanlon 1988) finds:

They tell of a divinely assisted canoe with sixteen voyagers – nine of whom were women – that sailed from a foreign shore to the south. Upon reaching a submerged reef these voyagers constructed a stone altar that served as a foundation for what later became Pohnpei. Using their supernatural powers, two of the female travellers covered the stone structures with soil they had carried with them on their journey. Six succeeding voyages brought more men and women to Pohnpei, carrying with them the necessities for life on a new island, including the first varieties of banana plants and yam seedlings which were brought by two women who accompanied the sixth voyage of settlement from Katau Peidi in the west.

A soil survey of Pohnpei divided the island into two generalized types of landscape (Laird 1982). The first includes the alluvial 'bottom lands', which are

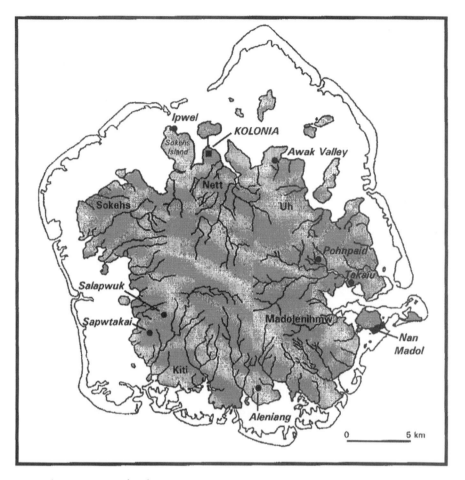

Fig. 7.6 Map of Pohnpei.

level to gently sloping in relief and account for 18 per cent of the land area. The remaining area consists of the upland soil unit very similar to that described for the islands in Chuuk Lagoon (see above).

The environmental history of Pohnpei is not well known, but Bloom's (1970b) cores showed that sediment has been constantly deposited in estuarine mangrove swamps, indicating Holocene submergence. In his doctoral research, Alan Haun (1984: v) took as one of his four aims an ecological approach, which sought to 'define the pre-human environmental setting [on Pohnpei] and to identify spatial and temporal variations that may explicate developmental changes and intra-island differences in subsistence strategy'. To address this issue, Haun took cores from three inland swamps in the Awak valley and one at a coastal mangrove location. Also, a small trench was excavated in upland fern country, to complement the results obtained from the cores.

Haun found that the mangroves of Pohnpei have been a feature of the shore-line from early in the Holocene and, more importantly, that beginning around 2500 to 2000 years ago, there is evidence from the upland area that indicates clearing by fire and subsequent soil erosion. However, there is not enough evidence to support the hypothesis that these locations ever had enough soil to support a dense forest which would require clearing. Also in this period the Leh en Luhk depression, located at 90 metres above sea level, appears to have switched a number of times from lake to swamp and vice versa.

Visitors to Pohnpei during the nineteenth century soon became aware of the existence of the large and apparently abandoned site of Nan Madol, consisting of monumental stone-built architecture on the fringing reef of the small lagoon island of Temwen (e.g., O'Connell 1972 [1836]; Clark 1852; Kubary 1874; Christian 1899b; see also Athens 1981). Interest in Nan Madol continued through the German and Japanese administrations (e.g., Yawata 1932b; Hambruch 1936; Muranushi 1942) and, as historian David Hanlon (1990) has pointed out, archaeological research through the second half of the twentieth century has led to a great deal of 'speculation and conjecture'. Nan Madol's size and complexity has attracted a great deal of modern archaeological attention (Athens 1980a; 1980c; 1983; 1984; 1990b; Saxe, Allenson and Loughbridge 1980b; Ayres, Haun and Mauricio 1983; Ayres 1988; 1990a; 1992; 1993; Bryson 1989; Bath and Athens 1990), and it is considered to be one of the most fascinating archaeological sites in the islands of Oceania. As sites such as this are prone to, it has also attracted other, rather more fantastic, non-archaeological theories (e.g., Morrill (1970), who thinks that Nan Madol proves that there had once been a vast inhabited land mass in the Pacific, which has been submerged; see also Von Däniken (1973) who survived the 'hot humid hell of Nan Madol').

The popular American author Willard Price, who provided the quote in the title of this chapter, was one of only a few foreigners allowed to travel in the Caroline Islands during the Japanese mandate years. On visiting Nan Madol, and helping with an archaeological excavation by the visiting Japanese noble Prince Saionji, he describes a scene that he imagines may have occurred at this place (1936: 236):

It is a stormy morning a few thousand years ago. Magnificent canoes, shaped somewhat like gigantic, sea-going gondolas, bravely decorated, move in procession through the water streets of Nanmatal [Nan Madol]. Some are double canoes with a platform between. On these decks maidens dance. Time is kept by the lion-roar of a great drum, five feet high, shaped like monstrous dice boxes, and covered with the skin of the stingray. In one canoe is King Chau-te-leur and his priests. He has proclaimed this festival in honour of the completion of his city. Flowers rain down from the hands of women who line the crests of the battlements high among the tops of palm trees.

Nan Madol is a site created from ninety-two artificial islets, separated by canals, upon a tidal fringing reef (Fig. 7.7). From the earliest date for construction

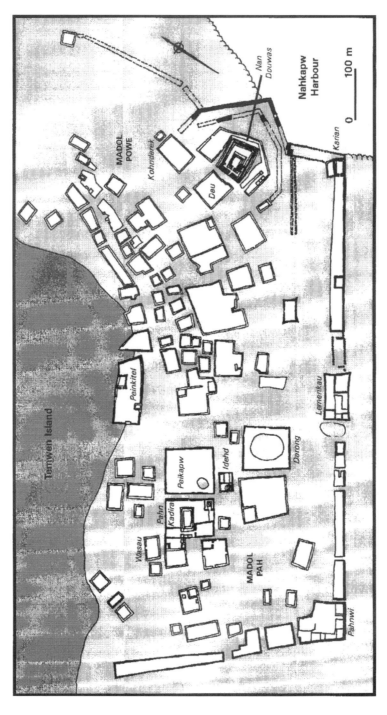

Fig. 7.7 Plan of Nan Madol (after Morgan 1988). The artificial islets and sea wall are constructed on the reef fringing Temwen Island.

Fig. 7.8 The mound on Idehd Islet, Nan Madol, was excavated during the Smithsonian Expedition. The residue recovered apparently included many turtle bones, consistent with local tradition that the mound and islet was related to a turtle ceremony.

derived from Wasau Islet (Ayres 1993), the site developed into a complex of monumental architecture probably serving secular, mortuary and, perhaps, other non-secular functions. Although the sandy substrate was occupied earlier (see chapter 4), the artificially raised islets appear to have been built starting around 1500 years ago, and islet construction slowly expanded towards the reef edge (Ayres 1993). Excavations on the mortuary islet of Nan Douwas, close to the reef edge, revealed a relict beach or sand bar beneath the platform. Charcoal scatters and concentrations on this surface reveal use of this area prior to islet construction. A radiocarbon date from this horizon suggests that the outer area of Nan Madol was not developed prior to 800 years ago (Ayres 1993), suggesting that the site developed over a period of at least 700 years.

Ayres places the demise of Nan Madol at around 450–350 years ago, and this is in part derived from the reconstructed oral history that proposes this date as the collapse of *Saudeleur* hegemony (see below). A 1963 Smithsonian expedition led by Reisenberg, Evans and Meggers investigated a mound traditionally related to a ritual turtle ceremony (Fig. 7.8). The mound, on Idehd Islet, certainly contained burnt turtle bone, and three radiocarbon dates indicated that it had been in use between 890 and 340 years ago (*Radiocarbon* 1965). The as yet not fully published information from the excavations by Steve Athens appears to propose use of Nan Madol, for fishing at least, up to very recent times (Leach, Davidson and Athens 1996). What is clear is that, by the time of European visits in the middle of the nineteenth century, the site was only in minimal use.

Given that there are no obvious outcrops or quarries in the immediate area of Nan Madol, there has been some attempt to source the stone used to construct the architecture. Gordon Goles, as part of Ayres' broader project aims, has started mapping locations and conducting petrographic and geochemical (INAA, XRF) analysis in order to match the potential sources for the boulders and columnar basalt material. The preliminary results indicate that stone from a variety of sources is used in the walls of Nan Douwas, but the investigators are not clear as to whether this can be interpreted as a result of initial construction or later repairs. The long-term goal of the project 'is to tie the Nan Madol complex and related sites together graphically, structurally and ideologically' (Ayres, Goles and Beardsley 1997: 57).

F.W. Christian, writing in 1899, describes the trees and creepers that were destroying the walls of the complex. However, in making clearings in order to pursue his investigations he ran into trouble with the local community, who believed that spirits of the ancestors resided in the vegetation that grew here. This is an interesting and continuing theme, because many Pohnpeians continue to believe that Nan Madol is inhabited by the spirits (*ani*), and this challenges archaeological notions of abandonment. That is, it might be said that although overgrown and uninhabited for at least two centuries, Nan Madol continues to be a place alive with meaning for Pohnpeian people. The contested interests surrounding the site in the present have been well described by Glenn Petersen (1995a).

Archaeological investigations at Nan Madol have led to the recovery of a wide range of artefacts, bone and shell from the islets. The ceramic assemblage shows that pottery was in use a great deal longer on Pohnpei than on the other islands of the eastern Carolines. As noted in chapter 4, pottery appears to have been present from initial colonization, and on Pohnpei has currency until at least 1100 years ago and possibly as recently as 800 years ago (Bryson 1989; Ayres 1993; Rainbird 1999a). The pottery falls into two basic types based on temper: the typically early Calcareous Sand Tempered (CST) ware, which virtually disappears by 1500 years ago (Bryson 1989), and Plainware, which is present in small quantities in the early period but then predominates until the demise of ceramics. However, it should be noted here that the identification of Plainware is not unproblematic, as Dickinson (1995) has found that the calcareous temper may be removed by water solution, leaving an apparently plain sherd. Pottery from Pohnpei shows little decoration, usually limited to notching on the lip and rim (Bryson 1989; Athens 1990b). Spatial analyses of the pottery distribution undertaken by Bryson (1989) showed that the great majority of pottery is found in Madol Powe, the northern half of Nan Madol, and this may indicate that this is the area where the earliest platforms were constructed.

Animal bones recovered in excavations show some general trends in the protein component of the diet (Kataoka 1991; 1996). Ayres (1993) reports that remains of fish, dog, turtle, rat and bird have been recovered (listed in order of their relative importance as a food source). Over time, there was a decrease in the diversity of seafood with an increased reliance on specific species of fish and shellfish, particularly the *Anadara* clam and the small gastropod *Strombus strombus*. Foss Leach, Janet Davidson and Steve Athens (1996) propose a convincing argument, based on fish remains and architecture, that in part at least, the canals at Nan Madol were used to trap the small reef fish that would normally inhabit this environment. They propose that trapping and then poisoning may have been the typical method and, although they did not note this, Christian (1899b: 91) reported that within Nan Douwas:

A tangle of grasses and creeper carpets the precinct; among them a poison-weed like a Wistaria, the bruised roots of which, tied in bundles, native fishermen dabble in the water of the surf-pools at low tide, to which they impart a milky tinge and stupify the fish. The [Pohnpeians] call it *Up*, the Malays *Tuba*.

The poison plant species is *Derris elliptica* and is known locally as *uhp kitik* (Rehg and Sohl 1979). Its compatibility with the artificial islet environment may indicate an easy association between the plant and fishing at Nan Madol.

Some of the earliest explorations of Nan Madol report the recovery of human remains. O'Connell (1972 [1836]), Christian (1899b) and Muranushi (1942) report the presence of human skeletal remains within the central tomb of Nan Douwas (Fig. 7.9). More recent archaeological research has uncovered other remains of the probable inhabitants of Nan Madol. Pahnwi, a massively constructed islet on the corner of the sea wall in Madol Pah, the south half of the site, was in 1984 subjected to excavations and survey by Ayres and his team. The large tomb (*lolong*) of Pahnwi is constructed in the typical header and stretcher method of Pohnpei. Such construction utilizes columnar basalt, with each layer at right angles to the last, as in the construction of log cabins, but using stone rather than timber. Excavation of the tomb found it to contain the remains of a minimum of six adults, and at least two children aged between 2 and 4 years (Tasa 1988). A subsidiary cist within the tomb contained the fragmentary remains of two children aged between 3 and 5 years.

In association with the human skeletal remains, the tomb on Pahnwi also contained approximately 10,000 artefacts, 9000 of which are shell beads (Tasa 1988). These, and the other artefacts collected, fall into the categories recovered by earlier excavators from other tombs around the site. They include pearl shell fishing lure shanks, *Tridacna* shell adzes, perforated shark teeth, shell pendants and/or needles, and armbands or rings manufactured from both *Conus* and

Fig. 7.9 The central tomb (*lolong*) at Nan Douwas, Nan Madol. This is
the central feature of perhaps the most spectacular walled islet in
Nan Madol. The tomb has been excavated a number of times by
antiquarians and interested individuals, with fragments of bone
presumably confirming its use as a tomb.

Tridacna shell. The fishing lure shanks have at times been regarded as valued
pendants, as opposed to basic fishing technology, and the petroglyph site at
nearby Pohnpaid may indicate they had a special status (see below). Rare basalt
stone adzes and imported obsidian flakes have also been reported from mortuary
contexts (Christian 1899b; Ayres and Mauricio 1987). The stone adzes appear
to be important artefacts and have been found in tombs outside of the Nan
Madol complex and on the island proper, but the occasional flaking of basalt
to provide basic cutting tools has also been identified (Ayres and Mauricio
1987).

The apparent specific spatial distribution of formal stone artefacts can be
matched at Nan Madol by the spatial distribution of mortuary architecture. As
can be observed in Figure 7.10, the islets that show some indication of mortuary
activity are, except for one special case which I will return to below, constructed
on the seaward side of the site. Many are actually on the sea wall itself, and
this spatial location indicates that they are some of the last structures to have
been constructed at Nan Madol. The only *lolong* within the core area of Nan
Madol that does not fit this pattern is that on the islet of Peinkitel. The islet
of Peinkitel is noteworthy for two reasons: the first is that it is the only islet

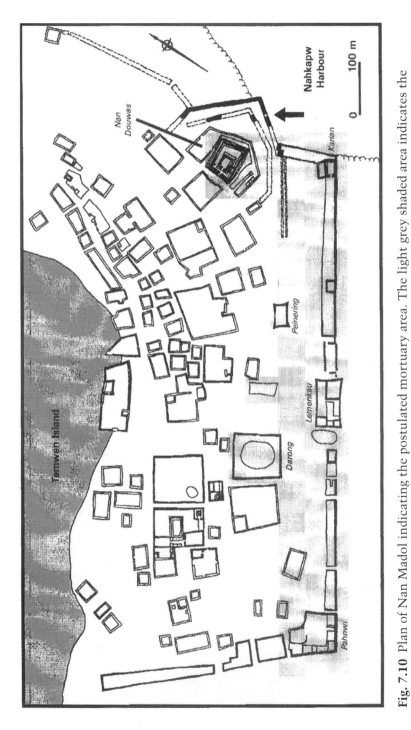

Fig. 7.10 Plan of Nan Madol indicating the postulated mortuary area. The light grey shaded area indicates the location of the majority of known mortuary features. The bold arrow below Nan Douwas (in the area of Nahkapw Harbour) indicates the deep-sea entrance through the breakwater (after Morgan 1988).

Fig. 7.11 Nan Douwas: a view from inside the breakwater entrance.

that appears to have been built half on the dry land of Temwen Island and half on the fringing reef; second, the tomb on Peinkitel is reputed in oral history to be the burial place of Isohkelekel.

Isohkelekel is the man reputed to have freed Pohnpeians from a long history of evil dictatorship by defeating the last of the *Saudeleur* dynasty. The *Saudeleur* dynasty is regarded as able to trace a direct ancestry to the brothers Olsipha and Olsopha, the founders of Nan Madol. The *Saudeleurs* are reputed to have ruled Pohnpei through a harsh regime that involved extracting massive tribute from the rest of the population, in order to maintain themselves in their island home. They were all-seeing over the island, and terrible retribution would follow any transgression of their law. If we can, in reality, find any material links between the oral history and archaeology, then the period of tomb construction on the seaward side of Nan Madol may be linked to the *Saudeleur* hegemony, and the greater expression of their power not only to locals, but also to visitors. The only entrance available to long-distance visitors is through the sea wall at a point adjacent to the greatest mortuary expression at Nan Douwas (Figs. 7.10 and 7.11).

The burial of Isohkelekel on the islet of Peinkitel may then be seen to link the man formally with his political history after death. Here, the architecture links the fringing reef with the dry land and metaphorically draws Isohkelekel in from the sea, from whence he came, and on to the dry land that he became part of as popular hero or 'stranger king' according to Hanlon (1988). However, as

Petersen (1990a) observes, Isohkelekel has his origins in Pohnpei and therefore cannot be considered a stranger king; nevertheless, we might consider that no longer was elite power separated from the land by being situated on the reef.

As Ayres and others have made clear in their research, Nan Madol should not be considered in isolation, and related and other sites on the main island have not been neglected. In 1977, a long-term project of survey and limited excavation was instigated under the direction of Ayres, and included investigation of Pohnpeian settlement in its economic and sociopolitical landscape (Ayres 1979; Ayres and Haun 1980; 1985; 1990; Ayres, Haun and Severance 1981; Haun 1984; Mauricio 1986; Falgout 1987; Ayres and Mauricio 1990; 1997; 1999). This research has been augmented by the survey and excavation work of Athens (1980b), Saxe, Allenson and Loughbridge (1980a), Streck (1980; 1984; 1985), Bath (1984a; 1984b) and Brulotte (1986).

Ayres and Mauricio (1990) found that approximately 90 per cent of main island archaeological sites are stone architectural features, which exhibit substantial diversity. Ayres (1993) notes that thousands of these 'dot the Pohnpei landscape' and range from house platforms to tombs, possible 'forts' and agricultural features. Other archaeological sites include earth constructions, artefact scatters and middens. In a survey of the area of the village of Salapwuk in Kiti Municipality, south-west Pohnpei, Ayres and Mauricio (1990) found that the typical site consisted of a cluster of earthen features and stone architecture.

Ayres and Mauricio's typical site description is as far as interpretation of the main island settlement pattern has been able to proceed. The detailed surveys at Awak and Salapwuk conducted by Ayres and his colleagues have only included excavation as a minor component, allowing notions of diachronic change to be related almost exclusively to the oral histories and ethnography of political factionism of questionable chronological depth. There is still much to be recorded, and we can see tantalizing glimpses in such things as Davidson's (1967b: 88) brief visit to a site high up in the mountains of Madolenihmw Municipality, where she observed numerous stone platforms in eighteen units on a narrow ridge which include '[e]ighty sites suitable for supporting houses'. Davidson's note forms the only archaeological description of this apparently complex site, but Pohnpeians often talk of sites deep in the interior that they relate to evacuation of lowland areas during periods of intra-island conflict, and Davidson may be describing one such site. Damon (1861) noted from missionary diaries that 'panic-struck' Pohnpeians fled to the mountains during a smallpox outbreak in the 1850s; Gorenflo and Levin (1992: 5) note that 'As a result of diseases the population of Pohnpei Island declined from more than 10,000 persons in the 1820s to as few as 2,000 in the 1850s.' Joyce Bath did take the opportunity to explore one hilltop site, albeit not in the mountains.

During 1980, Bath (1984a; 1984b) conducted survey and excavation in an area neighbouring Salapwuk. The hilltop site of Sapwtakai was central to this research, as Bath considered it 'a regional centre, contemporaneous with and architecturally reflective of Nan Madol' (1984b: 81). At 220 metres above sea level, the site of Sapwtakai consists of platforms and a tomb, surrounded on most sides by a wall, which is particularly large at the northern end of the site (Fig. 7.12). The total enclosed area is approximately 1.75 hectares and the removal of vegetation would probably allow extensive views of the lowland areas of Kiti and out to sea, including Ant Atoll. Other features consist of breadfruit storage pits, an oven area, a midden area, a pit probably for water storage and paved terraces (Bath 1984a; Morgan 1988).

The commanding hilltop position of Sapwtakai, along with the size of its northern perimeter walls, at the point of easiest access to the summit, may indicate a defensive function for the site. Bath collected possible slingstones and two 'basalt war clubs'. But as a regional centre, in a potentially difficult context of shifting allegiances, it may have played a more symbolic role in relation to the establishment and maintenance of authority. Although not necessarily contradicting this view, Bath concluded that no status-linked artefacts were recorded at the site, except for pounding stones typically used for crushing the roots of the *Piper methysticum* plant to make *sakau* (*kava*).

The *Piper methysticum* plant, which is used on various islands across Oceania to prepare the mildly narcotic drink *kava*, is found in Pohnpei as *sakau*, and prior to missionary intervention in Kosrae as *seka*. Utilizing a variety of techniques, including botanic, genetic and chemical evidence, northern Vanuatu has been identified as the most likely area for the domestication and initial dispersal of *P. methysticum* (Lebot 1991; Lebot, Merlin and Lindstrom 1992). Pounding stones for the preparation of *sakau* are a ubiquitous feature of sites on Pohnpei, and it appears that consuming this narcotic drink is probably an old practice, but introduced through contact with Polynesians (Crowley 1994). The societies of Pohnpei and Kosrae are alone in Micronesia in having a history of using *kava*. Its use on Pohnpei, as recorded ethnographically, follows strict protocol in a variety of social circumstances, but it is not necessarily restricted to elite sites, and thus the presence of the pounding stones cannot alone be used as an indicator of status.

Bath did not consider Sapwtakai to be an isolated and independent site, but actually the 'citadel' for higher-status settlement-clusters located on the piedmont of the hilltop at Panpei, Peinkareraua and the Kiti Rock complex (1984a; 1984b). Panpei, for example, is a group of four large stone platforms and an unusual type of tomb containing four crypts (Bath 1984a) (Fig. 7.13). All of these sites, and Sapwtakai itself, have columnar basalt prisms incorporated into their architecture, and the use of this type of stone, for Bath, provides a direct material indicator of a high-status site.

Unfortunately, once again, owing to minimal excavation it cannot be shown that these sites are contemporaneous with Sapwtakai. Bath appears to have been confident that her research dated the occupation of Sapwtakai to between about 500 through to approximately 100 years ago, but none of the radiocarbon

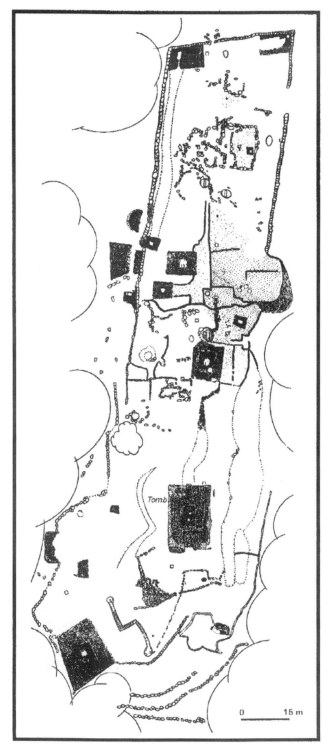

Tomb

0   15 m

Fig. 7.12 Plan of Sapwtakai, Kiti District. Possibly an alternative 'centre' to Nan Madol (after Morgan 1988).

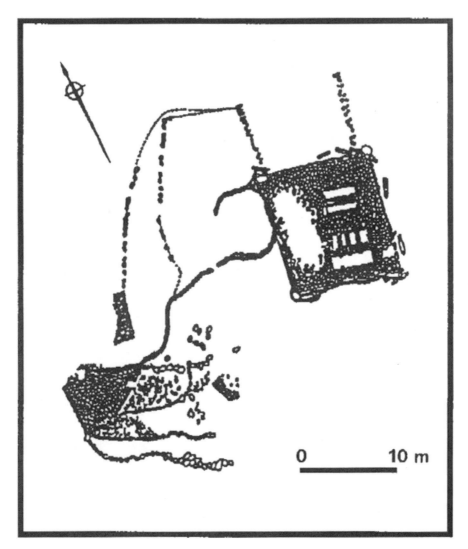

Fig. 7.13 Plan of tombs at Panpei West. These are located among other features below the summit of Sapwtakai and may form part of a larger linked complex (after Bath 1984a).

dates is directly related to the architecture. In reality, the most that can be said is that some of the stone construction started after 630 years ago.

This weak chronology does still provide some support for Bath's (1984a: 152) conclusion that Sapwtakai was developing as a special place at the same time that Nan Madol was declining, and that:

Rather than representing a secondary-level political centre in a unified island-wide system [under Nan Madol] Sapwtakai could represent a late district political centre, imitative of old traditions in stylistic construction but not necessarily organised in the same manner.

Such an imitative role for the architecture at Sapwtakai may represent more than simple mimesis, but rather an extension to a mnemonic device that leads back through the tombs (*lolong*) to ceramics at Nan Madol. I have suggested elsewhere (Rainbird 1999a) that during the first millennium of settlement on Pohnpei pottery became representative of the ancestors. After that time, the link between the ceramics and the exotic and distant origins of the ancestors became inappropriate, and the ancestors were more suitably and actively seen as local. This change in cosmology, perhaps a case of symbolizing formal appropriation of the island, was materialized in the construction of tombs that appear to start at the time pottery production ends. At Sapwtakai then, it would be essential to tie the ancestors to the regional centre, and *lolong* on the summit and on the slopes directly below would have been an essential physical manifestation of the ancestors' power and tenure.

Archaeologists and others have at times been guilty of not taking a critical stance in relation to historical and oral sources. In an assessment of the early Euro-American accounts of Nan Madol, many of which are used as an 'endpoint' for archaeologists, Hanlon (1990: 109) found that they are full of 'presumptions, ignorance, racism, self-justification, exploitation and factual errors'. In a more recent paper addressing one of the major published works of Pohnpeian oral history, *The Book of Luelen*, Hanlon accepts that although there is unease about such things, Bernart's book, and oral history more generally, can 'provide precious glimpses of a deeper, more distant past' (1992: 20), but he does express the need for understanding the context of its production and the localized and personal nature of its content. For Hanlon, plurality should be expected (1992: 32):

The issue then becomes not the discrediting of Luelen's book and other oral or orally informed sources of history because of their variations, ambiguities, contradictions, or general lack of agreement; rather, these are the very sources to value for the important reason that they give us a sense of event and of the multiple meanings and significance of those events to different and self-defining groups of people on the island.

Petersen has also pursued the issue of the value of oral history in reconstructions of Pohnpei history, and especially to archaeology, in a paper presented at the Micronesian Archaeology Conference held in Guam in 1987. Petersen (1990b: 149) makes the point as a warning that 'sociopolitical organisation was in considerable flux in the early nineteenth century'. Further, that owing to this flux, 'We cannot use modern images . . . as indicative of what Pohnpei life was like at the time of contact, nor can we use such an image of that period to explain what had been taking place 400 years earlier' (1990b: 149). Petersen concludes his paper by requesting that archaeologists stop relying on the historical sources and utilize the archaeological record to provide evidence to elucidate the complexities of Pohnpeian social organization through time. Petersen (1990a) is in conflict with the view of Hanlon regarding the use of oral sources, as he judges oral accounts unsuitable for reconstructing Pohnpei's past, seeing them as political devices of use only in the context of their oration.

Bath and Athens (1990) in their paper delivered at the same conference, address basic questions about the complexity of social and political organization on Pohnpei, by stating that their interest concerns the development of chiefdom societies from an evolutionary perspective. It is their wish to test the archaeological data from Nan Madol against the oral accounts of Luelen Bernart and his grandson Masao Hadley. In the first instance, the methodology is an admirable one: the examination of tension between parallel lines of information could be used to tease out new interpretations of the past. However, this potential is not realized and Bath and Athens take the majority of the available oral history as 'fact' and, where they are able, tie their interpretation of material remains into the accounts provided by the local historians.

Bath and Athens propose to account for the demise of Nan Madol as a priestly, ritual and elite centre through the indigenous stories that tell of the 'evil' *Saudeleur* dynasty being defeated and replaced by the Nahnmwarki system similar to that in operation in the present day. They see the demise of the central *Saudeleur* dynasty as 'devolution'. For me, it is not clear how the separation of Pohnpei into four or five independent units each with two 'chiefs', with each one the head of a parallel ritual and secular hierarchy, can be considered a 'simplification' of the sociopolitical organization of society. An interpretation of this type can only be possible when the evaluator is tied to a model of social evolution that expects centralization of power as the most complex form of social organization. This model is clearly inappropriate for assessing the island society of Pohnpei.

The complexity of Pohnpei's traditional social structure is not to be doubted. Matrilineality is the basis for title achievement in the multiple ranking systems; but as Petersen (1982a) has shown, the 'matrilineal puzzle' of the apparent growing separation of descent and authority in such a system, that caused consternation to a generation of anthropologists including David Schneider who worked in the Carolines, is maintained and still exists because of its flexibility. This flexibility (see also Petersen 1999) supports the overwhelming Pohnpeian desire to avoid centralization of authority, and is clearly reflected in the Pohnpeian term translated by Petersen (1982b) as 'one man cannot rule a thousand'. For Petersen the stories of the evil *Saudeleur* hegemony are not to be taken as direct historical account, but are moral directives told as warnings regarding the containing of political and ritual authority in a single centre.

Elements of traditional spatial correlates to gender and power have been mapped in contemporary gatherings at the community houses known as *nahs*. These community houses are distinctive in plan, having a U-shaped platform on top of which is erected a roof that also covers the area of earth within the U. In this space *sakau* is pounded, and on the occasion of feasts cooked breadfruit may also be pounded here. In his chronology of Pohnpei, outlined below, Ayres proposes that *nahs* were first constructed some 500 years ago and represent the advent of a new political system. The ethnographically recorded space within a *nahs* is tightly controlled (Mauricio 1993; Keating 1999). The chiefly persons have separate entrances by gender, which lead them directly on to the highest part of the platform at the base of the U. Other participants in the gathering are seated along the arms of the U, in descending ranking order towards their ends. I will return to issues of social organization below and in the final chapter, but here I will complete a description of the 'orthodox' view.

Ayres (1990b: 189) divides the history of Pohnpei into six 'culture-historical phases':

1. *Settlement and Adaptive Integration Phase*   pre-500 BC–AD 1
   Inland forest clearance, Awak; CST pottery in use.
2. *Peinais Phase*   AD 1–1000
   Stone house foundations, breadfruit storage pits, pottery with rim notching, rare punctate and incised line designs; Nan Madol islets with some columnar basalt construction as early as AD 500–600.
3. *Nan Madol Phase*   AD 1000–1500
   Expansion and formalization of Nan Madol complex and associated sociopolitical aspects (Deleur 'empire'), chiefly residential architecture, stylized tombs (*lolong*), pottery declining in use – increasingly Plainware – or absent.
4. *Isohkelekel Phase*   AD 1500–1826
   Disintegration of the Deleur polity, Nahnmwarki title in use, chiefly complexes and new style meeting houses (*nahs*), post-pottery.
5. *Early Contact Phase*   AD 1826–1885
   Western contact; Nan Madol occupation continues but in non-centre role.
6. *Historic Phase*   AD 1885–present
   Western contact and colonial governments.

In Ayres' culture-historical phases, the first two are defined by archaeology, with the subsequent two phases (3 and 4) defined almost wholly by oral-historical accounts that, for the most part, the archaeology merely serves to illustrate. For example, in Phase 3 the archaeology of Nan Madol cannot be separated as an entity worthy of consideration detached from its presumed 'sociopolitical aspects', which are derived from oral accounts relating the site with the 'Deleur Empire'. Phase 4 goes one step further in actually naming this period after a mythological (or mythologized) figure named in traditional stories.

For Ayres, it appears that the archaeology in the more recent pre-contact phases is of secondary importance in comparison to the 'primary' source of oral history. This history is made sense of by inclusion in an overall, but implicit, social evolutionary perspective which is evident, for example, in this statement: 'The primary hypothesis is that Nan Madol's development as a chiefly and priestly center reflects an *evolving chiefdom* that controlled a Pohnpei polity from c. AD 1000 to 1500' (Ayres 1990b: 202; my emphasis).

The final two phases defined by Ayres are also not as unproblematic as they look at first sight. He dates the beginning of the 'Early Contact Phase' with the first recorded visit to the island, but as I have suggested in chapter 2, the effects of encounters with difference were probably being felt long before the first actual record of encounter. The most recent phase is apparently of little concern to Ayres, but it should be, as it is a continuation of the process of encounters with difference. It is then extremely significant, in that it accounts for much of the 'ethnographic present', or 'endpoint', to which the evolutionary models of Ayres are aiming. In the model provided by Ayres it should surely be expected that more detailed and critical attention be paid to these late phases.

One site that on present evidence is unique in Pohnpei, and not comparable within the region, is that named Pohnpaid. Pohnpaid, also known as Indenlang, Takai-nin-Talang, Takai en Intolen, Tilen and Takaien, is a complex of engraved rocks and boulders situated above the Lehdau River in the Sapwalap village area of Madolenihmw. A detailed recording of the engravings (petroglyphs) identified over 750 individual motifs (Rainbird and Wilson 1999). The majority of the motifs consist of a number of repeated forms, which included human foot and hand prints, human figures (anthropomorphs), fishhooks, dots and circles. An especially interesting find was the presence of enveloped crosses that are a feature of much Melanesian rock-art (both painted and engraved).

The major motif type at Pohnpaid has sometimes been referred to as representing a 'sword' or 'dagger' (Fig. 7.14). These motifs Rainbird and Wilson (1999) propose may actually represent fishing lures. Lures are generally regarded as an item of fishing gear specifically for use in catching pelagic (deep-water) fish, but there is a limited amount of information to show that lures had more value than purely as fishing apparatus.

It is important to note here that in the earliest European records of Pohnpeian society no reference is made to seacraft, other than those suitable for use within the lagoon (Ayres 1993). Further support that lures would not have been used for deep-sea fishing on Pohnpei in late prehistoric times is found in the analysis of excavated material from Nan Madol where 'Fish bone remains . . . indicate that pelagic fishing, if practised at all, must have been a very minor activity' (Leach, Davidson and Athens 1996: 333). Indeed, Hambruch and Eilers (1936) found that pearl shell lures functioned as a shell valuable or type of money. The inferred prestige value of such lures perhaps explains the usual mortuary context for the recovery of such artefacts (Athens 1980a).

Ethnographic accounts from elsewhere in the Carolines emphasize the importance placed on the selection of raw materials for lures. In his study of tuna fishing amongst the Satawal islanders of the central Caroline Islands, Robert Gillett (1987: 11–14) reports that:

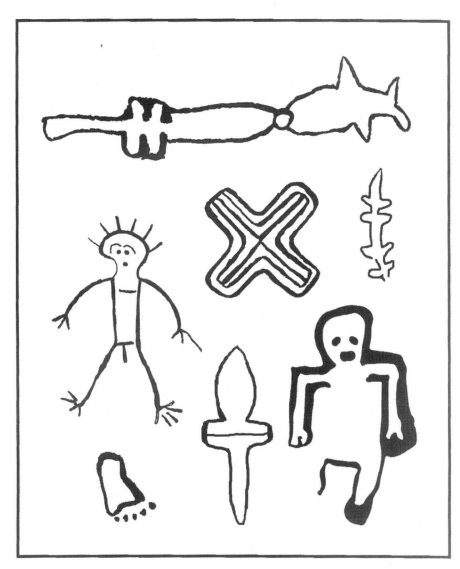

Fig. 7.14 A selection of engravings from the Pohnpaid site, Pohnpei. The top motif is one of two identified at the site, which may depict a fish on a lure. The central feature, between the two anthropomorphs, is an enveloped cross.

A large assortment of pearl-head squids, feather jigs, and large, exotic-looking lures are used on trolling lines . . . Pearl shell does not occur naturally on Satawal and must be imported . . . New Guinea pearl shell, although thick and strong, was not quite as highly prized as that from Truk [Chuuk] due to its colour . . . the Truk variety was 'like a rainbow,' with red, yellow, and orange mixed with gold . . . The pearl shell lures . . . ranged from 5 to 15 centimetres long, excluding the feathers.

Although actually used for fishing, these lures have a value beyond the purely mundane, and if indeed they took on further significance as prestige objects in Pohnpei, their marking on rock may be less remarkable. It is perhaps the case that as ocean-going sailing became moribund, in part because of the enormous attracting potential of Nan Madol, the lure took on a new role as a symbol of former voyaging, which had been a source for gaining cultural capital.

Another feature at Pohnpaid provides a glimpse of local cosmologies that may link into the broader ones of voyaging and ancestry. One facet of this feature consists of low piles of stones forming a flat surface. Such stone piles have elsewhere on Pohnpei been identified as shrines, where offerings are left for the spirits. Ayres, Haun and Severance (1981: 20) report 'a small shrine platform (1 × 1.5 × 0.5 m high) of basalt stones used in offering ferns to local spirits (ani)' in the rock shelter at Pahn Takai in Uh. Hanlon (1988: 179) mentions a number of stone piles built as shrines and states that: 'Pohnpeians believed that ritual supplication accompanied by appropriate offerings induced their gods to release the bounty of the land and the sea.' Of course, a literal translation of the name Pohnpei is 'upon a stone altar'.

The Pohnpaid 'shrine' is situated in the centre of four hollows that have been ground into the rock outcrop, and in plan these form the corners of a rectangle measuring 1.5 by 2 metres. These hollows were capable of holding wooden posts that may have supported a cover over the shrine. The example from Uh was in a rock shelter, so the addition of a cover may not be inappropriate. Located as it is on the highest terrace of the main engraved outcrop, it is possible to look south-easterly along the long axis of the rectangular feature, and find that there is a direct alignment with the prominent and sharp summit of Mount Takaiu, located on the shore of Madolenihmw Bay. This not only provides a direct visual link between the engraving site and the sea, it also hints at a sophisticated cultural landscape inherent with meaning.

Elsewhere I have proposed (Rainbird 2002b) that the importance of the creation of the engravings at Pohnpaid is potentially related more to the aural than to the visual. I developed this idea in two local ways, one in regard to the current sound-producing propensity of the apparently exfoliating rock, which attracts children to hit it with sticks and produce sounds of different pitch. The second is the sound and ethnography related to *sakau* preparation (Riesenberg 1968; Petersen 1995b). That is, the sound produced by beating stone pounders on the basalt slabs resonates far through the forest, and in the various rhythms created by the multiple pounding persons, messages are imparted to the community at large about things such as the stage of production of the *sakau*, or if anyone of importance is present in the *nahs* (community meeting house). I argue, and this very much follows from Alfred Gell (1995) talking of a different circumstance, that in heavily forested situations the aural has higher sensory importance in some circumstances than the visual, thus overturning common western hierarchies of the senses.

Robert Langdon (1992) provides controversial evidence to suggest that Spanish castaways were present in the Caroline Islands as early as the sixteenth century, but for Pohnpei there is no certain evidence of foreign settlement until that of Euro-American beachcombers who had arrived by around 1830: some 200–300 years after the first recorded sightings of the island (Zelenietz and Kravitz 1974). An Irish castaway James O'Connell, who later achieved fame as the 'Tattooed Irishman', lived on the island in the 1820s, and in 1836 published his account of the five years he spent there. By 1850 it is recorded that approximately 150 foreigners were residing on Pohnpei (Marshall and Marshall 1976). By the end of the nineteenth century Pohnpei was fully incorporated within the Spanish and later German colonial spheres.

In the Wene district at the south of the island, Suzanne Falgout (1987) has recorded the remains of the Spanish Fort Aleniang and an adjacent Catholic mission. According to the information collected by Falgout, the Spanish structures in Wene were established next to the 'royal compound' of Aleniang. Features within the walled compound of Aleniang include a number of stone-built platforms, a well and a sacred rock. Clearly the local community considered the location important prior to the construction of the Spanish installation. Although the site is undated and not excavated, this interpretation appears to be supported by the construction of the adjacent fort. Falgout does not consider the importance that either the Pohnpeians or the Spanish, or perhaps both, may have placed on the establishment of the new site at an already significant locale. With these aspects of association in mind, it is interesting to consider the site of the initial Spanish colony at Kolonia. Here Hanlon (1981: 11–15, 53), who has conducted historical research regarding the town, finds:

the area called Kolonia was once, and still is to some, a very special place . . . The modern boundaries closely approximate to an area known as 'Mesenieng', a [Pohnpeian] word that translates as 'face of the wind' . . . It is said that, before the coming of the Spanish colonial rule, there were numerous shrines and spirit dwellings throughout [this area] . . . The Spanish broke apart a large *pehi* or altar at a place close by to build the walls.

It is impossible to tell, at present, whether power through this association of sites was reflected on the Spanish, or the local elite felt that they had appropriated Spanish power by guiding them to construct in these locations. But the location of the fort and colony at these already significant locales is not likely to have been accidental. Such issues are starting to be addressed by historical anthropologists, ethnohistorians and archaeologists. Certainly Hanlon (1988) has made an excellent case in 'God versus gods' for the manipulation of the early missionaries by the local chiefs in order to suit their own outcomes. More recent historical archaeology has been explored by D. 'Colt' Denfield in his report on the Second World War material remains from Pohnpei (1981a).

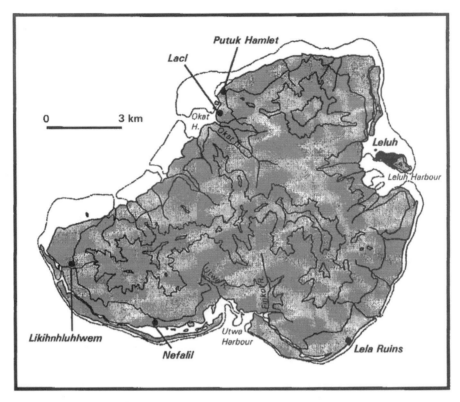

Fig. 7.15 Map of Kosrae.

Kosrae

Although a third the size of Pohnpei in land area, Kosrae has a similar environment, but in having a fringing reef it lacks the lagoon of Pohnpei (Fig. 7.15). Jerome Ward (1988) confirms Bloom's (1970b) assertion that Kosrae has experienced constant subsidence throughout the Holocene. Laird (1983a) splits the general soil units of Kosrae into three landscape types as follows: coastal strand and coastal tidal marshes comprising 16 per cent of total land area; level and nearly level alluvial bottom lands making up 12 per cent of the total area; and upland soils on moderately steep to very steep slopes forming the remaining 72 per cent of the island land area.

Ward (1988; 1995; Athens *et al.* 1989; Athens, Ward and Murakami 1996) found that, from the time of Kosrae's formation some 1.4 million years ago (Keating *et al.* 1984), the basalt substrate of the island has become worn and degraded. This has allowed soil to form, which has been displaced by rainfall out to sea or deposited in alluvial fans at the point where the streams meet the coast. Holocene mangrove forests developed in the river/stream mouths, and enough sediment was trapped to keep pace with the submerging island. Approximately

2000 years ago, Kosrae would have appeared quite different from today, with the hillsides descending directly from the mountain peaks into the sea or fringing reef. Along with the mangroves at the mouths of the four small rivers draining the uplands, a few small lagoons behind sand bars that had formed on the fringing reef may have been apparent (Athens 1995). Also, at this time, there is a rise in the amount of charcoal, indicating that forest fires become a more regular phenomenon than previously experienced on the island. From about 1500 years ago, coastal progradation adds significantly to the land area, and the form of the island as it appears today takes shape. The coastal strand noted by Laird appears to have come into existence only at this time, a time, as discussed in chapter 2, that coincides, within a few centuries, with the earliest date for human settlement of the island.

Work by Athens (1995; Athens, Ward and Murakami 1996) and his colleagues show that an agroforest dominated by breadfruit appears to have been present since earliest human settlement, and continued until the European demand for copra led to the development of coconut plantations. Taro appears to have been a back-up crop. There is some confusion as to whether citrus fruit, a highly unusual crop in ancient Oceania and of South-East Asian origin (Sauer 1993), was cultivated prior to a supposed European introduction. The journal of René Primevère Lesson, a surgeon and naturalist aboard Duperrey's *La Coquille*, regarded as the first European ship to visit Kosrae, lists the local words for orange tree and orange as *menezioko* and *meozasse* respectively (Ritter and Ritter 1982). Ward's (1995) palynological work of 1988 recorded a single palynomorph of the citrus family and, although he only lists its presence, a correlation with the age-depth graph provided by Ward for the core from which it derives would date its presence to over 1000 years ago.

Ruins of monumental architecture matching those found at Nan Madol on Pohnpei exist in Kosrae, and are similarly built on the fringing reef of a small coastal island. In this case, the island and site are named Leluh (Lelu) and are joined to the mainland by the shallow fringing reef (Fig. 7.16). Ethnographic work and recording at the ruins of Leluh were conducted by Ernst Sarfert (1919) during the German administration while the earliest, rudimentary, archaeological investigations are those of Yawata (1932a; 1932b; also Muranushi 1943) during the Japanese period.

A local understanding of the place of Leluh in Kosrae history relates that the villages of the main island, Tafunsak, Malem and Utwe, were established and named by the children of a mother inhabiting Leluh. The youngest son stayed at Leluh after the death of his mother, and gave the island its name which means 'inside of the lake' (Ashby 1985).

Leluh has provided less of a focus for pure research than Nan Madol, with much modern archaeological work taking place in order to mitigate damage caused by infrastructure improvements on the main island and Leluh. Much of this work was, of course, informed by research objectives, with a few projects solely for

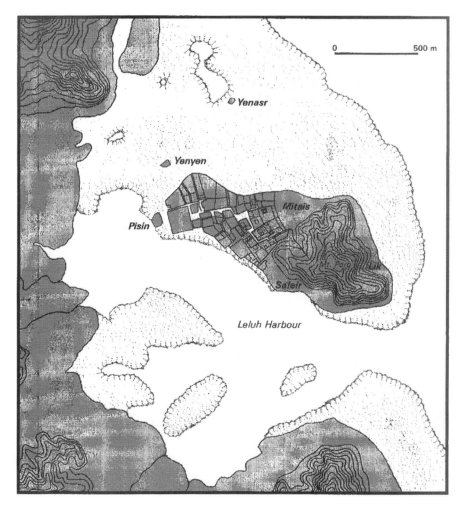

Fig. 7.16 Map of the Leluh area, Kosrae (after Morgan 1988). The Leluh complex was constructed on the fringing reef west of a reef island and next to the deep channel forming Leluh Harbour.

research purposes (Sinoto nd; Craib 1978b; Cordy 1981; 1982a; 1982b; 1983a; 1985a; 1993; Bath and Shun 1982; Bath, Shun and Cordy 1983; Ueki 1984; Cordy *et al.* 1985; Swift, Harper and Athens 1990; Welch, McNeill and Athens 1990).

Presently Kosrae possesses 16 square kilometres of land area suitable for habitation and terrestrial subsistence, with much of this only becoming available since human settlement. Excavations at Wiya (Cordy 1981) and Lacl (Welch, McNeill and Athens 1990) have revealed evidence of undated archaeological features, stone paving and stone walls, up to a metre below the surface.

Following the initial settlement at Leluh by pottery-using people (discussed in chapter 4), the continuing evidence for human occupation is extremely limited until about 1000 years ago. This may be due to the abandonment of pottery within the first 500 years, reducing site visibility. It may also, in a similar way to the long gap in Chuuk, be due to the significant landscape transformations that are indicated by the palaeoenvironmental evidence as discussed above.

Construction of landfill at Leluh begins at approximately 750 years ago, physically continuing the process of landscape enhancement started at first settlement. There is, however, no evidence for the construction of large architectural features at Leluh in this early stage. At this time though, on the main island, new settlements appear in many locations.

Takeshi Ueki (1984) recorded many other stone enclosures in the Finkol and Yawal sections, with some forming compounds of three or four enclosures grouped together. Typically no artefacts are recovered in these sites. One enclosure in the Finkol section of the island is situated about 10 metres from a river tributary. The walls reach 40 centimetres in height, are from 0.8 to 1 metre wide and enclose an area of 106 square metres, with a stone partition across the centre. No entrance could be discerned, and the northern area was paved and contained a 3 by 3 metre stone platform raised 40 centimetres above the ground. Although no artefacts are reported, a dated charcoal sample indicated occupation of the site after between 710 and 550 years ago.

Located in the Utwe section, 40 metres from a river and 25 metres from a mangrove swamp, is a large square enclosure consisting of walls built of rough and columnar basalt with a coral core (Ueki 1984). These walls have an average length of 33 metres and enclose an area of 1089 square metres. External wall heights were measured as reaching 1.4 metres and the width averaged about 90 centimetres. The more acceptable of two radiocarbon determinations from the four 1 by 1 metre test pits indicate occupation of the enclosure starting between 700 and 300 years ago.

Cordy *et al.* (1985) describe an enclosure located next to the Sipien River and below the first inland escarpment. The enclosure defines an area of 783 square metres and is bordered on three sides by wall and on the fourth by the river (Fig. 7.17). The height of the wall varies between 0.45 and 1.3 metres and the width is on average 70 centimetres. Of particular note, as this is usually associated with larger monumental sites in the region, the north corner of the enclosure is constructed in header and stretcher style using columnar basalt (this style is typical of Pohnpei – see above). An ephemeral alignment of stones in the west side of the enclosure appears to outline a rectangle (4 by 6 metres) 24 square metres in area. A small excavation in the centre of the enclosure revealed an earth oven and adjacent posthole. A single date from the oven was used by the excavators to propose use of this site between approximately 1030 and 790 years ago.

This corner, architecturally embellished by header and stretcher construction, was built next to the path and would have been the first major element of the enclosure wall seen by visitors or passers-by traversing the valley floor. Can it be that this is a material manifestation resulting directly from inter-island

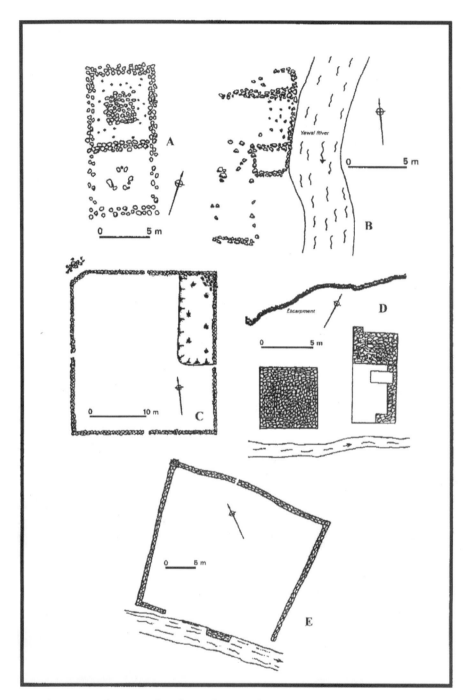

Fig. 7.17 Selection of early enclosure plans: A   Ko-C2-17; B   Ko-C3–14; C   Ko-C6-29 (all after Ueki 1984); D   Ko-C7-2; E   Ko-C7-7 (both after Cordy *et al.* 1985).

contact? The date of the enclosure coincides with a time when header and stretcher construction was at its zenith at Nan Madol on the island of Pohnpei. In Kosrae the corner of the Sipien River enclosure, assuming that it was not a later addition, is the only contemporary example outside of Pohnpei of this style of construction. It is certainly possible that the header and stretcher construction at this site is as a direct result of contact with Pohnpei. This log cabin style architecture may be considered to serve as a 'ship's ledger' to record at least one instance of a direct encounter involving Pohnpeians and Kosraeans a thousand years ago.

As evidenced by the distribution of particular adze types, it appears that inter-island communication was maintained throughout the last 1000 years, and for those involved it was a prestigious activity that would have accrued cultural capital for the individual or community. Connections between separate island communities can be shown in the material remains, but there is no indication that this contact necessarily determined the organization of each society.

In relation to this it might be regarded as odd that reports both from the Duperrey expedition and a few years later by Lütke in 1827 point to the lack of sails on the seacraft of Kosrae, or much desire by the Kosraeans to go far beyond the reef in their paddled boats. I will return to this issue in the final chapter but here note that Lesson reports (Ritter and Ritter 1982: 67):

We noticed a singular trait that never did the inhabitants use sails and masts. We did not even see a vestige. They only use a paddle; this latter has a long handle, very narrow and ending in a sharp point, which could, if need be, serve as a defensive weapon, and which is little useful to swimming. The ability of the natives to manoeuvre their canoes is hardly worth mentioning, and as this people are not fishermen in the true significance of the word, and as they never have felt the necessity of subsisting on the ocean, they have lost the practice of an art in which the Carolinians excel.

Here I have provided just a small selection of the enclosed sites that appear to be typical of the period beginning in the first half of the second millennium AD. In general, these sites are not restricted to any particular land type, ranging from almost zero altitude on the coast up to a height, in the valley of the Finkol River, of nearly 100 metres above sea level. Some of these enclosed sites incorporate internal stone structural remains of walls, paving and platforms. Although not showing any patterns in regard to location, the structures that apparently date to this period appear to fit into two groups based on size.

Two of the enclosures, one in Utwe and the other next to the Sipien River, are clearly different from the smaller paved and compound sites (see Fig. 7.17). It is likely that within the large walled enclosures other structures, some on paving and some on earth, were located and the size of these structures may have been similar to the group of smaller enclosures. Evidence for this comes from the Sipien River enclosure where a rectangular alignment of stones traced out an area of 24 square metres, and a posthole was identified close to the centre of the enclosure. The excavated areas are small, and one can only wonder how many more postholes would have been located if a larger area had been excavated.

A problem arises when it comes to actually interpreting the smaller structures. Little, if anything, in the way of portable artefacts is found in association with them, and the lack of large-scale excavation reduces the clues to internal arrangement. Such apparently spartan spaces are supported by the texts of the Duperrey and Lütke expeditions. Activities associated with food preparation appear to have been conducted here, since a number of the dates come from what have been interpreted as earth ovens and firepits. Perhaps some of the small architectural units are cookhouses, but this interpretation can only account for units with unpaved floors, otherwise digging an earth oven would be problematic. The lack of obvious entrances into the walled units and the provision of paved floors also create a problem when trying to imagine the type of superstructure that may have been constructed. The lack of doorways suggests that a person would have to enter by using wooden steps or a stile over the wall into the building. If this was the case, then this is an interesting movement of the body, requiring a very noticeable threshold to be crossed when entering and leaving the structure.

It is likely that wood was the common medium used for shelter construction since initial settlement of the island. Why then was stone introduced as a material for construction? A general explanation might be that stone became preferable to wood for building as more of the endemic tree species of the island were replaced by introduced subsistence plants. However, this does not provide any suggestion as to how this change in material culture was consciously perceived by the builders and/or occupants.

At present it is not known how the preceding and contemporary wooden architecture restricted movement or physically represented cosmology, or if elaborate (even monumental) structures were constructed in this medium. The difference between wood and stone structures comes in the (almost) indelible mark imprinted on the landscape by the construction of stone walls. Wooden structures are ephemeral, as an archaeologist knows only too well. In a tropical environment, once abandoned, these buildings soon decay and are lost from sight. In contrast, stone structures are solid and can remain for centuries, unheeding of climate.

The physical act of bounding a space registers an extremely significant message in regard to the perception of land, the fundamentals of ownership and the operation of social competition. If it is not the case that archaeologists have missed the evidence for earlier bounded spaces (which may not have been constructed of stone), then it is in this period that these aspects are first recorded in the material record of Kosrae.

What may have taken place is a shift from the unmarked or uninscribed knowledge of land use and rights through aural and visual means, to the inscription of place by architectural features. That is, the visual knowledge of

Fig. 7.18 Plan of Leluh, Kosrae (after Cordy 1993). Standing walls marked in bold line and modern roads marked.

an area through natural features, and the ability to recognize the existence of people in that area through further visual and probably aural means, is replaced by a bounded landscape where tenure of some type becomes inscribed and perhaps less yielding to change.

Although space was being altered, and probably in certain senses controlled, prior to the construction of stone enclosures, the control of space in this period takes on a new solidified form. This could indicate the presence of social competition in at least two senses: the ownership of a piece of land, and the ability to organize labour and possess access to skills required to construct the new form of architecture.

Scholars have proposed that around 600 to 500 years ago population grew rapidly on Kosrae, leading to expansion of settlement, a diversity of settlement types and a new hierarchical order (Ueki 1984; 1990; Cordy *et al.* 1985). This is identified in the archaeology by a three-tiered settlement hierarchy: (1) the monumental multi-functional settlement at Leluh; (2) four or five multi-compound complexes distributed around the island; and (3) small dispersed hamlets. I will discuss each of these in this order.

Leluh

As at Nan Madol, the site of Leluh is constructed on artificial ground, on the fringing reef of a small island on the eastern coast of the main island (Fig. 7.18). Leluh has walls up to 6.4 metres in height constructed of basalt, some of it columnar and in header and stretcher style, and coral rubble. Unlike Nan Madol, the majority of these compounds are not separated by water, but can be approached along coral-paved paths. A tidal canal runs as a central artery through the complex. The best-reported investigations by Cordy (1993) and Athens (1995) have established a chronology for the development of the site (Fig. 7.19).

---→

Fig. 7.19 Development phases of Leluh, Kosrae (after Morgan 1998): A   Prior to 600 years ago the beach area around Leluh Island was occupied, probably continuing from the very first human settlement of Kosrae. Minimal traces of these settlements have been found and consist mostly of shell midden material. B   After 600 years ago the shallow reef area on the west side of Leluh Island begins to be purposefully filled, and on the artificial land the compounds, surrounded by large stone walls, are constructed. C   This area remained the monumental core of the site and was completed by 400 years ago. Between 400 and 200 years ago more artificial land was created, and extended the site further west towards the main island (Fig. 7.18). By this time, a complex of walled compounds, paths, tombs and a canal had been created.

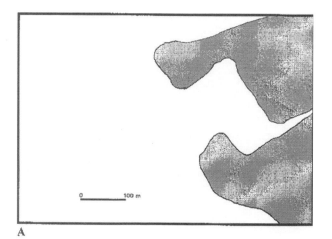

A

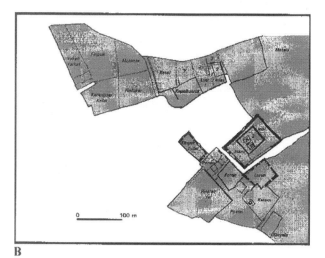

B

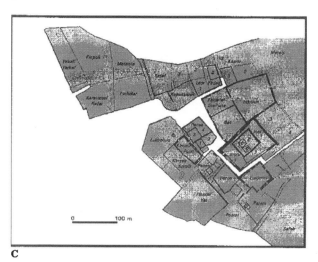

C

Although later developments have removed much, in final form, perhaps only 200 years ago the fringing reef was covered by more than 100 compounds where the sea had previously cooled the coral bed of the fringing reef. The whole area measured approximately 800 by 500 metres, covering 27 hectares, with coral-paved 'streets' up to 6 metres wide connecting the compounds. All of the compounds appear to have been separated by walls constructed of basalt and coral rocks, but were modest in comparison to the ones constructed in the core area. Indicated by historical accounts and the compounds that remain in the present day, the largest and most impressive of the compound walls were located in the early eastern area of the complex.

The archaeological remains indicate that the construction of Leluh was a massive undertaking, which required much labour and planning. Unlike Nan Madol, at the time of European visits in the nineteenth century Leluh was a flourishing settlement and was recorded in a number of journals. Dumont D'Urville, who was second in command of the 1824 expedition, described his approach to Leluh thus (Ritter and Ritter 1982: 29–30):

beautiful huts surrounded by high walls, well paved streets and, on the beach, the entire population of Leilei [Leluh], in the number of 800 people at least . . . in silence [we were led] one hundred steps from the shore to an immense hut which seemed to be for public ceremonies. It was open on all sides, and only a little corner provided with a partition seemed to be reserved for the principal chief.

Lesson described his first impressions of Leluh in these terms (Ritter and Ritter 1982: 53):

in front of us lay the little island of *Lélé* [Leluh], where the king and most of the population resided. This little island was connected to the big one by a plateau of reef, upon which one could walk, with water only coming to the waist. They let us off on the shore . . . we crossed a large number of twisting roads . . . We observed with astonishment a huge wall composed of blocks, and we wondered how and why they had raised these massive structures fifteen feet high. The elegant houses of the islanders bordered the streets on raised mounds, for the sloping part of *Lélé* seemed to be covered by sea water and it is for this reason, no doubt, that it is entirely surrounded by a belt of walls.

The historical records, supported by archaeological and ethnographic studies, indicate that there were three types of compound. The first type, defined by the largest walls, were habitations of 'high chiefs' and Ross Cordy believes that there were about ten of these. One was apparently the paramount ruler (*Tokosra*), and resided in the compound named Posral (Fig. 7.20), but Lütke found that 'we could not recognize in any way Togoja [Tokosra] as king of all the island' (Ritter and Ritter 1982: 133). Each of these compounds had a feasting/meeting house at the main entrance and behind this, hidden by bamboo screens, were houses for the wives, children and servants and the chief's sleeping house.

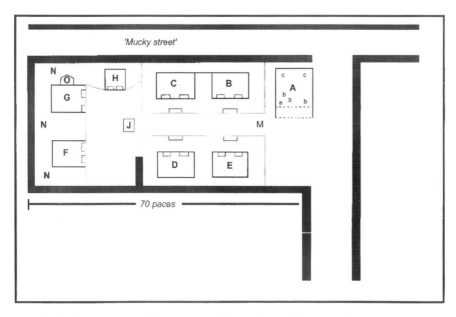

Fig. 7.20 Compound of Posral, Leluh, Kosrae (after Sarfert 1919). Annotated from the description provided by the Lütke expedition of 1827. A   Chief's feast and entertaining house (a = chief's sitting place; b = guests; c = people involved in other activities); B   Children's house; C   First wife's house; D   Second wife's house; E   Unknown function; F   Guests' house; G   Chief's sleeping house; H   Wife's sleeping house; J   *Seka* pounding stone under roofed structure; M   Entry to compound proper from street: N   Garden area of coconut, breadfruit and banana; O   Pig enclosure; Grey borders Bamboo screens.

Also in the compound was a garden area for trees and a place for burials. The *Tokosra*, however, had a particular form of burial, and this involves the second compound type.

Neighbouring the high-status residences are mortuary and ritual enclosures and their associated tombs. What eventually became the central area of Leluh, where the tombs are located, is accessible from the open sea through the arterial canal. The tomb architecture is standardized, with the five tombs constructed in the style of a four-sided truncated pyramid, with a crypt placed in the centre, only accessible from the top. Investigations by Cordy (1993) found that the central Insru compound tombs are the earliest, built between 600 and 400 years ago, with the 'wall tomb' in the north corner of the Insru compound constructed most recently, at approximately 200 years ago. Each of the tomb compounds appears to have had a large feasting house next to its main entrance.

The core of the tomb is constructed using quarried columnar basalt, and is covered by a layer of coral rubble collected from the reef. Similarly, the boundary walls of the mortuary compounds, unlike other walls at Leluh, are constructed of basalt capped with coral rubble. Excavations in the Inol tomb compound by Athens (1995) also show that, unlike the deposits in other excavated compounds, there is no evidence of domestic use or the presence of vegetation in the mortuary precinct. It is possible to infer from the clean soils in this compound that there is something different about its use compared to the others.

The third type of compound is undistinguished in comparison, and most are located in the western portion of the site. According to Cordy these formed the residences of the servants/retainers of the chiefs and contained two or three houses, but no meeting or feasting structure. These compounds, being more ephemeral, are the least well known of the types.

The range of artefacts collected from Leluh includes pounding stones, adzes of *Tridacna* and *Terebra*, and five of basalt representing 8 per cent of the adze assemblage (Cordy 1993). The most common portable artefacts collected during Cordy's project were *Anadara* sp. shell 'peelers', usually regarded as being related to breadfruit processing. These are made from one side of the bivalve shell and are also sometimes interpreted as netsinkers.

According to Cordy, Leluh represents the dwelling place of the two highest strata of the four-strata Kosraean society that developed after *c.* 1400 AD. Other than those members of the lower strata who were required to serve the needs of the high chiefs, the rest of the population lived on the main island, which was separated into some fifty or so sections (*facl*) (Fig. 7.21). The sections were managed by a stratum of lower chiefs, and labour for agricultural production was provided by the lowest and most populous level of society, the 'commoners'. Each of the sections was linked to a specific high chief and provided food tribute to sustain him and his retinue at Leluh. Once again, although other historical commentators agree with the presence of highly differentiated class-based strata, Lütke finds that Lesson, a chronicler of Duperrey's visit three years earlier, was wrong. He says (Ritter and Ritter 1982: 133): 'We did not notice this rigorous distinction between the various classes, nor the striking difference between the exterior of the chiefs and that of the common people of which Mr Lesson speaks.'

The main island complexes

The second level of sites dating to this period are the relatively large multi-compound enclosures located on the coast of the main island, and Cordy regards these as the residences of the lower chiefs. These sites are less architecturally impressive than Leluh, but do represent a major investment in the establishment of significant places. They are located at Lacl, Likihnluhlwen, Nefalil and Putuk Hamlet (Figs. 7.22, 7.23, 7.24 and 7.25). A fifth possible contender for this group, at Lela Ruins, I believe is a special case and this will be described separately below.

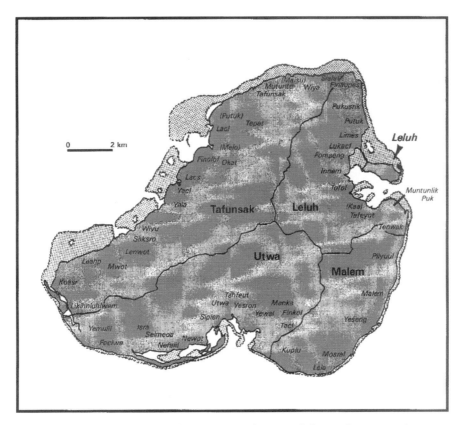

Fig. 7.21 Map showing the sections of Kosrae (after Athens 1995).

The site at Lacl was in use at the time of both Duperrey's and Lütke's visits in 1824 and 1827/28 respectively and in both cases it was where the expedition members first set foot ashore. Dumont D'Urville wrote (Ritter and Ritter 1982: 26):

At Lual [Lacl], we were received in a big public hut, which also served as a workshop, for I noticed a large canoe being shaped by two or three workers with their sharp, *tradacne* [*Tridacna*] shell adzes. I had always imagined that it took a long time for savages to finish such undertakings with such imperfect tools, but I saw they were going at it fairly rapidly; each blow of the shell adze sent fairly large chips of wood flying, and I even noticed that the form of their blades suited their work much better than our steel instruments. The master of the workshop, admiring the ax which we had brought . . . especially the prodigious power of its cutting edge, tried to use it for a while. Then he gave it back to us saying that it cut too much.

A few years after Dumont D'Urville, Lütke came ashore at Lacl and left this account (Ritter and Ritter 1982: 95–6):

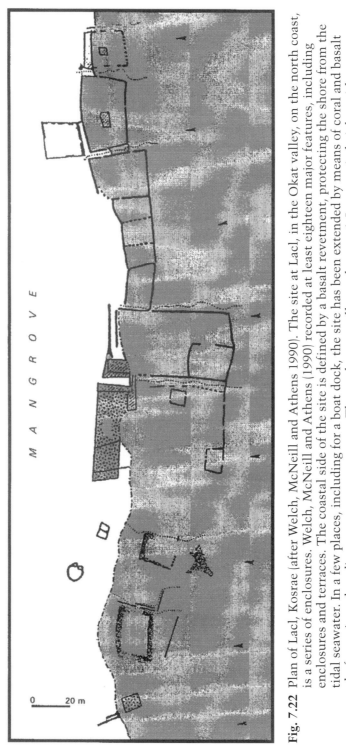

Fig. 7.22 Plan of Lacl, Kosrae (after Welch, McNeill and Athens 1990). The site at Lacl, in the Okat valley, on the north coast, is a series of enclosures. Welch, McNeill and Athens (1990) recorded at least eighteen major features, including enclosures and terraces. The coastal side of the site is defined by a basalt revetment, protecting the shore from the tidal seawater. In a few places, including for a boat dock, the site has been extended by means of coral and basalt platforms into the adjacent mangrove swamp. The enclosure walls reach up to 1.5 metres in height, with revetments over 2 metres high. Internal features include large areas of paving, earth ovens and pounding stones. Radiocarbon dates, all from probable earth ovens, extend from 710 years ago to modern. Artefacts collected included forty pounding stones, ten basalt pounders, two basalt adzes and two *Tridacna* clam shell pounders.

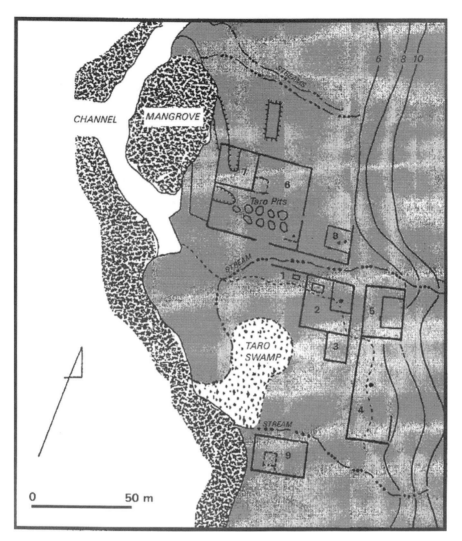

Fig. 7.23 Plan of Likihnluhlwen, Kosrae (after Bath, Shun and Cordy 1983). This site is located on the western coast of Kosrae and consists of eight walled compounds situated on a small alluvial plain. The compound walls are built of basalt and survive up to 1.5 metres in height. Within Compound 2 there is a raised platform with an area of 150 square metres, and a smaller paved area 20 square metres in area. Bath, Shun and Cordy (1983) conducted survey and excavation at the site and, apart from pounding stones on the surface, found very little in the way of artefacts. The two radiocarbon dates associated with the site indicate that there was activity here in the last 500 years.

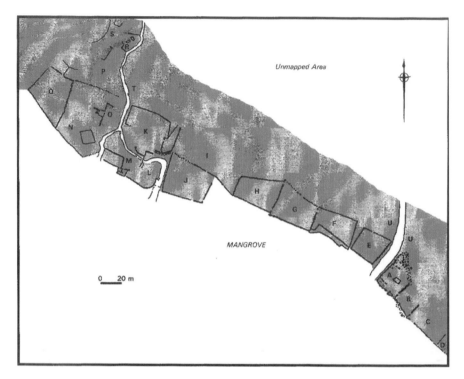

Fig. 7.24 Plan of Nefalil, Kosrae (after Ueki 1984). Nefalil is a complex of eighteen walled enclosures spread along 430 metres of the coast on the south side of the island. Ueki (1984) conducted survey and limited excavation, finding wall heights reaching a maximum of 1.9 metres. Features within the enclosures included pavement, possible foundations and pounding stones. No portable artefacts or midden were reported, and a single radiocarbon date indicated occupation between 340 years ago and modern times.

——→

Fig. 7.25 Plan of Putuk Hamlet, Kosrae (after Cordy 1982). Although undated, Putuk Hamlet on the north coast appears to fit into the group of main island complexes. It consists of twelve contiguous walled enclosures running along the shoreline. The walls reach a height of 1.8 metres and internal features include pavement and, in Compound 6, a platform raised 1 metre above ground level and measuring 6 by 8 metres (Cordy 1981). Compound 5 has a well-defined path leading from an entrance. Many of the enclosures have stone and coral rubble-built extensions into the tidal zone. This is of little surprise, as the site is located on a very narrow shoreline backed by steep slopes and enclosed by ridges to east and west where they meet the shore. Boat docks attest to this form of transport as the major means of communication. No portable artefacts or midden are reported from the site.

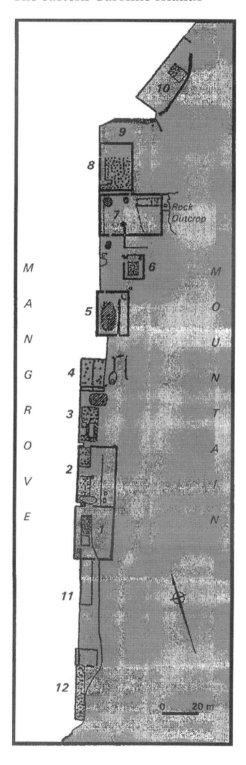

To get there [from the ship], we had to cross a skirt of mangroves and other shrubs that surrounded the shore at a distance of more than 100 fathoms [about 180 metres]. It is strange and interesting to paddle through a thick grove of trees, forming with a thousand vaults an arcade which rises out of the water in an innumerable multitude of branches, whose interlacings present an impenetrable wall. The village . . . is situated on a very steep shore, in a thick wood of breadfruit trees, banana trees and pandanus. The houses, or rather the huts, that made up the village were scattered here and there without any sense of order or regularity. We found them entirely deserted. Not one soul came to meet us, and without two or three individuals of the common people, whom we already knew, carelessly lounging about on mats under a big tent, inviting us to sit down, we would have believed that the village was completely abandoned. We did not know how to explain these circumstances. The confident and warm welcome of the inhabitants, our affable conduct toward them and the gifts which we showered on them did not allow us to suppose that it was out of jealousy or fear that they hid their families from us. It was not reasonable either that if they had absented themselves momentarily to go elsewhere, that they would have taken everything with them.

The middle level of the identified settlement hierarchy forms a consistent group of multi-compound enclosures situated in shoreside locations. They each have high walls and revetments, often have boat docks, and have material evidence linking in with basic domestic settlement activities. I will now describe the third level of settlement type in Kosrae, which consists of smaller and much more diverse types of site that may have been inhabited by the lowest strata of society.

Dispersed settlements

The site of Mosral Wan (#1) is located in Malem section in the south-east of Kosrae. It is a single enclosure of approximately 177 square metres in area, and situated on an alluvial fan approximately a kilometre from the shore and 10 m above sea level. Swift, Harper and Athens (1990) conducted survey and excavation at the site and reported that the walls are constructed of basalt rubble and stand to a height of 1.4 metres on its southern external side overlooking a marsh (see Fig. 7.26a). No artefacts or midden material were observed, the acidity of the soil being regarded as responsible for poor preservation, but one radiocarbon date from a hearth feature indicates occupation between 590 and 370 years ago.

Ueki (1984) recorded a site near the head of the Finkol valley at nearly 100 metres above sea level. It consists of two enclosed areas abutting one another, but at different levels (Fig. 7.26b). There is a high platform measuring 3 by 3.8 metres at its base, but reducing to 1.5 by 2 metres at the top, which is 1.2 metres above ground level and although Ueki does not notice the similarity,

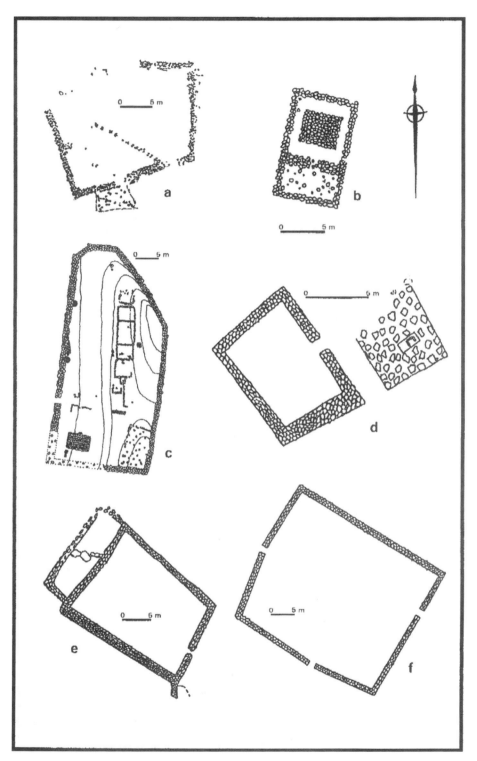

Fig. 7.26 Selection of later enclosure plans, Kosrae: a   Mosral Wan 1 (after
Swift, Harper and Athens 1990); b   Ko-C2-24; c   Ko-C2-29 (both
after Ueki 1984); d   Ko-C6-25; e   Ko-C7-5; f   Ko-C8-3 (all after
Cordy *et al.* 1985).

and regards the platform as 'unusual', I find a parallel with the truncated pyramid shape of the tombs at the site of Leluh. The single date indicates that
the lower platform was paved after 490 years ago, and this may be a late prehistoric tomb with an associated enclosure. I will return to this possibility
below.

Next to the Finkol River, at an altitude of approximately 75 metres, is an
enclosure that at approximately 930 square metres in area makes it the largest
site with an associated date in the uplands of Kosrae. The internal arrangement
of walls, enclosures and platforms makes this a rather more complex site than
the others in this group (Fig. 7.26c). A number of pounding stones, of the style
probably used for *seka* production, are associated with the group of enclosed
spaces in the centre of the site. Although Ueki (1984), who surveyed and excavated this site, does not report any artefacts or midden, he does conclude that
this is a site dated to before the onset of continuous European contact in the
nineteenth century.

Further sites that appear to be contemporaneous with these late period settlements are illustrated in Figure 7.26.

Lela Ruins

A site that I have not discussed as yet is that of the Lela Ruins (Fig. 7.27). I have
avoided discussion of it in previous sections as it is difficult to place within
the three groups. Swift, Harper and Athens (1990) during survey and excavation
found evidence of activity at the Lela Ruins prior to the construction of a walled
settlement at the site. It was in the later period, under discussion here, that
the walls were built. Samples for radiocarbon dating in association with the
surface architecture provided determinations of 690 years ago and modern. The
architecture consists of four adjacent enclosures defined by low walls, mostly of
coral rubble. (A fifth isolated and undated enclosure which is subsumed under
the Lela Ruins name is not considered here as the association appears tenuous.)
Within the enclosures, there are paved areas and a pit, possibly for breadfruit
storage. The site is located on a sandy rise, surrounded by mangrove swamp, and
is some 250 metres from the present shoreline. Artefacts and other finds from
the site include pounding stones, *Tridacna*, *Mitra* and *Terebra* adzes, *Anadara*
'scrapers', and human skeletal remains in Compound 1. The human bones
had been brought to the surface by crab burrowing, allowing no assessment of
context or method of deposition.

These are large enclosures and are dissimilar to the other Kosrae main island
complexes. With the siting on the reef and with large walls and compounds, the
Lela Ruins shares similarities only with Leluh. Prior to the building of the road
through the site, the walls are considered to have been much larger. It might
be that the Lela Ruins and Leluh served similar functions in this late period of

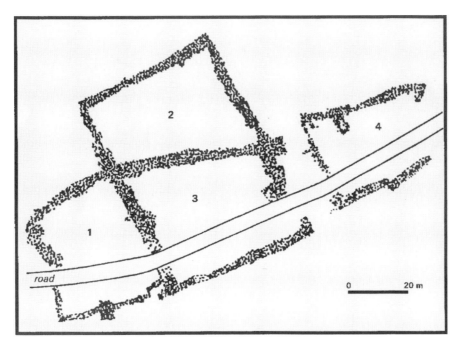

Fig. 7.27 Plan of Lela Ruins (after Swift, Harper and Athens 1990). The site morphology as identified by the plan suggests there are at least two phases of enclosures here.

Kosraean history. These functions may have initially been non-secular, with their reef locations chosen for the purpose of being non-confrontational, while at the same time highlighting aspects of cosmology.

A major similarity between the Lela Ruins and Leluh is the use of coral rubble for wall construction. The use of coral rubble at Leluh appears to be spatially distinct and, given its contexts, may have imparted specific meaning. As noted above, at Leluh the mortuary enclosures and their associated tombs are central to the complex and the tombs are constructed using basalt in the style of a four-sided, truncated pyramid, covered by a layer of coral rubble. Similarly, the boundary walls of the mortuary compounds, unlike other walls at Leluh, are constructed of basalt capped with coral rubble. It is interesting to note that as one approaches the central tomb complex, either along the canal or along one of the pathways through the complex, the white coral capping of the mortuary enclosure walls attracts the eye in the dark basalt environment. The coral clearly demarcates these non-domestic enclosures, and this must have been the intention of the builders. Coral covers the tombs and forms a clear boundary around them. That coral is significant in a non-secular context appears likely, and may indicate a non-secular function for the Lela Ruins.

A three-tier settlement hierarchy model for Kosrae may then be too simple and not able to portray the different functions of enclosure sites. The settlements on the main island show a clear division between the coastal complexes and the scattered individual dwelling units, which are located away from the coast up to 150 metres above sea level in upland river valleys. This perhaps indicates a two-tier habitation model that excludes Leluh and Lela Ruins as quite different, but also interconnected, as a simple mundane and sacred functional model is not likely to be appropriate either. It is possible that the inhabitants of Leluh gradually gained power over time as the role of the site changed from one that was peculiar and on the fringe, to one that became the container of power through both chiefly habitation and control of the mortal remains of the ancestors.

In further attempting to elucidate the role of Leluh, Cordy (1993) takes as his starting point the 'historic baseline' which for him is the record provided by the early European visitors to the site. These nineteenth-century visitors, on 'scientific' expeditions, presented the occupied site as 'the capital of Kosrae, a feudal society . . . [And] the hub of this society . . . [as] it was here that the king and nobility lived' (Cordy 1993: 1). He accepts that massive changes occurred in Kosraean society as a consequence of the European encounters, but that these did not occur until after AD 1850: more than 25 years after the first recorded European visit to the island.

In addition to data collected from mainland sites, Cordy concludes that the 'four strata feudal society' recorded in the historical documents can be traced back to at least AD 1400. The 'ethnographic present' (the 'endpoint') is used to explain as much of the archaeology as possible (see Graves 1986a). In an evolutionary framework such as Cordy's, all understanding of the archaeology prior to the 'development' of the recorded 'traditional' society is based on the notion that incremental evolution took place in Kosraean society starting at initial colonization and continuing until the supposed endpoint.

Sarfert was a member of the *Südsee-Expedition* which travelled with a group of scientists through Germany's colonial holdings in the north-west tropical Pacific. The full team spent seventeen days on Kosrae while Sarfert remained for three months and, although the work produced is an admirable piece of recording, this record took place nearly 100 years after the earliest recorded encounters between Kosraeans and Europeans. The century that elapsed between the first direct encounter and Sarfert's visit witnessed massive depopulation and significant changes in society. The arrival of missionaries and the consequent introduction of Christianity had probably significantly altered knowledge of the past that Sarfert was trying to collect. Sarfert talked mainly to old people, as 'The younger generation do not know their own past and their culture at all' (Sarfert 1919: vii).

By the 1850s, when missionaries arrived, the positive accounts of Leluh by members of the Duperrey and Lütke expeditions were, within a generation, ridiculed as outdated. Gulick reported (Damon 1861: 36–7) that:

From M. D'Urville's reports and from the accounts of sea captains we had received glowing ideas of the architectural exhibitions at Lila [Leluh]; we were to find a native city handsomely laid out, with paved streets, and at frequent intervals handsome piles of stone-cut masonry. On the contrary, we found nothing but muddy paths, zigzagging hither and thither over rubbish and stones . . . Along the south western shore are a number of canals communicating with the harbor and in which the sea ebbs and flows. The sides of the canals are in some cases crumbled, but boar [*sic*] evident tokens of having been artificially built . . . Mangrove trees have in many cases choked up these watery courses, and with other types of trees on the islets have nearly buried the whole in a shade most congenial with the thoughts excited by these relics of a dimmer age than that which we might hope had now dawned upon them.

Obviously it suited the missionaries to find a people in a state of despair and 'uncivilised', and thus ready to be 'saved'. But that the situation had changed dramatically in the twenty-five years or so since the first recorded European contact may have been the case. The population collapse recorded by the missionaries (Damon 1861) may have already been in progress when they arrived (see Gorenflo 1993).

Summary

The historical high island societies of the eastern Carolines offer a diverse range of organizational types. This range has attracted scholars interested in the processes of understanding the varied evolution in similar, but not the same, environments. I will turn to some critical issues in relation to such claims in the final chapter. Here, it is important to note that the durable and, at times, monumental stone architectural remains of these islands have acted as attractors to research scholars in the present as, undoubtedly, they lured other island visitors in the past.

The ancient monuments of the eastern Carolines are unprecedented elsewhere in the Pacific islands, and need to be studied in their local and regional contexts. Arguments that they were constructed by people other than the islanders themselves have abounded since Europeans first started writing about these places, and in these contexts the Japanese, Chinese, Spanish and many others have been mentioned. Perhaps one of the major contributions of archaeological research in the last three decades of the twentieth century has been to show that stone architecture developed over a millennium or more on these islands, and cannot be seen as a recent introduction. Further support in regard to these long-term developments comes, I would argue, from evidence of anthropogenic landscape modification, that from the time of initial human settlement extended the coastal lowlands for habitation, and is most dramatically witnessed in the artificial land creation at Nan Madol and Leluh.

Chronological issues are not completely resolved, and there is a dearth of evidence centring on an approximately 500-year span in the second half of the second millennium BP. The eastern Carolines are not alone in this, and in chapter 9 I will return to issues regarding the long gaps.

CHAPTER 8

ISLANDS AND BEACHES: THE ATOLL
GROUPS AND OUTLIERS

Despite their enormous geographical distribution, spreading as they do 20 degrees in longitude, and starting from a little south of the Equator to nearly 12 degrees north, there are three factors that link the islands discussed in this chapter. The first is that they are all low atolls or limestone islands whose residents, as I write, are particularly concerned about rising sea levels that threaten to submerge their homes; and second, they have received the least archaeological attention in Micronesia. Third, if the Caroline Islands were considered part of a 'Breadfruit Culture Complex' (Ishikawa 1987), then perhaps these islands ought to be considered part of a 'Pandanus Pattern', given the traditional importance of the pandanus tree for many of the communities discussed here (Grimble 1933–34; Stone 1963).

The Marshall Islands

The Ralik (sunset) and Ratak (sunrise) chains of twenty-nine atolls and five raised limestone islands form the Marshall Islands (Fig. 8.1). Although producing some of the earliest dates for colonization in this part of Oceania (see chapter 4), they have until recently resisted attempts to gain a clear understanding of the sequences of settlement and land use of this widely dispersed and numerous group of islands. This is typical of atoll groups, as noted in chapter 6 in relation to the Carolinian atolls, in that they appear to be some of the last to be subjected to intensive archaeological investigation.

According to Marshall Weisler (2001b), the atolls of the Marshall Islands are not likely to have formed until about 3000 years ago, and the islets, although attractive to human settlement once developed, probably took another 1000 years to develop into viable places for habitation. The local view of such creation processes includes stories from the Marshalls presented in chapter 4 and another, the story of Lijebake, that links the Marshalls with Kiribati in the south and helps explain the distribution of non-human animal species in the archipelago (Downing, Spennemann and Bennett 1992: 36–8):

Lijebake was the wife of Wullep, a high god living in the land of Eb. Lijebake had a daughter who married an *Irooj* (chief) among the people of Kiribati ([known as] *ri-Pit* by the Marshallese) and Lijebake lived with them. Unfortunately, her

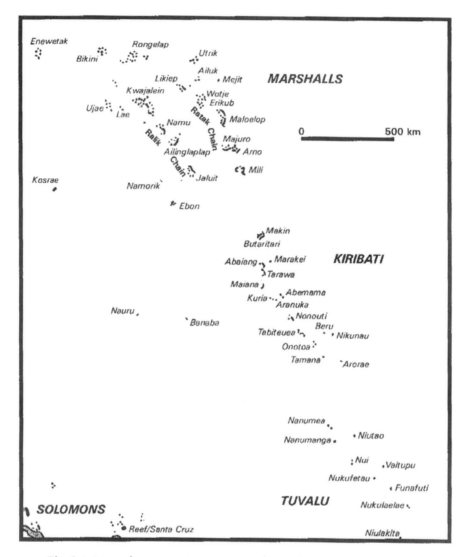

Fig. 8.1 Map of eastern Micronesia and Tuvalu.

daughter died, leaving behind Lijebake's grand daughter Limaninbit, who had to work hard and was ill-treated for many years by the *Irooj*'s second wife. One day, Limaninbit was left at home by her father and stepmother who told her to clean the house. Limaninbit took all the mats out of the house and spread them in the sun. Limaninbit went back in the house and fell asleep.

[While asleep a variety of rains came and the mats received a soaking and on the return of her parents they were so angry that they threw her out of the household.] On that day her grand mother [Lijebake], incensed at the bad treatment her grand daughter had received by the people from Kiribati, turned herself into a turtle, and her husband into a frigate bird. With Limaninbit riding on her back, Lijebak swam north until she reached Mili.

'Can you see the *ri-Pit*?' she asked her husband, who flew high in the sky. 'Yes'
he said 'I can see them'. So they swam further north [arriving at a number of
atolls where the same process was repeated]. And she swam further to the north
until they reached Jemo. 'Can you see *ri-Pit*?' she asked her husband . . . 'No'
he said 'I can no longer see them'. And he flew as high as he could, and he could
no longer see the islands of Kiribati.

Here Lijebake stopped swimming and put Limaninbit ashore. And from this
day on until today, turtles and frigate birds prefer the island of Jemo and the
atolls north of it for nesting purposes.

In developing archaeological understandings of the archipelago, surveys by Paul
Rosendahl in 1977, Thomas Riley in 1979 and Tom Dye in 1980 (all reported in
Dye 1987b) achieved only minimal success in elucidating further the sequence
of prehistoric occupation on these islands. Rosendahl (1987) surveyed thirteen
different atolls and islands and identified forty-two individual sites. Subsurface
testing was conducted on the four atolls of Majuro, Mili, Arno and Lae.

On Majuro Islet, Rosendahl (1987) excavated six test pits that revealed substantial subsurface features including pits, earth ovens (*um*) and possible postholes. One *um* produced a radiocarbon date indicating that it was approximately
750 years old, but the sample consisted of a mix of charcoal and burnt coral.
Stratified cultural deposits were present below the dated feature, and subsequently Riley (1987) found evidence of earlier occupation. During the survey,
4122 artefacts were collected from both surface and subsurface contexts. The
assemblage included adzes, gouges and chisels of *Tridacna*, *Cassis* and *Lambis*
that accounted for 1627 of the artefacts. Other shell artefacts, ranging from
fishing gear to ornaments and scrapers for food preparation, account for most
of the remaining assemblage, except for 502 items attributed to the historic
period.

Riley (1987) followed up Rosendahl's initial findings with an intensive survey
and excavation project on a number of Majuro Atoll islets. Excavating close to
Rosendahl's trench in Laura Village on Majuro Islet, Riley found evidence for
dense occupation over a period of 2000 years, with multiple use of the location
in the centre of the islet, ranging from cooking to taro production and postholes
indicating the former presence of wooden structures. More recent work in the
vicinity found mixed archaeological deposits, including some human remains,
to a depth of 90 centimetres, with seven radiocarbon dates indicating that these
were less than 1000 years old (Walker, Donham and Rosendahl 1992).

Dye (1987a) conducted archaeological reconnaissance survey and test excavations on the islets of Arno Atoll. The range of sites and artefacts mirrors that
of Rosendahl (1987), except for the identification of a new site type, which he
classified as 'pillars'. Of the two sites thus identified, only one, on Aneran Islet,
had more than one pillar remaining, and it consists of two parallel rows of three
upright pillars of quarried slabs of reef rock, standing to a height of 1.05 metres
and defining an area of 5 by 3.35 metres. As suggested for the *latte* sets of the

Marianas (see chapter 5), informants stated that a house rested atop the pillars. Other Marshallese houses are built on top of pillars in the present day, and this may represent a relatively recent phenomenon. However, Marshall Weisler (1999a) has noted that such settings of pillars are typical of early historic period burials.

In reporting his 1817 expedition that visited the Marshall Islands, Otto von Kotzebue (1821: 126–7) described houses as having:

a square roof, neatly made of reeds pointed at the top, rested upon four columns, five feet from the ground, forming a shelter from the sun, while the cool breeze blew through the columns; the ground was paved with coral-stones, the internal space from the top of the roof down to the columns was separated by a pretty lattice-work, in the middle of which was a square opening, large enough to creep through. The rats have undoubtedly induced the inhabitants to build their houses upon columns, for I perceived that their pantry was within the lattice-work, where the rats could not gain entry due to the smooth pillars. Their sleeping houses are built on the ground, and consist only of a roof with two entrances: their day houses are large enough to contain from twenty to thirty people.

All of the archaeological expeditions discussed above located coral stone-lined earthen platforms, house foundations represented by a coral rubble scatter, coral slab-lined graves and walled enclosures. The researchers excavated, or at least assessed, some of these features and present no evidence to show that any of these types pre-date the historic period (Dye 1987a; Riley 1987; Rosendahl 1987). Unlike the sites on the high islands of the eastern Carolines, at present there is little evidence for traditional coral/coral limestone construction in the Marshalls. Although, intriguingly, Kotzebue's (1821: 132) account does comment on stone built tombs:

Near the shore we saw a plain tomb, forming a square, built of coral-stone: it seemed to me that the natives were not permitted to enter it, and I afterwards learnt that the chiefs are buried there, and all other corpses are thrown into the sea.

From more recent ethnographic accounts the avoidance behaviour described by Kotzebue sounds very close to that practised in relation to burial sites more recently and reported by Lin Poyer (1997: 62):

Sites associated with the lives and deaths of *irooj lablab* [chiefs] are valued and marked by Marshallese throughout the Marshall Islands. Burial sites of *irooj* (wuliej lap, literally 'big' or 'great cemetery') are usually *mo*, taboo – places where shouting and casual walking is prohibited, readily identified in any community.

Stone constructions have sometimes been used to identify the supposed highly hierarchical nature of Marshallese society noted by early commentators (e.g., see Dye 1987a; Cordy 1985b). Coral pebble and cobble pavings have been attested for in an 'upper prehistoric layer', covering an area over 200 metres wide, on Kwajalein Atoll (Shun and Athens 1990). The lack of evidence for stone architecture pre-dating the historic period might be seen as lending support to Laurence Carucci's (1988) contention that a highly hierarchical society only developed in the Marshalls as a product of European intervention, and was not present prior to this. Certainly, Carucci's view, which also recognizes significant diversity in social organization across the Marshall Islands, highlights major historical contradictions in the views of earlier anthropologists. This certainly brings into question, and considerable doubt, Cordy's (1986b) estimate of traditional Marshallese society at 'contact' consisting of four strata, being the most hierarchical in the region along with those of Pohnpei and Kosrae.

According to Carucci (1988), although the atolls and islands of the Marshalls were in a constant renegotiation of fusion and fission that might often see a chief as ruling over more than one atoll, a significant shift in the conception of chieftainship occurred starting in the mid-nineteenth century that changed the nature of social relations and how these were perceived as distinct strata. For Carucci it is the shift from the typical symbolic role of the chief, who is provided with first fruits, etc., but is in reality alienated from the holding of land apart from that belonging to his matrilineage, through to the chief remodelled on Western concepts and supported by Western technology to allow possession of land, which in turn supported Western requirements for land for copra production. So when formal colonial control of the Marshall Islands began in 1885, a social system was fossilized, and was one that was quite distinct from the inherent flux of only two generations earlier.

Moving back to the archaeology, Chuck Streck's (1990) work on Bikini Atoll, in the northern Marshall Islands, uncovered evidence for long and intensive occupation of the islets. On Eneu Islet, for example, a 2 to 3 metre high eroding scarp on the shoreline revealed three distinct archaeological deposits. In interpreting the radiocarbon dates, Streck suggests that the majority fall into the period between 950 and 700 years ago, with few younger than 400 years. He concludes that the paucity of later sites is probably due to twentieth-century alterations to the islets for military purposes.

Surface survey and excavation on the islets of Kwajalein Atoll, a US military base, have shown that intact prehistoric deposits can survive, even where no surface indication is present (Craib 1989; 1998b; Beardsley 1994). These projects have established an antiquity for initial human settlement of at least 2000 years. On Kwajalein, rich deposits of earth ovens, coral pavements, midden and faunal remains have been excavated (Beardsley 1994).

Most recently, Marshall Weisler (1999a; 1999b; 2001a; 2001b; 2001c) has been conducting a project designed to test for variability in prehistoric settlement types, by selecting four atolls in different parts of the 150 to 350 centimetres north to south precipitation gradient. Weisler chose Utrik in the dry north, Ebon in the wet south, and Ujae and Maleolap in the centre.

Weisler finds that, in most cases, individual atolls should be regarded as single settlement landscapes. In this scenario, each atoll has a single major settlement that is located on the largest islet of the atoll. The components of this settlement site will normally include the earliest date for habitation within the atoll, the largest and most developed giant taro (*Cyrtosperma*) cultivation pits in the centre of the islet, and fish traps (and perhaps turtle enclosures) on the reef immediately adjacent to this islet.

On Maleolap and Ujae, evidence from excavation and subsequent analyses place initial settlement in the first few centuries after 2000 years ago. In both cases these early dates come from close to the taro pits at the centre of the island. The habitation area then expands from the centre towards the lagoon, and may be aided by progradation. Weisler (1999a) finds that the habitation area of Kaven Islet, the largest of Maleolap Atoll, grew to approximately 25 hectares in extent prior to European contact, and guesses that 200 to 300 people may have been resident there.

The largest islet of an atoll would be chosen, because of its obvious advantages in having the largest store of fresh water (the Ghyben–Herzberg lens) for drinking and the cultivation of taro, and a central area providing protection from coastal environmental perturbations. The other islets of the atoll, being smaller, were then utilized by inhabitants of the main village as 'resource locales', where birds, turtles and shellfish were collected, or people on fishing expeditions could camp for a few days at a time.

This model is best worked out at present for Maleolap Atoll, and Weisler may find that different settlement organizations are to be found on other atolls, especially if the difference in rainfall when comparing north and south does have an effect. It also appears that systems of exchange and inter-islet support, as witnessed in the Caroline Islands (see previous chapter), may play a role in overcoming environmental parameters, along with seeding islets prior to habitation (Rainbird 1995a). It should also be noted here that the islet-building evidence from Kapingamarangi Atoll (a Polynesian Outlier, see below) should caution against assuming that the largest islet of an atoll in the present has always been so in the past.

Although Weisler states generally that his fascination with atolls comes from what he perceives as their marginality in terms of sustaining human populations, he does find that they would be attractive to initial human colonizers; he says (2001a: 124):

What attracted human colonists to atolls, at least in part, were the previously untapped stocks of marine fauna (fish, molluscs, turtles and crabs) as well as massive colonies of sea birds. With an extremely high ratio of reef to land area – a situation unique to atolls – marine resources could sustain human colonists until bananas and arrowroot were harvested, aroid pits became productive, and longer-term resources such as pandanus, coconut and breadfruit yielded food some years after planting.

Although the scenario provided by Weisler is an attractive one, it is clear, given that all of his earliest dates for settlement come from below soil tossed up for the construction of taro pits in the centre of the islet, that the colonizers knew that the production of crops and the maintenance of the introduced populations of rats and dogs were also necessary for the long-term viability of the community – these were not strandloopers.

Typical of interpretations of such low island environments as exist in the Marshall Islands, there are expectations that interaction with neighbouring and other island communities would be maintained to allow for inter-community support in times of food shortage, perhaps caused by drought or typhoon. Weisler (2000) and colleagues (Swindler and Weisler 2000; Weisler *et al.* 2000) have used a variety of techniques in order to identify such interaction. In discussing the ornaments found with an apparently 'high status' single inhumation on Kwajalein Atoll, Weisler *et al.* (2000: 214, references removed) conclude:

The polished Pinctada valve, an ornament more common in Polynesia, may signal some form of long-distance interaction between eastern Micronesia and island groups to the south . . . Certain plant names (e.g., for swamp taro, *Cyrtosperma*) are also shared between eastern Micronesia and the Polynesian atoll group of Tuvalu. And it is realistic to assume that the discrete geographical position of the 'Micronesian–Polynesian' boundary we identify today may have been blurred in the distant past. The 15th century date for the Kwajalein burial fits well within the period of long-distance interaction throughout Polynesia and it would not be surprising that some manner of contact was made between the Marshalls and island groups farther afield.

Weisler (2000) has also pointed to a distinctive pearl shell trolling lure, excavated in a cemetery on Majuro Atoll (see Spennemann 1999), as evidence of contacts with the Solomon Islands. This contact would appear to date between 2000 and 1000 years ago and may be linked to the direction of arrival of the first human colonists in the Marshalls.

A number of sources record contact along the island chains of the Marshalls, for warfare, tribute and trade. Nancy Pollock (1975: 259) noted that:

Trading up and down the chain, which was particularly common in precontact times, enabled the various atoll populations to increase the range of foodstuffs available to each. From north to south through the Marshalls the annual rainfall increases. Thus the drier northern atolls were able to trade turmeric and arrowroot for breadfruit and other fruits that grew in the wetter southern atolls. Navigational skills, for which the Marshallese are renowned, were of great assistance in this broadening the resource base of any particular atoll.

Kiribati (the Gilbert Islands)

The Republic of Kiribati was formed in 1979, following independence from Britain, and consists of three island groups, the Gilberts, the Phoenix Islands and the majority of the Line Islands. The nation also includes the island of Banaba, located near to the Equator in the west. The Phoenix and Line groups are located far to the east, and fall outside of the area normally regarded as Micronesia. The archaeology of the Line Islands was discussed briefly in chapter 4, and although traces of archaeological remains have been reported from the Phoenix group (Emory 1939) they appear to have been abandoned until the emigration of overflow population from the Gilberts starting in 1938 (Maude 1952; Knudson 1965; Lundsgaarde 1966). In this section, I will deal only with the eleven atolls and five raised limestone coral islands of the Gilbert group (Kiribati is a local corruption of Gilbert), and consider separately below the geographically distant island of Banaba.

The Gilberts form a distinct elongated north-west to south-east cluster of low islands, rarely reaching heights more than 4 metres above sea level, situated between the Marshall Islands to the north and the Tuvalu (formerly Ellice) group to the south (Fig. 8.1). The people of Tuvalu are generally regarded as Polynesian, making the people of the Gilberts, whose islands straddle the Equator, the most south-easterly of the Micronesians. However, links with Polynesian areas are manifest in architecture and words. There appears to be a local acceptance (in the southern islands at least: Anne Di Piazza personal communication), derived from oral history, of I-Kiribati (the people of the Gilberts) originating from Samoa (Kirion and Karaiti 1979) and displacing or assimilating the original inhabitants, who may have been 'dark-skinned' (Uriam 1995).

There are many local accounts for the origin of the islands (see in particular Maude and Maude 1994); one of them is provided by Alexandria Brewis (1996: 1):

In the beginning when earth and sky were still sealed together there was only the giant spider Nareau. He cleft the earth and the sky and then walked out across the ocean. In those places where his feet touched the sea, islands welled up. And so, the islands of Tungara [Gilberts] are the footprints of Nareau.

The people of the Gilberts (and Banaba) achieved international recognition through the immensely popular autobiographical works of Sir Arthur Grimble in two books, *A Pattern of Islands* (published in the US as *We Chose the Islands*) (1952) and *Return to the Islands* (1957). Grimble, a British colonial officer, lived on the islands for many years in the first half of the twentieth century (1918 to 1930). His popular publications offer only one facet of his work, and he is credited with recording much of traditional culture, as remembered in the early twentieth century, through detailed ethnography (Maude 1989). Harry Maude, also a colonial officer, overlapped with Grimble for three years, and having been trained in anthropology at Cambridge, continued and complemented Grimble's studies (e.g., Maude 1979; 1980).

The southern islands of the group are generally considered to receive less rainfall than the northern ones, with the raised coral limestone islands at most risk from drought (Luomala 1953; Lundsgaarde 1968). The atolls rely on the Ghyben–Herzberg lens for water supply and typically, as discussed for the Marshall Islands above, have taro cultivation pits in the centre, although the role of this crop appears to be less for subsistence and more as food for special occasions. Traditional subsistence is based on agroforestry (Thaman 1990) incorporating coconut, pandanus and breadfruit, supplemented by seafood. Although differences occur between islands within the group, Gerd Koch's (1986: xv) statement that 'this is one of the most inhospitable areas of our world' stands in stark contrast to Agassiz (1903, cited in Luomala 1953: 10), who found that two of the northern islands probably had 'the finest coconut groves of the tropical Pacific'.

Archaeological work in the Gilberts has been extremely limited, and the first reported excavations did not take place until 1983. As appears to be the case for the Marshalls, and other low islands in the region, the perceived impoverished nature of atolls is probably in part to blame for this late start (see Di Piazza 1998a). Also, the paucity of work may be linked to the Gilberts lying outside of the former US Trust Territory of the Pacific Islands and thus not receiving the same development impact and consequent funds. To date, much of Kiribati history is drawn from oral history, but the I-Kiribati historian Kambati Uriam (1995: 85) warns:

Even the *aomata* [true or real human beings] stories in the reconstructions, stories that are supposed to be real and true because they are close to our time, are in many cases not considered to be historical. They may be genuine, and possibly refer to actual events and people, but this does not necessarily guarantee them as historical. What is historical in Gilbertese oral tradition is an account that serves the people best in their daily activities and in their relationships with one another.

Takayama, Takasugi and Nakajima (1985) report that Richard Shutler had conducted brief surface surveys of Abemama, Butaritari, Makin and Tarawa, and had reported that the shell artefacts he observed were typologically indistinguishable from those that he had collected in Vanuatu. However, it was the project led by Jun Takayama that instigated the first archaeological excavations in the Gilberts.

Takayama (Takayama, Takasugi and Nakajima 1983; Takayama 1988) chose to excavate on the reef island of Makin at the very north end of the group. He believed it was likely to possess deeply stratified deposits and provide direct comparisons with sites, many excavated by him and his colleagues, in the rest of Micronesia to the north. Indeed a site, named Utiroa by the excavators, was discovered with cultural material located up to 3.5 metres below the current ground surface and in semi-submerged deposits. A single date on shell indicated that the deepest buried material may be approximately 1600 years old, with dog, not known at European contact, apparently present during earlier times. The preliminary conclusions drawn from this single season of excavation were that shell artefact types common elsewhere in Micronesia did not appear to be present, for example items such as cowrie-shell scrapers and *Terebra* adzes with the cutting edge at the aperture (rather than the pointed) end. Fishing gear with apparent east Polynesian relationships was regarded as a major discovery.

For Takayama and Takasugi (1987), one complete and two parts (proximal ends) of *Cassis* shell lure shafts, excavated in the lower levels of the Utiroa site, provided interesting parallels. In comparisons of ethnographic and archaeological specimens, they concluded that their excavated examples 'exhibit greatest resemblance to early Eastern Polynesian specimens from the typological point of view' (1987: 36). Thus, they suggest that the east Polynesian type developed in the Gilbert–Tuvalu–Rotuma region, prior to moving with the earliest settlers of eastern Polynesia.

Grimble (1921) noted that lure shanks and other items of material culture were sometimes made from bones excavated from the graves of human ancestors. The skull was also at times exhumed and treated with care within the home, or the complete skeleton of an ancestor might be preserved in the community meeting house (Roberts 1952). On occasion, when the teeth fell out of the skull, these were incorporated into necklaces (Grimble 1921: 47). Takayama, Takasugi and Kaiyama (1990) reported a fragment of 'human tooth pendant' from their excavation at the Nukantekainga site, Tarawa.

In 1988 Takayama, Takasugi and Kaiyama (nd; 1990) returned to the Gilberts and excavated at sites in Tarawa, in the central area of the group, and on Tamana in the south. At Bekaka village in Tamana, excavations revealed coral slab alignments, paving, and large quantities of shell beads. Fishing gear was recovered, including lure shanks and one-piece shell fishhooks, with one reported to be extremely similar to a type found in Hawaii, and others similar to types excavated in the Cook Islands. They conclude that (Takayama, Takasugi and Kaiyama nd: 5):

excavations on Makin, Tamana, and Vaitupu [in Tuvalu, see Takayama, Eritaia and Saito (1987)] have led us to postulate that Makin has closer parallels in the Marshalls and the Carolines to the west than Tamana, whereas Tamana has [a] closer historical relationship with Polynesia than Makin.

Koch (1984; 1986) conducted studies of contemporary material culture in the Gilbert Islands and that of neighbouring Polynesian Tuvalu to the south. He found that there was little similarity between the artefacts of the two archipelagos. As such, he concluded that it was not appropriate to describe the area as 'transitional' or as a 'migrational bridge' within the history of the settlement of Oceania. However, there are certainly indications from the minimal archaeological, as noted above, and ethnographic work so far conducted to suggest otherwise.

As noted above, much oral history refers to strong links with Samoa, and one of the most distinctive features of traditional Gilbertese architecture was the *maneaba*, a large community meeting house, basically consisting of a roof placed on quarried coral rock pillars (*boua*) (Lundsgaarde 1978; Maude 1980; Hockings 1989). Although they varied in size, Grimble (1952: 82–3) describes the *maneaba* regarded as typical of earlier times in his *A Pattern of Islands*:

Every Gilbertese village of any size had its own maneaba, or speak-house, in those days. The building was the focus of social life, the assembly hall, the dancing lodge, the news-mart of the community. Under the gigantic thatch, every clan [*boti*] had its ordained sitting place up against the overhang of the eaves . . . The ridge soared 60 feet high, overtopping the coconut-palms; the deep eaves fell to less than a man's height from the ground. Within, a man could step fifty paces clear from end to end, and thirty from side to side.

Apart from the secular functions listed by Grimble, the *maneaba* was also a ritual place where, if custom did not prevail, the spirits of ancestors might easily be offended (Maude 1979). A link to Polynesia is evidenced in the fact that the crushed coral gravel floor of the *maneaba* extended beyond the eaves to create an area called *te marae*, which is a typical name for such places in Polynesia (Hockings 1989). Linguistic interpretation has been proposed that points to the swamp taro, *Cyrtosperma chamissonis*, typical of the eastern Micronesian atolls, being introduced from there into western Polynesia (see Whistler 1991).

The most recent archaeological investigation is the small-scale work of Anne Di Piazza (1998a; 1999) on Nikunau, in the south of the group. As discussed in chapter 4, these excavations have produced the earliest dates for settlement of the Gilberts. The excavations revealed two earth ovens, both exhibiting a layer of lime powder. Interesting experimental work resulted in the discovery that the coral and clam shell used as 'oven stones', when treated with water, are much more efficient than the volcanic stones commonly used elsewhere in the Pacific (Di Piazza 1998b).

Apparently unique to the low islands of the region are the engravings marked on concreted sand rocks on the islets of Tarawa Atoll, and perhaps elsewhere in the Gilberts. The only information for these petroglyphs is provided in a rather confusing short report by I.G. Turbott (1949). With an obvious, although probably not direct, similarity to the petroglyphs from Pohnpei (see previous chapter), the engravings reported by Turbott consist mostly of footprints pecked out of the rock. The old men told him that they were places where giants, their names for the most part remembered in oral history, had stood during various 'historic' events. Indeed, that these are the footprints of giants is certainly consistent with their size: the largest has twelve toes and measures 1.35 metres in length. It is said to be the right foot of Tabuariki, an ancestral giant commonly mentioned in stories, and although not confirmed by Turbott, the left foot was apparently to be found on the neighbouring island of Maiana, over 30 kilometres to the south. Other larger than life footprints are reported in association with representations of a basket and lizards, and at a location on the

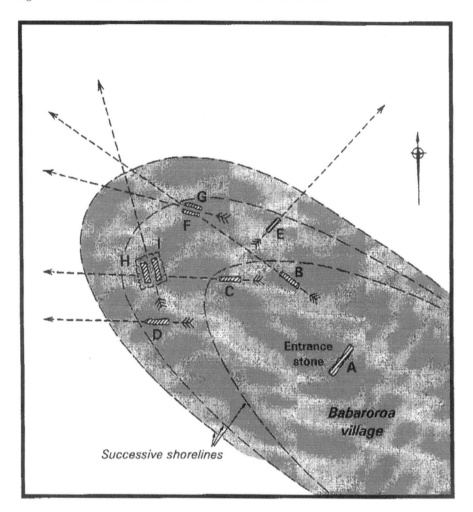

Fig. 8.2 Stone setting at Arorae (after Hilder 1959). A setting of stones that have been proposed to mark sailing directions for a navigational school. The arrows mark the alignments.

neighbouring islet of Bikenbiu, a boat with outrigger and sail. Each of these elements was incorporated by the old men into various historical narratives.

Brett Hilder (1959) reported another special feature of Gilbertese archaeology, after he was taken to a group of nine stones on the north-west tip of Arorae Island. The stone slabs set on end and in two cases paired were found to be oriented in the direction of three neighbouring islands (Fig. 8.2). The stone labelled 'E' appears anomalous as its orientation does not seem to relate to the direction of a local island, and Hilder proposes that this is the direction of exile – although some 3000 kilometres in this direction leads to Hawaii. Hilder's general conclusion was that these stones marked the site of a navigational school.

Alkire (1977) recognized a basic division in diversity of social organization between the Gilbert Islands to south and north. In the north he pointed to ambilineality, in which an individual can choose to trace a relationship with an ancestor through either the female or male line. In these islands the social structure tended to greater hierarchy than in the southern islands where there were no 'paramount chiefs' making the meeting house of greater importance in organizing district affairs. Residence was patrilocal, and although ambilineality was practised here as in the north, its outward tendency appeared to be patrilineal. Alkire's description only touches upon some of the complexities of social organization in the Gilberts, but this is not the place for further detail.

Banaba (Ocean Island) and Nauru

Banaba (formerly Ocean Island) lies some 450 kilometres west of the Gilberts, and Nauru a further 300 kilometres west of Banaba, and they are individual raised limestone islands spread 'along-the-line' of the Equator. Banaba is presently within the Republic of Kiribati, while Nauru is an independent country, but they previously shared much in the way of material culture. The Banabans were famed seafarers, and even though Nauruan is regarded as a linguistic isolate, there appears to have been much contact between the two islands (Maude and Lampert 1967). The two islands also share a poorly known archaeology and twentieth-century exploitation of phosphate deposits, which has removed much of the land surface. I will consider each island separately.

Banaba

Banaba is 3 kilometres long by 2 wide, and rises to a maximum elevation of 82 metres, with cliffs dropping sharply to a small fringing reef on all sides. The island is prone to drought, and subsistence was based on the most hardy of plants, pandanus and coconut, with a heavy reliance on fish (Maude and Lampert 1967). A positive attribute is the honeycomb of natural caves (*bangabanga*) within the island, which retain potable water in all but the most severe of droughts (Grimble 1957). The oral history regarding origins is very similar to that recorded for the Gilberts, with an early dark-skinned people later joined by fairer-skinned settlers (Maude 1995). Early commentators made much of the fact that Banabans are culturally and linguistically linked with the Gilberts. Harry and Honor Maude (1932: 263) made much of the Banabans being:

identical with the inhabitants of the neighbouring Gilbert group ... They speak the Gilbertese language, but with a distinct local accent and with the addition of a considerable number of words not used in the Gilbert Islands.

Maude and Maude (1932: 270–1) pursue further differences between the Banabans and the Gilbertese (I-Kiribati) in regard to the organization of social ties. They state:

The hamlet is the central pivot of the Banaban social structure . . . for on it depends the locality of his home and his lands, the *maneaba* in which he will have a right to sit and the *uma-n anti* in which he will make his food offerings to the gods, the terrace where his son will learn the mysteries of magic, his position in the dance and in all ceremonies, and numberless other things.

In the Gilberts, on the other hand, the hamlet is comparatively unimportant, the supreme factor in social organization being the clan. Now a comparison between the Gilbertese clan and the Banaban *kawa* [hamlet] will show them to be two similar but distinct social groupings. Both are patrilineal and both determine the sitting place in the maneaba, but here the resemblance ends, as the *kawa* is essentially a geographical unit and the Gilbertese clan is certainly not, members of the same clan being found scattered over all the sixteen islands of the group. Again, the Gilbertese clan is an exogamous unit while no evidence has ever been obtained suggesting that the *kawa* is, or was at any time, exogamous.

In this passage by the Maudes we see not only an example of the problematic essentializing of social practices across the whole of the Gilberts group as discussed in the previous section above, but also an apparent desire to make clear by juxtaposition the links between the Banabans and the I-Kiribati. Recent scholarship has made clear some of the political motivations in trying to group these islands together, and is also politicized as there is a strong contemporary movement for the full resettlement of Banaba and independence of the island from the Republic of Kiribati. Raobeia Ken Sigrah and Stacey King (2001) not only argue that the Banabans had a language distinct from the I-Kiribati, but that many of the similarities of social organization and customs attributed to them and the neighbours to the west are the result of missionary and other outside intervention in the late nineteenth century.

Among his papers, Grimble (1989b) left a note on the archaeology of Banaba in which he records the presence of long terraces on the east coast of the island, constructed of dry-stone walls backed by earth and rock to make a level area (Fig. 8.3). Although apparently abandoned when Grimble visited, the old men informed him that in the past unmarried boys lived here as a colony, while they learned the 'arts of life'. In the vicinity of the long terraces, Grimble also observed small platforms, and a line of seven stone monuments consisting of flat stones and monoliths. The monoliths suggested a vague resemblance to a human head and neck. Interestingly, elsewhere on Banaba Grimble was shown stones, some of them apparently unmodified natural projections, which were regarded as unspecified ancestors. A link can perhaps be made to a report elsewhere in the Grimble (1989a) papers, to ceremonial monoliths often with associated flat stones for the presentation of offerings to 'various spiritual powers'. Like the pillar stones of the *maneaba*, which were all named and associated to

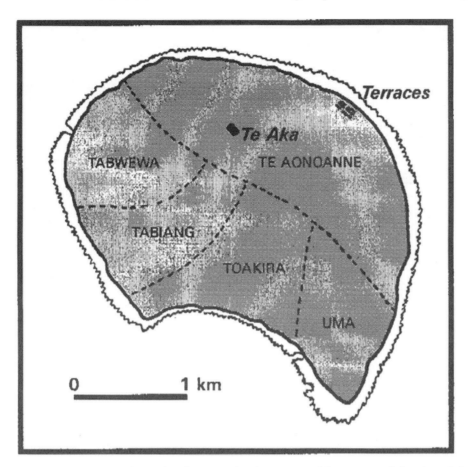

Fig. 8.3 Map of Banaba showing the districts and locations of the site of the te Aka village and north-east coast terraces.

ancestors and the sun (on the east) and the moon (on the west), these shrines were also named *boua* (Hockings 1989).

Although the terraces were apparently out of use by the time Maude and Maude (1932) studied them, they assessed them as having many of the same functions that club-houses for unmarried men had in other island societies of the region. Although everywhere they found evidence for the practice of *kouti* magic, which involved the performer sitting on a small platform and awaiting the rising of the sun, in discussing the terraces they find that they were not linked to this practice (1932: 281):

According to all our informants the terraces were primarily made not as a rendezvous for *kouti* devotees but usually for the catching and taming of the frigate-birds, which took up a large part of the leisure hours of the Banabans. Catching the frigate-bird was far more than a mere pastime . . . as an elaborate ritual was attached to it and to attain skill involved a lifetime of study and practice.

The only professional excavation reported from Banaba is that directed by Ron Lampert (1968) in advance of phosphate extraction. A possible *maneaba*, house site and burial were excavated at an inland village site identified as te Aka. The *maneaba* had already been partially removed by bulldozing, but the excavation of the north-west end showed that it had been rebuilt and extended on at least three occasions. Prior to the *maneaba*, a structure measuring 4 by 3 metres, defined by holes for four corner posts and a central post, had been constructed. It is possible that two shallow earth ovens pre-date this. This structure is consistent with the size and construction of the domestic building excavated on the site. A piece of wood taken from one of the excavated postholes provided a date for site use of less than 250 years ago. Although such a date is supported by all of the identified elements, except for the burial, being consistent with the ethnography, charcoal from cooking pits dated subsequent to publication provided a range of 300 to 400 years ago (Sigrah and King 2001).

The burial was found to be in a flexed position, within a box structure of coral slabs that had been placed around the edge. The skull was missing, and it is likely to have been as prized on Banaba as noted above for the Gilberts. All of these elements, including the lack of grave-goods, are consistent with the ethnography, with the only deviation being the orientation, with the head end oriented north-west instead of east, as would be expected in regard to the information provided to Grimble (1921). Further burials and house posts were found in excavations by amateur enthusiasts in 1968, with inconclusive results. The minimal information has usefully been published by Sigrah and King (2001).

Items unique to the material culture repertoire of Banaba are the fishing lures made from pieces of stalactite derived from the caves. Owing to the relatively poor fringing reef resources, the usual shell lures were not easy to produce. Maude and Lampert (1967), who discuss these lures in detail, note that they took weeks to manufacture and were highly prized, being regarded as far superior to shell lures in their ability to attract fish.

Nauru

Moving west, Nauru, rising to a height of some 60 metres above sea level, has a similar environment to Banaba. Within its area of 21 square kilometres, it contains an inland lake, Buada Lagoon, and Alkire (1978) proposes that only in this area and the coastal fringe was horticulture possible. The main subsistence crops were coconut and pandanus, with milkfish (*Chanos chanos*) raised in the lagoon, and shellfish collected from the narrow fringing reef; however, adverse currents reportedly restricted fishing by boat (Alkire 1978). Solange Petit-Skinner (1981) notes that the milkfish were not a staple food, and frigate birds, noddies and terns supplemented the diet, along with chickens, argued to have been present prior to nineteenth-century European contact.

First reported contact by Europeans was with the merchant ship *Hunter* in 1798. Wilhelm Fabricus (1992: 160) summarizes this brief encounter from the writings in the logbook of Captain John Fearn:

he had sighted an island which he called 'Pleasant Island' on account of its pleasing aspect and the friendly demeanour of its inhabitants. He did not land but received gifts of coconuts and fruit from the natives, who came out to him on boats through the surf. The large numbers of boats, manned by more than 300 natives, led him to conclude that the population was large and the island was closely settled and very fertile. In the opinion of Captain Fearn, the bearing of the natives suggested that they had already had previous contact with white people.

This and other historical reports rather contradict Alkire's view, noted above, that fishing by boat was not possible because of adverse currents. A German Navy report of 1888 states (Fabricus 1992: 219):

As in all other places in the South Seas, the canoes are fitted with an outrigger. As the natives of Nauru, unlike those of the neighbouring island groups, have never undertaken long sea voyages, their vessels are small and unadorned and intended purely for fishing.

Power (1905, cited in Maude and Lampert 1967) reports that fossilized shells were extracted from the base of holes 6 metres deep, to be manufactured into adzes and fishhooks.

As far as I am aware, no detailed archaeological investigations have been conducted on Nauru. The twentieth-century developments related to phosphate mining and the wartime defence and attacks on the island mean that there are only a few places where archaeological deposits may survive (Specht 1982). Petit-Skinner (1981) reports that many standing stones, called *tabuerik*, had stood around the island and represented 'ancient family gods'. People would leave offerings at these stones in a similar fashion to the *boua* of Banaba. However, all but one of these monoliths was removed during the Second World War.

Nukuoro and Kapingamarangi

The atolls of Nukuoro and Kapingamarangi are located to the west and north of Nauru and may be grouped in two ways. The first is as part of Micronesia, and the second as two of the eighteen island societies known collectively as the 'Polynesian Outliers'. The 'Outliers' are defined as islands located outside of the traditional Polynesian triangle formed by Hawaii, Rapa Nui (Easter Island) and Aotearoa/New Zealand, and where the people speak Polynesian languages. They have been variously considered as either relict populations left behind, as their colonizing friends and relatives moved east, or as representing a return west after most of the eastern Pacific islands had been settled. A more complicated picture, including a combination of both and later rather more complex histories, perhaps including cultural replacement, has more recently been considered (Bayard 1976; Kirch 1984b; Davidson 1992). The two northern-most (the 'Northern Outliers' (Kirch 1984b)), Nukuoro and Kapingamarangi, are discussed here as they fall within that first grouping of Micronesia.

Nukuoro

Davidson's pioneering work of 1965 began on Nukuoro, an almost circular atoll with a lagoon 28 square kilometres in area, located 400 kilometres south of Pohnpei. The atoll fringe consists of forty-six reef islets, making a total land area of approximately 1.7 square kilometres. Deeply stratified archaeological deposits were located through excavation, but Davidson could not find any indication of the settlement by 'Polynesians', and indeed she states that 'there is nothing unambiguously Polynesian . . . from the excavations' (1992: 296). New dates from the excavations now contradict the anomalous date of 1970 ± 90 bp (Davidson 1971). Evidence for the earliest settlement is derived from a dog tooth dated to 1300 years ago (Davidson 1992).

The excavations revealed a number of diachronic changes. Dogs, although numerous in the early deposits, disappear by 500 years ago (Davidson 1971). Fish remains were reported to reveal a change, from an emphasis on trolling for deep-sea fish to other methods for catching reef and shallow-water species (Leach and Davidson 1988; Davidson 1992), but the vast majority of the fish bone recovered is not derived from pelagic fish, while the 759 one-piece fishhooks and fragments collected in the excavations are those mostly associated with fishing for pelagic species (Davidson and Leach 1996). Davidson and Leach (1996) conclude that deep-sea fishing was probably socially important, but that the majority of fishing for subsistence purposes was achieved by netting. However, Michael Lieber (1992) found that on Kapingamarangi the netting of pelagic fish in a group expedition was regarded as a prestigious activity and of course did not require the type of fishing gear reported from the archaeological deposits on Nukuoro.

Davidson (1967a; 1971) was able to create a typology for the one-piece fish-hooks, which could be partially seriated. The majority of hooks are rotating rather than jabbing types and lack barbs. *Terebra* and *Mitra* adzes are not found in deposits containing dog bones (Davidson 1992), suggesting a late introduction on the atoll and reflecting a trend already noted for the Carolines. In conclusion, Davidson (1992) finds little to support Kirch's (1984b: 229) statement that the two Northern Outliers 'may well exemplify the east-to-west drift voyage model of outlier settlement, with relatively shallow time depth', and further suggests that the vulnerability of the atoll deposits to environmental perturbations may preclude the discovery of the earliest evidence of settlement.

Kapingamarangi

The other Northern Outlier, Kapingamarangi, is some 225 kilometres due south of Nukuoro. With a land area on its thirty-two islets of just over 1 square kilometre, the reef forms a thin band around the large 60 square kilometre lagoon. Four localities on the main currently inhabited islet of Touhou were excavated by Leach and Ward (1981). Stratified archaeological deposits were found to a depth of over 4 metres below current ground surface. That artefacts were less common than on Nukuoro is explained by Leach and Davidson (1988) as due, at least in part, to the virtual absence of pearl shell and black mussel, the usual raw material for fishhooks on Nukuoro. Kapingamarangi fishhooks would probably have been manufactured from less durable materials such as wood, coconut shell and turtle carapace. Alkire (1978: 70, following Lieber 1968) suggests the surprising scenario that inter-island contact was unknown to the inhabitants of Kapingamarangi until the Spanish administration of the 1880s; this might provide an explanation of the limited artefact repertoire.

Leach and Ward (1981) made the extremely important discovery that Touhou Islet was almost completely an artificial creation. The first occupation, dating to about 750 years ago, was only a little above sea level. Subsequently the islet has been built up, with the aid of sea walls, to a height of 4 metres above sea level. A few differences can be noted from the findings from Nukuoro. There is no evidence for dog in the prehistory of Kapingamarangi, and all the adzes recovered are of *Tridacna*, with no *Terebra* or *Mitra* shell adzes being found. One pot sherd provided inconclusive evidence of origin or age. Unlike Nukuoro, the fish bone assemblage from Kapingamarangi shows evidence of more specialized forms of fishing developing over time, with a possible increase in baited hook fishing, as judged from the species represented (Leach and Davidson 1988).

Following his 1947 ethnographic survey, Te Rangi Hiroa (Buck 1950: 4–5) was able to write that 'The people, friendly and hospitable, are taller and more robust than the Micronesians. Their skin color is typical Polynesian brown and their hair is wavy or curly . . . The language is a pure Polynesian dialect with few, if any, intrusions from Micronesia.' The excavations, however, did not reveal unambiguous evidence regarding the origins of the Kapingas.

Summary

These island groups and outliers of Micronesia are only slowly yielding parts of their histories to archaeological investigation. In this, in many circumstances, they are challenging the ethnographic, linguistic and historical records and revealing, through the material remains, complex but currently opaque histories of contact and independent innovation. Concerted and long-term projects, like that instigated in the Marshall Islands by Weisler, are clearly what is required if a more detailed archaeological understanding of these islands is to be gained.

The varying colonial histories of the low island groups have led to significant changes in the Marshall Islands, including the displacement of people from their home islands. The I-Kiribati have been similarly affected, although in this case because of perceived over-population. A number of plans have been proposed in an effort to raise some of the Marshall Islands artificially in order to ameliorate the apparent threat of global sea level rise, and the urgency has recently been sharpened by reports in the media of flooding in the Gilbert Islands. Given these factors, it is likely that in the next few decades the people of this part of Micronesia will be less concerned with digging holes in their islands than with building them up.

CHAPTER 9

THE TROPICAL NORTH-WEST PACIFIC IN CONTEXT

In the first three chapters of this book I introduced the motifs of fusion and fluidity that have helped in the understanding and contextualization of the long-term human history of the tropical north-west Pacific. Emerging through the chapters has been a third motif, that of flux. This last motif is strongly linked to those of fusion and fluidity, and all three together highlight similarity and difference through time. In this chapter, although they can only be artificially separated, I will assess aspects of the region's history under the heading of each of them. In conclusion, I will draw these motifs back together and consider the future for the archaeological past in the region.

Fusion

In his 1832 publication, at a time when the region was still little known in the European literature, Dumont d'Urville in defining 'Micronesia' mentioned the likelihood of 'fusion' between the 'races' of Micronesia and Melanesia. Further, he proposed that the original people who inhabited the islands of the tropical north-west Pacific were derived from populations in the Philippines who had already 'fused' with Japanese or Chinese people who had landed there. Thus, the notion of fusion in regard to the region discussed in this volume is by no means a new concept. The question then might be asked as to why I have reintroduced it here. In the 170 years since Dumont D'Urville defined the boundaries of the region, which are the ones generally recognized in the present day, academic scholarship has shifted to a preferred view that islands are isolated and that internal development related to the potential of the environment has accounted, for the most part, for the variety of island existence encountered on the arrival of Europeans willing to provide written accounts of their experiences. This perception, I argued at the beginning of this book, is not satisfactory for providing the basis for understanding the long-term history of Oceania. The material presented here, and the constructions of that material from the perspective of developing an archaeological anthropology of the region, I hope has gone some way to revealing the complexity of the history of these islands: a history of contact and communication continuing processes of fusion and revealing little evidence of isolation.

As I prepared this book I started to think that one of the real barriers to thinking differently about the history of these island peoples, at least for archaeologists, has been their reading of linguistic distributions placed on the maps by linguists as actual boundaries to communication. I once thought of these linguistic groupings as indicators of localized 'spheres of interaction', but such a reading of this single strand of evidence runs against the tide of ethnographic and archaeological indicators that reveal interaction across such boundaries. Perhaps the best example is the *sawei* system that links the Chuukic speakers with the Yapese, or perhaps the quarrying of stone disks by the Yapese on Palau. Each case crosses linguistic boundaries. We need to imagine islanders in the region possessing the ability to communicate in more than one language, in a way similar to Indigenous communities in central Australia that are fluent in their own language and those of a number of their immediate neighbours. The recent history of Micronesia has illustrated the local ability to adopt successfully the language of successive colonial governments while maintaining their own. Elizabeth Keating's (e.g., 2001) work on Pohnpei is developing an approach that is beginning to identify the nuances of the fusion of such language contacts in the region.

It must also be kept in focus that European influence in this corner of Oceania was centuries old by the time that Cook happened upon islands elsewhere. These influences, as I proposed in chapter 2, need not have been direct to have an effect. Early on in the aftermath of Magellan there were already down-the-line consequences of floating settlements containing a fusion of humanity born of the colonial experience. These consequences of remote contacts may not be easy to detect archaeologically, but certainly must be worthy of further consideration. Fusion came in many forms.

Reporting his visit to Palau in 1876 and following an account of local antipathy towards Europeans, the Russian naturalist and ethnographer Nikolai Miklouho-Maclay provides a list of the 'foreigners' he encountered there (Parmentier and Kopnina-Geyer 1996: 106):

1.) I saw, especially in Koror, a significant number of Beluulechab [Island of Ashes] natives (as Palauans call Yap Island), which . . . come here to get *fei* [stone money]; 2.) a native from Niningo (Exchequer on the maps); four women in Koror who were brought over a few years ago by a German skipper. They were taken from Niningo against their wills and were left in Koror; 3.) a few Javanese sailors from the one which I have been a passenger; 4.) a Chinese man who was brought here by one of the skippers; 5.) a West Indian Negro (Mr. Gibbons), who has long been married and had a large family; there were three European traders living on the islands during my visit (Irish, Swedish, and German); also, many skippers have their own temporary houses on Melekeok, where they live from time to time awaiting the shipment of goods.

Ocean settlement *is* fusion. Colonialism brought with it displacement and relocation for many islanders. That in many cases this was forced, such as following the Sokehs Rebellion on Pohnpei, should not be forgotten, but other cases such as the establishment of the Refalawasch in the Mariana Islands appear to have been requested. However, the movement of people across the fluid boundaries provided by the ocean would not have been an unfamiliar concept, and undoubtedly would have been incorporated within local cosmological understanding.

Fluidity

Hunter-Anderson and Butler (1995) in their overview of the archaeology of the Commonwealth of the Northern Mariana Islands found that the date for the arrival of *Rattus exulans* in the archipelago is 'unclear'. In chapter 5 I presented a case for the arrival of rats and rice in the Marianas at around 1000 years ago and at about the same time that *latte* structures appear to have been constructed for the first time. Together this suite of evidence forms a strong basis for proposing significant contact with island South-East Asia at that time. Further evidence of widespread connections between western Micronesia and the islands and lands to the west and south may be derived from the glass beads in Yap and Palau. Although the connections with South-East Asia may have been quite different for the people of the Marianas compared to those of the Palauans and Yapese.

Yap was undoubtedly incorporated into a number of networks, including the *sawei*. The material remains of the *rai/fei* and evidence of quarry sites in Palau, and the exotic materials excavated in the outer islands, along with the ethnography indicating the vast distances travelled in the *sawei*, and elsewhere, using traditional seacraft and navigational techniques, must be regarded as echoes of regular inter-island voyaging, at least over the last 1000 years or so. Other indicators include the adoption of the *Terebra* adze type across the whole of the Caroline Islands after about 1000 years ago and the material similarities of architecture between Pohnpei and Kosrae in the eastern Carolines (Fig. 9.1). Craib (nd) has argued for the widespread adoption of the 'beaked adze', dating to a few centuries later, another, distinctive style that indicates the sharing of ideas or materials (Fig. 9.2).

My own work (with Meredith Wilson) on the rock-art of Pohnpei has recorded the presence of the enveloped cross, a motif only previously known in Melanesia, suggestive of wider communication and contact, but presently undated (Rainbird and Wilson 1999). Also undated is the introduction of *kava* into the eastern Carolines, but it is highly likely that its immediate origins were in western Polynesia. As I discussed in chapter 3, there are also suggestions in the form of maritime technology and swamp taro, amongst other things, of influences going in the other direction.

The evidence for these widespread seaways is slowly starting to amount to significant material confirmation of widespread contact and communication in Micronesia prior to Magellan's arrival (and long after, see D'Arcy 2001). It was

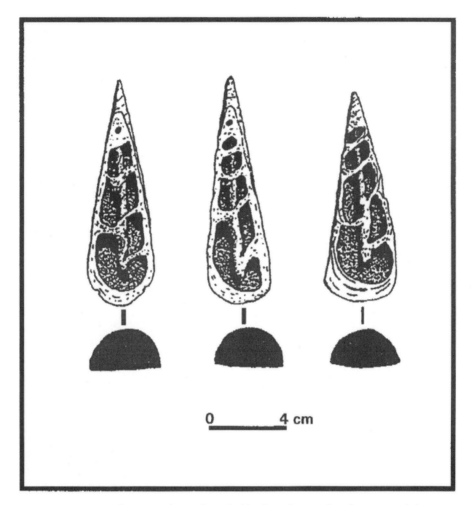

Fig. 9.1 A selection of *Terebra* shell adzes from Chuuk Lagoon (after King and Parker 1984).

into this milieu of local seaways and social networks across fluid boundaries that the Europeans stumbled.

Flux

The evidence from Micronesia is that islanders did alter the landscape of their islands in order to enhance the physical attributes. On some islands, where the required variables were absent, there was a limitation to the possible alterations; on others, natural processes such as tectonic change ran ahead of the settlers. On some islands the necessary variables were present, and the potential for habitation expanded through valley infilling and coastal progradation.

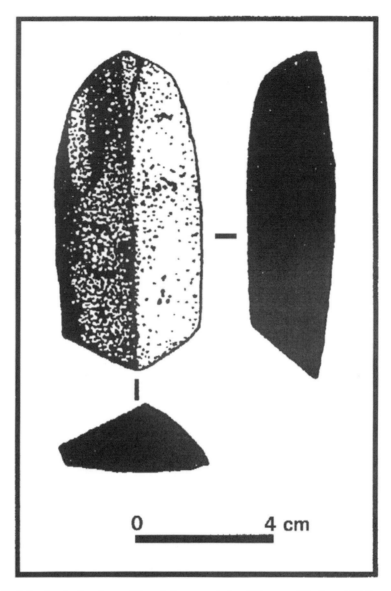

Fig. 9.2 A beaked adze from Chuuk Lagoon (after King and Parker 1984).

There can be no greater indication of purposeful environmental change in Micronesia than the massive terraces of the Palau archipelago, but, as Weisler has shown in the Marshall Islands, less spectacular but rather more subtle environmental changes purposefully caused by humans have made the atoll islets what they are today. What is still not satisfactorily resolved is when the atolls of the region presented themselves for human occupation. That a number of the high islands in the region had already been settled by this time seems likely, and the variable distribution of other lands to settle added another dimension of flux in the sensing of place and the possibilities of dwelling.

In proposing in earlier chapters that some of the orthodox methods of interpreting the archaeology of the islands are flawed, how then are we to interpret the monumental material remains of places such as Nan Madol and Leluh? If we follow the archaeologists who have worked in these places, then they represent local social evolution available in regard to the environmental parameters of the high islands. In one case, that of Nan Madol, devolution occurred when what was believed to be centralized society based at Nan Madol was destroyed and replaced by a system of five independent polities that became fossilized shortly after prolonged contact with Euro-Americans. If Petersen is right, however, then sociopolitical organization should have been resistant to any form of centralized or feudal control. Indeed, his research on Pohnpei finds that there is a long-term resilience in the matrilineal conical clan system, a politically manipulated system based on both genealogy and competition. How could we envisage Nan Madol and Leluh operating under such conditions? Do we need to get away from reading these monuments in the classic Giddensian sense as 'containers of power'? How is labour mobilized for such projects when there are only 'chiefs among chiefs'?

Perhaps we should be looking at the role of ancestry, given that the overriding ideal principle of the conical clan, whether it is reckoned through the female or male lines, is the identification of links to the ancestors and through this the kinship ties that bind individuals and clans to the land. Perhaps in relation to this is a telling report from missionaries, who said that according to informants each wall at Leluh was built in honour of the dead, and that 'one of their most decisive evidences of public grief is to rebuild the wall about the premises of a bereaved chief' (Damon 1861: 37). Further evidence of the importance placed on honouring and commemorating the ancestors can be seen in the tombs of both Leluh and Nan Madol. If then we can perceive of these places as the stages for maintaining the ancestors, something that became solidified in stone over the last 1000 to 1500 years, then competition for worthy deeds could have led to a gradually accretative locale, with competitive emulation occurring not only internally, as I am suggesting here, but also externally and leading to the structures that were built at a later date at Leluh. So we may have in these places both manifestations of ancestry, with the maintenance of genealogical ties, with tombs, walls and platforms perhaps all acting as mnemonics in the recounting of genealogies and this manifested as competition seen as goodly works that would allow chiefs among chiefs greater opportunity to gain higher titles. In the past, archaeologists may have envisaged Nan Madol in completely the wrong way in the expectation that this was some sort of urban centre, with the multitude of roles that term implies. Rather, parts may have been more or less permanently occupied, with perhaps a chief in residence whose status was heightened by physical and mythical closeness to the ancestors, and within whom sacredness was embodied, but nothing like absolute power. The other islets and tombs may have acted as monuments where on occasions ceremonies were enacted, and depending on which ancestor was being referenced at any particular time, for politically expedient reasons, some islet or tombs would take on more importance than others. This would leave some islets deserted and overgrown, while others were cleared and the ancestor was revered. At Leluh we may be observing the expected variations on the conical clan theme. The emulation of Nan Madol, in at least the smallest way, cannot, I think, be doubted – although Ross Cordy (1993), as a necessary corollary of maintaining a 'founder effect' type philosophy for Kosrae social evolution, argues that no links can be observed.

Of course, the particular manifestations of eastern Carolinian high island style conical clanship still require explaining: that is why did this happen here and not elsewhere in the region? In answering this and part of the issue of mobilization of labour, one thing that Pohnpei and Kosrae had was large and probably stable populations compared to neighbouring atoll populations, owing to resource availability. They also were not fragmented high islands like those in Chuuk Lagoon. Elsewhere on the high islands, monumental and prestige elements can be identified in the terraces of Palau, the stone money of Yap and the *latte* stones of the Marianas.

Nan Madol and Leluh may be regarded as places where power, through genealogy and competition, was negotiated. It may be no surprise that these locales were chosen, given the importance of primary domain in the conical clan system, as they are archaeologically the earliest dated settlement sites on their islands. So rather than being individual containers of power in centralized systems, they may actually have been central to negotiation in dynamic systems of fragmentation and fusion, each pulling in opposite directions and creating the multiple polities as witnessed on Pohnpei historically.

Through the 1980s and 1990s archaeologists have interpreted Nan Madol and Leluh as representing urban centres in centralized political systems led by a single ruler in a pyramidal hierarchy with three or four basic levels of social stratification. These were seen to have evolved, and in the case of Nan Madol eventually devolved, in their bounded island environments, with little notion of outside contact or a prior history of social organization possessed by the settlers. Although much difference is exhibited, the basic underlying similarities in sociopolitical organization across the region do suggest, in much the same way as linguistics, that there is some shared history between these island communities. It is patently clear that these communities did not need to evolve socially; they were already social and organized by historical understandings. As the communities settled into and adapted their new islands they also varied the sociopolitical organization around the themes they had inherited. As I have argued elsewhere, at some point in the first millennium of settlement ancestors stopped being regarded as overseas and became related to the island itself. Once this occurred then the local ancestors could be celebrated and commemorated and maintained as central to community organization as they always had been. As Petersen argues, the mythohistory of the *Saudeleurs* is one that warns of the evils of absolute power, a power that within the contradictions of the conical clan system is impossible to achieve.

What Leluh and Nan Madol, in their monumental glory, are most likely to represent is the importance of ancestry and place in the past negotiation of socio-political organization. They are not, as is so commonly reported, the apogee of sociopolitical systems in their social evolutionary march towards supposedly more complex levels of social hierarchy. The organization of society in these islands was already complex, negotiated, contingent and thoroughly historical. These places do not need to be interpreted as representing entirely new forms of sociopolitical organization; rather they are manifestations of an old, but very resilient system that is antithetical to the type of distinct hierarchical structure that archaeologists attempt to apply to them.

In celebrating their ancestors, the apparent lack of long-distance seacraft on Pohnpei and Kosrae at the time of earliest European reporting may not be so odd. The effort represented in the goodly works at these places acted as an attractor (Fig. 9.3). We have seen that stories from Ulithi Atoll, far to the west, recount visits to Pohnpei and Nan Madol. People came from the sea. Pohnpeians and Kosraeans, at various stages prior to and during periods of European and other visits, learnt to control visitors and, as Petersen has observed in regard to themes in Pohnpeian oral history, visitors were to be expected.

The future of the past

New understandings are likely to emerge from the continuing excavations in the Palau archipelago, many of which are related to long-term infrastructure development and other research-led projects. One includes applying expectations of island colonization developed elsewhere in Lapita pottery user contexts, and this already appears to be reaping rewards.

Development-led archaeology continues in the Mariana Islands, and as the islanders of Tinian and Rota get further embroiled in attracting tourist dollars a wealth of new data will be produced. Additionally, in this archipelago the large corpus of previously excavated material still awaits full analysis and will undoubtedly provide further insightful interpretations of the past in these islands.

Elsewhere in the region communities face an uncertain future. The dual effects of global warming and the reduction in external funding as former colonial countries step further back from post-colonial commitments mean that funding for archaeological research will need to be found from elsewhere. In this situation, further archaeological research will depend on the vagaries of research funding and the personal preferences of individuals.

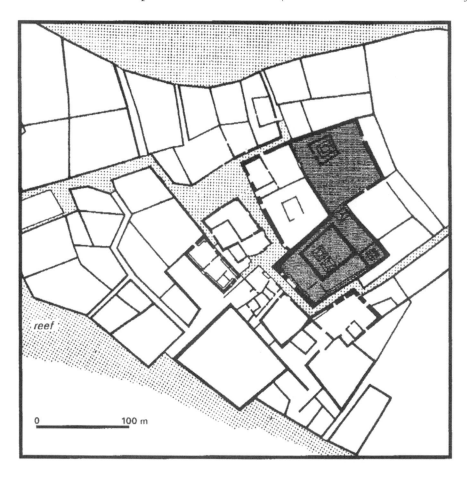

Fig. 9.3 Mortuary compounds at Leluh, Kosrae (after Morgan 1988). The compounds in dark shading are distinctive in their architecture and may mark special places that are related to the ancestors and ceremonies in their honour.

Archaeological anthropologies

In attempting to construct an archaeological anthropology for this non-region commonly termed Micronesia, I have been chasing chimeras and developing contradictions. Anthropologists along with sociologists and other social scientists are all painfully aware of the difficulty of representing people in all of their complexities in the present. How, they may ask, can it be possible for the distant past? Secondly, and in part because of the nature of area studies, but more importantly because of nineteenth-century decisions that could have turned out quite differently, I have been attempting to construct a long-term history of a place that I have in the material presented in this volume tried to show does not exist. So, what can I say that I have achieved?

In working through the motifs of fusion, fluidity and flux I have attempted to construct island lives by contextualizing the available information. This includes the direct archaeological materials from the particular place, as interpreted by me or the original reporter. These are considered within a broader comparative framework and then in regard to local information and broader anthropological understandings of the possibilities for human existence. The material I have used – and I am confident that I have not missed too much – has not resisted the interpretations I have constructed in this contextual approach. Thus, from a particular perspective, what I have provided here is a long-term history derived from the particularities of the fragmentary evidence available. As I write, I am aware that the work in progress may already be leading to certain fluxes in the veracity of elements of my interpretation. In a world defined less by boundaries and more by connections this is only to be expected.

REFERENCES

Adams, W.H. (ed.) 1997. *Archaeological Survey of Gachlaw Village, Gilman Municipality, Yap, Federated States of Micronesia. Micronesian Resources Study*. Micronesian Endowment for Historic Preservation, Federated States of Micronesia, US National Park Service: San Francisco.

Adams, W.H., Campbell, S.K. and Ross, R.E. 1997. Gachlaw Village. In W.H. Adams (ed.) *Archaeological Survey of Gachlaw village, Gilman Municipality, Yap, Federated States of Micronesia. Micronesian Resources Study*. 25–37. Micronesian Endowment for Historic Preservation, Federated States of Micronesia, US National Park Service: San Francisco.

Alkire, W.H. 1965. *Lamotrek Atoll and Inter-island Socioeconomic Ties*. Illinois Studies in Anthropology 5. Urbana: University of Illinois Press.

1977. *An Introduction to the Peoples and Cultures of Micronesia*. 2nd edition. Cummings: Menlo Park.

1978. *Coral Islanders*. AHM Press: Arlington Heights.

1980. Technical knowledge and the evolution of political system in the central and western Carolines of Micronesia. *Canadian Journal of Anthropology* 1: 229–37.

1993. Madrich: Outer Islanders on Yap. *Pacific Studies* 16(2): 31–66.

1999. Cultural ecology and ecological anthropology in Micronesia. In R.C. Kiste and M. Marshall (eds.) *American Anthropology in Micronesia: An Assessment*. 81–105. University of Hawaii Press: Honolulu.

Allen, J. 1996. The pre-Austronesian settlement of Island Melanesia: implications for Lapita archaeology. In W.H. Goodenough (ed.) *Prehistoric Settlement of the Pacific*. 11–27. American Philosophical Society: Philadelphia.

Ambrose, S.H., Butler, B.M., Hanson, D.B., Hunter-Anderson, R.L. and Krueger, H.W. 1997. Stable isotopic analysis of human diet in the Marianas Archipelago, western Micronesia. *American Journal of Physical Anthropology* 104: 343–61.

Ambrose, W. 1997. Contradictions in Lapita pottery, a composite clone. *Antiquity* 71: 525–38.

Amesbury, J.R. 1998. Changes in species composition of archaeological marine shell assemblages in Guam. *Micronesica* 31: 347–66.

Amesbury, J.R., Moore, D.R. and Hunter-Anderson, R.L. 1996. Cultural adaptations and late Holocene sea level change in the Marianas: recent excavations at Chalan Piao, Saipan, Micronesia. *Bulletin of the Indo-Pacific Prehistory Association* 15: 53–69.

Anderson, A. 1989. *Prodigious Birds: Moas and Moa-Hunting in Prehistoric New Zealand*. Cambridge University Press: Cambridge.

1994. Palaeoenvironmental evidence of island colonization: a response. *Antiquity* 68: 845–7.

2000. Slow boats from China: issues in the prehistory of Indo-Pacific seafaring. In S. O'Connor and P. Veth (eds.) *East of Wallace's Line: Studies of Past and Present Maritime Cultures of the Indo-Pacific Region. Modern Quaternary Research in South-East Asia*, 16. 13–50. A.A. Balkema: Rotterdam.

Anderson, A., Bedford, S., Clark, G., Lilley, I., Sand, C., Summerhayes, G. and Torrence, R. 2001. An inventory of Lapita sites containing dentate-stamped pottery. In G. Clark, A. Anderson and T. Vunidilo (eds.) *The Archaeology of Lapita Dispersal in Oceania: Papers from the Fourth Lapita Conference, June 2000, Canberra, Australia. Terra Australis* 17: 1–13.

Anderson, Benedict 1991. *Imagined Communities: Reflections on the Origin and Spread of Nationalism.* 2nd edition. Verso: London.

Anthony, D.W. 1990. Migration in archeology: the baby and the bathwater. *American Anthropologist* 92: 895–914.

Ashby, G. 1985. *Some Things of Value . . . Micronesian Customs and Beliefs.* Revised edition. Rainy Day Press: Eugene, Or.

Ashcroft, B. 2001. Language and race. *Social Identities* 7: 311–28.

Athens, J.S. 1980a. *Archaeological Investigations at Nan Madol: Islet Maps and Surface Artifacts.* Pacific Studies Institute Monograph Series, 2. Guam.

1980b. An archaeological inventory survey in the Palikir region of Ponape: the FSM and CCM relocation project. MS on file, Hamilton Library, University of Hawaii, Honolulu.

1980c. Pottery from Nan Madol, Ponape, eastern Caroline Islands. *Journal of the Polynesian Society* 89: 95–9.

1981. *The Discovery and Archaeological Investigation of Nan Madol, Ponape, Eastern Caroline Islands: An Annotated Bibliography.* Micronesian Archaeological Survey Report 3. Historic Preservation Office: Saipan.

1983. The megalithic ruins of Nan Madol. *Natural History* 92(12): 50–61.

1984. Surface artefact distributions at the Nan Madol site: a preliminary assessment of spatial patterning. *New Zealand Journal of Archaeology* 6: 129–53.

1986. *Archaeological Investigations at Tarague Beach, Guam.* Report for the Department of Air Force, San Francisco.

1990a. Kosrae pottery, clay and early settlement. In R.L. Hunter-Anderson (ed.) *Recent Advances in Micronesian Archaeology. Micronesica Supplement* 2: 171–86.

1990b. Nan Madol pottery, Pohnpei. In R.L. Hunter-Anderson (ed.) *Recent Advances in Micronesian Archaeology. Micronesica Supplement* 2: 17–32.

1995. *Landscape Archaeology: Prehistoric Settlement, Subsistence, and Environment of Kosrae, Eastern Caroline Islands, Micronesia.* International Archaeological Research Institute, Inc.: Honolulu.

Athens, J.S., Hunter-Anderson, R.L., Ward, J.V. and Welch, D.J. 1989. *Landscape Change, Agriculture, and Complex Societies on Tropical Pacific Islands.* Preprint Proceedings of the Circum-Pacific Prehistory Conference: bringing a million years to Washington State (Vol. IV), Seattle.

Athens, J.S. and Ward J.V. 1995. Paleoenvironment of the Orote Peninsula, Guam. *Micronesica* 28: 51–76.

Athens, J.S., Ward, J.V. and Murakami, G.M. 1996. Development of an agroforest on a Micronesian high island: prehistoric Kosraean agriculture. *Antiquity* 70: 834–46.

Ayres, W.S. 1979. Archaeological survey in Micronesia. *Current Anthropology* 20: 598–600.

1988. Preliminary report on the 1987 Nan Madol fieldwork. MS on file, Historic Preservation Office, Pohnpei State, Federated States of Micronesia.

1990a. Mystery islets of Micronesia. *Archaeology* 43(1): 58–63.

1990b. Pohnpei's position in eastern Micronesian prehistory. In R.L. Hunter-Anderson (ed.) *Recent Advances in Micronesian Archaeology. Micronesica Supplement* 2: 187–212.

1992. Nan Madol, Micronesia. *Society for American Archaeology Bulletin* 10: 4–5.

1993. Nan Madol archaeological fieldwork: final report. MS on file, Historic Preservation Office, Pohnpei State, Federated States of Micronesia.

Ayres, W.S., Goles, G.G. and Beardsley, F.R. 1997. Provenance study of lithic materials in Micronesia. In M.I. Weisler (ed.) *Prehistoric Long-Distance Interaction in Oceania: An Interdisciplinary Approach*. 53–67. New Zealand Archaeological Association Monograph 21.

Ayres, W.S. and Haun, A.E. 1980. Ponape Archaeological Survey: 1977 research. *Micronesian Archaeological Survey Report*, 1. Historic Preservation Office: Saipan.

1985. Archaeological perspectives on food production in eastern Micronesia. In I.S. Farrington (ed.) *Prehistoric Intensive Agriculture in the Tropics* (Part II). 455–73. British Archaeological Reports S232: Oxford.

1990. Prehistoric food production in Micronesia. In D. Yen and M.J.M. Mummery (eds.) *Pacific Production Systems: Approaches to Economic Prehistory*. 211–27. The Australian National University, Research School of Pacific Studies, Occasional Papers in Prehistory 18. Canberra.

Ayres, W.S., Haun, A.E. and Mauricio, R. 1983. Nan Madol archaeology: 1981 survey and excavations. MS on file, Historic Preservation Office, Pohnpei State, Federated States of Micronesia.

Ayres, W.S., Haun, A.E. and Severance, C. 1981. *Ponape Archaeological Survey: 1978 Research*. Micronesian Archaeological Survey Report 4. Historic Preservation Office: Saipan.

Ayres, W.S. and Mauricio, R. 1987. Stone adzes from Pohnpei, Micronesia. *Archaeology in Oceania* 22: 27–31.

1990. Salapwuk Archaeology: 1989 survey of historic and cultural resources of Pohnpei State. MS on file, Historic Preservation Office, Pohnpei State, Federated States of Micronesia.

1997. *Pohnpei Archaeology Component. Salapwuk Archaeology: A Survey of Historic and Cultural Resources on Pohnpei, Federated States of Micronesia. Micronesian Resources Study*. Micronesian Endowment for Historic Preservation, Federated States of Micronesia, US National Park Service: San Francisco.

1999. Definition, ownership and conservation of indigenous landscapes at Salapwuk, Pohnpei, Micronesia. In P.J. Ucko and R. Layton (eds.) *The Archaeology and Anthropology of Landscape*. 298–321. Routledge: London.

Bahn, P. and Flenley, J. 1992. *Easter Island, Earth Island*. London: Thames and Hudson.

Baker, R.R. 1989. *Human Navigation and Magnetoperception*. Manchester University Press: Manchester.

Barratt, G. 1984. *Russian Exploration in the Mariana Islands, 1817–1828*. Micronesian Archaeological Survey Report 17. Historic Preservation Office: Saipan.

1988a. *Carolinean Contacts with the Marianas: The European Record*. Micronesian Archaeological Survey Report 25. Historic Preservation Office: Saipan.

1988b. *H.M.S. Centurion at Tinian, 1742: The Ethnographic and Historic Records*. Micronesian Archaeological Survey Report 26. Historic Preservation Office: Saipan.

Bates, M. 1956. Process. In W.L. Thomas (ed.) *Man's Role in Changing the Face of the Earth*. 1136–40. University of Chicago Press: Chicago.

Bath, J.E. 1984a. *Sapwtakai: Archaeological Survey and Testing*. Micronesian Archaeological Survey Report 14. Historic Preservation Office: Saipan.

1984b. A tale of two cities: an evaluation of political evolution in the Eastern Caroline Islands of Micronesia since AD 1000. PhD dissertation, University of Hawaii, Honolulu.

1986. The San Vitores Road Project – Part 1. Final report. Unpublished report, Pacific Studies Institute.

Bath, J.E. and Athens, J.S. 1990. Prehistoric social complexity on Pohnpei: the *Saudeleur* to *Nahnmwarki* transformation. In R.L. Hunter-Anderson (ed.) *Recent Advances in Micronesian Archaeology. Micronesica Supplement* 2: 275–90.

Bath, J.E. and Shun, K. 1982. Archaeological salvage on Water Line 'C', Lelu, Kosrae. MS on file, Historic Preservation Office, Kosrae State, Federated States of Micronesia.

Bath, J.E., Shun, K. and Cordy, R. 1983. Archaeological investigations at Likihnhluhlwem and Leahp (The Kosrae phase 2 project). MS on file, Historic Preservation Office, Kosrae State, Federated States of Micronesia.

Bauman, Z. 1998. *Globalization: The Human Consequences*. Polity Press: Cambridge.

Bayard, D. 1976. *The Cultural Relationships of the Polynesian Outliers*. Studies in Prehistoric Anthropology 9. University of Otago: Dunedin.

Beaglehole, J.C. 1974. *The Life of Captain James Cook*. A. and C. Black: London.

Beardsley, F.R. 1993. *Archaeological Data Recovery and Monitoring of the Maneng-gon Hills Access Road Corridor, Guam*. International Archaeological Research Institute, Inc.: Honolulu.

1994. *Archaeological Investigations on Kwajalein Atoll, Marshall Islands*. International Archaeological Research Institute, Inc.: Honolulu.

1996. *Fragments of Paradise: Archaeological Investigations in the Republic of Palau, Palau Rural Water System Survey and Testing*. International Archaeological Research Institute, Inc.: Honolulu.

1997. *Fishponds, Taro Patches and Shell Middens: Archaeological Investigations on Peleliu, Republic of Palau, Data Recovery and Monitoring for the Palau Rural Water System Program*. International Archaeological Research Institute, Inc.: Honolulu.

1998. Monumental earthworks of Palau: the shaping of culture. Paper presented to the Indo-Pacific Prehistory Association Congress, Melaka.

Beardsley, F.R. and Basilius, U. 1998. Sngall Ridge, Belau: burials, spirit walks, and painted pottery. Paper presented to the Indo-Pacific Prehistory Association Congress, Melaka.

Beardsley, R.K. and Takashi, Nakano 1970. *Japanese Sociology and Social Anthropology: A Guide to Japanese Reference and Research Materials*. University of Michigan Press: Ann Arbor.

Beauclair, I. de 1961. 'Ken-pai', a glass bracelet from Yap. *Asian Perspectives* 5: 113–15.

1962. Addenda to 'Ken-pai': a glass bracelet from Yap. *Asian Perspectives* 6: 232–5.

1963. Some ancient beads of Yap and Palau. *Journal of the Polynesian Society* 72: 1–10.

Bellwood, P. 1978. *Man's Conquest of the Pacific*. William Collins: Auckland.

    1997a. *Prehistory of the Indo-Malaysian Archipelago*. 2nd edition. University of Hawaii Press: Honolulu.

    1997b. Taiwan and the prehistory of the Austronesian-speaking people. *The Review of Archaeology*, Fall: 39–48.

Berg, M.L. 1988. 'The wandering life among unreliable islanders': the Hamburg *Südsee-Expedition* in Micronesia. *Journal of Pacific History* 23: 95–101.

    1992. Yapese politics, Yapese money and the Sawei tribute network before World War I. *Journal of Pacific History* 27: 150–64.

    1993. German colonial influence in Chuuk. *Journal de la Société des Océanistes* 97: 195–210.

Black, P.W., Osborne, D. and Patricio, M. 1979. Appendix 7: Tobi Island artifacts. In D. Osborne *Archaeological Test Excavations, Palau Islands. 1968–1969. Micronesica Supplement* 1: 349–53.

Bloom, A.L. 1970a. Holocene submergence in Micronesia as the standard for eustatic sea-level changes. *Quaternaria* 12: 145–54.

    1970b. Paludal stratigraphy of Truk, Ponape, and Kusaie, Eastern Caroline Islands. *Geological Society of America Bulletin* 81: 1895–1904.

Bodner, C.C. 1997. On architecture and social power: some possible Philippine–Oceanic links. *Bulletin of the Indo-Pacific Prehistory Association* 16: 89–102.

Boughton, G. 1992. Revisionist interpretations of precontact Marianas society. In D.H. Rubenstein (ed.) *Pacific History: Papers from the 8th Pacific History Association Conference*. 221–4. Micronesia Area Research Center, University of Guam: Guam.

Bourdieu, P. 1977. *Outline of a Theory of Practice*. Translated by R. Nice. Cambridge University Press: Cambridge.

Brace, C.L., Brace, M.L., Dodo, Y., Hunt, K.D., Leonard, W.R., Yongi, L., Sangvichien, S., Xiang-qing, S. and Zhenbiao, Z. 1990. Micronesians, Asians, Thais and relations: a craniofacial and odontometric perspective. In R.L. Hunter-Anderson (ed.) *Recent Advances in Micronesian Archaeology. Micronesica Supplement* 2: 323–48.

Branco, J.F. 1988. From artefacts to archives. In Mary R. Bouquet and Jorge Freitas Branco (eds.) *Melanesian Artefacts: Postmodern Reflections/Artefactos Malanésios: Reflexõs Pós-modernistas*. 27–61. Museu de Etnologia: Lisbon.

Brewis, A. 1996. *Lives on the Line: Women and Ecology on a Pacific Atoll*. Harcourt Brace: Fort Worth.

Broodbank, C. 2000. *An Island Archaeology of the Early Cyclades*. Cambridge University Press: Cambridge.

Brooks, C.C. 1981. A contribution to the geoarchaeology of Truk, Micronesia. *Asian Perspectives* 24: 27–42.

Brulotte, R.K. 1986. Temwen causeway and road project: Nihkawad Village to Temwen Elementary School. MS on file, Historic Preservation Office, Pohnpei State, Federated States of Micronesia.

Bryan, E.H. Jr. 1971. *Guide to the Placenames in the Trust Territory of the Pacific Islands*. Bernice P. Bishop Museum: Honolulu.

Bryant, C.G.A. and Jary, D. (eds.) 1991. Introduction: coming to terms with Anthony Giddens. In C.G.A. Bryant and D. Jary (eds.) *Giddens' Theory of Structuration: A Critical Appreciation*. 1–31. Routledge: London.

Bryson, R.U. 1989. Ceramics and spatial archaeology at Nan Madol, Pohnpei. PhD dissertation, University of Oregon, Eugene.

Buck, P.H. (Te Rangi Hiroa) 1938. *Vikings of the Sunrise*. Lippincott: Philadelphia.

   1950. Material culture of Kapingamarangi. *Bulletin of the Bernice P. Bishop Museum*, 200: Honolulu.

Bukea, F. 1979a. Excavation project. MS on file, Historic Preservation Office, Chuuk State, Federated States of Micronesia.

   1979b. Tunnuk electrification survey. MS on file, Historic Preservation Office, Chuuk State, Federated States of Micronesia.

Burns, A.F. 1997. *Kosrae Ethnography. Kosrae Ethnography Project, Federated States of Micronesia: Micronesian Resources Study*. Micronesian Endowment for Historic Preservation/Federated States of Micronesia Government/US National Park Service: San Fancisco.

Burrows, E.G. 1963. *Flower in My Ear: Art and Ethos of Ifaluk Atoll*. University of Washington Publications in Anthropology 14. University of Washington Press: Seattle.

Buschmann, R.F. 1996. Tobi captured: converging ethnographic and colonial visions on a Caroline Island. *Isla: A Journal of Micronesian Studies* 4: 317–40.

Butler, B.M. 1990. Pots as tools: the Marianas case. In R.L. Hunter-Anderson (ed.) *Recent Advances in Micronesian Archaeology. Micronesica Supplement* 2: 33–46.

   1992a. *An Archaeological Survey of Aguiguan (Aguijan), Northern Mariana Islands*. Micronesian Archaeological Survey Report 29. Saipan.

   1992b. The future of Micronesia's past. In D.H. Rubenstein (ed.) *Pacific History: Papers from the 8th Pacific History Association Conference*. 441–6. MARC, University of Guam: Guam.

   1994. Early prehistoric settlement in the Mariana Islands: new evidence from Saipan. *Man and Culture in Oceania* 10: 15–38.

Butler, B.M. (ed.) 1988. *Archaeological Investigations on the North Coast of Rota, Mariana Islands*. Micronesian Archaeological Survey Report 28. Saipan.

   1995. *Archaeological Investigations, Achugao and Matansa Areas of Saipan, Mariana Islands*. Micronesian Archaeological Survey Report 30. Saipan.

Carson, M.T. 1998. Cultural affinities of monumental architecture in the Phoenix Islands. *Journal of the Polynesian Society* 107: 61–77.

Carucci, J. 1984. Archaeological survey of the Bai-ra-Irrai, Arrai State, Republic of Palau. MS on file, Center for Archaeological Investigations, Southern Illinois University at Carbondale (1984–14).

   1992. Cultural and natural patterning in prehistoric marine foodshell from Palau, Micronesia. PhD dissertation, Southern Illinois University at Carbondale.

   1993. *The Archaeology of the Orote Peninsula: Phase I and II Archaeological Inventory Survey of Areas Proposed for Projects to Accommodate Relocation of Navy Activities from the Philippines to Guam*. International Archaeological Research Institute, Inc.: Honolulu.

Carucci, L.M. 1988. Small fish in a big sea: geographical dispersion and sociopolitical centralization in the Marshall Islands. In J. Gledhill, B. Bender and M.T. Larsen (eds.) *State and Society: The Emergence and Development of Social Hierarchy and Political Centralization*. 33–42. Unwin Hyman: London.

   1995. Symbolic imagery of Enewetak sailing canoes. In R. Feinberg (ed.) *Seafaring in the Contemporary Pacific*. 16–33. Northern Illinois University Press: DeKalb.

Chamisso, A. von 1836 [1986]. *A Voyage around the World with the Romanzov Exploring Expedition in the Years 1815–1818 in the Brig Riurik*. University of Hawaii Press: Honolulu.

Chang, K. and Goodenough, W.H. 1996. Archaeology of southeastern coastal China and its bearing on the Austronesian homeland. In W.H. Goodenough (ed.) *Prehistoric Settlement of the Pacific.* Transactions of the American Philosophical Society 86(5): 36–56.

Chapman, P.S. 1964. Micronesian archaeology: an annotated bibliography. MA dissertation, Stanford University.

  1968. Japanese contributions to Micronesian archaeology and material culture. In I. Yawata and Y.H. Sinoto (eds.) *Prehistoric Culture in Oceania: A Symposium*. 67–82. Bishop Museum Press: Honolulu.

Christian, F.W. 1899a. Exploration in the Caroline Islands. *The Geographical Journal* 63(2): 105–36.

  1899b. *The Caroline Islands: Travel in the Sea of the Little Islands*. Methuen: London.

Clark, Rev. E.W. 1852. Remarkable ruins on Ascension. *The Friend* 1(12): 89–90.

Clark, J.T. and Terrell, J. 1978. Archaeology in Oceania. *Annual Review of Anthropology* 7: 293–319.

Clifford, J. 1997. *Routes: Travel and Translation in the Late Twentieth Century*. Harvard University Press: Cambridge, Mass.

Cloud, P.E. Jr., Schmidt, R.G. and Burke, H.W. 1956. *Geology of Saipan, Mariana Islands: Part 1, General Geology*. Professional Paper 280-A, US Geological Survey. Washington, DC.

Clune, F.J. Jr. 1974. Archaeological survey of Truk, Micronesia. *Micronesica* 10(2): 205–6.

  1977. Truk Islands, Eastern Caroline Islands, Trust Territory of the Pacific Islands, Archaeological Investigations. MS on file, Micronesian Seminar, Pohnpei.

Cole, F. 1913. *The Wild Tribes of Davao District, Mindanao*. Field Museum of Natural History, Publication 170, Anthropology Series 12(2).

Cordy, R. 1980. Archaeological survey of Sapuk Village, Moen, Truk. MS on file, Historic Preservation Office, Chuuk State, Federated States of Micronesia.

  1981. Archaeological investigations in Wiya and Tepat Fal, Kosrae. MS on file, Hamilton Library, University of Hawaii, Honolulu.

  1982a. Archaeological research on Kosrae (Eastern Caroline Islands). *Bulletin of the Indo-Pacific Prehistory Association* 3: 129–34.

  1982b. Lelu, the stone city of Kosrae: 1978–1981 research. *Journal of the Polynesian Society* 86: 103–19.

  1983a. *Archaeological Survey of Innem, Okat and Loal, Kosrae Island*. Micronesian Archaeological Survey Report 7. Historic Preservation Office: Saipan.

  1983b. Social stratification in the Mariana Islands. *Oceania* 53: 272–6.

  1985a. Investigations of Leluh's stone ruins. *National Geographic Research* 1: 255–63.

  1985b. Settlement patterns of complex societies in the Pacific. *New Zealand Journal of Archaeology* 7: 159–82.

  1986a. *Archaeological Settlement Patterns Studies on Yap*. Micronesian Archaeological Survey Report 16. Historic Preservation Office: Saipan.

  1986b. Relationships between the extent of social stratification and population in Micronesian polities at European contact. *American Anthropologist* 88: 136–42.

1993. *The Lelu Stone Ruins (Kosrae, Micronesia): 1978–1981 Historical and Archaeological Research*. Asian and Pacific Archaeology Series 10. Social Science Research Institute, University of Hawaii: Honolulu.

Cordy, R. and Allen, J. 1986. *Archaeological Investigations of the Agana and Fonte River Basins, Guam*. International Archaeological Research Institute, Inc.: Honolulu.

Cordy, R., Bath, J., Shun, K. and Athens, J.S. 1985. Archaeological data recovery in central Utwa, Kosrae Circumferential Road. MS on file, Library of Congress, Palikir, Pohnpei, Federated States of Micronesia.

Craib, J.L. 1977. A typological investigation of Western Micronesian adzes. MA dissertation, California State University, Long Beach.

1978a. Archaeological investigation of selected areas on Moen and Dublon, Truk District, Eastern Caroline Islands. MS on file, Historic Preservation Office, Chuuk State, Federated States of Micronesia.

1978b. Archaeological surveys for capital improvement projects on Kosrae, Kosrae District, Eastern Caroline Islands. MS on file, Hamilton Library, University of Hawaii, Honolulu.

1980. *Archaeological Survey of Ulithi Atoll, Western Caroline Islands*. Pacific Studies Institute Monograph Series 1. Guam.

1981. Settlement on Ulithi Atoll, Western Caroline Islands. *Asian Perspectives* 24: 47–55.

1983. Micronesian prehistory: an archaeological overview. *Science* 219: 922–7.

1986. Casas de los Antiguos: social differentiation in protohistoric Chamorro society, Mariana Islands. PhD dissertation, University of Sydney.

1988. Preliminary report on the archaeological fieldwork at Alaguan, Rota, Commonwealth of the Northern Mariana Islands. MS on file, Historic Preservation Office, Saipan, Commonwealth of Northern Mariana Islands.

1989. Archaeological reconnaissance survey and sampling. US Army Kwajalein Atoll Facility (USAKA), Kwajalein Atoll, Republic of the Marshall Islands, Micronesia. Unpublished report for US Army Engineering District, Honolulu, Hawaii.

1990. Archaeological excavations at Mochong, Rota, Mariana Islands. Unpublished report for the Historic Preservation Office, Saipan, Commonwealth of Northern Mariana Islands.

1993. Early occupation at Unai Chulu, Tinian, Commonwealth of the Northern Mariana Islands. *Bulletin of the Indo-Pacific Prehistory Association* 13: 116–34.

1994. Archaeological investigation at an inland latte site (M-221) in the Maneng-gon Hills, Yona District, Guam. Unpublished report prepared for Micronesian Archaeological Research Services, Guam.

1997. *Truk Archaeology: An Intensive Archaeological Survey of Pwene Village, Dublon, Truk State, Federated States of Micronesia. Micronesian Resources Study*. Micronesian Endowment for Historic Preservation, Federated States of Micronesia, US National Park Service: San Francisco.

1998a. *Archaeological Excavations in the Uyulan Region of Rota*. Micronesian Archaeological Survey 33. Saipan.

1998b. Archaeological monitoring and sampling during construction of a controlled humidity warehouse, Kwajalein Islet, USAKA, Republic of the Marshall Islands. Unpublished draft report for the US Army Corps of Engineers, Corps of Engineers District, Honolulu.

1999. Colonisation of the Mariana Islands: new evidence and implications for human movements in the western Pacific. In J.C. Galipaud and I. Lilley (eds.) *Le Pacifique de 5000 à 2000 avant le présent: suppléments à l'histoire d'une colonisation. The Pacific from 5000 to 2000 BP: Colonisation and Transformation. Actes du colloque Vanuatu, 31 Juillet – 6 Août 1996.* 477–85. Editions de l'ORSTOM. Collection Colloques et séminaires: Paris.

nd. The beaked adze in Oceania: implications for late prehistoric contacts within the western Pacific. MS in possession of author.

Craib, J.L. and Farrell, N.L. 1981. On the question of prehistoric rice cultivation in the Mariana Islands, Micronesia. *Micronesica* 17: 1–9.

Craib, J.L. and Mangold, G.R. 1999. Storm in a test pit: effects of cyclonic storms on coastal archaeological sites in western Micronesia. In J. Hall and I.J. McNiven (eds.) *Australian Coastal Archaeology*. 299–306. Research Papers in Archaeology and Natural History 31. Department of Archaeology and Natural History, Research School of Pacific and Asian Studies, The Australian National University: Canberra.

Craib, J.L. and Price, S. 1978. An archaeological reconnaissance of selected areas of Yap, Western Caroline Islands. MS on file, Historic Preservation Office, Saipan, CNMI.

Craib, J.L. and Ward, G.K. 1988. Archaeological investigations at Mochong, Rota, Mariana Islands. MS on file, Historic Preservation Office, Saipan.

Crowley, T. 1994. Proto who drank kava. In A. Pawley and M. Ross (eds.) *Austronesian Terminologies: Continuity and Change*. 87–100. Pacific Linguistics C-127. Department of Linguistics, Research School of Pacific and Asian Studies, Australian National University: Canberra.

CSHPO (Chuuk State Historic Preservation Office) 1980a. Archeological survey: report in Tunnuk. MS on file, Historic Preservation Office, Chuuk State, Federated States of Micronesia.

1980b. Archaeological survey report of Winipis. MS on file, Historic Preservation Office, Chuuk State, Federated States of Micronesia.

1980c. Report of the archeological survey in Sapuk. MS on file, Historic Preservation Office, Chuuk State, Federated States of Micronesia.

1981. Archaeological survey report of Piis Moen. MS on file, Historic Preservation Office, Chuuk State, Federated States of Micronesia.

Curray, J.R., Shepard, F.P. and Veeh, H.H. 1970. Late Quaternary sea-level studies in Micronesia: CARMARSEL expedition. *Geological Society of America Bulletin* 81: 1865–80.

Damm, H. 1938. *Zentralkarolinen (Vol. II). Visit by the Sudsee Expedition 1908–1910.* Friederichsen: Hamburg.

Damon, Rev. S.C. 1861. *Morning Star Papers (Supplement to The Friend)*. Honolulu: Hawaiian Missionary Society.

D'Arcy, P. 2001. Connected by the sea: towards a regional history of the Western Caroline Islands. *Journal of Pacific History* 36: 163–82.

Davidson, J.M. 1967a. An archaeological assemblage of simple fish-hooks from Nukuoro Atoll. *Journal of the Polynesian Society* 76: 177–96.

1967b. Preliminary archaeological investigations on Ponape and other Eastern Caroline Islands. *Micronesica* 3: 81–97.

1971. Archaeology on Nukuoro Atoll: a Polynesian Outlier in the Eastern Caroline Islands. *Bulletin of the Auckland Institute and Museum* 9, Auckland.

1988. Archaeology in Micronesia since 1965: past achievements and future prospects. *New Zealand Journal of Archaeology* 10: 83–100.

1992. New evidence about the date of colonisation of Nukuoro Atoll, a Polynesian Outlier in the Eastern Caroline Islands. *Journal of the Polynesian Society* 101: 293–8.

Davidson, J. and Leach, F. 1996. Fishing on Nukuoro Atoll: ethnographic and archaeological viewpoints. In M. Julien, M. Orliac and C. Orliac (eds.) *Mémoire de pierre, mémoire d'homme: tradition et archéologie de Océanie. Hommage a José Garanger.* 183–202. Collection "Homme et Société" 23, Université de Paris I, Panthéon-Sorbonne: Paris.

De Ishtar, Z. 1994. *Daughters of the Pacific*. Spinifex Press: North Melbourne.

Deleuze, G. and Guattari, F. 1988. *A Thousand Plateaus: Capitalism and Schizophrenia*, trans. B. Massnei. Athlone: London.

Denfield, D. 'Colt' 1981a. *Field Survey of Ponape: World War II Features*. Micronesian Archaeological Survey Report 2. Historic Preservation Office: Saipan.
   1981b. *Field Survey of Truk: World War II Features*. Micronesian Archaeological Survey Report 6. Historic Preservation Office: Saipan.

Dening, G. 1992. Towards an anthropology of performance in encounters in place. In D.H. Rubenstein (ed.) *Pacific History: Papers from the 8th Pacific History Association Conference.* 3–6. Micronesia Area Research Center, University of Guam: Guam.

Descantes, C. 1998. Integrating archaeology and ethnohistory: the development of exchange between Yap and Ulithi, Western Caroline Islands (Micronesia). PhD dissertation, University of Oregon.

Descantes, C., Neff, H., Glascock, M.D. and Dickinson, W.R. 2001. Chemical characterizaton of Micronesian ceramics through Instrumental Neutron Activation analysis: a preliminary provenance study. *Journal of Archaeological Science* 28: 1185–90.

Diaz, V. 1993. Pious sites: Chamorro culture between Spanish Catholicism and American liberal individualism. In Amy Kaplan and Donald E. Pease (eds.) *Cultures of United States Imperialism.* 312–39. Duke University Press: Durham, NC.

Diaz, V. and Kauanui, J.K. 2001. Native Pacific cultural studies on the edge. *The Contemporary Pacific* 13: 315–42.

Dickinson, W.R. 1982. Temper sands from prehistoric sherds excavated at Pemrang site on Yap and from nearby Ngulu atoll. *Bulletin of the Indo-Pacific Prehistory Association* 3: 115–17.
   1984. Indigenous and exotic sand tempers in prehistoric potsherds from the central Caroline Islands. In Y. Sinoto (ed.) *Caroline Islands Archaeology: Investigations on Fefan, Faraulep, Woleai and Lamotrek.* 131–5. Pacific Anthropological Records 35. Bernice P. Bishop Museum: Honolulu.
   1995. Temper sands in prehistoric sherds from Kosrae. In J.S. Athens *Landscape Archaeology: Prehistoric Settlement, Subsistence, and Environment of Kosrae, Eastern Caroline Islands, Micronesia.* 271–6. International Archaeological Research Institute, Inc.: Honolulu.

Dickinson, W.R. and Green, R.C. 1998. Geoarchaeological context of Holocene subsidence at the Ferry Berth Lapita site, Mulifanua, Samoa. *Geoarchaeology* 13: 239–63.

Dickinson, W.R. and Shutler, R. Jr. 2000. Implications of petrographic temper analysis for Oceanic prehistory. *Journal of World Prehistory* 14: 203–66.

Dilli, B., Haun, A.E., Goodfellow, S.T. and Deroo, B. 1998. Archaeological Mitigation Program, Mangilao Golf Course Project Area, Mangilao Municipality, Territory of Guam. Volume II, Data Analyses. Unpublished report by Paul H. Rosendahl, PhD, Inc.: Hilo.

Dilli, B.J., Ryan, E.M. and Workman, L.W. 1993. Archaeological Monitoring and Limited Data Recovery, Royal Palm Resort, Tumon, Tamuning Municipality, Territory of Guam. Unpublished report by Paul H. Rosendahl, PhD, Inc.: Hilo.

Di Piazza, A. 1998a. Archaeobotanical investigations of an earth oven in Kiribati, Gilbert Islands. *Vegetation History and Archaeobotany* 7: 149–54.

1998b. Efficiency of calcium carbonate oven stones. *Archaeology in Oceania* 33: 84–7.

1999. Te Bakoa site. Two old earth ovens from Nikunau Island (Republic of Kiribati). *Archaeology in Oceania* 34: 40–2.

2001. Forward. *Journal de la Société des Océanistes* 112: 9–11.

Di Piazza, A. and Pearthree, E. 2001. L'art d'être pirogues de voyage. *Journal de la Société des Océanistes* 112: 61–72.

Dobres, M. and Robb, J. (eds.) 2000. *Agency in Archaeology*. Routledge: London.

Dodson, J. and Intoh, M. 1999. Prehistory and palaeoecology of Yap, Federated States of Micronesia. *Quaternary International* 59: 17–26.

Domeny de Rienzi, M.G.L. 1836. *Océanie ou Cinquième Partie du Monde*. Firmin Didot Frères: Paris.

Donham, T.K. 1989. Historic Resources Survey and Inventory, North Field, Island of Tinian, Commonwealth of the Northern Mariana Islands. Unpublished report by Paul H. Rosendahl, PhD, Inc.: Hilo.

Douglas, B. 1999. Art as ethno-historical text: science, representation and indigenous presence in eighteenth and nineteenth century oceanic voyage literature. In N. Thomas and D. Losche (eds.) *Double Vision: Art Histories and Colonial Histories in the Pacific*. 65–99. Cambridge University Press: Cambridge.

Douglas, M.T., Pietrusewsky, M. and Ikehara-Quebral, R. 1997. Skeletal biology of Apurguan: a precontact Chamorro site on Guam. *American Journal of Physical Anthropology* 104: 291–314.

Downing, J., Spennemann, D.H.R. and Bennett, M. 1992. *Bwebwenatoon Etto: A Collection of Marshallese Legends and Traditions*. Historic Preservation Office: Republic of the Marshall Islands.

Driver, M.C. 1989. *The Account of Fray Juan Pobre's Residence in the Mariana Islands*. Micronesia Area Research Center, University of Guam: Guam.

Dumont d'Urville, J-.S-.C. 1832. Sur les Iles du Grand Océan. *Bulletin de la Société de Géographie* 105: 1–21.

1987. *An Account in Two Volumes of Two Voyages to the South Seas by Captain (later Rear-Admiral) Jules-S-C Dumont d'Urville of the French Navy to Australia, New Zealand, Oceania 1826–1829 in the Corvette Astrolabe and to the Straits of Magellan, Chile, Oceania, South East Asia, Australia, Antarctica, New Zealand and Torres Strait 1837–1840 in the Corvettes Astrolabe and Zelee*. Melbourne University Press: Melbourne.

Dunmore, J. 1992. *Who's Who in Pacific Navigation*. Melbourne University Press: Melbourne.

Dye, T.S. 1979. Archaeological reconnaissance survey in the Inarajan River valley, Territory of Guam. MS on file, Department of Anthropology, B.P. Bishop Museum, Honolulu, Hawaii (031379).

1987a. Archaeological survey and test excavations on Arno Atoll, Marshall Islands. In T.S. Dye (ed.) *Marshall Islands Archaeology*. 271–399. Pacific Anthropological Records 38. Bernice P. Bishop Museum, Honolulu: Hawaii.

Dye, T.S. (ed.) 1987b. *Marshall Islands Archaeology*. Pacific Anthropological Records 38. Bernice P. Bishop Museum, Honolulu: Hawaii.

Dye, T.S. and Cleghorn, P.L. 1990. Prehistoric use of the interior of southern Guam. In R. L. Hunter-Anderson (ed.) *Recent Advances in Micronesian Archaeology. Micronesica Supplement* 2: 261–74.

Dye, T.S., Price, S.T. and Craib, J.L. 1978. Archaeological and historical reconnaissance survey of the Ugum River valley, Guam, Mariana Islands. MS on file, Department of Anthropology, B.P. Bishop Museum, Honolulu, Hawaii (061578).

Earle, T. (ed.) 1991. *Chiefdoms: Power, Economy, and Ideology*. Cambridge University Press: Cambridge.

Edge-Partington, J. 1896. The ethnography of Matty Island. *Journal of the Anthropological Institute* 25: 288–95.

Edwards, J. and Edwards, R. 1978. Fauba: a past waiting for a future. MS on file, Hamilton Library, University of Hawaii, Honolulu.

Edwards, R. 1978. Report of the Tol Island Road Archaeological Survey, Truk District, Trust Territory of the Pacific Islands. MS on file, Hamilton Library, University of Hawaii, Honolulu.

Emory, K. 1939. Archaeology of the Phoenix Islands. *Bernice P. Bishop Museum Special Publication* 34: 7–8.

Eriksen, T.H. 1993. In which sense do cultural islands exist? *Social Anthropology* 1: 133–47.

Fabricus, W. 1992. *Nauru 1888–1900*. Trans. and ed. Dymphna Clark and Stewart Firth. Division of Pacific and Asian History, Research School of Pacific Studies, Australian National University: Canberra.

Falanruw, M.C., Cole, T.G., Ambacher, A.H., McDuffie, K.E. and Maka, J.E. 1987. *Vegetation Survey of Moen, Dublon, Fefan, and Eten, State of Truk, Federated States of Micronesia*. Resource Bulletin PSW-20. US Department of Agriculture, Forest Service: Berkeley.

Falgout, S. 1987. *Master Part of Heaven: The Ethnohistory and Archaeology of Wene, Pohnpei, Eastern Caroline Islands*. Micronesian Archaeological Survey Report 22. Historic Preservation Office: Saipan.

Finney, B. 1992. *From Sea to Space: The Macmillan Brown Lectures*. Massey University: Palmerston North.

 1995. A role for magnetoperception in human navigation? *Current Anthropology* 36: 500–6.

 1998. Nautical cartography and traditional navigation in Oceania. In D. Woodward and G.M. Lewis (eds.) *The History of Cartography, Volume 2, Book Three, Cartography in the Traditional African, American, Arctic, Australian, and Pacific Societies*. 443–92. University of Chicago Press: Chicago.

Firth, S. 1973. German firms in the Western Pacific Islands, 1857–1914. *Journal of Pacific History* 8: 10–28.

Fischer, J.L. and Fischer, A.M. 1957. *The Eastern Carolines*. Human Relations Area Files: New Haven.

Fitzpatrick, S.M. 2000. Micronesia. *Society for Historical Archaeology Newsletter* 33(4): 18.

 2001. Archaeological investigation of Omis Cave: a Yapese stone money quarry in Palau. *Archaeology in Oceania* 36: 153–62.

Fitzpatrick, S.M. and Kanai, V.N. 2001. An applied approach to archeology in Palau. *Cultural Resource Management* 1: 41–3.

Flecker, M. 2001. A ninth-century AD Arab or Indian shipwreck in Indonesia: first evidence for direct trade with China. *World Archaeology* 32: 335–54.

Force, R.W. 1959. Palauan money: some preliminary comments on material and origins. *Journal of the Polynesian Society* 68: 40–4.

Force, R.W. and Force, M. 1972. Just One House: a description and analysis of kinship in the Palau Islands. *Bernice P. Bishop Museum Bulletin*, 235. Honolulu.

Forster, J.R. 1996 [1778]. *Observations Made During a Voyage Round the World* (ed. N. Thomas, H. Guest and M. Dettelbach). University of Hawaii Press:Honolulu.

Fosberg, F.R. 1991. Polynesian plant environments. In P.A. Cox and S.A. Barnack (eds.) *Islands, Plants, and Polynesians: An Introduction to Polynesian Ethnobotany*. 11–23. Dioscorides: Portland.

Fosberg, F.R., Sachet, M.-H. and Oliver, R. 1987. A geographical checklist of the Micronesian Dictyledonae. *Micronesica* 15: 41–295.

Fox, J.J. 1993. Comparative perspectives on Austronesian houses: an introductory essay. In J.J. Fox (ed.) *Inside Austronesian Houses: Perspectives on Domestic Designs for Living*. 1–28. Department of Anthropology, Research School of Pacific and Asian Studies, The Australian National University: Canberra.

Frazer, J.G. 1924. *The Belief in Immortality and the Worship of the Dead. Vol. III. The Belief Among the Micronesians*. Macmillan: London.

Freeman, D. 1974. The evolutionary theories of Charles Darwin and Herbert Spencer. *Current Anthropology* 15: 211–37.

Freycinet, Rose Marie de 1996. *A Woman of Courage: The Journal of Rose de Freycinet on Her Voyage around the World, 1817–1820*. National Library of Australia: Canberra.

Fried, M.H. 1967. *The Evolution of Political Society: An Essay in Political Economy*. Random House: New York.

Fritz, G. 2001. *The Chamorro: A History and Ethnography of the Mariana Islands*. 3rd English edition. Occasional Historical Papers Series 1. Commonwealth of the Northern Mariana Islands Division of Historic Preservation: Saipan.

Fujimura, K. and Alkire, W.R. 1984. Archaeological excavations on Faraulep, Woleai, and Lamotrek. In Y. Sinoto (ed.) *Caroline Islands Archaeology: Investigations on Fefan, Faraulep, Woleai and Lamotrek*. 65–149. Pacific Anthropological Records 35. Bernice P. Bishop Museum: Honolulu.

Gale, M.K. and Fitzpatrick, S.M. 2001. The Micronesia and South Pacific Program: a decade of cultural resource preservation assistance. *Cultural Resource Management* 1: 38–40.

Galipaud, J.-C. 2001. Le peuplement initial de Pohnpei. *Journal de la Société des Océanistes* 112: 49–60.

Garanger, J. 1982 [1972]. *Archaeology of the New Hebrides*. Trans. R. Groube. Oceania Monograph 24. Sydney.

Garrett, J. 1996. *Island Exiles*. ABC Books: Sydney.

Gell, A. 1985. How to read a map: remarks on the practical logic of navigation. *Man* (NS) 20: 271–86.

    1995. The language of the forest: landscape and phonological iconism in Umeda. In E. Hirsh and M. O'Hanlon (eds.) *The Anthropology of Landscape: Perspectives on Place and Space*. 232–54. Oxford University Press: Oxford.

Gerhard, P. 1972. *A Guide to the Historical Geography of New Spain*. Cambridge University Press: Cambridge.

Gibson, R. 1994. Ocean settlement. *Meanjin* 4: 665–78.

Giddens, A. 1984. *The Constitution of Society: Outline of the Theory of Structuration*. Polity Press: Cambridge.

Gifford, E.W. and Gifford, D.S. 1959. *Archaeological Investigations on Yap*. University of California Press: Berkeley.

Gilbert, T. 1789 [1968]. *Voyage from New South Wales to Canton in 1788, with Views of the Islands Discovered*. N. Israel: Amsterdam.

Gillett, R. 1987. *Traditional Tuna Fishing: A Study at Satawal, Central Caroline Islands*. Bishop Museum Bulletin in Anthropology 1. Honolulu.

Gillilland, C.L.C. 1975. *The Stone Money of Yap: A Numismatic Survey*. Smithsonian Studies in History and Technology 23. Smithsonian Institute: Washington.

Gladwin, T. 1970. *East Is a Big Bird*. Harvard University Press: Cambridge, Mass.

Gladwin, T. and Sarason, S.B. 1953. *Truk: Man in Paradise*. Viking Fund Publications in Anthropology 20.

Godard, P. 1995. *Latt: The Mysterious Megaliths of the Marianas*. Abrolhos: Perth.

Goodenough, W.H. 1951. *Property, Kin and Community on Truk*. Yale University Publications in Anthropology 46.

   1957. Oceania and the problem of controls in the study of cultural and human evolution. *Journal of the Polynesian Society* 66: 146–55.

   1986. Sky world and this world: the place of Kachaw in Micronesian cosmology. *American Anthropologist* 88: 551–68.

Goodwin, L. 1983. Change is continuity: the maritime and subsistence economics of Ponape, Micronesia. PhD dissertation, University of Oregon.

Gorenflo, L.J. 1993. Demographic changes in Kosrae State, Federated States of Micronesia. *Pacific Studies* 16: 67–118.

Gorenflo, L.J. and Levin, M.J. 1991. Regional demographic change in Yap State, Federated States of Micronesia. *Pacific Studies* 14: 97–145.

   1992. Regional demographic change in Pohnpei State, Federated States of Micronesia. *Pacific Studies* 15: 1–49.

   1994. The evolution of regional demography in the Marshall Islands. *Pacific Studies* 17: 93–158.

Gosda, R. 1958. Notes on archeological specimens from Truk Atoll sent to the US National Museum on July 8th 1958, including a brief description of sites. MS on file, Historic Preservation Office, Chuuk State, Federated States of Micronesia.

Gosden, C. 1994. *Social Being and Time*. Blackwell: Oxford.

Gosden, C., Allen, J., Ambrose, W., Anson, D., Golson, J., Green, R., Kirch, P., Lilley, I., Specht, J. and Spriggs, M. 1989. Lapita sites of the Bismarck Archipelago. *Antiquity* 63: 561–86.

Gosden, C. and Knowles, C. 2001. *Collecting Colonialism: Material Culture and Colonial Change*. Berg: Oxford.

Gosden, C. and Pavlides, C. 1994. Are islands insular? Landscape vs. seascape in the case of the Arawe Islands, Papua New Guinea. *Archaeology in Oceania* 29: 162–71.

Gosden, C. and Webb, J. 1994. The creation of a Papua New Guinean landscape: archaeological and geomorphological evidence. *Journal of Field Archaeology* 21: 29–51.

Gould, S.J. 1986. Evolution and the triumph of homology, or why history matters. *American Scientist* 74: 60–9.

Graves, M. 1986a. Late prehistoric social complexity on Lelu: alternatives to Cordy's model. *Journal of the Polynesian Society* 95: 479–89.

1986b. Organization and differentiation within late prehistoric ranked social units, Mariana Islands, Western Pacific. *Journal of Field Archaeology* 13: 139–54.

1991. Architectural and mortuary diversity in late prehistoric settlements at Tumon Bay, Guam. *Micronesica* 24: 169–94.

Graves, M. and Green, R.C. (eds.) 1993a. *The Evolution and Organisation of Prehistoric Society in Polynesia*. New Zealand Archaeological Association Monograph 19. Auckland.

Graves, M. and Green, R.C. 1993b. The study of archaeological variability in Polynesia. In M. Graves and R.C. Green (eds.) *The Evolution and Organisation of Prehistoric Society in Polynesia*. 6–8. New Zealand Archaeological Association Monograph 19. Auckland.

Graves, M., Hunt, T.L. and Moore, D. 1990. Ceramic production in the Mariana Islands: explaining change and diversity in prehistoric interaction and exchange. *Asian Perspectives* 29: 211–33.

Graves, M. and Ladefoged, T.N. 1995. The evolutionary significance of ceremonial architecture in Polynesia. In P.A. Telser (ed.) *Evolutionary Archaeology: Methodological Issues*. University of Arizona Press: Tucson.

Green, R.C. 1991. Near and remote Oceania – disestablishing 'Melanesia' in culture history. In A. Pawley (ed.) *Man and a Half: Essays in Pacific Anthropology and Ethnobiology in Honour of Ralph Bulmer*. 491–502. Memoirs of the Polynesian Society 48. Auckland.

1999. Integrating historical linguistics with archaeology: insights from research in Remote Oceania. *Bulletin of the Indo-Pacific Prehistory Association* 18: 3–16.

2000. Lapita and the cultural model for intrusion, integration and innovation. In A. Anderson and T. Murray (eds.) *Australian Archaeologist: Collected Papers in Honour of Jim Allen*. 372–92. Coombs Academic Publishing, The Australian National University: Canberra.

Gregory, L. and Osborne, D. 1979. The Aulong 4 pictographs. In D. Osborne *Archaeological Test Excavations. Palau Islands. 1968–1969. 299–315. Micronesica Supplement* 1.

Grimble, A. 1921. From birth to death in the Gilbert Islands. *Journal of the Royal Anthropological Institute* 51: 25–54.

1933–4. The migrations of a pandanus people: as traced from a preliminary study of food, food-traditions and food-rituals in the Gilbert Islands. Memoir 12 (uncompleted) *Journal of the Polynesian Society*, Supplement 42: 1–84 and Supplement 43: 85–112.

1952. *A Pattern of Islands*. John Murray: London.

1957. *Return to the Islands*. John Murray: London.

1989a. Ancestor cult. In H.E. Maude (ed.) *Tungaru Traditions: Writings on the Atoll Culture of the Gilbert Islands* (by A.F. Grimble). 20–7. Melbourne University Press: Melbourne.

1989b. Archaeology. In H.E. Maude (ed.) *Tungaru Traditions: Writings on the Atoll Culture of the Gilbert Islands* (by A.F. Grimble). 37–40. Melbourne University Press: Melbourne.

Groube, L.M. 1971. Tonga, Lapita pottery, and Polynesian origins. *Journal of the Polynesian Society* 80: 278–316.

Gumerman, G.J. 1986. The role of competition and cooperation in the evolution of island societies. In P.V. Kirch (ed.) *Island Societies: Archaeological*

Approaches to Evolution and Transformation. 42–9. Cambridge University Press: Cambridge.

Gumerman, G.J., Snyder, D. and Masse, W.B. 1981. *An Archaeological Reconnaissance of the Palau Archipelago, Western Caroline Islands, Micronesia*. Southern Illinois University Center for Archaeological Investigations Research Paper 23. Carbondale.

Gunn, M.J. 1980. *Etak* and the ghost islands of the Carolines. *Journal of the Polynesian Society* 89: 499–507.

Haddon, A.C. and Hornell, J. 1936. *Canoes of Oceania. Vol. I. The Canoes of Polynesia, Fiji, and Micronesia*. Bernice P. Bishop Museum Special Publication 27. Honolulu.

Hage, P. and Harary, F. 1991. *Exchange in Oceania: A Graph Theoretical Analysis*. Clarendon Press: Oxford.

Hage, P., Harary, F. and Milicic, B. 1996. Tattooing, gender and social stratification in Micro-Polynesia. *Journal of the Royal Anthropological Institute* (NS) 2: 335–50.

Hagelberg, E., Kayser, M., Nagy, M., Roewer, L., Zimdahl, H., Krawczak, M., Lió, P. and Schiefenhöfel, W. 1999. Molecular genetic evidence for the human settlement of the Pacific: analysis of mitochondrial DNA, Y chromosome and HLA markers. In M. Jones, D.E.G. Briggs, G. Eglington and E. Hagelberg (eds.) *Molecular Information and Prehistory. Philosophical Transactions of the Royal Society of London, Series B: Biological Sciences* 354: 141–52.

Hale, H. 1968 [1846]. *United States Exploring Expedition during the Years 1838, 1839, 1840, 1841, 1842, Under the Command of Charles Wilkes, U.S.N. Ethnography and Philology*. Gregg Press: Ridgewood, NJ.

Hall, K.R. 1992. Economic history of early south-east Asia. In Nicholas Tarling (ed.) *The Cambridge History of Southeast Asia. Vol. I. From Early Times to c. 1800*. 183–275. Cambridge University Press: Cambridge.

Hambruch, P. 1936. *Ponape (Vol. III): The Ruins. Visit to Ponape by the Sudsee Expedition 1908–1910*. Friederichsen: Hamburg.

Hambruch, P. and Eilers, A. 1936. *Ponape (Vol. II). Visit to Ponape by the Sudsee Expedition 1908–1910*. Friederichsen: Hamburg.

Hanlon, D. 1981. *From Mesenieng to Kolonia*. Micronesian Archaeological Survey Report 5. Historic Preservation Office: Saipan.

1988. *Upon a Stone Altar: A History of the Island of Pohnpei to 1890*. University of Hawaii Press: Honolulu.

1989. Micronesia: writing and rewriting the history of a nonentity. *Pacific Studies* 12: 1–21.

1990. 'The pleasure of speculation and conjecture': early Euro-American visions of Nan Madol and their relevance to post-modern archaeological investigations. In R.L. Hunter-Anderson (ed.) *Recent Advances in Micronesian Archaeology. Micronesica Supplement* 2: 99–116.

1992. The path back to Pohnsakar: Luelen Bernart, his book, and the practice of history on Pohnpei. *Isla* 1: 13–35.

1998. *Remaking Micronesia: Discourses over Development in a Pacific Territory, 1944–1982*. University of Hawaii Press: Honolulu.

1999. Magellan's chroniclers? American anthropology's history in Micronesia. In R.C. Kiste and M. Marshall (eds.) *American Anthropology in Micronesia: An Assessment*. 53–79. University of Hawaii Press: Honolulu.

Hanson, D. 1988. Prehistoric mortuary practices and human biology. In B. Butler (ed.) *Archaeological Investigations on the North Coast of Rota.* 375–435. Southern Illinois University Center for Archaeological Investigations Occasional Paper 3. Carbondale.

Hardach, G. 1997. Defining separate spheres: German rule and colonial law in Micronesia. In Hermann J. Hiery and John M. MacKenzie (eds.) *European Impact and Pacific Influence: British and German Colonial Policy in the Pacific Islands and the Indigenous Response.* 231–58. Tauris: London.

Hau'ofa, E. 1975. Anthropology and Pacific islanders. *Oceania* 45: 283–9.

  1993. Our sea of islands. In E. Waddell, V. Naidu and E. Hau'ofa (eds.) *A New Oceania: Rediscovering Our Sea of Islands.* 2–16. University of the South Pacific Press: Fiji.

Haun, A.E. 1984. Prehistoric subsistence, population, and sociopolitical evolution on Ponape, Micronesia. PhD dissertation, University of Oregon, Eugene.

Haun, A., Jimenez, J.A. and Kirkendall, M. 1999. Archaeological Investigations at Unai Chulu, Island of Tinian, Commonwealth of the Northern Mariana Islands. Unpublished report by Paul H. Rosendahl, PhD, Inc.: Hilo.

Hempenstall, P. 1994. Imperial manouvres. In K.R. Howe, R.C. Kiste and B.V. Lal (eds.) *Tides of History: The Pacific Islands in the Twentieth Century.* 29–39. Allen and Unwin: Sydney.

Henrickson, P.R. 1968. Two forms of primitive art in Micronesia. *Micronesica* 4: 39–48.

Henry, J.D., Boudreau, M. and Haun, A.E. 1994. Talofofo Golf Resort Project Area Archaeological Mitigation Program Phases II and III, Data Recovery and Monitoring, Talofofo Municipality, Territory of Guam. Unpublished report by Paul H. Rosendahl, PhD, Inc.: Hilo.

Henry, J.D. and Haun, A.E. 1994. Archaeological Data Recovery Rota Industrial Park to Tatachog Satellite Campus Waterline Project (Contract No. C30185), Island of Rota, Commonwealth of the Northern Mariana Islands. Unpublished report by Paul H. Rosendahl, PhD, Inc.: Hilo.

Henry, J.D., Ryan, E.M. and Haun, A.E. 1993. DFS Saipan, Ltd. Main Store Expansion Archaeological Mitigation Program Phases II and III Data Recovery and Monitoring, Island of Saipan, Commonwealth of the Northern Marianas. Unpublished report by Paul H. Rosendahl, PhD, Inc.: Hilo.

Hezel, F.X. 1973. The beginnings of foreign contact with Truk. *Journal of Pacific History* 8: 51–73.

  1979. *Foreign Ships in Micronesia: A Compendium of Ship Contacts with the Caroline and Marshall Islands, 1521–1885.* Trust Territory of the Pacific Islands Historic Preservation Office: Saipan.

  1983. *The First Taint of Civilization. A History of the Caroline and Marshall Islands in Pre-Colonial Days, 1521–1885.* Pacific Islands Monograph Series 1. University of Hawaii Press: Honolulu.

  1995. *Strangers in Their Own Land: A Century of Colonial Rule in the Caroline and Marshall Islands.* Pacific Islands Monograph Series 13. University of Hawaii Press: Honolulu.

Hiery, H.J. 1997. Germans, Pacific Islanders and sexuality: German impact and indigenous influence in Melanesia and Micronesia. In Hermann J. Hiery and John M. MacKenzie (eds.) *European Impact and Pacific Influence: British and German Colonial Policy in the Pacific Islands and the Indigenous Response.* 299–323. Tauris: London.

Highness, D.E., Brown, R.S. and Haun, A.E. 1992. Archaeological Inventory Survey, InterPacific Hotel and Country Club, Fadian, Mangilao Municipality, Territory of Guam. Unpublished report by Paul H. Rosendahl, PhD, Inc.: Hilo.

Highness, D.E., Dixon, A., Brown, R.S., and Haun, A.E. 1993. Archaeological inventory survey, Mount Sasalaguan access road corridor, Inarajan Municipality, Territory of Guam. Unpublished report by Paul H. Rosendahl, PhD, Inc.: Hilo.

Hijikata, H. 1956. Report on the consecrated stone images and other stoneworks in Palau, Micronesia. *Minzokugaku Kenkyu* 20(3–4): 103–56. [In Japanese] (English translation in the Micronesian Area Research Center, University of Guam).

Hilder, B. 1959. Polynesian navigational stones. *Journal of the Institute of Navigation* 12: 90–7.

Hockings, J. 1989. *Traditional Architecture in the Gilbert Islands: A Cultural Perspective*. University of Queensland Press: St Lucia.

Hodder, I. 1990. *The Domestication of Europe: Structure and Contingency in Neolithic Societies*. Blackwell: Oxford.

Hodder, I., Shanks, M., Alexandri, A., Buchli, V., Carmen, J., Last, J. and Lucas, G. (eds.) 1995. *Interpreting Archaeology: Finding Meaning in the Past*. Routledge: London.

Holden, H. 1975 [1836]. *A Narrative of the Shipwreck, Captivity and Sufferings of Horace Holden and Benj. H. Nute*. Ed. K. Huntress. Ye Galleon Press: Fairfield, Washington.

Hunter-Anderson, R.L. 1981. Yapese stone fish traps. *Asian Perspectives* 24: 81–90.

1983. *Yapese Settlement Patterns: An Ethnoarchaeological Approach*. Pacific Studies Institute: Guam.

1985. *Settlement Patterns in Nlul Village, Map Island, Yap, Western Caroline Islands*. Micronesian Archaeological Survey Report 20. Historic Preservation Office: Saipan.

1987. *Indigenous Fresh Water Management Technologies of Truk, Pohnpei and Kosrae, Eastern Caroline Islands, and of Guam, Mariana Islands, Micronesia*. Water and Energy Research Institute Technical Report 65. University of Guam.

1989. *Archaeological Investigations in the Small Boat Harbor Project Area, Agat, Guam*. International Archaeological Research Institute, Inc.: Honolulu.

1991. A review of traditional high island horticulture in Belau, Yap, Chuuk, Pohnpei, and Kosrae. *Micronesica* 24: 1–56.

2000. Ethnographic and archaeological investigations in the south-west Islands of Palau. *Micronesica* 33: 11–44.

Hunter-Anderson, R.L. and Butler, B.M. 1995. *An Overview of Northern Marianas Prehistory*. Micronesian Archaeological Survey Report 31. Historic Preservation Office: Saipan.

Hunter-Anderson, R.L. and Graves, M.W. 1990. Coming from where? An introduction to recent advances in Micronesian archaeology. In R.L. Hunter-Anderson (ed.) *Recent Advances in Micronesian Archaeology. Micronesica Supplement* 2: 5–15.

Hunter-Anderson, R.L. and Moore, D.R. 1987. Report on a survey of *Latte* sites in the Magpo Valley, Tinian, Commonwealth of the Northern Mariana Islands. MS on file, Historic Preservation Office, Saipan.

1995. Archaeology and oral history of the Japanese lighthouse at Yap. *Isla: A Journal of Micronesian Studies* 3: 257–77.

2001. The Marianas pottery sequence revisited. Unpublished paper prepared for the Ceramic Tradition Workshop, International Symposium on Austronesian Cultures: Issues Relating to Taiwan, December 8–12, Institute of Linguistics, Academia Sinica, Taipei, Taiwan.

Hunter-Anderson, R.L., Thompson, G.B. and Moore, D.R. 1995. Rice as a prehistoric valuable in the Mariana Islands, Micronesia. *Asian Perspectives* 34: 69–89.

Hunter-Anderson, R.L. and Zan, Y. (Go'opsan) 1996. Demystifying the Sawei, a traditional interisland exchange system. *ISLA: A Journal of Micronesian Studies* 4: 1–45.

Huntress, K. (ed.) 1975. *A Narrative of the Shipwreck, Captivity and Sufferings of Horace Holden and Benj. H. Nute* by Horace Holden. Ye Galleon Press: Fairfield, Washington.

Ikehara-Quebral, R. and Douglas, M.T. 1997. Cultural alteration of human teeth in the Mariana Islands. *American Journal of Physical Anthropology* 104: 381–91.

Intoh, M. 1981. Reconnaissance archaeological research on Ngulu Atoll in the Western Caroline Islands. *Asian Perspectives* 24: 69–80.

1986. Pigs in Micronesia: introduction or re-introduction by the Europeans. *Man and Culture in Oceania* 2: 1–26.

1988. Changing prehistoric Yapese pottery technology: a case study of adaptive transformation. PhD dissertation, University of Otago.

1989. Water absorption testing of Pacific pottery. In D. Sutton (ed.) *Saying So Doesn't Make it So: Essays in Honour of B. Foss Leach*. 132–52. New Zealand Archaeological Association Monograph 17. Auckland.

1990. Ceramic environment and technology: a case study in the Yap Islands in Micronesia. *Man and Culture in Oceania* 6: 35–52.

1991. Archaeological research on Fais Island: preliminary report. MS on file, Historic Preservation Office, Yap State, Federated States of Micronesia.

1992a. Pottery traditions in Micronesia. In J. C. Galipaud (ed.) *Poterie Lapita et peuplement*. ORSTOM: Noumea.

1992b. Why were pots imported to Ngulu Atoll? *Journal of the Polynesian Society* 101: 159–68.

1996. Multi-regional contacts of prehistoric Fais islanders in Micronesia. *Bulletin of the Indo-Pacific Prehistory Association* 15: 111–17.

1997. Human dispersals into Micronesia. *Anthropological Science* 105: 15–28.

1998. *The Catalogue of Prehistoric Micronesian Artifacts Housed in Japan.* Micronesian Archaeological Survey Report 34. Historic Preservation Office: Saipan.

1999. Culture contacts between Micronesia and Melanesia. In J.-C. Galipaud and I. Lilley (eds.) *Le Pacifique de 5000 à 2000 avant le présent: suppléments à l'histoire d'une colonisation. The Pacific from 5000 to 2000 BP: Colonisation and Transformation. Actes du colloque Vanuatu, 31 Juillet – 6 Août 1996.* 407–22. Editions de l'ORSTOM, Collection colloques et séminaires: Paris.

Intoh, M. and Leach, F. 1985. *Archaeological Investigations in the Yap Islands, Micronesia: First Millennium BC to the Present Day*. British Archaeological Reports S277. Oxford.

Irwin, G. 1992. *The Prehistoric Exploration and Colonisation of the Pacific*. Cambridge University Press: Cambridge.

1998. The colonisation of the Pacific plate: chronological, navigational and social issues. *Journal of the Polynesian Society* 107: 111–43.

2000. No man is an island: the importance of context in the study of the colonisation and settlement of the Pacific Islands. In A. Anderson and T. Murray (eds.) *Australian Archaeologist: Collected Papers in Honour of Jim Allen*. 393–411. Coombs Academic Publishing, The Australian National University: Canberra.

Ishida, H. and Dodo, Y. 1997. Cranial variation in prehistoric human skeletal remains from the Marianas. *American Journal of Physical Anthropology* 104: 399–410.

Ishikawa, E. 1987. The breadfruit culture complex in Oceania. *Senri Ethnological Series* 21: 9–27.

Ito, M. 1998. Distribution of terraced earthwork remains, Babeldaob, Palau. *Man and Culture in Oceania* 14: 121–9.

Jernigan, E.W. 1973. Lochukle: a Palauan art tradition. PhD dissertation, University of Arizona.

Johannes, R.E. 1981. *Words of the Lagoon: Fishing and Marine Lore in the Palau District of Micronesia*. University of California Press: Berkeley.

Johannes, R.E. and Black, P.W. 1981. Fishing in the South West Islands. In R.E. Johannes *Words of the Lagoon: Fishing and Marine Lore in the Palau District of Micronesia*. 85–100. University of California Press: Berkeley.

John, T. 1992. Historic preservation and development in the Federated States of Micronesia: an overview. In D.H. Rubenstein (ed.) *Pacific History: Papers from the 8th Pacific History Association Conference*. 455–9. MARC, University of Guam: Guam.

Jolly, M. 1992. 'Ill-natured comparisons': racism and relativism in European representations of ni-Vanuatu from Cook's second voyage. *History and Anthropology* 5: 348–56.

1996. Desire, difference and disease: sexual and venereal exchanges on Cook's voyages in the Pacific. In R. Gibson (ed.) *Exchanges: Cross-cultural Encounters in Oceania*. 185–217. Museum of Sydney: Sydney.

2001. On the edge? Deserts, oceans, islands. *The Contemporary Pacific* 13: 417–66.

Karolle, B.G. 1993. *Atlas of Micronesia*. 2nd edition. Bess Press: Honolulu.

Kataoka, O. 1991. Faunal analysis of Nan Madol, Pohnpei, Micronesia. *Man and Culture in Oceania* 7: 71–105.

1996. Prehistoric and historic faunal utilization in Pohnpei: an ecological and ethnoarchaeological understanding. PhD dissertation, University of Oregon.

Keate, G. 1789. *An Account of the Pelew Islands*. G. Nichol: London.

Keating, B.H., Mattey, D.P., Naughton, J., Helsley, C.E., Epp, D., Lararwicz, A. and Schwank, D. 1984. Evidence for a hot spot origin of the Caroline Islands. *Journal of Geophysical Research* 89: 9937–48.

Keating, E. 1999. Contesting representations of gender stratification in Pohnpei, Micronesia. *Ethnos* 64: 350–71.

2001. Language, identity, and the production of authority in new discursive contexts in Pohnpei, Micronesia. *Journal de la Société des Océanistes* 112: 73–80.

Kihleng, K.S. 1992. Kinswomen in production and exchange: Pohnpei women in the nineteenth century. In D. H. Rubenstein (ed.) *Pacific History: Papers from the 8th Pacific History Association Conference*. 169–76. MARC, University of Guam: Guam.

King, T.F. 1984. A note on Winikopos, a complex of stone structures on Tonowas (Dublon) Island, Truk. MS on file, Micronesian Seminar, Pohnpei, Federated States of Micronesia.

King, T.F. and Parker, P.L. 1984. *Pisekin Noomw Noon Tonaachaw: Archaeology in the Tonaachaw Historic District, Moen Island.* Southern Illinois University Center for Archaeological Investigations, Occasional Paper 3.

Kirch, P.V. 1984a. *The Evolution of the Polynesian Chiefdoms.* Cambridge University Press: Cambridge.

1984b. The Polynesian Outliers: continuity, change, replacement. *Journal of Pacific History* 19: 224–38.

1986. Introduction: the archaeology of island societies. In P.V. Kirch (ed.) *Island Societies: Archaeological Approaches to Evolution and Transformation.* 1–5. Cambridge University Press: Cambridge.

1987. Lapita and Oceanic cultural origins: excavations on Mussau Islands, Bismarck Archipelago. *Journal of Field Archaeology* 14: 163–80.

1988a. Long distance exchange and island colonization. *Norwegian Archaeological Review* 21: 105–16.

1988b. The Talepakemalai Lapita site and Oceanic prehistory. *National Geographic Research* 4: 328–42.

1993. Ofu Island and the To'aga site: dynamics of the natural and cultural environment. In P.V. Kirch and T.L. Hunt (eds.) *The To'aga Site: Three Millennia of Polynesian Occupation in the Manu'a Islands, American Samoa.* 9–22. Contributions of the University of California Archaeological Research Facility 51. Berkeley.

1997a. Microcosmic histories: island perspectives in global change. *American Anthropologist* 99: 30–42.

1997b. Introduction: the environmental history of Oceanic Islands. In P.V. Kirch and T.L. Hunt (eds.) *Historical Ecology in the Pacific Islands: Prehistoric Environmental and Landscape Change.* 1–21. Yale University Press: New Haven.

1997c. *The Lapita Peoples: Ancestors of the Oceanic World.* Blackwell: Oxford.

2000. Pigs, humans, and trophic competition on small Oceanic islands. In A. Anderson and T. Murray (eds.) *Australian Archaeologist: Collected Papers in Honour of Jim Allen.* 427–39. Coombs Academic Publishing, The Australian National University: Canberra.

Kirch, P.V. (ed.) 2001. *Lapita and Its Transformations in Near Oceania: Archaeological Investigations in the Mussau Islands, Papua New Guinea, 1985–88. Vol. I. Introduction, Excavations, Chronology.* University of California at Berkeley, Archaeological Research Facility, Contribution 59.

Kirch, P.V. and Ellison, J. 1994. Palaeoenvironmental evidence for human colonization of remote Oceanic islands. *Antiquity* 68: 310–21.

Kirch, P.V. and Green, R.C. 1987. History, phylogeny, and evolution in Polynesia. *Current Anthropology* 28: 431–56.

Kirch, P.V. and Hunt, T.L. (eds.) 1988. *Archaeology of the Lapita Culture Complex: A Critical Review.* Thomas Burke Memorial Washington State Museum Research Report 5. Seattle.

1997. *Historical Ecology in the Pacific Islands: Prehistoric Environmental and Landscape Change.* Yale University Press: New Haven.

Kirch, P.V. and Weisler, M.I. 1994. Archaeology in the Pacific Islands: an appraisal of recent research. *Journal of Archaeological Research* 2: 285–328.

Kirion, M.T. and Karaiti, B. 1979. Migration from Samoa and beyond. In Multiple Authors (eds.) *Kiribati: Aspects of History.* 10–17. Ministry of Education, Training and Culture, Kiribati Government: Tarawa.

Kiste, R.C. 1974. *The Bikinians: A Study in Forced Migration*. Cummings: Menlo Park.

1994a. Pre-colonial times. In K.R. Howe, R.C. Kiste and B.V. Lal (eds.) *Tides of History: The Pacific Islands in the Twentieth Century*. 3–28. Allen and Unwin: Sydney.

1994b. United States. In K.R. Howe, R.C. Kiste and B.V. Lal (eds.) *Tides of History: The Pacific Islands in the Twentieth Century*. 227–57. Allen and Unwin: Sydney.

1999. A half century in retrospect. In R.C. Kiste and M. Marshall (eds.) *American Anthropology in Micronesia: An Assessment*. 433–67. University of Hawaii Press: Honolulu.

Kiste, R.C. and Marshall, M. 2000. American anthropology in Micronesia, 1941–1997. *Pacific Science* 54: 265–74.

Kiste, R.C. and Marshall, M. (eds.) 1999. *American Anthropology in Micronesia: An Assessment*. University of Hawaii Press: Honolulu.

Kluge, P.F. 1991. *The Edge of Paradise: America in Micronesia*. University of Hawaii Press: Honolulu.

Knudson, K.E. 1965. *Titiana: A Gilbertese Community in the Solomon Islands*. Department of Anthropology, University of Oregon: Eugene.

Koch, G. 1984. *The Material Culture of Tuvalu*. Institute of Pacific Studies, University of the South Pacific: Suva.

1986. *The Material Culture of Kiribati*. Institute of Pacific Studies, University of the South Pacific: Suva.

Kotzebue, O. von 1821. *Voyage of Discovery in the South Sea, and to Behring's Straits: in Search of a North-east Passage, Undertaken in the Years 1815, 16, 17, and 18, in the Ship Riurik*. Sir Richard Phillips: London.

1830 [1967]. *A New Voyage Round the World in the Years, 1823, 24, 25, and 26*. N. Israel: Amsterdam.

Krämer, A. 1929. *Palau. Vol. V. Visit to Palau by the Südsee Expedition 1908–1910*. Friederichsen: Hamburg.

1932. *Truk: Visit to Truk by the Südsee Expedition 1908–1910*. Friederichsen: Hamburg.

Kubary, J.S. 1874. Die Ruinen von Nanmatal auf der Insel Ponape (Ascension). *Journal des Museums Godeffroy* 3: 123–31.

1895. *Ethnographische Beiträge zur Kenntnis des Karolinen Archipels*. Verlag von P.W.M. Trap: Leiden.

Kurashina, H. and Clayshulte, R. 1983. Site formation processes and cultural sequence at Tarague, Guam. *Bulletin of the Indo-Prehistory Association* 4: 114–22.

Laird, W.E. 1982. *Soil Survey of Island of Ponape, Federated States of Micronesia*. US Department of Agriculture, Soil Conservation Service.

1983a. *Soil Survey of Island of Kosrae, Federated States of Micronesia*. US Department of Agriculture, Soil Conservation Service.

1983b. *Soil Survey of Islands of Truk, Federated States of Micronesia*. US Department of Agriculture, Soil Conservation Service.

Lampert, R.J. 1968. An archaeological investigation on Ocean Island, Banaba. *Archaeology and Physical Anthropology in Oceania* 3: 1–18.

Langdon, R. 1992. Sixteenth century Spanish castaways in the Caroline and Mariana Islands. In D. H. Rubenstein (ed.) *Pacific History: Papers from the 8th Pacific History Association Conference*. 7–16. MARC, University of Guam: Guam.

Larsen, C.S. and Milner, G.R. (eds.) 1994. *In the Wake of Contact: Biological Responses to Conquest*. Wiley-Liss: New York.

Leach, F. and Davidson, J.M. 1988. The quest for the Rainbow Runner: prehistoric fishing on Kapingamarangi and Nukuoro. *Micronesica* 21: 1–22.

Leach, F., Davidson, J. and Athens, J.S. 1996. Mass harvesting of fish in the waterways of Nan Madol, Pohnpei, Micronesia. In J.M. Davidson, G. Irwin, B.F. Leach, A. Pawley and D. Brown (eds.) *Oceanic Culture History: Essays in Honour of Roger Green*. 319–41. New Zealand Journal of Archaeology Special Publication: Dunedin.

Leach, F. and Ward, G.K. 1981. *Archaeology on Kapingamarangi Atoll, a Polynesian Outlier in the Eastern Caroline Islands*. Privately published by F. Leach.

Leach, H.M. and Green, R.C. 1989. New information for the Ferry Berth site, Mulifanua, Western Samoa. *Journal of the Polynesian Society* 98: 319–29.

LeBar, F.M. 1964. *The Material Culture of Truk*. Yale University Publications in Anthropology 68. Yale University Press: New Haven.

Lebot, V. 1991. Kava (*Piper methysticum* Forst. f.): the Polynesian dispersal. In P. A. Cox and S. A. Barnack (eds.) *Islands, Plants, and Polynesians: An Introduction to Polynesian Ethnobotany*. 169–201. Dioscorides: Portland.

Lebot, V., Merlin, M. and Lindstrom, L. 1992. *Kava: The Pacific Drug*. Yale University Press: New Haven.

Legge, J.D. 1964. *Indonesia*. Prentice Hall: Englewood Cliffs, NJ.

Leigh, R.W. 1929. *Dental Morphology and Pathology of Prehistoric Guam*. Bernice P. Bishop Museum Memoir 11(3).

Lessa, W.A. 1950. Ulithi and the outer native world. *American Anthropologist* 52: 27–52.

1959. Diving knots in the Carolines. *Journal of the Polynesian Society* 68: 188–204.

1961. *Tales from Ulithi Atoll: A Comparative Study in Oceanic Folklore*. Folklore Studies 13. University of California Press: Berkeley.

1962. An evaluation of early descriptions of Carolinian culture. *Ethnohistory* 9: 313–403.

1966. *Ulithi: A Micronesian Design for Living*. Holt, Rinehart and Winston: New York.

1975a. The Portuguese discovery of the Isles of Sequeira. *Micronesica* 11: 35–70.

1975b. *Drake's Island of Thieves: Ethnological Sleuthing*. University of Hawaii Press: Honolulu.

1978. The Mapia Islands and their affinities. In N. Gunson (ed.) *The Changing Pacific: Essays in Honour of H.E. Maude*. 228–46. Oxford University Press: Oxford.

1980. *More Tales from Ulithi Atoll: A Content Analysis*. Folklore and Mythology Studies 32. University of California Press: Berkeley.

Lévesque, R. 1992. *History of Micronesia. Vol. I. European Discovery*. Lévesque Publications: Québec.

1993. *History of Micronesia. Vol. III. First Real Contact*. Lévesque Publications: Québec.

Lévi-Strauss, C. 1987. *Anthropology and Myth: Lectures 1951–1982*. Trans. R. Willis. Basil Blackwell: Oxford.

Lewis, D. 1994 *We, the Navigators: The Ancient Art of Landfinding in the Pacific*. 2nd edition. University of Hawaii Press: Honolulu.

Lieber, M.D. 1968. *Porakiet: A Kapingamarangi Colony on Ponape*. Department of Anthropology, University of Oregon: Eugene.

1992. Wringing it dry – Kenneth Emory's reconstruction of the ancient religion of Kapingamarangi Atoll: a lesson in historiography. In D.H. Rubenstein (ed.) *Pacific History: Papers from the 8th Pacific History Association Conference*. 381–4. MARC, University of Guam: Guam.

Lilley, I. 1999. Lapita as politics. In J.-C. Galipaud and I. Lilley (eds.) *Le Pacifique de 5000 à 2000 avant le présent: suppléments à l'histoire d'une colonisation. The Pacific from 5000 to 2000 BP: Colonisation and Transformation. Actes du colloque Vanuatu, 31 Juillet – 6 Août 1996*. 21–9. Editions de IRD, Collection Colloques et séminaires: Paris.

Lingenfelter, S.G. 1975. *Yap: Political Leadership and Culture Change in an Island Society*. University of Hawaii Press: Honolulu.

Liston, J. 1996. *The Legacy of Tarague Embayment and Its Inhabitants, Andersen AFB, Guam. Vol. I. Archaeology*. International Archaeological Research Institute, Inc.: Honolulu.

1999. *Lab Analysis, Synthesis, and Recommendations: Archaeological Data Recovery for the Compact Road, Babeldaob Island, Republic of Palau*, Vol. V. International Archaeological Research Institute, Inc.: Honolulu.

Liston, J., Kaschko, M. and Welch, D. 1998. *Archaeological Inventory Survey of the Capital Relocation Site, Melekeok, Republic of Palau*. International Archaeological Research Institute, Inc.: Honolulu.

Liston, J., Mangieri, T., Grant, D., Kaschko, M. and Tuggle, H.D. 1998. *Fieldwork Reports: Archaeological Data Recovery for the Compact Road, Babeldaob Island, Republic of Palau*, Vol. II. International Archaeological Research Institute, Inc.: Honolulu.

Liston, J., Tuggle, H.D., Mangieri, T., Kaschko, M. and Desilets, M. 1998. *Fieldwork Reports: Archaeological Data Recovery for the Compact Road, Babeldaob Island, Republic of Palau*, Vol. I. International Archaeological Research Institute, Inc.: Honolulu.

Lucking, L.J. 1984. An archaeological investigation of prehistoric Palauan terraces. PhD dissertation, University of Minnesota.

Lucking, L.J. and Parmentier, R.J. 1990. Terraces and traditions of Uluang: ethnographic and archaeological perspectives on a prehistoric Belauan site. In R.L. Hunter-Anderson (ed.) *Recent Advances in Micronesian Archaeology. Micronesica Supplement* 2: 125–36.

Lum, K.J. 1998. Central and eastern Micronesia: genetics, the overnight voyage, and linguistic divergence. *Man and Culture in Oceania* 14: 69–80.

Lum, K.J. and Cann, R.L. 1998. mtDNA and language support a common origin of Micronesians and Polynesians in Island South-east Asia. *American Journal of Physical Anthropology* 105: 109–19.

2000. mtDNA lineage analyses: origins and migrations of Micronesians and Polynesians. *American Journal of Physical Anthropology* 113: 151–68.

Lundsgaarde, H.P. 1966. *Cultural Adaptations in the Southern Gilbert Islands*. Department of Anthropology, University of Oregon: Eugene.

1968. *Social Changes in the Southern Gilbert Islands: 1938–1964*. Department of Anthropology, University of Oregon: Eugene.

1978. Post-contact changes in Gibertese *maneaba* organisation. In N. Gunson (ed.) *The Changing Pacific: Essays in Honour of H.E. Maude*. 67–79. Oxford University Press: Melbourne.

Luomala, K. 1953. *Ethnobotany of the Gilbert Islands*. Bernice P. Bishop Museum Bulletin 213. Honolulu.

Lütke, Fedor P. 1835–6 [1971]. *Voyage autour du Monde, 1826–1829*. N. Israel: Amsterdam.

McKnight, R.K. 1964. *Orachl's Drawings*. Micronesian Research Working Papers 1. Literature Production Center: Saipan.

McNeill, J.R. 1998. Human spear points and speared humans: the procurement, manufacture and use of bone implements in prehistoric Guam. Paper presented to the Indo-Pacific Prehistory Association Congress, Melaka.

Marshall, M. 1979. *Weekend Warriors: Alcohol in a Micronesian Culture*. Mayfield: Palo Alto, Calif.

1999. 'Partial connections': kinship and social organization in Micronesia. In R.C. Kiste and M. Marshall (eds.) *American Anthropology in Micronesia: An Assessment*. 107–43. University of Hawaii Press: Honolulu.

Marshall, M. and Marshall, L.B. 1976. Holy and unholy spirits: the effects of missionization on alcohol use in eastern Micronesia. *Journal of Pacific History* 11: 135–66.

1990. *Silent Voices Speak: Women and Prohibition in Truk*. Wadsworth: Belmont, Calif.

Martin, K.R. (ed.) 1980. *'Naked and Prisoner': Captain Edward C. Barnard's Narrative of a Shipwreck in Palau 1832–1833*. Kendall Whaling Museum: Sharon, Mass.

Masse, W.B. 1989. The archaeology and ecology of fishing in the Belau Islands, Micronesia. PhD dissertation, Southern Illinois University at Carbondale.

1990. Radiocarbon dating, sea-level change and the peopling of Belau. In R.L. Hunter-Anderson (ed.) *Recent Advances in Micronesian Archaeology. Micronesica Supplement* 2: 213–30.

Masse, W.B. and Snyder, D. 1982. The final report of the 1981 field season of the Southern Illinois University Palau Archaeological Project. MS on file, Historic Preservation Office, Saipan.

Masse, W.B., Snyder, D. and Gumerman, G.J. 1984. Prehistoric and historic settlement in the Palau Islands, Micronesia. *New Zealand Journal of Archaeology* 6: 107–27.

Matsumura, A. 1918. Contributions to the ethnography of Micronesia. *Journal of the College of Science, Imperial University of Tokyo* 40(7).

Maude, H.C. and Maude, H.E. 1932. The social organization of the Banaba or Ocean Island, central Pacific. *Journal of the Polynesian Society* 41: 262–301.

1994. *An Anthology of Gilbertese Oral Tradition*. Institute of Pacific Studies, University of the South Pacific: Suva.

Maude, H.E. 1952. The colonization of the Phoenix Islands. *Journal of the Polynesian Society* 61: 62–89.

1979. *The Evolution of the Gilbertese* Boti. Institute of Pacific Studies, University of the South Pacific: Suva.

1980. *The Gilbertese* Maneaba. Institute of Pacific Studies, University of the South Pacific: Suva.

1989. A.F. Grimble as anthropologist. In H.E. Maude (ed.) *Tungaru Traditions: Writings on the Atoll Culture of the Gilbert Islands* (by A.F. Grimble). xix–xxvi. Melbourne University Press: Melbourne.

1995. History of Banaba. In A. Talu and M. Quanchi (eds.) *Messy Entanglements: Papers of the 10th Pacific History Association Conference, Tarawa, Kiribati*. 83–90. Pacific History Association: Brisbane.

Maude, H.E. and Lampert, R.J. 1967. The stalactite fishhooks of Ocean Island. *Journal of the Polynesian Society* 76: 415–25.

Mauricio, R. 1986. Ethnoarchaeological observations of Pohnpei Chiefdoms: 1984 field research on Temwen Island and Wene community. MS on file, Historic Preservation Office, Pohnpei State, Federated States of Micronesia.

    1993. Ideological bases for power and leadership on Pohnpei, Micronesia: perspectives from archaeology and oral history. PhD dissertation, University of Oregon.

Moore, D.R. 1983. Measuring change in Marianas pottery: the sequence of pottery production at Tarague, Guam. MA dissertation, University of Guam.

Moore, D.R. and Hunter-Anderson, R.L. 1999. Pots and pans in the Intermediate Pre-Latte (2500–1600 BP), Mariana Islands, Micronesia. In J.-C. Galipaud and I. Lilley (eds.) *Le Pacifique de 5000 à 2000 avant le présent: suppléments à l'histoire d'une colonisation. The Pacific from 5000 to 2000 BP: Colonisation and Transformation. Actes du colloque Vanuatu, 31 Juillet – 6 Août 1996.* 487–503. Editions de l'ORSTOM. Collection Colloques et séminaires: Paris.

Moorehead, A. 1966. *The Fatal Impact: An Account of the Invasion of the South Pacific.* Hamilton: London.

Morgan, A. 1996. Mystery in the eye of the beholder: cross-cultural encounters on 19th-century Yap. *Journal of Pacific History* 31: 27–41.

Morgan, W.N. 1988. *Prehistoric Architecture in Micronesia.* University of Texas Press: Austin.

Morrill, S.S. 1970. *Ponape: Where American Colonialism Confronts Black Magic, Five Kingdoms, and the Mysterious Ruins of Nan Madol.* Cadleon: San Francisco.

Murakami, G.M. 1995. Identification of charred plant remains. In J.S. Athens *Landscape Archaeology: Prehistoric Settlement, Subsistence, and Environment of Kosrae, Eastern Caroline Islands, Micronesia.* 337–48. International Archaeological Research Institute, Inc.: Honolulu.

Muranushi, I. 1942. Brief account of human remains on Ponape and relics on Nan Madol. *Kagaku Nanyo* 4: 218–25. [In Japanese]. Translation in the Bishop Museum, Honolulu.

    1943. Summary of the ruins, Kusaie Island. *Kagaku Nanyo* 5(2) (in Japanese). Translation in the Bishop Museum, Honolulu.

Nelson, S.M. 1999. Megalithic monuments and the introduction of rice into Korea. In C. Gosden and J. Hather (eds.) *The Prehistory of Food: Appetites for Change.* 147–65. Routledge: London.

Nero, K.L. 1999. Missed opportunities: American anthropological studies of Micronesian arts. In R.C. Kiste and M. Marshall (eds.) *American Anthropology in Micronesia: An Assessment.* 255–99. University of Hawaii Press: Honolulu.

Nunn, P.D. 1993. Beyond the naïve lands: human history and environmental change in the Pacific Basin. In E. Waddell and P.D. Nunn (eds.) *The Margin Fades: Geographical Itineraries and a World of Islands.* 5–27. Institute of Pacific Studies, University of the South Pacific: Fiji.

O'Connell, J.F. 1972 [1836]. *A Residence of Eleven Years in New Holland and the Caroline Islands.* New edition, ed. S. H. Riesenberg. University of Hawaii Press: Honolulu.

Olmo, R.K. 1995. *Archaeological Subsurface Testing of a Portion of the Achang Bay Site, Merizo, Guam.* International Archaeological Research Institute, Inc.: Honolulu.

Olmo, R.K. and Goodman, W.L. 1994. *Archaeological investigations for Ypao Beach Park Ground Penetrating Radar Survey, Guam*. International Archaeological Research Institute, Inc.: Honolulu.

Olsudong, R. 1995. Reconstructing the indigenous political structure in the recent prehistory of Belau, Micronesia. Unpublished MA dissertation, La Trobe University.

 1998. Oral history and archaeology in Micronesia. Paper presented to the Indo-Pacific Prehistory Association Congress, Melaka.

Osborne, D. 1947. Archaeology on Guam: a progress report. *American Anthropology* 49: 518–24.

 1966. *The Archaeology of the Palau Islands: An Intensive Survey*. Bernice P. Bishop Museum Bulletin 230. Honolulu.

 1979. *Archaeological Test Excavations. Palau Islands. 1968–1969. Micronesica Supplement* 1.

 1980. Palau prehistory: a brief summary. In P.L. Prematilleke, W.T.T.P. Gunawardana and R. Silva (eds.) *P.E.P. Deraniyagala Commemoration Volume*. 274–82. Lake House: Sri Lanka.

Parker, P.L. 1981. Preliminary report: archaeological data recovery in advance of sewer lateral and water facility construction, Iras, Mechchitiw, and Sapuuk villages, Moen Island, Truk. MS on file, Historic Preservation Office, Chuuk State, Federated States of Micronesia.

Parker, P.L. and King, T.F. 1981. Recent and current archaeological research on Moen. *Asian Perspectives* 24: 11–26.

 1987. Intercultural mediation at Truk International Airport. In R.M. Wulff and S.J. Fiske (eds.) *Anthropological Praxis: Translating Knowledge into Action*. 160–73. Westview: Boulder.

Parkes, A. 1997. Environmental change and the impact of Polynesian colonization: sedimentary records from central Polynesia. In P.V. Kirch and T.L. Hunt (eds.) *Historical Ecology in the Pacific Islands: Prehistoric Environmental and Landscape Change*. 166–99. Yale University Press: New Haven.

Parmentier, R.J. 1987. *The Sacred Remains: Myth, History, and Polity in Belau*. University of Chicago Press: Chicago.

 1991. The rhetoric of free association and Palau's political struggle. *The Contemporary Pacific* 3: 146–58.

Parmentier, R.J. and Kopnina-Geyer, H. 1996. Miklouho-Maclay in Palau, 1876. *ISLA: A Journal of Micronesian Studies* 4: 71–108.

Pate, F. Donald, Craib, John L. and Heathcote, Gary M. 2001. Stable isotopic analysis of prehistoric human diet in the Mariana Islands, western Pacific. *Australian Archaeology* 52: 1–4.

Pavlish, L.A., Hancock, R.G.V., Snyder, D. and Lucking, L. 1986. INAA study of pottery from Palau, Micronesia. In J.S. Olin and M.J. Blackman (eds.) *Proceedings of the 24th International Archaeometry Symposium*. Smithsonian Institute Press: Washington, DC.

Pawley, A. and Ross, M. 1995. The prehistory of the Oceanic languages: a current view. In P. Bellwood, J.J. Fox and D. Tryon (eds.) *The Austronesians: Historical and Comparative Perspectives*. 39–74. The Australian National University: Canberra.

Peattie, M.R. 1988. *Nan'yo: The Rise and Fall of the Japanese in Micronesia, 1885–1945*. Pacific Islands Monograph Series 4. Center for Pacific Island Studies, University of Hawaii Press: Honolulu.

Penny, G. 1998. Municipal displays. Civic self-promotion and the development of German ethnographic museums, 1870–1914. *Social Anthropology* 6: 157–68.

Peoples, J.G. 1990. The evolution of complex stratification in eastern Micronesia. In R.L. Hunter-Anderson (ed.) *Recent Advances in Micronesian Archaeology. Micronesica Supplement* 2: 291–302.

    1993. Political evolution in Micronesia. *Ethnology* 32: 1–17.

Peter, J. 2000. Chuukese travellers and the idea of horizon. *Asia Pacific Viewpoint* 41: 253–67.

Petersen, G. 1982a. Ponapean matriliny: production, exchange, and the ties that bind. *American Ethnologist* 9: 129–44.

    1982b. *One Man Cannot Rule a Thousand: Fission in a Ponapean Chiefdom.* University of Michigan Press: Ann Arbor.

    1990a. *Lost in the Weeds: Theme and Variation in Pohnpei Political Mythology.* Center for Pacific Island Studies, University of Hawaii, Occasional Paper 35. Honolulu.

    1990b. Some overlooked complexities in the study of Pohnpei social complexity. In R.L. Hunter-Anderson (ed.) *Recent Advances in Micronesian Archaeology. Micronesica Supplement* 2: 137–52.

    1995a. Nan Madol's contested landscape: topography and tradition in the Eastern Caroline Islands. *Isla: A Journal of Micronesian Studies* 3: 105–28.

    1995b. The complexity of power, the subtlety of *kava*. *Canberra Anthropology* 18: 34–60.

    1999. Sociopolitical rank and conical clanship in the Caroline Islands. *Journal of the Polynesian Society* 108: 367–410.

    2000. Indigenous island empires: Yap and Tonga considered. *Journal of Pacific History* 35: 5–27.

Petit-Skinner, S. 1981. *The Nauruans.* McDuff: San Francisco.

Pickering, R.B. 1990. An ethno-archaeological investigation of Yapese mortuary behavior. In R.L. Hunter-Anderson (ed.) *Recent Advances in Micronesian Archaeology. Micronesica Supplement* 2: 153–70.

Pitt-Rivers, George Lane Fox 1925. Aua Island: ethnographical and sociological features of a South Sea pagan society. *Journal of the Royal Anthropological Institute* 55: 425–38.

Plaza, F. 1973. The Lattes of the Marianas. *Guam Recorder* (Second Series) 3(1): 6–9.

Pollock, N.J. 1975. The risks of dietary change: a Pacific atoll example. In R.W. Casteel and G.I. Quimby (eds.) *Maritime Adaptations of the Pacific.* 255–64. Mouton: The Hague.

    1983. The early use of rice in Guam: the evidence from the historical records. *Journal of the Polynesian Society* 92: 509–20.

Poyer, L. 1993. *The Ngatik Massacre: History and Identity on a Micronesian Atoll.* Smithsonian Institution Press: Washington, DC.

    1995. Yapese experiences of the Pacific War. *Isla: A Journal of Micronesian Studies* 3: 223–55.

    1997. *Marshall Islands Ethnography. Ethnography and Ethnohistory of Taroa Island, Republic of the Marshall Islands. Micronesian Resources Study.* Micronesian Endowment for Historic Preservation, Republic of the Marshall Islands, US National Park Service: San Francisco.

Pregill, G.K. and Steadman, D.W. 2000. Fossil vertebrates from Palau: a resource assessment. *Micronesica* 33: 137–52.

Price, W. 1936. *Pacific Adventure.* Reynal and Hitchcock: New York.

Purcell, D.C. Jr. 1976. The economics of exploitation: the Japanese in the Mariana, Caroline and Marshall Islands. *Journal of Pacific History* 11: 189–211.

Radiocarbon 1965. Ponape Series. *Radiocarbon* 7: 253–4.

Rainbird, P. 1994a. Prehistory in the north-west tropical Pacific: the Caroline, Mariana, and Marshall Islands. *Journal of World Prehistory* 8: 293–349.

1994b. Report of an archaeological survey conducted on Fefen Island, Chuuk Lagoon, Federated States of Micronesia. MS on file, Historic Preservation Office, Chuuk State, Federated States of Micronesia.

1995a. Kosrae's place in Pacific prehistory. *Archaeology in Oceania* 30: 139–45.

1995b. Pacific Island societies: a non-evolutionary approach to the archaeological interpretation of difference. PhD dissertation, University of Sydney.

1996. A place to look up to: a review of Chuukese hilltop enclosures. *Journal of the Polynesian Society* 105: 461–78.

1999a. Entangled biographies: western Pacific ceramics and the tombs of Pohnpei. *World Archaeology* 31: 214–24.

1999b. The use of landscape in identifying potential sources of Caroline Island colonisation. In J.-C. Galipaud and I. Lilley (eds.) *Le Pacifique de 5000 à 2000 avant le présent: suppléments à l'histoire d'une colonisation. The Pacific from 5000 to 2000 BP: Colonisation and Transformation. Actes du colloque Vanuatu, 31 Juillet – 6 Août 1996.* 451–60. Editions de IRD. Collection Colloques et séminaires: Paris.

1999c. Islands out of time: towards a critique of island archaeology. *Journal of Mediterranean Archaeology* 12: 218–36.

2000a. The non-use of archaeology in Chamorro land rights: a comparison with Aboriginal Australia. In I. Lilley (ed.) *Native Title and the Transformation of Archaeology in the Postcolonial World.* 153–63. Oceania Monographs 50.

2000b. 'Round, black and lustrous': a view of encounters with difference in Chuuk Lagoon, Federated States of Micronesia. In R. Torrence and A. Clarke (eds.) *The Archaeology of Difference: Negotiating Cross-cultural Engagements in Oceania.* 32–50. Routledge: London.

2001a. Deleuze, turmeric and Palau: rhizome thinking and rhizome use in the Caroline Islands. *Journal de la Société des Océanistes* 112: 13–19.

2001b. The remote effects of European exploration and colonialism in Micronesia: implications for archaeology and anthropology. Paper presented to the Second European Colloquim on Micronesia, University of the Basque Country, Donostia/San Sebastian, Spain, April 17–20.

2002a. A message for our future? The Rapa Nui (Easter Island) ecodisaster and Pacific island environments. *World Archaeology* 33: 436–51.

2002b. Making sense of petroglyphs: the sound of rock-art. In B. David and M. Wilson (eds.) *Inscribed Landscapes: Marking and Making Place.* 93–103. University of Hawaii Press: Honolulu.

in press. Pohnpei petroglyphs, communication and miscommunication. *Bulletin of the Indo-Pacific Prehistory Association* 22.

Rainbird, P. and Wilson, M. 1999. Pohnpaid Petroglyphs, Pohnpei. MS on file, Historic Preservation Office, Pohnpei State, Federated States of Micronesia.

Reed Smith, DeVerne 1983. *Palauan Social Structure.* Rutgers University Press: New Brunswick.

1997. *Palau Ethnography. Vol. II. Recommendations for the Preservation of Historic and Cultural Resources in Palau. Micronesian Resources Study.* Micronesian Endowment for Historic Preservation, Republic of Belau, US National Park Service: San Francisco.

Rehg, K.L. 1995. The significance of linguistic interaction spheres in reconstructing Micronesian prehistory. *Oceanic Linguistics* 34: 305–26.

Rehg, K.L. and Sohl, D.G. 1979. *Ponapean–English Dictionary*. University of Hawaii Press: Honolulu.

Reid, L. 1997. On linguistic evidence for early Philippine contact with Chamorro. *Bulletin of the Indo-Pacific Prehistory Association* 17: 63.

  1998. On linguistic evidence for early Philippine contact with Chamorro. Paper presented to the Indo-Pacific Prehistory Association Congress, Melaka.

Reinman, F.M. 1965. Maritime adaptation: an aspect of Oceanic economy. PhD dissertation, University of California, Los Angeles.

  1967. Fishing: an aspect of Oceanic economy. An archaeological approach. *Fieldiana: Anthropology* 54(2): 95–208.

Reinman, F.R. 1977. *An Archaeological Survey and Preliminary Test Excavations on the Island of Guam, Mariana Islands, 1965–1966*. Miscellaneous Publications 1. Micronesian Area Research Center: Guam.

Riesenberg, S. 1968. *The Native Polity of Ponape*. Smithsonian Contributions to Anthropology 10. Washington, DC.

Riley, T.J. 1987. Archaeological survey and testing, Majuro Atoll, Marshall Islands. In T.S. Dye (ed.) *Marshall Islands Archaeology*. 169–270. Pacific Anthropological Records 38. Bernice P. Bishop Museum: Honolulu.

Ritter, L. and Ritter, P. 1982. *The European Discovery of Kosrae Island. Accounts by Louis Isidore Duperrey, Jules-Sébastien-César Dumont d'Urville, René Primevère Lesson, Fyedor Lütke and Friedrich Heinrich von Kittlitz*. Micronesian Archaeological Survey Reports 13. Historic Preservation Office: Saipan.

Ritzenhaler, R.E. 1954. *Native Money in Palau*. Milwaukee Public Museum, Publications in Anthropology 1. Milwaukee.

Roberts, R. 1952. Bathing the bones. *Journal of the Polynesian Society* 61: 319–21.

Robinson, D. 1970. The Micronesian canoe. In D. Robinson (ed.) *Canoes in Micronesia*. 2–3. University of Guam, Gallery of Art, Micronesian Working Papers 2. Guam.

Rosendahl, P.H. 1987. Archaeology in eastern Micronesia: a reconnaissance survey in the Marshall Islands. In T.S. Dye (ed.) *Marshall Islands Archaeology*. 17–168. Pacific Anthropological Records 38. Bernice P. Bishop Museum: Honolulu.

Ross, M.D. 1996. Is Yapese Oceanic? In B. Nothofer (ed.) *Reconstruction, Classification, Description: Festschrift in Honor of Isidore Dyen*. 121–66. Abera: Hamburg.

Russell, S. 1998a. Gani revisited: a historical overview of the Mariana Archipelago's northern islands. *Pacific Studies* 21(4): 83–105.

  1998b. *Tiempon I Manmofo'na: Ancient Chamorro Culture and History in the Northern Mariana Islands*. Micronesian Archaeological Survey 32. Saipan.

Ryan, E.M. 1998. Intrasite spatial distribution of gender at the Tumon Bay–Hyatt Site, Guam. In M. Casey, D. Donlon, J. Hope and S. Wellfare (eds.) *Redefining Archaeology: Feminist Perspectives*. 234–8. ANH Publications, Research School of Pacific and Asian Studies, The Australian National University: Canberra.

Sahlins, M. 1958. *Social Stratification in Polynesia*. University of Washington Press: Seattle.

  1995. *How 'Natives' Think: About Captain Cook for Example*. University of Chicago Press: Chicago.

Sanderson, S.K. 1990. *Social Evolutionism: A Critical History*. Blackwell: Oxford.

Sarfert, E.G. 1919. *Kusrae: Report of the Südsee Expedition*. Friederichsen: Hamburg. [In German.]

Sather, C. 1995. Sea nomads and rainforest hunter-gatherers: foraging adaptations in the Indo-Malaysian Archipelago. In P. Bellwood, J.J. Fox and D. Tryon (eds.) *The Austronesians: Historical and Comparative Perspectives*. 229–68. The Australian National University: Canberra.

Sauer, J.D. 1993. *Historical Geography of Crop Plants: A Select Roster*. CRC Press: Boca Raton.

Saxe, A.A., Allenson, R. and Loughbridge, S.R. 1980a. Archeological survey of sections of the circumferential road on Ponape Island. MS on file, Hamilton Library, University of Hawaii, Honolulu.

 1980b. The Nan Madol area of Ponape: researches into bounding and stabilizing an ancient administrative center. MS on file, Hamilton Library, University of Hawaii, Honolulu.

Schmidt, L.W. 1974. An investigation into the origin of a prehistoric Palauan rock art style. MA dissertation, University of California, Long Beach.

Seki, T. 1977. Truk Islands as seen from the perspective of archaeological data and [oral] tradition. *Festschrift for Dr. T. Mikami, S.54*. [In Japanese.]

Semper, K. 1982 [1873]. *The Palau Islands in the Pacific Ocean*. Trans. Mark L. Berg. Micronesian Area Research Center, University of Guam: Agana.

Service, E. 1962. *Primitive Social Organization: An Evolutionary Perspective*. Random House: New York.

Shun, K. and Athens, J.S. 1990. Archaeological investigations at Kwajalein Atoll, Marshall Islands, Micronesia. In R.L. Hunter-Anderson (ed.) *Recent Advances in Micronesian Archaeology. Micronesica Supplement* 2: 231–40.

Shutler, R. Jr., Sinoto, Y. and Takayama, J. 1984. Preliminary excavations of Fefan Island sites, Truk Islands. In Y. Sinoto (ed.) *Caroline Islands Archaeology: Investigations on Fefan, Faraulep, Woleai and Lamotrek*. 1–64. Pacific Anthropological Records 35. Bernice P. Bishop Museum: Honolulu.

Sica, A. 1991. The California–Massachusetts strain in structuration theory. In C.G.A. Bryant and D. Jary (eds.) *Giddens' Theory of Structuration: A Critical Appreciation*. 32–51. Routledge: London.

Sigrah, R.K. and King, S.M. 2001. *Te Rii ni Banaba*. Institute of Pacific Studies, University of the South Pacific: Suva.

Simmons, D.R. 1970. Palau cave paintings on Aulong Island. *Records of the Auckland Institute and Museum* 7: 171–3.

Sinoto, Y. 1988. *Abstracts of Translated Japanese Articles: Anthropological Research in Micronesia under the Japanese Mandate, 1908–1945*. Department of Anthropology, Bernice P. Bishop Museum: Honolulu.

 nd. Report on the test excavation of the Bird Cave, Site D-16, on Kosrae Island, Eastern Caroline Islands. MS on file, Bernice P. Bishop Museum. Honolulu.

Smith, A. 1995. The need for Lapita: explaining change in the Late Holocene Pacific archaeological record. *World Archaeology* 26: 366–79.

Smith, A.H. 1958. Micronesia. *Asian Perspectives* 2: 68–85.

Smith, G. 1991. *Micronesia: Decolonisation and US Military Interests in the Trust Territory of the Pacific Islands*. The Australian National University, Research School of Pacific Studies, Peace Research Centre Monograph 10. Canberra.

Snyder, D. 1985. An archaeological survey of Koror State, Republic of Palau. MS on file, Center for Archaeological Investigations, Southern Illinois University at Carbondale (1985–13).

1989. Towards chronometric models for Palauan prehistory: ceramic attributes. PhD dissertation, Southern Illinois University at Carbondale.

Snyder, D. and Butler, B.M. 1997. *Palau Archaeology: Archaeology and Historic Preservation in Palau.* Micronesian Resources Study. US National Park Service: San Francisco.

Souder, L.M. 1987. *Daughters of the Island: Contemporary Chamorro Women Organizers on Guam.* Micronesian Area Research Center: Agana, Guam.

1992. Unveiling herstory: Chamorro women in historical perspective. In D.H. Rubenstein (ed.) *Pacific History: Papers from the 8th Pacific History Association Conference.* 143–61. MARC, University of Guam: Guam.

Specht, J. 1982. Some shell artefacts from Nauru and Ocean Island. *Bulletin of the Indo-Pacific Prehistory Association* 3: 135–42.

Specht, J. and Gosden, C. 1997. Dating Lapita pottery in the Bismarck Archipelago, Papua New Guinea. *Asian Perspectives* 36: 175–99.

Spennemann, D.H.R. 1999. No room for the dead: burial practices in a constrained environment. *Anthropos* 94: 35–56.

Spennemann, D.H.R. and Downing, J. (eds.) 2001. *My Adventures and Researches in the Pacific. By a 'Master Mariner' (Handley Bathurst Sterndale).* Mulini Press: Canberra.

Spennemann, D.H.R., Look, D.W. and Graham, K. 2001. Heritage eco-tourism in Micronesia: expectations of government officials. *Cultural Resource Management* 1: 30–2.

Spoehr, A. 1957. Marianas prehistory: archaeological survey and excavations on Saipan, Tinian, and Rota. *Fieldiana: Anthropology* 48. Natural History Museum: Chicago.

Spriggs, M. 1982. Taro cropping systems in the south-east Asian–Pacific region: archaeological evidence. *Archaeology in Oceania* 17: 7–15.

1984. Early coconut remains from the South Pacific. *Journal of the Polynesian Society* 93: 71–6.

1990. God's police and damned whores: images of archaeology in Hawaii. In P. Gathercole and D. Lowenthal (eds.) *The Politics of the Past.* 118–29. Unwin Hyman: London.

1991. Facing the nation: Hawaiians and archaeologists in an era of sovereignty. *Contemporary Pacific* 3: 379–92.

1995. The Lapita Culture and Austronesian prehistory in Oceania. In P. Bellwood, J.J. Fox and D. Tryon (eds.) *The Austronesians: Historical and Comparative Perspectives.* 112–33. The Australian National University: Canberra.

1997a. Early agriculture and what went before in island Melanesia. In D.R. Harris (ed.) *The Origins and Spread of Agriculture and Pastoralism in Eurasia.* 524–37. University College London Press: London.

1997b. *The Island Melanesians.* Blackwell: Oxford.

1997c. Landscape catastrophe and landscape enhancement: are either or both true in the Pacific? In P.V. Kirch and T.L. Hunt (eds.) *Historical Ecology in the Pacific Islands: Prehistoric Environmental and Landscape Change.* 80–104. Yale University Press: New Haven.

1999a. Archaeological dates and linguistic sub-groups in the settlement of the island Southeast Asian–Pacific region. *Bulletin of the Indo-Pacific Prehistory Association* 18: 17–24.

1999b. Pacific archaeologies: contested ground in the construction of Pacific history. *Journal of Pacific History* 34: 109–21.

2000. The Solomon Islands as bridge and barrier in the settlement of the Pacific. In A. Anderson and T. Murray (eds.) *Australian Archaeologist: Collected Papers in Honour of Jim Allen.* 348–64. Coombs Academic Publishing, The Australian National University: Canberra.

2001a. Future eaters in Australia, future eaters in the Pacific? Early human environmental impacts. *Australian Archaeology* 52: 53–9.

2001b. Who cares what time it is? The importance of chronology in Pacific archaeology. In A. Anderson, I. Lilley and S. O'Connor (eds.) *Histories of Old Ages: Essays in Honour of Rhys Jones.* 237–49. Pandanus Books, The Australian National University: Canberra.

Spriggs, M. and Anderson, A. 1993. Late colonization of East Polynesia. *Antiquity* 67: 200–17.

Steadman, D. 1992. Extinct and extirpated birds from Rota, Mariana Islands. *Micronesica* 25: 71–84.

1998. The prehistory of vertebrates, especially birds, on Tinian, Aguiguan, and Rota, Northern Mariana Islands. *Micronesica* 31: 319–45.

Steadman, D. and Intoh, M. 1994. Biogeography and prehistoric exploitation of birds from Fais Island, Yap State, Federated States of Micronesia. *Pacific Science* 48: 116–35.

Steager, P.W. 1979. Where does art begin on Puluwat? In S.M. Mead (ed.) *Exploring the Visual Art of Oceania.* 342–53. University of Hawaii Press: Honolulu.

Steinberg, D.J. 1982 *The Philippines: A Singular and Plural Place.* Westview: Boulder.

Stepan, N. 1982. *The Idea of Race in Science: Great Britain 1800–1960.* Macmillan: London.

Stocking, G.W. 1991. Maclay, Kubary, Malinowski: archetypes from the dreamtime of anthropology. In G.W. Stocking (ed.) *Colonial Situations: Essays on the Contextualization of Ethnographic Knowledge.* 9–74. History of Anthropology 7. University of Wisconsin Press: Madison.

Stone, B.C. 1963. The role of pandanus in the culture of the Marshall Islands. In J. Barrau (ed.) *Plants and the Migrations of Pacific Peoples.* 61–74. Bishop Museum Press: Honolulu.

Streck, C.F. Jr. 1980. Ponape: an archaeological survey of the south portion of the Ponape circumferential road. MS on file, Historic Preservation Office, Pohnpei State, Federated States of Micronesia.

1984. Archaeological reconnaissance survey for the proposed Nanpil River Hydropower Project, Net Municipality, Ponape, Federated States of Micronesia. MS on file, Hamilton Library, University of Hawaii, Honolulu.

1985. Intensive archaeological site survey for the Proposed Nanpil River Hydropower Project, Net Municipality, Pohnpei, Federated States of Micronesia. MS on file, Hamilton Library, University of Hawaii, Honolulu.

1990. Prehistoric settlement in eastern Micronesia: archaeology on Bikini Atoll, Republic of the Marshall Islands. In R.L. Hunter-Anderson (ed.) *Recent Advances in Micronesian Archaeology. Micronesica* Supplement 2: 247–60.

Sudo, K. 1996. Rank, hierarchy and routes of migration: chieftainship in the central Caroline Islands of Micronesia. In J.J. Fox and C. Sather (eds.) *Origins, Ancestry and Alliance: Explorations in Austronesian Ethnography.* 55–69. Department of Anthropology, Research School of Pacific and Asian Studies, Australian National University: Canberra.

Summerhayes, G.R. 2000. *Lapita Interaction*. Terra Australis 15. Department of Archaeology and Natural History and Centre for Archaeological Research, Research School of Pacific and Asian Studies, Australian National University: Canberra.

2001. Far Western, Western, and Eastern Lapita: a re-evaluation. *Asian Perspectives* 39: 109–38.

Swadling, P. 1996. *Plumes from Paradise: Trade Cycles in South-east Asia and Their Impact on New Guinea and Nearby Islands until 1920*. Papua New Guinea National Museum: Boroko.

Swift, M.K., Harper, R.A. and Athens, J.S. 1990. *Studies in the Prehistory of Malem Municipality: Kosrae Archaeology, Micronesian Resources Study*. International Archaeological Research Institute, Inc.: Honolulu.

Swindler, D.R. and Weisler, M. 2000. Dental size and morphology of precontact Marshall Islanders (Micronesia) compared with other Pacific Islanders. *Anthropological Science* 108: 261–82.

Takayama, J. 1979. Archaeological investigation of PAAT-2 in the Palaus: an interim report. In H. Kusakabe (ed.) *Report: Cultural Anthropological Research on the Folkculture in the Western Caroline Islands of Micronesia in 1977*. 81–103. Committee for Micronesian Research, Tokyo University of Foreign Studies: Tokyo.

1982. A brief report on archaeological investigations of the southern part of Yap Island and nearby Ngulu Atoll. In M. Aoyagi (ed.) *Islanders and Their Outside World*. 77–104. St Paul's (Rikkyo) University: Tokyo.

1988. A pandanus fruit scraper from Makin Island, Kiribati, Central Pacific. *Bulletin of the Indo-Pacific Prehistory Association* 8: 162–6.

Takayama, J. and Egami, J.T. 1971. *Archaeology on Rota in the Mariana Islands*. Reports of the Pacific Archaeology Survey 1. Tokai University: Hiratsuka.

Takayama, J., Eritaia, B. and Saito, A. 1987. Preliminary observation of the origins of Vaitupuans in view of pottery. In E. Ishikawa (ed.) *Cultural Adaptations to Atolls in Micronesia and West Polynesia: A Report of the Cultural Anthropological Research in the Caroline, Marshall and Ellice Islands, 1985*. 1–13. Tokyo Metropolitan University: Tokyo.

Takayama, J. and Intoh, M. 1978. *Archaeological Excavation at Chukienu Shell Midden on Tol, Truk*. Reports of Pacific Archaeological Survey 5. Tezukayama University: Nara City.

1980. *Reconnaissance Archaeological Survey in the Lower Mortlocks, Truk State*. Reports of Pacific Archaeological Survey 6. Tezukayama University: Nara City.

Takayama, J., Intoh, M. and Takasugi, H. 1980. *The Brief Archaeological Survey on Kayangel and Angaur in the Palaus*. Reports of Pacific Archaeological Survey 7. Tezukayama University: Tokyo.

Takayama, J. and Seki, T. 1973. *Preliminary Archaeological Investigations on the Island of Tol in Truk*. Reports of Pacific Archaeological Survey 2. Azuma Shuppan: Tokyo.

Takayama, J. and Takasugi, H. 1978. Preliminary report on the archaeological excavation of PAAT-2, in Palau. MS on file, Historic Preservation Office, Saipan.

1987. The significance of lure shanks excavated in the Utiroa site of Makin Island in the Gilberts. In I. Ushilima and S. Kenichi (eds.) *Cultural Uniformity and Diversity in Micronesia*. 29–41. Senri Ethnological Studies 21.

Takayama, J., Takasugi, H. and Kaiyama, K. 1985. Preliminary report of archaeological excavation on Makin Island in the Gilberts, Central Pacific. In E. Ishikawa (ed.) *The 1983–84 Cultural Anthropological Expedition to Micronesia: An Interim Report*. 85–100. Tokyo Metropolitan University: Tokyo.

1990. Test excavations of the Nukantekainga site on Tarawa, Kiribati, Central Pacific. In I. Ushijima (ed.) *Anthropological Research on the Atoll Cultures*. 1–19. Committee of Micronesian Research 1988, University of Tsukuba: Tsukuba-shi.

nd. The 1988 archaeological expedition to Kiribati: a preliminary report of Tamana. Unpublished MS in possession of the author.

Tasa, G.L. 1988. Report of the human skeletal remains from Pahnwi and Wasau, Nan Madol, Pohnpei. MS on file, Historic Preservation Office, Pohnpei State, Federated States of Micronesia.

Tcherkézoff, S. 2001. The archaeology and history of Dumont d'Urville's 'Melanesia/Polynesia' opposition. Paper presented to the Foreign Bodies: Oceania and Racial Science 1750–1940 Workshop, Australian National University, Canberra, 18–19 October.

Teaiwa, T.K. 1992. Microwomen: US colonialism and Micronesian women activists. In D.H. Rubenstein (ed.) *Pacific History: Papers from the 8th Pacific History Association Conference*. 125–41. MARC, University of Guam: Guam.

Terrell, J. 1986. *Prehistory in the Pacific Islands: A Study of Variation in Language, Customs, and Human Biology*. Cambridge University Press: Cambridge.

1988. History as a family tree, history as an entangled bank: constructing images and interpretations of prehistory in the South Pacific. *Antiquity* 62: 642–57.

Terrell, J., Hunt, T.L. and Gosden, C. 1997. The dimensions of social life in the Pacific. *Current Anthropology* 38: 155–95.

Terrell, J., Kelly, K. and Rainbird, P. 2001. Foregone conclusions? In search of 'Papuans' and 'Austronesians'. *Current Anthropology* 42: 97–107.

Tetens, A. 1958. *Among the Savages of the South Seas: Memoirs of Micronesia, 1862–1868*. Trans. F. Mann Spoehr. Stanford University Press: Stanford.

Thaman, R. 1990. Kiribati agroforestry: trees, people and the atoll environment. *Atoll Research Bulletin* 333: 1–29.

Thilenius, G. (ed.) 1913–38. *Ergebnisse der Südsee Expedition, 1908–1910*, Part 2, B, *Mikronesien*. 12 volumes in 25 parts. Friederichsen: Hamburg.

Thomas, J. (ed.) 2000. *Interpretive Archaeology: A Reader*. Leicester University Press: Leicester.

Thomas, N. 1989. The force of ethnology. *Current Anthropology* 30: 27–34.

1991. *Entangled Objects: Exchange, Material Culture, and Colonialism in the Pacific*. Harvard University Press: Cambridge, Mass.

1997. *In Oceania: Visions, Artifacts, Histories*. Duke University Press: Durham, NC.

2000. George Keate: benevolence on the beach. In J. Lamb, V. Smith and N. Thomas (eds.) *Exploration and Exchange: A South Seas Anthology, 1680–1900*. 112–16. University of Chicago Press: Chicago.

Thompson, L.M. 1932. *Archaeology of the Mariana Islands*. Bernice P. Bishop Museum Bulletin 100. Honolulu.

1940. The function of *latte* in the Marianas. *Journal of the Polynesian Society* 49: 447–65.

1945. *The Native Culture of the Mariana Islands*. Bernice P. Bishop Museum Bulletin 185. Honolulu.

Tilley, C. 1999. *Metaphor and Material Culture*. Blackwell: Oxford.

Tilley, C. (ed.) 1993. *Interpretative Archaeology*. Berg: Oxford.

Torrence, Robin 1993. Ethnoarchaeology, museum collections and prehistoric exchange: obsidian-tipped artifacts from the Admiralty Islands. *World Archaeology* 24: 467–81.

Trigger, B.G. 1989. *A History of Archaeological Thought*. Cambridge University Press: Cambridge.

Tryon, D. 1995. Proto-Austronesian and the major Austronesian sub-groups. In P. Bellwood, J.J. Fox and D. Tryon (eds.) *The Austronesians: Historical and Comparative Perspectives*. 17–38. Australian National University: Canberra.

Turbott, I.G. 1949. The footprints of Tarawa. *Journal of the Polynesian Society* 58: 193–7.

Uchinomi, F. [Huzio Utinomi] (compiler) 1952. *Bibliography of Micronesia (Bibliographia Micronesica: Scientae naturalis et cultis)*. University of Hawaii Press: Honolulu.

Ueki, T. 1984. Processes of increasing social complexity on Kosrae, Micronesia. PhD dissertation, Brown University, Rhode Island.

   1990. Formation of a complex society in an island situation. In R.L. Hunter-Anderson (ed.) *Recent Advances in Micronesian Archaeology*. *Micronesica Supplement* 2: 303–16.

Uriam, K.K. 1995. *In Their Own Words: History and Society in Gilbertese Oral Tradition*. Journal of Pacific History: Canberra.

Ushijima, I. 1982. The control of reefs and lagoons: some aspects of the political structure on Ulithi Atoll. In M. Aoyagi (ed.) *Islanders and Their Outside World*. 35–75. St Paul's (Rikkyo) University: Tokyo.

Van Tilburg, J.A. 1991. *Anthropomorphic Stone Monoliths on the Islands of Oreor and Babeldaob, Republic of Belau (Palau), Micronesia*. B.P. Bishop Museum Occasional Papers 31: 3–62.

Von Däniken, E. 1973. *The Gold of the Gods*. Trans. M. Heron. G.P. Putnam's Sons: New York.

Walker, A.T., Donham, T.K. and Rosendahl, P.H. 1992. Archaeological Monitoring, Laura Water Line Project. Majuro Atoll, Republic of the Marshall Islands. Unpublished report by Paul H. Rosendahl, PhD, Inc.: Hilo.

Ward, J.V. 1988. Palynology of Kosrae, Eastern Caroline Islands: recoveries from pollen rain and Holocene deposits. *Review of Palaeobotany and Palynology* 55: 247–71.

   1995. Sediment coring and palynology. In J.S. Athens, *Landscape Archaeology: Prehistoric Settlement, Subsistence, and Environment of Kosrae, Eastern Caroline Islands, Micronesia*. 299–335. International Archaeological Research Institute, Inc.: Honolulu.

Ward, M.C. 1989. *Nest in the Wind: Adventures in Anthropology on a Tropical Island*. Waveland Press: Prospect Heights, Ill.

Warner van Peenan, M. 1974. *Chamorro Legends of the Island of Guam*. Micronesian Area Research Center, Publication 4.

Weisler, M. 1996. Origins, development, and transformation of Marshallese society: summary of a multi-year investigation. Paper presented to the Third Pacific Archaeology Conference, Vanuatu National Museum, Vanuatu.

   1999a. Atolls as settlement landscapes: Ujae, Marshall Islands. *Atoll Research Bulletin* 460: 1–51.

   1999b. The antiquity of aroid pit agriculture and significance of buried A horizons on Pacific atolls. *Geoarchaeology* 14: 621–54.

   2000. Burial artifacts from the Marshall Islands: description, dating and evidence for extra-archipelago contacts. *Micronesica* 33: 111–36.

2001a. Life on the edge: prehistoric settlement and economy on Utrok Atoll, northern Marshall Islands. *Archaeology in Oceania* 36: 109–33.

2001b. *On the Margins of Sustainability: Prehistoric Settlement of Utrok Atoll, Northern Marshall Islands*. British Archaeological Reports International Series 967. Archaeopress: Oxford.

2001c. Precarious landscapes: prehistoric settlement of the Marshall Islands. *Antiquity* 75: 31–2.

Weisler, M., Lum, J.K., Collins, S.L. and Kimoto, W.S. 2000. Status, health, and ancestry of a late prehistoric burial from Kwajalein Atoll, Marshall Islands. *Micronesica* 32: 191–220.

Weisler, M. and Swindler, D. 2002. Rocker jaws from the Marshall Islands: evidence for interaction between Eastern Micronesia and West Polynesia. *People and Culture in Oceania* 18: 23–33.

Welch, D. 1998a. Integration of the archaeological and paleoenvironmental evidence of early human settlement in Palau. *Bulletin of the Indo-Pacific Prehistory Association* 17: 80.

1998b. Integration of the archaeological and paleoenvironmental evidence of early human settlement in Palau. Paper presented to the Indo-Pacific Prehistory Association Congress, Melaka,

Welch, D., McNeill, J.R. and Athens, J.S. 1990. *Intensive Archaeological Survey of the RS-3 Circumferential Road Corridor, Okat Valley, Kosrae, Eastern Caroline Islands, Micronesia*. International Archaeological Research Institute, Inc.: Honolulu.

Welsch, R.L. 2000. One time, one place, three collections: colonial processes and the shaping of some museum collections from German New Guinea. In Michael O'Hanlon and Robert L. Welsch (eds.) *Hunting the Gatherers: Ethnographic Collectors, Agents and Agency in Melanesia, 1870s–1930s*. 155–79. Berghahn: New York.

Wesley-Smith, T. 2000. Introduction. *The Contemporary Pacific* 12: 307–17.

Whistler, W.A. 1991. Polynesian plant introductions. In P.A. Cox and S.A. Banack (eds.) *Islands, Plants, and Polynesians: An Introduction to Polynesian Ethnobotany*. 41–66. Dioscordes: Portland, Or.

White, G.M. and Tengan, T.K. 2001. Disappearing worlds: anthropology and cultural studies in Hawai'i and the Pacific. *The Contemporary Pacific* 13: 381–416.

Wickler, S. 1990a. Prehistoric Melanesian exchange and interaction: recent evidence from the northern Solomon Islands. *Asian Perspectives* 29: 135–54.

1990b. *Archaeological Testing of the C.U.C. Underground Power Cable Right-of-way, Garapan, Saipan, Commonwealth of the Northern Mariana Islands*. International Archaeological Research Institute, Inc.: Honolulu.

1994. *Archaeological Inventory Survey, Damage Assessment and Mitigation Plan for Sites T-97, T-98 and T-99, Babeldaob Road Project, Ngaraad State, Republic of Palau*. International Archaeological Research Institute, Inc.: Honolulu.

1998a. The Palauan cultural sequence: a Babeldaob perspective. Paper presented to the Indo-Pacific Prehistory Association Congress, Melaka.

1998b. Villages and terraces: transformations of the cultural landscape on Babeldaob, Palau. Paper presented to the Indo-Pacific Prehistory Association Congress, Melaka.

1998c. Oral traditions and archaeology: modeling village settlement in Palau, Micronesia. In P. Wallin (ed.) *Archaeology, Communication and Language*.

14–23. The Kon-Tiki Museum, Institute for Pacific Archaeology and Cultural History, No Barriers Seminar Papers 1.

2000. Building a 4,500 year culture sequence in Palau (Belau): a multidisciplinary approach to modelling Neolithic settlement in western Micronesia. A paper presented to the Fiji Museum–ANU Conference: Prehistory of the west and central Pacific during the last 5000 years, Suva.

2001a. *The Prehistory of Buka: A Stepping Stone Island in the Northern Solomons*. Terra Australis 16. Department of Archaeology and Natural History and Centre for Archaeological Research, Research School of Pacific and Asian Studies, Australian National University: Canberra.

2001b. The colonization of western Micronesia and early settlement of Palau. Paper presented to the Second European Colloquium on Micronesia, University of the Basque Country, Donostia/San Sebastian, Spain, April 17–20.

in press. Terraces and villages: transformations of the cultural landscape in Palau. In T. Ladefoged and M. Graves (eds.) *Pacific Landscapes: Archaeological Approaches in Oceania*.

Wickler, S., Addison, D., Kschko, M. and Dye, T. 1997. *Intensive Archaeological Survey for the Palau Compact Road, Babeldaob Island, Palau. Historic Preservation Investigations Phases 1, Vol. 2: Area Survey Reports*. International Archaeological Research Institute, Inc.: Honolulu.

Wickler, S., Welch, D., Tomanari-Tuggle, M.J., Liston, J. and Tuggle, H.D. 1998. *Intensive Archaeological Survey for the Palau Compact Road, Babeldaob Island, Palau. Historic Preservation Investigations Phases 1, Vol. 1: Scope, Background, Results, Evaluation and Recommendations*. International Archaeological Research Institute, Inc.: Honolulu.

Wilson, L.B. 1995. *Speaking to Power: Gender and Politics in the Western Pacific*. Routledge: London.

Workman, L.W. and Haun, A.E. 1993. Archaeological Inventory Survey and Limited Data Recovery, Hyatt Temporary Parking Lot, Tumon, Tamuning Municipality, Territory of Guam. Unpublished report by Paul H. Rosendahl, PhD, Inc.: Hilo.

Yawata, I. 1932a. Hidden treasures in the excavations. *Dorumen* 1: 15–18. [In Japanese.] Trans. in P. S. Chapman (1964). Micronesian archaeology: an annotated bibliography. MA dissertation, Stanford University.

1932b. On the megalithic structures in the Eastern Carolines, Ponape and Kusaie. *The Geographical Review of Japan* 8(4): 50–66. [In Japanese.] Trans. Shigeo Ofuji on file at the Micronesian Area Research Center, University of Guam.

1963. Rice cultivation of the ancient Mariana islanders. In J. Barrau (ed.) *Plants and the Migration of Pacific Peoples*. 91–2. Bishop Museum: Honolulu.

Yoffee, N. 1993. Too many chiefs? (or safe texts for the 90s). In N. Yoffee and A. Sherratt (eds.) *Archaeological Theory: Who Sets the Agenda?* 60–78. Cambridge University Press: Cambridge.

Young, J.A., Rosenberger, Nancy, R. and Harding, Joe R. 1997. *Truk Ethnography. Ethnography of Truk, Federated States of Micronesia. Micronesian Resources Study*. Micronesian Endowment for Historic Preservation, Federated States of Micronesia, US National Park Service: San Francisco.

Zelenietz, M. and Kravitz, D. 1974. Absorption, trade and warfare: beachcombers on Pohnpei, 1830–1854. *Ethnohistory* 21: 223–49.

INDEX

Abemama, *see* Kiribati
Achang Bay, Guam, *see* Marianas
Achugao, Saipan, *see* Marianas
Adams, William 155–6, 162
Admiralties 52
Africa 19, 94
Agana Bay, Guam, *see* Marianas
Aguiguan, *see* Marianas
Alaguan, Rota, *see* Marianas
Alkire, William 43, 44, 45, 46, 158–9, 161, 163, 236–7, 240, 241
American English 9
Amesbury, Judith 83, 133
Anderson, Atholl 56–7, 58
Angaur, Palau, *see* Caroline Islands
Anson, George 20, 117, 127–9
Ant (And) Atoll, Pohnpei, *see* Caroline Islands
Anthony, David 74
Aotearoa/New Zealand 6, 7, 34, 57, 61, 97, 116, 241
Aplog, Rota, *see* Marianas
Apra Harbour, Guam, *see* Marianas
Apurguan, Guam, *see* Marianas
Arabia 19
Arellano, Alonso de 177
Arno, *see* Marshall Islands
Arorae, *see* Kiribati
art 35–6, 45, 48–9, 145–6
As Nieves, Rota, *see* Marianas
Athens, J. Stephen 86, 87, 88, 92, 97, 183, 185, 194, 201, 208, 212, 220
Aua, *see* Western Islands
Australia 30–1, 34, 61, 74, 153, 246
Austronesian 9, 47, 51–2, 75, 81, 97, 120
Awak Valley, Pohnpei, *see* Caroline Islands
Ayres, William 34, 88, 92, 165, 183, 185, 189, 195–6

Babeldaob, Palau, *see* Caroline Islands
Badrulchau, Palau, *see* Caroline Islands
Bahn, Paul 1
Baker, Robin 57

Banaba (Ocean Island) 29, 30–1, 40, 43, 231–2, 237–40, 241
  te Aka 240
banana 41, 96, 125, 166, 179, 212–18
Barnard, Edward 21, 149
Barnett, Homer 33
Barratt, Glynn 18, 127, 130
Bath, Joyce 34, 107, 189–93, 194
Beaglehole, John 19
Beardsley, Felicia 113, 142, 147
Beauclair, Inez de 147, 161
bêche de mer 150, 162
Bekaka Village, Tamana, *see* Kiribati
Belau, Palau, *see* Caroline Islands
Belau, Republic of 21–2, 58–9
Bellwood, Peter 141, 147
Berg, Mark 25, 26–7, 159–60, 169–70
Berlin Ethnological Museum 23, 26
Bernart, Luelen 194
betel nut 162
Bikenbiu, *see* Kiribati
Bikini, *see* Marshall Islands
Bismarck Archipelago 25, 74, 82, 85, 92, 94
Black, Peter 147
Boas, Franz 25
Bodner, Connie 120
Boeder, Gustav 28
Borneo 7, 74
Boughton, George 119
Bourdieu, Pierre 142
Branco, Jorge 25
breadfruit 41, 42, 87, 94, 95, 96–7, 125, 127, 163, 165, 176, 190, 201, 212–18, 220, 230, 231, 233
Brewis, Alexandria 232
Britain 20–1, 27, 34, 61
Bryson, Robert 63, 89, 184–5
Buada Lagoon, *see* Nauru
Buck, Peter (Te Rangi Hiroa) 66–7, 243
Buka 74
Burns, Alan 56
Burrows, Edwin 35–6
Butaritari, *see* Kiribati